John Lennon
Listen To
This Book

John Blaney

Paper Jukebox

Contents

Acknowledgements

I would like to thank everyone who helped make this book possible. In particular I would like to thank the staff of EMI Archives, MFSL and Rykodisc Records, the Hard Rock Café Headquarters and the British Library Newspapers. I would also like to thank my family and friends without whom...

Introduction

As one quarter of the Beatles John Lennon recorded some remarkable music. The music he made as a solo artist was every bit its equal. In just twelve-years he recorded an extraordinary body of work that encompassed avant-gardism, agitprop, rock 'n' roll and pop. Although Lennon's music-making took many forms, he always stayed true to the ideas and ideals he'd established with the Beatles. Themes that encompassed personal and universal love, self-knowledge, liberation, utopianism and idealism were honed to perfection. He also perfected his song writing which, like him, could be simple or complex, transparent or opaque, base or urbane. Lennon used his songs to tell the world of his feelings, his thoughts and desires. Whatever the subject, Lennon expressed himself with a compelling honesty. At times he was perhaps too honest. His probity challenged, it questioned and it shocked. It made him all the more intriguing, all the more human.

The records he made are tangible reminders of a quixotic mind, visceral musician, sensitive songwriter, passionate individual and family man. If you want to trace Lennon's development as a musician, thinker and rock star, then his records provide an audible map for you to follow. But Lennon's records did more than reflect, they redefined popular music and had a marked impact on the cultural and political landscape from which they emerged. To say that they changed people's lives wouldn't be an over statement. Jerry Rubin, for one, had his life turned around by one of Lennon's songs, long before he met him. Through his song writing, Lennon touched the hearts and minds of people from Liverpool to Tokyo. At their best his songs challenge the listener to reconsider and question the world they inhabit. They are personal epistles that resonate around the globe, offering hope and inspiration. They proffer a genuine desire for change, for personal development, for a revolution in the head that will benefit all humanity. In the years following his death, Yoko Ono has maintained her late husband's legacy with a string of archival releases that have contributed to his slim but select oeuvre. The amount of material issued has been considerable: respectfully and carefully managed, it now outweighs that released in his lifetime. These albums have revealed aspects of his work that, had he survived, would have remained unknown. All too often posthumous releases betray an artist's reputation. This can't be said for the majority of Lennon's posthumous albums, which have sustained the exceedingly high standards set in his lifetime. Whether recording a home demo, leading a band through a rehearsal or recording a guide vocal, Lennon simply couldn't give less than 100%.

Listen To This Book sets out to trace the recordings that Lennon left behind and, I hope, shed some new light on them. While it is primarily a discography, it also reveals the influences and stories behind the songs. It collects together for the first time in one book information about label variations, promotional records chart positions, recording locations and much more. Entries are arranged chronologically. The book begins with Lennon's debut solo album, Two Virgins, and ends with his latest, John Lennon Acoustic. Information about each record is broken down into discrete parts. Song titles are followed by the artist's name, release date and catalogue number. Chart positions from Billboard and BMRB | Music Week are provided for American and British releases. Japanese chart positions, taken from 'Oricon', are also provided. As a comparison, I've included an appendix that gives chart positions for Lennon's single releases, excluding re-entries, from Billboard and Cash Box and Music Week and NME. In addition, each song has been assigned an index number followed by the song title, composer credit, recording personnel, recording studio, recording date and producer credit. Where songs appear on more than one release, a cross reference is provided.

Appendices for British, American and Japanese discographies provide the following information: release date, title, record label, catalogue numbers for LPs, 8-tracks, reel-to-reel tapes (US only), CDs, 7-inch singles, 12-inch singles, cassette singles (UK only), CD singles and promo singles. An appendix to the main John Lennon discography details interview records and discs issued with books. Information about Capitol, Geffen and Polydor label variations issued in America is also provided.

1968 to 1969: Evolution Of An Odd Couple

UNFINISHED MUSIC NO. 1: TWO VIRGINS
JOHN LENNON AND YOKO ONO

Side 1 'Two Virgins 1', 'Together' (De Silva, Brown, Henderson), 'Two Virgins 2', 'Two Virgins 3', 'Two Virgins 4', 'Two Virgins 5'.
Side 2 'Two Virgins 6', 'Hushabye, Hushabye', 'Two Virgins 7', 'Two Virgins 8', 'Two Virgins 9', 'Two Virgins 10'.

UK release November 29 1968; Apple APCOR 2 (mono), SAPCOR 2 (stereo); failed to chart.
US release January 6 1969; LP Apple T 5001 (stereo); 4-track cartridge (distributed by Tetragrammation) Apple TNX-45001 (white shell and slip cover) or (distributed by GRT) Apple 473 5001; 8-track cartridge Apple TNM-85001; 8-track cartridge Tetragrammation 873 5001; chart high No.124.

'Two Virgins' (Lennon, Ono)
John Lennon (various instruments), Yoko Ono (voice). Recorded at Home Studio, Kenwood, Wood Lane, St George's Hill Estate, Weybridge, Surrey. Produced by John Lennon and Yoko Ono.

TWO VIRGINS

A lot had happened in the two years since the release of McCartney's music for the film *The Family Way*. In 1966, Beatlemania had forced the group into the studio and further from their audience. Entrenched at Abbey Road Studios, they developed new ways of writing and recording that transformed their music and enthralled their listeners. A thirst for knowledge and a delight in experimentation ensured that The Beatles embraced new ideas faster than Marshall McLuhan could say "the medium is the message". By the time the public had caught up with them, The Beatles had moved on.

They were absorbing complex ideas and incorporating them into their work with remarkable speed and ease. Although their music had become more sophisticated and at times difficult to understand, a new record by The Beatles was always eagerly awaited. What new direction had they taken? What had they to say? What would it sound like? If by the mid 1960s their music and message had grown increasingly oblique, there were still legions of fans eager to hear it.

What then would Lennon have to say with the release of his debut solo album? Whatever it was, surely it would be worth hearing? After all, hadn't it been Lennon who with McCartney had written some of the most insightful songs of the 1960s? Obviously The Beatles had changed. No longer mop-tops, they had grown and matured. Few would have expected Lennon's debut to contain twee boy-meets-girl ballads. But when it was eventually issued, what listeners heard came as a shock.

Two Virgins was as far removed from pop music as one could get. Inspired by the avant-garde and musique concréte recordings that supplied London's art scene with its soundtrack, Lennon was partnered by a relatively obscure Japanese artist, Yoko Ono, whom he'd met in November 1966.

Ono was exhibiting at the Indica Gallery in central London and Lennon was invited to the preview. "I'd been going around to galleries a bit on my days off in between records," he recalled. "I got the word that this amazing woman was putting on a show next week, and there was going to be something about people in bags, in black bags, and it was going to be a bit of a happening and all that. So I went down to a preview of the show. There was an apple on sale there for 200 quid. I thought it was fantastic: I got the humour in her work immediately. But there was another piece which really decided me for or against the artist: a ladder which led to a painting which was hung on a ceiling. It looked like a blank canvas with a chain and a spyglass hanging on the end of it. I climbed the ladder, looked through the spy glass, and in tiny little letters it said, "Yes". So it was positive. I felt relieved.

"I was very impressed, and [gallery owner] John Dunbar sort of introduced us; neither of us knew who the hell we were. And Dunbar had been sort of hustling her, saying, 'That's a good patron, you must go and talk to him or do something,' because I was looking for action. John Dunbar insisted she say hello to the millionaire, you know what I mean? And she came up and handed me a card which said "breathe" on it, one of her instructions, so I just went [pant!]. This was our meeting!"

Having established contact, Ono asked Lennon if he would consider giving a manuscript of one of his songs to avant-garde composer John Cage for his 50th birthday. Ono had originally asked McCartney, but he turned her down. Lennon obliged and donated a multicoloured manuscript that he and McCartney had created for their song 'The Word'. Lennon probably didn't know it at the time but his gift was significant, especially for Ono.

By the time Ono met Lennon, she had been a professional artist for several years. Like Lennon, she began her career in the late 1950s. Working in New York City, she developed a conceptual and performance practice that drew on Zen Buddhism, Haiku poetry, and philosophy. She shared these interests with a number of artists, including Cage, who was then teaching at the New School for Social Research. His scores were often written as instructions: his most famous, '4' 33"', directs the performer(s) to make no sounds. As with many of Ono's pieces, the audience play an important role in the piece. The intention was for the audience to create something, either real or in their imagination, thereby establishing a reciprocal dialogue with the composer that blurred the relationship between artist and spectator, art and life.

Ono met Cage through her first husband, Toschi Ichiyanagi. He too was an avant-garde composer, whom she met while attending the Julliard School of Music in New York. Ichiyanagi studied at the New School for Social Research, where a number of visual artists interested in music were working with Cage. This small circle, which included George Brecht, Dick Higgins, Allan Kaprow, and Mac Low, would eventually have a considerable impact on the contemporary New York art scene. Ichiyanagi returned to Japan in 1960, but Ono stayed in New York to continue working as an artist.

One of the events Ono produced, a series of concerts organised with composer La Monte Young, became the catalyst for these artists to form themselves into a collective, Fluxus. George Maciunas conceived of the name and organized the first Fluxus Festival in September 1962 and then established the official Fluxus Headquarters a year later. An enthusiastic promoter of Fluxus, he suggested that artists should produce work that evoked a sense of flux. (The Lennons would work on several projects with Maciunas when they moved to New York in the early 1970s.) As Fluxus scores or performances often involved audience participation, they could never be performed the same way twice. They could, therefore, evoke a sense of fluidity that Maciunas's 'Fluxus Manifesto' described as a "continuous moving on or passing by, as of a flowing stream: a continuous succession of changes".

This notion of fluidity is clearly audible in the music that Lennon and Ono created. Their collage of made and found sounds flows from one improvised motif to another. Lennon's stream-of-consciousness utterances and Ono's vocalisations oscillate from visceral to contrived. Both were well versed in the kind of spontaneous creativity needed to produce this kind of music: Ono through her work as a multimedia artist; Lennon through his studio experimentation with The Beatles.

Thanks to their producer George Martin, The Beatles developed a healthy appetite for audio experimentation that found its way onto their records. As early as the 1950s, Martin used the recording studio as a sound laboratory, where sounds were dramatically manipulated. Working with The Goons and on his own Ray Cathode recordings, Martin took the art of recording to new areas. Within a few years, the recording techniques he'd developed were influencing and being used by The Beatles. Backwards tapes first appeared on 'Rain', the B-side of 'Paperback Writer', while sound effects and sound collages were scattered throughout *Sgt. Pepper's Lonely Hearts Club Band*. Once The Beatles discovered what could be done with tape, a few studio tricks, and a lot of imagination, there was no stopping them.

With The Beatles no longer committed to touring, the group had more time to take in London's burgeoning avant-garde scene and develop ideas of their own. While McCartney embraced London's artistic milieu, Lennon viewed it with cynicism. Although The Beatles had incorporated pioneering ideas in their music, Lennon had long been suspicious of the avant-garde. It was he who famously said that avant-garde was "French for bullshit". Unlike McCartney, Lennon remained ambivalent. "I'd get very upset about it being intellectual or all fucking avant-garde, then I'd like it, then I wouldn't," he explained. Nevertheless, it had a huge affect on the pair, who began experimenting with sound recordings at their respective home studios. Inspired by the work of Cardew, Cage, and Stockhausen, McCartney produced a number of tape loops that were superimposed onto Lennon's 'Tomorrow Never Knows'. While some of McCartney's experiments made it onto Beatles records, most of Lennon's did not. However, Lennon's experimental recordings did reveal that he too was thinking beyond the pop envelope, long before he met Yoko Ono.

Although Lennon and Ono had met on several occasions, it had always been in public and never as a couple. Lennon had sponsored the *Yoko Plus Me* exhibition at the Lisson Gallery in September 1967, but as far as the media were concerned, he was still happily married to Cynthia. In truth, the marriage had been failing for some time. By the time Lennon returned from India in early 1968, it was over. Ono maintained contact with Lennon through a series of letters and notes that intrigued and infuriated him. He was smitten, and later, while Cynthia was on holiday in Italy, he invited Ono to his house for the evening. To break the ice, he suggested that they retire to his attic studio, where he could play her some of his experimental recordings. Ono was impressed and suggested that they make a recording together. Their collaboration was significant. Not only did it mark the beginning of a long and fruitful career together, it also marked the beginning of the end of The Beatles.

Two Virgins was a powerful statement that effectively distanced Lennon from his cute mop-top image. As George Melly noted, The Beatles and their contemporaries turned "revolt into style". But by the mid 1960s there was too much style and not enough revolt. The Establishment quickly absorbed The Beatles by bestowing gifts of MBEs. The teenage consumer revolt, spearheaded by The Beatles, was turning sour and losing impetus. Consumerism was becoming a drag, and where it had once been fashionable to care passionately, by 1967 it was time to drop out and bite the hand that fed you. The teenage revolution that started with rock'n'roll in the 1950s had done little to change things. There may have been more freedoms, but there was also more oppression. The Cold War raged, as did the war in Vietnam, and by 1968, with riots spreading across America and Europe, the West was in turmoil.

A culture of dissent emerged, with its roots in the late 1950s and the establishment of CND and civil protest. One way of showing your displeasure with the status quo was through public demonstration, and the artistic community was quick to respond. In 1962, George Maciunas published a *Fluxus Policy Newsletter* in which he advocated civil disruption. For many artists within the group, Maciunas's suggestion went too far. For them, art should be less interventionist and more consciousness changing. By the mid 1960s, a growing number of artists were committed to this idea and, like them, Lennon and Ono wanted to expand artistic perimeters and pursue a socially-engaged public art. They believed that anything could be considered art, including avant-garde recordings, and that this art had the potential to change society for the better.

On Saturday August 24 1968 they appeared on the British television programme *Frost On Saturday* to explain their ideas. Speaking to the presenter, David Frost, Lennon and Ono suggested that anything that could be sensed could be considered art. They went on to point out that as individuals we are all works of art and that when the body and mind come together to make something creative it should be considered as art, in the same way as a critic might consider a painting or sculpture. Their argument was that the world is one vast gallery, one enormous art exhibition, that sends out vibrations which, they believed, could create positive changes.

Frost: Now, what have we got here? You were pointing at this as you were explaining that Yoko, tell us about this, it's what - a broken cup, right?

Yoko : It's just an example, this is supposed to be a sculpture, and it's a broken cup, an unfinished sculpture that will be just made by people just gradually re-building it into a cup.

Frost : Is the sculpture then, the broken cup? or the way people re-build it with the glue?

John : The thing is, there's no such thing as sculpture or art or anything, it's just a bit of - it's just words, you know, and actually saying everything is art. We're all art, art is just a tag, like a journalists' tag, but artists believe it. But sculpture is anything you care to name. This is sculpture - us sitting here, this is a happening, we are here, this is art, but yeah, if you gave that to a child, he wouldn't have any preconceived ideas, so you wouldn't have to say "This is sculpture!" Or "This is a broken cup", you'd say "There's that - there's glue, what do you do? You stick it together"

Yoko : In reply to your question I think that people say that this is just a process of things, everything is just a process.

If everyone is an artist and anything art, then anyone could add to Lennon and Ono's 'Unfinished Music'. But John and Yoko wanted to take it one step further. If it was possible for an individual to transform a work of art by adding to it, it was possible for them to transform their life and others for the better. The idea was to create a "revolution in the head" that would become an engine for change for the better.

Speaking less than a week after the release of *Two Virgins*, Lennon explained how he thought the music he'd made with Ono could bring about this change. "You can change people, you know, change their heads. A lot of people have changed my head, just with their records. I believe you can change, that's what Yoko and my singing is, to change it like that. All I'm saying is I think you should do it by changing people's heads, and they're saying, 'Well, we should smash the system.' Now the system-smashing scene has been going on forever, you know. The Irish did it, the Russians did it, and the French did it, and where's it got them? It's got them nowhere. That's the same old game."

For Lennon, *Two Virgins* spoke in bold terms of new beginnings. The album certainly loosened his bond with The Beatles and did much to debunk the myth of celebrity. A year earlier, he attempted to destroy his ego with LSD. Now, intent on reworking his public image, he released what many considered an unlistenable album with an unflattering naked image plastered over its front cover.

The photograph was taken at 34 Montagu Square in central London, in a flat that Lennon shared with Ono. Tony Bramwell, an Apple employee, set up the camera before leaving Lennon to take the photograph. "We were both a bit embarrassed when we peeled off for the picture, so I took it myself with a delayed action shutter," Lennon explained. "The picture was to prove that we are not a couple of demented freaks, that we are not deformed in any way, and that our minds are healthy. If we can make society accept these kind of things without offence, without sniggering, then we shall be achieving our purpose."

Lennon then asked another Apple employee Jeremy Banks (assistant to Derek Taylor) to get the film processed. Apple's Neil Aspinall explains: "John had just given Jeremy a roll of film and said, 'Get that developed please.' And when he got it back and saw the nude pictures he said, 'This is mind-blowing.' Everything was always 'mind-blowing' to Jeremy, but – just that one time – he was actually right. He couldn't believe it."

It wasn't as if male and female nudes hadn't been depicted before, but few, if any, had appeared on the cover of a long-playing record. Most nudes are perfect, idealised representations of the human form, not "two flabby bodies naked", which is how George Harrison described them. By 1968, a growing number of artists, including Yoko Ono, had taken to using their bodies to make art. Ono's *Cut Piece*, for example, involved members of the audience cutting off her clothes. She also made *Film No. 4 (Fluxfilm 16)*, consisting of naked bottoms, which the British Board of Film Censors banned by refusing to issue it with a certificate.

Ono considered the *Two Virgins* album cover part of her artistic endeavours and an important statement. "From my point of view, I was in the artistic community, where a painter did a thing about rolling a naked woman with blue paint on her body on a canvas; nakedness was part of the event 'happening' kind of thing that was going on at the time. The only difference was that we were going to stand together, which I thought was very interesting, instead of always exploiting women's bodies. This was: we are together, man and woman. And also it wasn't a sexy scene; it was just standing straight. I liked that concept. And that's why I had this filmic idea about us standing naked and being filmed in a way that was part of nature or something like that. But John's idea about putting it on an album cover, wow! That was very good."

The deliberately unglamorous image was another way for Lennon to break the illusion of his celebrity. The Beatles were the quintessence of glamour, the Four Kings of EMI, who mixed with the cream of London's swinging hipsters. By presenting himself in as unglamorous a manner as possible, he asked his audience to question the entire celebrity-making machine. "We felt like two virgins, because we were in love, just met, and we were trying to make something. And we thought to show everything. People are always looking at people like me, trying to see some secret. 'What do they do? Do they go to the bathroom? Do they eat?' So we just said, 'Here.' What we did purposely is not have a pretty photograph; not have it lighted so as we looked sexy or good. There were a couple of other takes from that session where we looked rather nice, hid the little bits that aren't that beautiful; we looked good. We used the straightest, most unflattering picture just to show that we were human."

Two Virgins data

Although Lennon owned a share in Apple Records, when it came to releasing *Two Virgins* he ran into problems. EMI had no problems manufacturing the record, but it would not distribute it in the sleeve he wanted. Lennon appealed to Sir Joseph Lockwood, chairman of EMI, but even though he was part of the company's greatest asset, EMI refused to distribute the album with the naked cover. Apple overcame the problem by employing some fans, known as "Apple scruffs", to put the records in the covers. Jack Oliver, an Apple employee, explained: "I had a bunch of Apple scruffs sleeve the record in the basement of the old Apple shop and then Track picked them up to distribute to the shops."

Two Virgins was scheduled for release on November 29, but distribution problems may have caused this date to slip. Speaking to John Peel on BBC Radio 1 on December 11 1968, Lennon not only gave the LP's catalogue number, which he cited as SAPCOR 12093, but he also said that the LP had sold 700 copies on its first day of release, December 10.

In Britain, the LP was to have been issued in mono and stereo. However, the mono edition was scrapped when Lennon decided to remix the album in stereo. (This would have further delayed the original November release date.) George Peckham, who worked for Apple at the time as a cutting engineer, explained what happened to the mono pressing in *Record Collector*: "We only received 50 pressings from the factory and it hadn't got the final sleeves at that point. When John remixed the album into stereo all of those pressings had sleeves, and I don't believe that there were any sleeves made with the mono markings." Of the handful of mono pressings that survived (APCOR 2) they have the 'Sold in U.K.' legend top centre, the title and composer credit in two lines above the spindle hole and the artist credit and publisher in three lines below the spindle hole. There are two sleeve variations; one with the text on the front, the other with the text on the back. It has been suggested that sleeves with the text on the front were intended for the mono edition.

The stereo edition (SAPCOR 1) has the title above the spindle hole, and the track listing in four lines followed by publisher and artist credits below the spindle hole. The stereo edition also has Track Records' logo and catalogue number (603012) in the top right corner above the Apple catalogue number. Technik printed the cover, which differs from its American counterpart in that the quote from McCartney and the album title appear on the rear.

Tetragrammaton Records, a company co-owned by US entertainer Bill Cosby, handled distribution of the album in America. As in Britain, the release date was held up because of problems with the cover. The scheduled release date of November 11 slipped, and the album was not issued until January 6 1969. The LP was issued in stereo, with Apple labels with title and composer credits in two lines above the spindle hole and artist credit and publisher below.

Although Capitol had nothing to do with the album, it distributed promotional blank picture discs of *Two Virgins* in a moulded plastic cover to its employees at their annual sales meeting in June 1969. Because the album was deleted quickly, counterfeit copies of *Two Virgins* were manufactured in America. Original Tetragrammaton pressings were issued in a brown paper outer cover, sealed with a circular white sticker; counterfeits do not have the white paper seal. Original pressings have glossy Apple labels; counterfeits have matte Apple labels.

In America, *Two Virgins* was issued by Apple on 8-track cartridge. It was originally distributed by Tetragrammaton and later GRT (General Recording Tape) for Tetragrammaton. The cartridge itself was manufactured by Ampex, North American Leisure Corp, and GRT.

In 1991, Rock Classics issued *Two Virgins* on CD (SSI 9999). A semi-legal CD, it was obviously dubbed from a vinyl source. Rykodisc issued the CD (RCD 10411) on June 3 1997. Taken from the original master tapes, it removes the last 30 seconds from side two of the album. It does, however, have a bonus Yoko Ono track, 'Remember Love', originally the B-side of 'Give Peace A Chance'.

On November 11 2017, Secretly Canadian in collaboration with Chimera Music released the first batch of re-mastered Yoko Ono solo albums on CD and vinyl. The vinyl editions were re-mastered from the original tapes by Greg Calbi and Sean Lennon. The first batch included *Unfinished Music No. 1: Two Virgins* (black or white vinyl), 1969's *Unfinished Music No. 2: Life with the Lions* (black or white vinyl), and 1970's *Yoko Ono Plastic Ono Band* (black or clear vinyl).

Above: front and back sleeve for the mono edition of *Unfinished Music No. 1: Two Virgins*. Note that the text is on the front cover. Sleeves for the stereo edition have the text on the back cover.

"When two great Saints meet it is a humbling experience. The long battles to prove he was a Saint." - Paul McCartney

Unfinished Music No. 1. Two Virgins. Yoko Ono/John Lennon. Apple Records. May, 1968. ● Made in Merris England.
Printed by Technica Limited. Photographs by John Lennon.

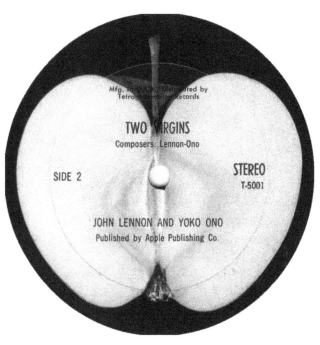

UNFINISHED MUSIC NO. 2: LIFE WITH THE LIONS
JOHN LENNON AND YOKO ONO

Side 1 'Cambridge 1969'.
Side 2 'No Bed For Beatle John', 'Baby's Heartbeat', 'Two Minutes Silence', 'Radio Play'.

UK release May 2 1969; Zapple ZAPPLE 01; failed to chart.
US release May 26 1969; LP Zapple ST 3357; 8-track cartridge Zapple 8XT-3357; chart high No.179.

'Cambridge 1969' (Lennon, Ono)
John Lennon (guitar), Yoko Ono (voice), John Tchicai (saxophone), John Stevens (percussion). Live recording at Lady Mitchell Hall, Cambridge University, Cambridge, England. Produced by John Lennon and Yoko Ono.
'Baby's Heartbeat' (Lennon, Ono)
Yoko Ono and John Lennon. Recorded at Queen Charlotte Hospital, Second West Ward, Room 1, London, England. Produced by John Lennon and Yoko Ono.
'Two Minutes Silence' (Lennon, Ono)
No personnel. Recording location unknown but probably Abbey Road Studios, London, England. Produced by John Lennon and Yoko Ono.

Remaining tracks see *Aspen* flexi.

LIFE WITH THE LIONS

Lennon and Ono's second album of avant-garde music appeared in early 1969 on Apple's new and short-lived imprint Zapple. The original intention was that Zapple would issue budget-price spoken word and avant-garde albums by the likes of Lenny Bruce, Richard Brautigan, Allen Ginsberg, and Charles Bukowski. The label was intended to respond quickly to cultural changes; the records would only be listened to once or twice and then disposed. Barry Miles, owner of the Indica gallery and bookshop, was made label manager and told to compile a list of releases. Besides approaching literary figures, Miles also intended to record world leaders such as Mao Tse Tung and Fidel Castro for the label. Although several writers including poet Charles Olon, Fugs drummer Ken Weaver, and author Lawrence Ferlinghetti were recorded for Zapple, only albums by Lennon and George Harrison were issued.

Zapple was launched on February 3 1969, with a press release explaining what it intended to issue and that some of its albums would sell at budget prices – UK LPs were intended to retail for 15/-, 21/- and 30/6 (75p, £1.05, £1.52) and US albums would sell for $1.98 and $4.98. However, by the time Zapple was up and running, The Beatles' manager Allen Klein had slashed funding, and what would have been a memorable series of recordings was shelved. When Zapple did issue records, they were little more than self-indulgent solo projects and sold at full price.

Life With The Lions documents two significant events in the life of Lennon and Ono. Side 1 was recorded at the couple's first concert performance together; side 2 features recordings made at Queen Charlotte's Hospital, London, some of which had already been issued by *Aspen* magazine (see previous entry). The album's title was a reference to a BBC radio programme, *Life With The Lyons*, that ran from 1951 to 1960. It was unique in that it featured a real family and real events, albeit exaggerated for comic effect. It isn't clear whether Lennon chose to name this album after the programme because of its documentary quality or simply because he remembered it from his childhood. What is clear is that the records and films he and Ono made were a very public diary. "I'm trying to get over as quickly as I can what exactly is happening to me at this given time, and so we collect photos, tape it, or make films of what's happening," he explained.

Some people were open to what the pair were attempting to do with their music; others were less receptive to their ideas. Writing for *Rolling Stone* magazine, Edmund Ward had nothing but contempt for the album. "*Life With The Lions* is utter bullshit, and perhaps a bit in poor taste. There is absolutely nothing on it to justify the expenditure of four bucks. Oh, wait – there is, too. One of the cuts on side 2 is called 'Two Minutes Silence,' and it is just that. Not only is it a much needed respite from the rest of the record, but it is also useful for checking the amount of rumble caused by your turntable's motor. See any hi-fi manual for instructions." The album was never going to sell to a mainstream audience, and Ward should have taken that into consideration. Although his criticism is a little harsh, it's true that *Life With The Lions* is hard-going.

It's unlikely that it was, or will ever be, a turntable favourite, but it is, nevertheless, an important historical document.

Life With The Lions songs

Only weeks after recording what would become *Let It Be*, Lennon made his first solo live appearance in support of Yoko Ono. The event was a free jazz concert at Cambridge University's 500-seat Lady Mitchell Hall. Ono was no stranger to events such as these, having performed a similar concert at the Albert Hall on February 29 1968 with jazzman Ornette Coleman. Although Lady Mitchell Hall was somewhat smaller than the Albert Hall, this time Ono was second on the bill to jazz pianist Chris McGregor. The concert had been booked long before Ono teamed up with Lennon, and she had intended to cancel, but Lennon insisted that she should go ahead with the concert.

Ono explained: "Cambridge asked me to come and do it before they knew about John and me. When we got together, there's a few appointments I missed because we were so involved with each other. But John was saying, 'Call them back, call them back,' so I said, 'OK, I'll call back,' and I said, 'Yes, I will come.' And then John was saying, 'Say that you'll bring your own band.' OK. 'I'm bringing my own band.'"

Tickets for the concert were priced at a reasonable 16/- (80p, about $2 then), and the audience was urged to bring their own "voice, flute or little shaker". The first act took to the stage at approximately three o'clock in the afternoon and immediately set the tone for what was to follow. Maggie Nichols, backed by two pianos, two basses, a trumpet, three woodwind instruments, and two drum kits, performed an ambitious free-form improvisation. Nichols' vocalisations echoed those of Ono's and were described by Douglas Oliver of *The Cambridge Evening News* as "epic wailing, weird pulses of sound, or cries – almost – of help".

After a short break, Yoko Ono strolled on stage followed by her accompanist, John Lennon. Positioning himself in front of a large Fender amplifier, he sat with his back to the audience throughout the performance. Dressed in black and standing behind two microphones – one for the PA, the other for recording – Ono announced timidly: "This is a piece called 'Cambridge 1969'." Then, without any further word of warning, she let out a long, sustained note, joined a few seconds later by ear-splitting guitar feedback. This atonal aural assault, formless and without melody or rhythm, continued for 26 minutes. Towards the end of the piece, saxophonist John Tchicai and percussionist John Stevens joined them on stage. After a few minutes of squawking saxophone and thumping percussion, Lennon and Ono left the stage and, one suspects, a traumatised audience behind them.

Whatever the audience thought of the performance, Lennon certainly found the experience liberating. "I just turned my guitar on and blew my mind out. She blew hers out, and you either get it or you don't. Just pure feedback and whatever is on that track," said Lennon. "If you hear it, it's just pure sound, because what else can you do when a woman's howling, you know, you just go along with it, right? … Yoko and I went to Cambridge, did the show and I discovered more about the guitar than I did for all these years. I enjoyed it!"

Just as the cover of *Two Virgins* had freed Lennon from the restrictions of being a Beatle, so performing with Ono freed him creatively. Here he was, one half of the world's greatest songwriting team, abandoning all the musical rules and concepts that had placed him at the top of his profession. He walked away from the concert a changed man. Ono's total abandonment of her classical training gave him the confidence to experiment. "What she did for guitar playing was to free it, the way she'd freed her voice from all the restrictions," Lennon explained.

Clearly, he was intent on destroying barriers, and performing with Ono was one way of doing so. Interviewed by B.P. Fallon for the *NME* around April 1969, he said: "All the musicians talk about no barriers between music and poetry. Yet most of them show it. We're doing it. Yoko will make pop records with me to show 'em."

The Lennons quest for artistic freedom would not be an easy one. The music they produced was often unsettling, for not only did it mirror their own feelings of pain and frustration but also the troubled atmosphere of the period. The *Cambridge Evening News* reviewer recognised the nexus that their music established between art and life. "The concert was strange and chilling. Not in a bad sense, but because there was so much unusual texture. At no time did the music become comforting. It was an extraordinary experience."

While at Queen Charlotte's with Ono, Lennon recorded the sound of their unborn baby's heartbeat. Sadly, the baby, named John Ono Lennon II, was stillborn. Lennon took the recording he'd made, looped it, and produced this recording. In light of Ono's miscarriage, issuing 'Baby's Heartbeat' was a very public reminder of their loss and a brave statement. It was not the first time Ono had alluded to child mortality in her work. The subject first appeared in a work from 1960, *A Grapefruit In The World Of Park*, and would reappear in later work such as 'Greenfield Morning I Pushed An Empty Baby Carriage All Over The City' from *Yoko Ono/Plastic Ono Band*.

'Baby's Heartbeat' is followed by 'Two Minutes Silence'. Whether they intended it as a memorial for their lost baby is not clear. Programming it to follow the recording of their lost child certainly strengthens the sense of loss and makes the baby's heartbeat seem all the more fragile.

It was also a sly reference to John Cage, as Ono explained, the piece was conceived as a tribute to the avant-garde composer. "In 'Two Minutes Silence', we sent a tribute to John Cage in a way. Cage did '4' 33''', and the title was the timing, the time. And he was saying the music is the sound that comes in, the sounds that come in during the silence, like environmental sounds, that was the music. So we were going to make a piece called 'Two Minutes Silence', and we were giggling, because we did the opposite, which was we made it totally dead silence! Like, this is the real silence, baby! So we were just being rebellious."

Unfortunately, the joke falls flat: like Cage's piece, 'Two Minutes Silence' does consist of extraneous sounds. Pressed on vinyl, there were inevitably static pops and clicks to interrupt the silence and, of course, the same external environmental sounds that Cage's '4' 33''' had set out to incorporate. Not content with borrowing Cage's idea wholesale, the pair even had the gall to copyright the silence and claim it as their own (and John would later do the same with his 'Nutopian International Anthem'). But when composer Mike Batt tried the same thing in July 2002, Cage's publishers sued for infringement of copyright. Batt had placed one minute's silence on his CD *Classical Graffiti* and credited it as a Batt/Cage composition. Because Batt jokingly claimed to have written the piece in collaboration with Cage, he was forced to pay the American composer's publishers a six-figure sum. In claiming it for their own, the Lennons got away with it.

Life With The Lions data

This time, EMI and Capitol manufactured and distributed the album – not that it made any difference to a poor sales performance. Original pressings came with a white paper inner sleeve printed with song titles and details of who played on which track. There are two UK label variations; with and without "Sold in the UK subject to …" text. There are several US label variations, which appear to be caused by variations in printing label backdrops and text. The album was issued in Japan with Apple labels (AP-8782). Promotional copies were pressed on low-noise red vinyl with white labels with an Apple logo top centre. Finished copies were issued with Zapple labels. The Japanese reissue (EAS-80701) came with a four-page lyric sheet rather than a printed inner sleeve. Rykodisc issued the album on CD (RCD10412) on June 3 1997 with enhanced packaging and two bonus tracks, 'Song For John' and 'Mulberry'.

On November 11 2017, Secretly Canadian in collaboration with Chimera Music released *Unfinished Music No. 2: Life with the Lions* on black or white vinyl and CD. The CD version includes the same 'bonus' tracks that first appeared on the Rykodisc edition.

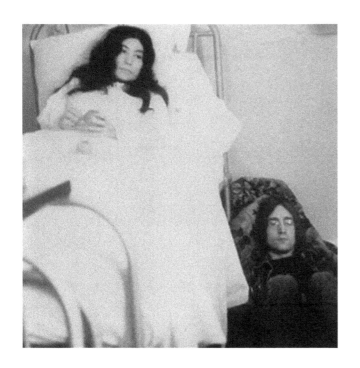

21

'NO COMMENT' — GEORGE MARTIN
UNFINISHED MUSIC NO. 2: LIFE WITH THE LIONS
JOHN LENNON/YOKO ONO   APPLE RECORDS
MADE IN MERRIE ENGLAND. NOV. '68

UNFINISHED MUSIC NO. 2:
LIFE WITH THE LIONS
JOHN LENNON AND YOKO ONO

STEREO   ST-3357
                      (ST 1-3357)
                      SIDE 1

1. CAMBRIDGE 1969 BMI 26:30

All Songs Composed by John Lennon and Yoko Ono
Produced by John Lennon and Yoko Ono
Recorded in England

UNFINISHED   JOHN LENNON
MUSIC NO. 2:   AND YOKO ONO
LIFE WITH THE LIONS

STEREO   ST-3357
                      (ST 2-3357)
                      SIDE 2

1. NO BED FOR BEATLE JOHN ASCAP 4:45
2. BABY'S HEARTBEAT ASCAP 5:10
3. TWO MINUTES SILENCE ASCAP 2:00
4. RADIO PLAY ASCAP 12:35

All Songs Composed by John Lennon and Yoko Ono
Produced by John Lennon and Yoko Ono

Recorded
in England

MFD. BY APPLE RECORDS, INC.

UNFINISHED MUSIC NO. 2:
LIFE WITH THE LIONS
JOHN LENNON AND YOKO ONO

STEREO   ST-3357
                      (ST 1-3357)
                      SIDE 1

1. CAMBRIDGE 1969 BMI 26:30

All Songs Composed by John Lennon and Yoko Ono
Produced by John Lennon and Yoko Ono
Recorded in England

UNFINISHED   JOHN LENNON
MUSIC NO. 2:   AND YOKO ONO
LIFE WITH THE LIONS

STEREO   ST-3357
                      (ST 2-3357)
                      SIDE 2

1. NO BED FOR BEATLE JOHN ASCAP 4:45
2. BABY'S HEARTBEAT ASCAP 5:10
3. TWO MINUTES SILENCE ASCAP 2:00
4. RADIO PLAY ASCAP 12:35

All Songs Composed by John Lennon and Yoko Ono
Produced by John Lennon and Yoko Ono

Recorded
in England

MFD. BY APPLE RECORDS, INC.

John Lennon: 'Radio Play'.
Yoko Ono: 'Song for John / Let's Go On Flying', 'Snow Is Falling All The Time', 'Mum's Only Looking For Her Hand In The Snow'.
Yoko Ono & John Lennon: 'No Bed For Beatle John'.

US release magazine published spring/summer 1970 by Roaring Fork Press, New York City, with 8-inch square flexible plastic record, 33-1/3 rpm, mono; edited by Mario Amaya; designed by John Kosh.

'Song For John / Let's Go On Flying', 'Snow Is Falling All The Time' (Ono)
Yoko Ono (voice).
'Mum's Only Looking For Her Hand In The Snow' (Lennon, Ono)
Yoko Ono (voice), John Lennon (guitar).
'No Bed For Beatle' (Lennon, Ono)
Yoko Ono (voice), John Lennon (voice).
'Radio Play' (Lennon, Ono)
Yoko Ono (voice), John Lennon (voice, radio).

All recorded at Queen Charlotte Hospital, Second West Ward, Room 1, London. All produced by John Lennon and Yoko Ono.

ASPEN FREE DISC

Aspen magazine was the brainchild of Phyllis Johnson, a former editor of *Women's Wear Daily* and *Advertising Age*. Johnson got the idea to publish a multimedia magazine while on holiday in Aspen, Colorado. Each issue would employ a different designer in order to capture a certain period, point of view, or person. Abandoning the traditional magazine format, which Johnson thought too restrictive, *Aspen* would consist of a variety of communication media, including print, film, and sound recordings.

The first two issues looked at the Aspen festival scene, but the magazine's scope was broadened with No.3, a Pop Art issue designed by Andy Warhol and David Dalton and devoted to New York's art and counterculture scenes. Issue 7, designed by John Kosh (who would also design The Beatles' *Get Back* book), explored new voices in British arts and culture. This issue arrived in a hinged box measuring 10 by 9-1/2 by 1-1/4 inches, shipped flat, designed by Richard Smith. Besides contributions from the Lennons, the magazine featured offerings from several of Britain's leading artists, writers, and designers including Ossie Clark, Edward Lucie-Smith, J. G. Ballard, Eduardo Paolozzi, Peter Blake, and David Hockney.

Issued on an 8-inch square 33-1/3 rpm 'flexi' record, the recordings were made under difficult circumstances. Ono was expecting their first child and had been admitted to Queen Charlotte's because her pregnancy was not going well. Only weeks earlier, on October 18 1968, Lennon's flat had been raided by the Scotland Yard Drug Squad. Headed by Detective-Sergeant Norman Pilcher, who had already busted several members of Britain's rock aristocracy, the 12-strong squad discovered a small quantity of cannabis resin and arrested Lennon and Ono, who were taken to Paddington Green police station. Charged with possession of cannabis and wilfully obstructing the police in the execution of their search warrant, the two were ordered to appear at Marylebone Magistrates Court the following day. Lennon took full responsibility, pleading guilty to save Ono from a criminal record – a decision he would live to regret. Released on bail, they had to battle through a 300-strong crowd and the waiting press.

Lennon subsequently claimed that the cannabis had been planted in his flat. Pilcher was seeking promotion by busting high-profile individuals and was not beyond planting evidence to ensure a conviction. However, Lennon's drug consumption was legendary, and had Pilcher bothered to search the flat he would surely have found what he was looking for without having to plant it. Years later, Pilcher was imprisoned for perjury and Lennon was forced to fight a long battle with the US authorities because of his criminal record.

This high-profile drugs bust did little to improve Ono's health. Several months' pregnant, she was admitted to hospital for observation. Lennon, of course, insisted on being by her side. To begin with, he slept in the bed next to her, but when that bed was needed, he slept on the floor in a sleeping bag. A Conservative Member of Parliament thought Lennon's presence in the hospital ward an invasion of privacy and raised the matter in Parliament. Although it says more about prevailing attitudes to the presence of men during childbirth than it does about Lennon's desire to be with Ono, that his presence should be remarked upon in Parliament says much about the couple's media profile. Besides being recorded in a hospital room, these recordings are made all the more remarkable as an indication of the pair's unquenchable desire to document every moment of their life together.

Aspen songs

Ono began writing 'Song For John / Let's Go Flying' before she met her future husband. She was already looking for a record deal and recalled that 'Song For John' was originally destined for what would have been her debut album. "A record company had suggested I do an album of my sort of freak-type freestyle things, one of which was 'Song For John'. When I was writing it, I was thinking about wanting to meet somebody who could fly with me. Then suddenly, [Lennon] came into the picture and was the first person who listened to the demo – so I felt a sentimental reason for the name to be John."

Several of Ono's early works employ the sky as a metaphor for intellect and transcendence. Besides writing scores and songs that referred to the sky, she made several 'paintings', intended as conceptual pieces, to act as conduits for transcendence.

'Song For John' was later reworked and re-recorded for her album *Approximately Infinite Universe*.

'Snow Is Falling All The Time' is reminiscent of a nursery rhyme and, if anything, is even more fragile than the first two parts of this recording. It was later reworked into 'Listen, The Snow Is Falling', issued as the B-side of 'Happy Christmas (War Is Over)'.

For 'Mum's Only Looking For Her Hand In The Snow', Lennon improvises some bluesy riffs on a nylon-string acoustic guitar to back Ono on an early version of 'Don't Worry Kyoko (Mummy's Only Looking For Her Hand In The Snow)'.

'No Bed For Beatle' finds Ono singing in the style of Gregorian chant, with Lennon in the background, intoning lines from newspaper articles about their stay in hospital and the impending release of the *Two Virgins* album. It's another example of their desire to document almost everything they did and said, and would not be the last.

'Radio Play' is an attempt at John Cage-like avant-garde composition, using nothing other than a radio. It sounds like the kind of early electronic music produced by the BBC's Radiophonic Workshop – without the tunes. A series of truncated blips eventually become recognisable as spoken and sung word fragments, which nevertheless remain the briefest of segments and unrecognisable. Meanwhile, in the background, Lennon and Ono have a conversation and Lennon makes a telephone call. As with several of Ono's pieces, it evokes a sense of absence, balance, and unity. Absence – the missing fragments of speech – are balanced by their conversation, when combined they create a whole. Ironically, this is an edited version of the complete recording, a longer version of which would be made available on the album *Life With The Lions*.

'GIVE PEACE A CHANCE' / 'REMEMBER LOVE'
PLASTIC ONO BAND

UK release July 4 1969; Apple APPLE 13; chart high No.2 (re-enters January 24 1981, chart high No.33).
US release July 21 1969; Apple APPLE 1809; chart high No.14.

'Give Peace A Chance' (Lennon, McCartney)
John Lennon (vocals and guitar), Yoko Ono (vocals), Tommy Smothers (guitar), Allen Ginsberg, Dr Timothy Leary, Petula Clark, Rosemary Woodruff, Derek Taylor, Murray The K, Dick Gregory, Abraham Feinberg, the Canadian chapter of the Radha Krishna Temple (hand drums, finger cymbals), unknown others (backing vocals).
'Remember Love' (Ono)
John Lennon (guitar), Yoko Ono (vocals).

Both recorded at Room 1742, La Hotel Reine Elizabeth, Montreal, Canada. Both produced by John Lennon and Yoko Ono.

'GIVE PEACE A CHANCE'

Lennon and Ono arrived in Toronto, Canada on May 25 1969 to begin their second bed-in for peace. The following day, the couple and their entourage moved into room 1742 of La Hotel Reine Elizabeth in Montreal. Inviting the world's media into their suite, the pair spent the week discussing peace.

Their original plan had been to stage the bed-in in America, but Lennon's conviction for possession of cannabis meant he was denied a visa. With no direct access to American media networks, Lennon considered The Bahamas. But this location proved to be unsuitable. The next logical location was Canada, because it shares a border with the USA.

The Lennons had staged their first bed-in in Suite 902 at the Amsterdam Hilton from March 25 to 29. Besides publicly celebrating their honeymoon – they were married in Gibraltar on March 20 – Lennon and Ono orchestrated the 'event' as part of a concerted peace campaign that would occupy them for the best part of ten months. The world's media were invited and were again baffled by the couple's antics. How could staying in bed for a week contribute to world peace? As usual they missed the point.

The bed-ins were part of a massive multimedia advertising campaign that was intended to get people, including world leaders, talking about peace rather than war. Speaking to David Frost, Lennon explained: "We're trying to sell peace, like a product, you know, and sell it like people sell soap or soft drinks, [because it's] the only way to get people aware that peace is possible and it isn't just inevitable to have violence; not just war – all forms of violence. People just accept it and think, 'Oh they did it,' or, 'Harold Wilson did it,' or, 'Nixon did it,' they're always scapegoating people. And it isn't Nixon's fault: we're all responsible for everything that goes on, you know, we're all responsible for Biafra and Hitler and everything. So we're just saying 'sell peace,' anybody interested in peace just stick it in the window, it's simple but it lets somebody else know that you want peace too. Because you feel alone if you're the only one thinking, 'Wouldn't it be nice if there was peace and nobody was getting killed.' So advertise yourself that you're for peace if you believe in it."

Bed-ins were only part of the marketing strategy. Poster campaigns, films, radio, television, and of course records all played their part in getting the message across. Lennon's first solo single was intended as part of the campaign and became the most successful element in his multimedia armoury.

Although this was his first solo single, it was not issued under John Lennon's name. The release of 'Give Peace A Chance' introduced another Fluxus-inspired concept, Plastic Ono Band. The band would have an ever changing line-up, echoing the Fluxus ideas of conceptualisation and fluidity: advertisements for the band's first single stated: "You Are The Plastic Ono Band."

The group was launched with a press reception at Chelsea Town Hall on July 3. Lennon and Ono should have attended the event, but they had been injured in a car accident and were hospitalised. Ringo and Maureen Starr took their place and Perspex boxes containing recording equipment represented the band. The Beatles' press officer, Derek Taylor, told *Disc*: "The band was made in Perspex in Hoylake, in Cheshire (where Selwyn Lloyd and I were brought up separately) by an inventor I know called Charles Melling. It was Yoko's idea, with John, made to her specifications; four pieces – like John, Paul, George, and Ringo, three taller and one shorter. Two rectangular, one cylindrical, and a cube. One column holds a tape recorder and amplifier, another a closed-circuit TV set with live camera, a third a record player with amplifier, and the fourth has a miniature lightshow and a loudspeaker. But they could hold anything; they are as adaptable as The Beatles. The Perspex columns were fitted with their equipment by Apple electronics under the direction of [Magic] Alexis Mardas, and here ends the first and last technological press release you will have from me."

Taylor also remarked upon the group's Fluxus credentials and their fluid nature. "The band may be the property of Apple, but it also belongs to everyone because what it represents is freedom, freedom for performers to be themselves, taking no heed of who they are or what they look like or where they have been or what their music is supposed to be. It could be children in a playground screaming their release from the bondage of the classroom or it could be John and Yoko screaming their love for one another. It could be anything. The band will tour – the British band will tour here, and in the US another band is to be built, built to withstand the long hauls across that amazing continent and maybe beyond, maybe far beyond one day. Who knows, any more?" Taylor's predictions were spot on: the band went through many changes on both sides of the Atlantic. The only thing he didn't get right was Lennon's commitment to touring. The Plastic Ono Band never did tour America and their live performances were few and sporadic.

'Give Peace A Chance' was recorded in room 1742 at La Hotel Reine Elizabeth, Montreal, on the night of May 31 and was completed in the early hours of June 1 1969. The Lennons had spent all week speaking with the media about peace and their message was simple: "All we are saying is give peace a chance," a phrase Lennon used during an interview he gave on arrival in Toronto on May 25. In the days that followed, he fleshed out his chorus with a simple verse, and on the final day of the Montreal bed-in he decided to record it.

While the song was credited to Lennon–McCartney, Paul McCartney played no part in its composition. Although Lennon was growing apart from The Beatles, he still felt obliged to stand by his original agreement with McCartney and split songwriting credits with him.

Taylor was asked to arrange for some recording equipment to be set up in the hotel room and contacted a local studio proprietor to provide it. André Perry got a call from Capitol asking him to provide 4-track recording gear, which he hired from RCA Victor because his was already in use, and deliver it to the hotel. Once everyone was assembled, there was a quick rehearsal and soundcheck, and then the recording proper. Perry, who engineered the session, recalls that the song was captured in one take. Although Lennon was happy with the take, Perry was not so sure, as conditions in the room were not ideal. Perry noted that the recording was suffering from distortion, so the following day he overdubbed additional vocals to mask the defects. Back in his studio, Perry transferred the 4-track tape to 8-track and invited some friends and singers to contribute to the recording. Lennon approved of Perry's work and the tape was sent back to the UK for mastering, and it was issued as Lennon's debut solo single a few weeks later.

'Give Peace A Chance', with just two chords, the stream-of-consciousness verses, and a simple repeated chorus, was deliberately simple. A mantra for peace, it was undeniably catchy and gave the peace movement something to sing besides 'We Shall Overcome'. While it's not one of his finest compositions, it is one of Lennon's best-known songs and has become a present-day folk song.

Although it was rumoured that Ringo Starr added percussion to the track, Perry insists that no further overdubs were added to the tape other than those he applied in Montreal. The later release of an excerpt from a rehearsal of 'Give Peace A Chance', on *John Lennon Anthology*, features the unnamed percussionist, proving that Starr did not overdub percussion at a later date. What the rehearsal take highlights is Ono's off-key singing, which was placed well down in the final mix.

Having completed 'Give Peace A Chance', Lennon and Ono turned to recording what would be the record's B-side. Written by Ono, 'Remember Love' took about four hours to make. Recording started at about one o'clock in the morning of June 1 and finished around five. Unlike her earlier avant-garde recordings, 'Remember Love' is a gentle ballad that borrowed from another recent Lennon composition, 'Sun King'.

'Give Peace A Chance' data

Apple issued 'Give Peace A Chance' in Britain with generic Apple labels and a picture sleeve. Three label variations were produced. The first has a dark green Apple label, is without 'Sold in U.K. subject to resale price conditions, see price lists', has 'Mfd. in U.K.' and song publishers 'Northern Songs NCB', and has a Parlophone catalogue number, R 5795, below the Apple catalogue number. The second has a dark green Apple label, with 'Sold in U.K. subject to resale price conditions, see price lists', 'Mfd. in U.K.', and song publishers 'Northern Songs.' The third has a light green Apple label without 'Sold in U.K. subject to resale price conditions, see price lists' but with 'Mfd. in U.K.' and song publishers 'Northern Songs'. EMI reissued 'Give Peace A Chance' (G 45 2) on March 12 1984 with a new B-side, 'Cold Turkey', and picture sleeve.

In America, Apple issued the single with generic Apple labels and a picture sleeve. The American single lacks the introductory count-in, which appears on the British version. An alternative colour picture sleeve, with different machines in the Perspex tubes, was created for the American market. Although proofs were printed, the alternative design was never produced commercially. The image was, however, used to advertise the band's *Live Peace In Toronto* album.

American pressings were produced with two label variations. The first has a dark green Apple label with song title at nine o'clock with composer credits and 'STEREO' below. Catalogue number and artist credit appear at three o'clock. This variant has thin text. The second has a dark green Apple label with song title at ten o'clock and composer credits below. 'STEREO' is at two o'clock and catalogue number at three o'clock, with artist credit centre bottom. This version has bold text.

'Give Peace A Chance' was produced as a 4-inch flexi-disc Pocket Disc by Americom. This company began working with Capitol in late 1968 and produced three Beatles singles in the new format. The discs were intended as an affordable alternative to the more expensive 7-inch single and originally aimed at the very young, although later research showed that they were being bought by people who rarely purchased pop records. The flexi-discs were printed with silver text and a line drawing of Apple A- and B-side labels. The Pocket Disc single was issued with two catalogue numbers, one assigned by Capitol, 1809P (the 'P' standing for Pocket Disc), the other M-435A, which was the Americom catalogue number. The discs were not issued in picture sleeves but in blue or red generic card sleeves.

Capitol's Special Markets Division produced gold-plated copies of 'Give Peace A Chance' in 1994 with purple Capitol labels (S7-17783). About 100 copies escaped the plating and found their way into the collectors' market.

'Give Peace A Chance' was issued as a 12-inch single (1C052-90372YZ) in Germany in 1981 with a picture sleeve based on an illustration from the *Shaved Fish* album cover.

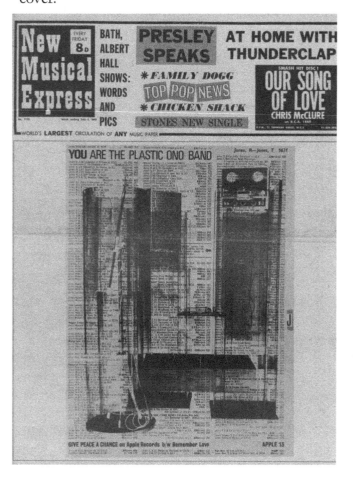

'THE KYA 1969 PEACE TALK'
FEATURING JOHN LENNON OF THE BEATLES WITH KYA'S TOM CAMPBELL AND BILL HOLLEY

US release 1969; KYA Records 1259; failed to chart.

KYA 1969 PEACE TALK

The Lennons' second bed-in was intended to reach an American audience. However, because John was unable to enter the country they went to Canada; he spent hours on the telephone speaking to American radio stations from his hotel room in Montreal. His interview with KYA in San Francisco was issued as a 7-inch single.

Interviewed by Tom Campbell and Bill Holley, Lennon sounded lively and engaging. Although he was primarily promoting peace, he was happy to answer questions on everything from the bed-in to The Beatles' latest single.

'COLD TURKEY' / 'DON'T WORRY KYOKO (MUMMY'S ONLY LOOKING FOR A HAND IN THE SNOW)'
PLASTIC ONO BAND

UK release October 24 1969; Apple APPLES 1001; chart high No.14.
US release October 20 1969; Apple APPLE 1813; chart high No.30.

'Cold Turkey' (Lennon)
John Lennon (vocals, guitar), Eric Clapton (guitar), Klaus Voormann (bass), Ringo Starr (drums). Recorded at Abbey Road Studios and Trident Studios, London, England. Produced by John and Yoko (BAG).

'Don't Worry Kyoko (Mummy's Only Looking For A Hand In The Snow)' (Ono)
Yoko Ono (vocals), John Lennon (guitar), Eric Clapton (guitar), Klaus Voormann (bass), Ringo Starr (drums). Recorded at Studio A, Lansdowne Studios, Lansdowne Road, London, England. Produced by John and Yoko (BAG).

'COLD TURKEY'

John Lennon had to have a drug of one kind or another. He admitted as much. "I've always needed a drug to survive. The others, too, but I always had more, more pills, more of everything, because I'm more crazy probably." By 1969, his drug of choice was heroin. It was a drug that he and Ono used to alleviate their pain. Although he appeared to have everything, Lennon suffered a lot in the late 1960s.

The cause of his pain was the reaction of others to the woman he loved. Above all else, Lennon wanted his friends to accept Ono as he did. But The Beatles and their circle were a tight unit. They didn't accept outsiders and never approved of Ono, whose presence they barely tolerated. Worse still, the media openly criticised Lennon for his relationship with her. At the time, women, particularly those married to rock stars, were meant to be glamorous and subservient. Ono was neither of these. Furthermore, she was an Oriental, a weird Japanese artist who made films of people's bottoms.

Naturally, Lennon felt troubled by the private and public reaction to his relationship with Ono. His troubles were compounded by a high-profile drugs bust, a conviction for possession of cannabis, Ono's miscarriage and the loss of their child, a divorce from his wife of six years, a growing discontent with The Beatles, a worsening relationship with McCartney, and vicious press coverage that labelled him and Ono as freaks. All this consolidated Lennon and Ono's misery. Outcasts, their only escape was through drugs. Speaking about his drug problem, Lennon said: "It just was not too much fun. I never injected it or anything. We sniffed a little when we were in real pain. … And we get into so much pain that we have to do something about it. And that's what happened to us. We took H because of what The Beatles and others were doing to us."

It has been suggested that Ono dabbled with heroin while Lennon was in India and that Lennon had been a user before meeting Ono. But it doesn't matter who took heroin first – what mattered was the grip it had on the couple. At first, Lennon was attracted to heroin's reputation as an artistic indulgence, but he quickly grew horrified at how difficult it was to kick it. Determined to rid himself of the monkey on his back, so he could father a child with Ono, Lennon decided on total abstinence. Rehab clinics were almost unheard of and hospitalisation would have attracted more adverse publicity, so Lennon had no other choice than to go cold turkey. Withdrawing from heroin is a little like having a bad bout of flu. Symptoms begin six to eight hours after the last dose and peak between 48 and 72 hours later. The symptoms include chills, goose bumps (hence the name), stomach cramps, and vomiting, and usually subdue after seven days.

Lennon had written songs about drugs before 'Cold Turkey'. Even some of his songs that had absolutely nothing to do with drugs were assumed to allude to them. He wasn't the first to write about his drug experiences and he wouldn't be the last, but he was perhaps the most honest. 'Cold Turkey' was another reading from Lennon's personal diary that he was determined to make public. Documenting his withdrawal from heroin, the song's bleak warning was a disturbing wake-up call to those naive about the danger of hard drugs.

The song was demoed in the summer of 1969. Lennon backed himself on acoustic guitar, which he then double-tracked. To this he added an acoustic lead guitar and a second vocal (and the result was issued later on *John Lennon Acoustic*). The tape was then spooled back to the start for Ono to add her contribution. Although it was only intended as a demo recording, the acoustic setting failed to match Lennon's harrowing lyric. The song failed to convince when it was performed at the Toronto Rock & Roll Revival festival on September 13 1969 (see the *Live Peace In Toronto* album featured later in this chapter). Still in embryonic state, it sounded no more shocking than any of the old rockers that Lennon performed that night.

Before its Toronto debut, Lennon offered 'Cold Turkey' to The Beatles, suggesting that they issue it as their next single. The offer was made prior to his performance in Toronto, as it was during that trip that he decided to leave the group. With The Beatles having turned it down, Lennon recorded it with Plastic Ono Band. As Clapton and Voormann knew the song from the Toronto show, they were asked to play on the studio recording. And although he had decided to quit The Beatles, Lennon invited Ringo Starr to play drums.

Convening at Abbey Road Studios on the evening of September 25, this line-up recorded 26 takes before calling it quits. Lennon was obviously unhappy with the results because the group were recalled to remake the song at Trident Studios on the 28th. Things went better this time, and the tape was mixed the following evening at Abbey Road. On October 5 more overdubs were added at Abbey Road and the final mix completed.

The finished product is a raw, stark confessional, almost as harrowing to listen to as the experience of going cold turkey. Voormann's bass pounds like blood pulsing in the ear, while Clapton's guitar howls like a banshee, or a junkie suffering the pain of withdrawal. It's little wonder that several radio stations banned the record. It would have frightened the living daylights out of most listeners.

On November 26, Lennon returned his MBE in protest against Britain's involvement in Nigeria, its support of America's war in Vietnam – and because 'Cold Turkey' was slipping down the charts. Legitimate protest that it was, Lennon's humorous reference to his latest single's decline was controversial. It was, of course, all part of a carefully planned publicity stunt to benefit the Lennons' peace campaign. It also gave Lennon the opportunity to distance himself from the Establishment and stake a claim as counterculture politico, a persona he would embrace wholly in the early 1970s.

Recorded by the same line-up that played on the A-side, Ono's 'Don't Worry Kyoko (Mummy's Only Looking For A Hand In The Snow)' had appeared in embryonic form on the *Aspen* magazine flexi-disc. The song would also appear on her double album, *Fly*, issued as a companion to Lennon's *Imagine*.

'Cold Turkey' data

Apple issued 'Cold Turkey' in Britain in a picture sleeve and generic Apple labels with "PLAY LOUD" printed in large bold type in the centre of both the A- and B-side labels.

American pressings were issued with two label variants. The first has a dark green Apple label and thin text, the song title at ten o'clock with the composer credits below, and "STEREO" at eight o'clock. "PLAY" appears at twelve o'clock and "LOUD" at six o'clock. The artist's name appears centre bottom. The second type has a light green Apple label with bold text, song title at ten o'clock, and artist's name at eight o'clock. "STEREO" appears at two o'clock, with the catalogue number and producer credits on the right-hand side of the label.

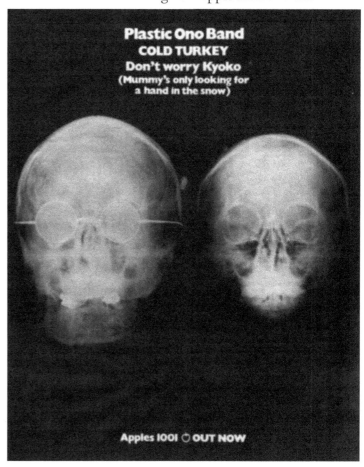

33

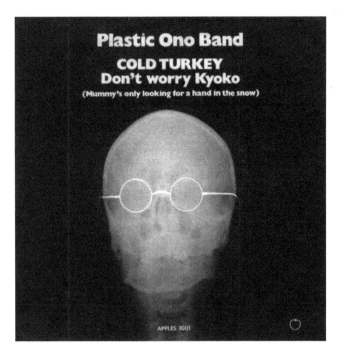

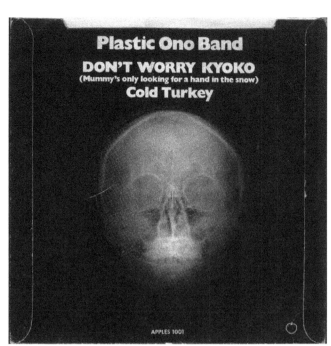

34

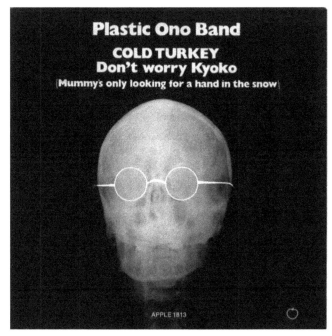

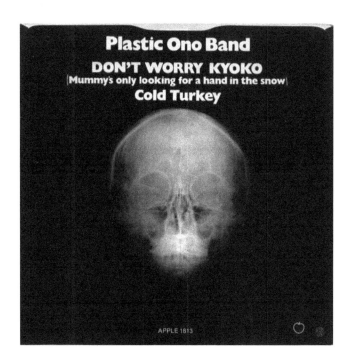

35

THE WEDDING ALBUM
JOHN LENNON AND YOKO ONO

Side 1 'John And Yoko'.
Side 2 'Amsterdam'.

UK release November 14 1969; Apple SAPCOR 11; failed to chart.
US release October 20 1969; LP Apple SMAX 3360; 8-track cartridge Apple 8AX-3360; chart high No.178.

'John And Yoko' (Lennon, Ono)
John Lennon (vocals, heartbeat), Yoko Ono (vocals, heartbeat). Recorded at Abbey Road Studios, London, England.
'Amsterdam' (Lennon, Ono)
John Lennon (vocals, guitar), Yoko Ono (vocals). Recorded at Room 902, The Hilton Hotel, Amsterdam, Netherlands.
Both produced by John Lennon.

THE WEDDING ALBUM

Lennon and Ono's third album of avant-garde recordings was a celebration of their honeymoon and, by implication, their art. Side two of the record was a montage of recordings made during the Lennons' first bed-in in Amsterdam. Knowing that the media would report their honeymoon whether they wanted the publicity or not, Lennon and Ono decided to use the occasion to promote world peace. Turning their honeymoon into a Fluxus based 'event', they blurred the boundary between art and life. Speaking at the time, Lennon said: "Our life is our art. That's what the bed-ins were. When we got married, we knew our honeymoon was going to be public, anyway, so we decided to use it to make a statement."

The Lennons' honeymoon was the perfect Fluxus event. It transgressed the boundaries of art and life; it confounded the media and the public alike; and as a mass media event it was available to all for the price of a newspaper. For those who wanted a more substantial and lasting reminder of the event, the couple issued a lavishly packaged album.

They entered Abbey Road Studio Two on Tuesday April 22 1969 to record a new avant-garde composition they named after themselves, 'John And Yoko'. The piece consisted of their heartbeats, over which they called each other's names. The recording was influenced by Ono, who had previously used bodily sounds for her avant-garde compositions. For one of her early pieces she attached microphones to people so that when they moved the amplified sounds were transformed into a bizarre form of music. John Cage, who had a strong influence on Ono, argued that all sound could be considered as music, but she was one of the first composers to use bodily noises and sounds that exist outside our normal range of hearing as a medium for generating music.

Although the Lennons had previously issued the sound of their unborn child's heartbeat, this was the first time they had recorded the sound of their own bodies to create music. Writing in *Melody Maker*, Richard Williams acknowledged the musical nature of the piece. He contended that "the rhythm of the heartbeats, constantly colliding and separating, resembles (albeit accidentally) the playing of African drummers, and in the middle, when the voices quieten, the metabolic sound surges through with considerable strength".

As simple as it is, this avant-garde piece had as many nuances as music made with conventional instruments. It was a challenging piece of experimentation, but Ono's use of unconventional sounds expressed universal emotions. The heart traditionally symbolises love; the sound of two heartbeats coming together created an equally powerful metaphor. If the sound of their unborn baby's heartbeat could represent loss, then the sound of their own heartbeats could stand as a metaphor for the intimacy of their relationship.

The session began at 11:00pm and continued until 4:30 the following morning. Five days later, on Sunday April 27, the pair returned to Abbey Road and remade the track. This time, recording and mixing was completed between 3:00 and 8:00pm. The piece was completed on May 1, when Lennon combined elements from both recordings. Three attempts were made to create the finished stereo mix, which he took away with him at the end of the session.

'Amsterdam' is a collage of songs, soundbites, and interviews recorded during their Amsterdam bed-in. Although the title suggests a specific location, parts of the recording were probably made in London after the event, as the bed-in is often discussed in the past tense. The musical content is similar to that found on the *Aspen* flexi-disc, although this time the mood was more up-beat.

The Wedding Album data

Apple issued *The Wedding Album* as a boxed set that included a booklet of press cuttings, a poster of drawings by Lennon and Ono, a large poster of black-and-white photographs taken on their wedding day, a postcard, a strip of passport photographs, a photograph of a slice of wedding cake, a plastic bag (not included in the Japanese reissue), and a copy of their marriage certificate. Because the packaging was so extravagant, the album was issued a good six months after the event it was intended to celebrate.

Richard Williams's review of the album for *Melody Maker* earned him a place in rock history. He was sent two one-sided test pressings of the LP, each including a blank side on the reverse containing nothing but an engineer's test signal. Assuming that the album was a double, and the 'tones' further examples of Lennon and Ono's minimalist pieces, Williams reviewed the blank sides. He suggested that "constant listening reveals a curious point: the pitch of the tones alters frequency, but only by microtones or, at most, a semitone. This oscillation produces an almost subliminal, uneven 'beat' which maintains interest. On a more basic level, you could have a ball by improvising your very own raga, plainsong, or even Gaelic mouth music against the drone." Lennon loved the review and sent Williams a personal thank-you.

Rykodisc issued a CD (RCD10413) on June 3 1997 with three bonus Yoko Ono tracks, 'Who Has Seen the Wind?' (originally the B-side of 'Instant Karma!'), 'Listen, The Snow Is Falling' (originally the B-side of 'Happy Xmas War Is Over') and 'Don't Worry, Kyoko (Mummy's Only Looking For Her Hand in the Snow)' (the *Aspen* magazine version, where it had the working title 'Mum's Only Looking For Her Hand In The Snow').

'Amsterdam'

'John and Yoko'

WEDDING ALBUM

STEREO
SAPCOR 11

33⅓
Mfd. in U.K.
SIDE 1

(SAPCOR 11A)
℗ 1969

JOHN AND YOKO (2:23)
Composed: John and Yoko
Published: Apple Publishing Ltd.
(for Bag Productions)
Produced: John and Yoko (Bag Productions)

JOHN AND YOKO

WEDDING ALBUM

STEREO
SAPCOR 11

33⅓
Mfd. in U.K.
SIDE 2

(SAPCOR 11B)
℗ 1969

AMSTERDAM (24:52)
Composed: John and Yoko
Published: Apple Publishing Ltd.
(for Bag Productions)
Produced: John and Yoko (Bag Productions)

JOHN AND YOKO

WEDDING ALBUM
JOHN ONO LENNON
& YOKO ONO LENNON

STEREO
SMAX-3361

(SMAX-1-3361)
SIDE 1

1. JOHN & YOKO BMI 22:23
(John Ono Lennon - Yoko Ono Lennon)

Produced by John Ono Lennon & Yoko Ono Lennon
Recorded in Europe

WEDDING ALBUM

JOHN ONO LENNON
&
YOKO ONO LENNON

STEREO
SMAX-3361

(SMAX-2-3361)
SIDE 2

1. AMSTERDAM BMI 24:52
(John Ono Lennon - Yoko Ono Lennon)

Produced by John Ono Lennon & Yoko Ono Lennon
Recorded in Europe

MFD. BY APPLE RECORDS, INC.

WEDDING ALBUM
JOHN AND YOKO

EMI
Odeon

EAS-80702 1 33⅓ r.p.m.
STEREO
(SAPCOR-11-A)

JOHN AND YOKO
Composed: John and Yoko
Published: Apple Publishing Ltd.
(for Bag Productions)
Produced: John and Yoko (Bag Productions)

WEDDING ALBUM
JOHN AND YOKO

EMI
Odeon

EAS-80702 2 33⅓ r.p.m.
STEREO
(SAPCOR-11-B)

AMSTERDAM
Composed: John and Yoko
Published: Apple Publishing Ltd.
(for Bag Productions)
Produced: John and Yoko (Bag Productions)

'YOU KNOW MY NAME (LOOK UP THE NUMBER)' / 'WHAT'S THE NEW MARY JANE'
PLASTIC ONO BAND

UK proposed release December 5 1969; Apple APPLES 1002; not issued.

'You Know My Name (Look Up The Number)' (Lennon, McCartney)
John Lennon (vocals, guitar, maracas), Paul McCartney (vocals, piano, bass), George Harrison (backing vocals, guitar, vibes), Ringo Starr (vocals, drums, bongos), Mal Evans (spade in gravel), Brian Jones (alto saxophone). Recorded at Abbey Road Studios, London, England. Produced by George Martin.
'What's The New Mary Jane' (Lennon, McCartney)
John Lennon (vocals, piano), George Harrison (vocals, acoustic guitar), Yoko Ono (vocals), Mal Evans (?) (handbell). Recorded at Abbey Road Studios. Produced by George Martin / Geoff Emerick / John Lennon.

'YOU KNOW MY NAME'

By September 1969, John Lennon had decided to quit The Beatles. He'd already formed a new band for solo projects and by mid 1969 issued two singles. Despite the decision to quit, he was determined to issue two offbeat recordings he'd made with The Beatles. Apple announced the release of Plastic Ono Band's third single on Friday December 5. It was mastered and test pressings made – one acetate was inscribed 'Look Up The Number Johnny' – but commercial copies failed to materialise. As the record was effectively a new Beatles single, it was put on permanent hold. What would have been the A-side was eventually issued as the B-side of The Beatles' last UK single, 'Let It Be'.

'You Know My Name (Look Up The Number)' began to take shape on Wednesday May 17 1967, when 14 takes of the first part of the song were recorded at Abbey Road. Work on the song began again on Wednesday June 7, when overdubs were applied to take 9. The rest of the evening was spent improvising on the song's main theme. The Beatles returned to the song the following evening, at which point Brian Jones of The Rolling Stones added his saxophone parts. The Beatles returned to the song the next evening, Friday June 8, to record another rhythm track (lasting 6:08). And that is were The Beatles left the song.

Twenty-two months later, on Wednesday April 30 1969, Lennon and Paul McCartney returned to the song to add their vocals. It was mixed at the end of the session, with three mono mixes completed, the third marked 'best'.

Recorded in a marijuana haze during the summer of love, 'You Know My Name (Look Up The Number)' is little more than a throwaway. It consists of the title sung to different musical settings, but is nevertheless one of the funniest records The Beatles ever recorded. Often cited by McCartney as one of his favourite Beatles recordings, it recalls the work of Lennon's heroes The Goons and the group's own Christmas records.

Lennon booked Abbey Road Studio Two on Wednesday November 26 1969 with the intention of producing finished masters for both 'You Know My Name (Look Up The Number)' and 'What's The New Mary Jane'. A copy was made of the mono mix of 'You Know My Name' from April 30 and edited down from 6:08 to 4:19. Lennon then turned his attention to 'What's The New Mary Jane'.

When interviewed for *NME* in May 1969, Lennon suggested he had written 'Mary Jane' with Alex Mardas. Magic Alex, as he was known, was employed by Apple as their resident mad inventor and head of Apple Electronics. Lennon claimed: "There was a mad thing I wrote half with our electronics genius, Alex. It was called 'What A Shame Mary Jane Had A Pain At The Party', and it was meant to be on the last Beatles album. It was real madness, but we never released it. I'd like to do it again."

Why would Lennon collaborate with the amateur Mardas when he had his pick of the world's greatest musicians? It does seem unlikely that Mardas helped with the song: he certainly wasn't credited as co-author and he didn't appear on the finished recording. Probably Lennon just threw in the comment during the interview simply to promote Apple Electronics – which, as it was failing to produce anything of worth, needed all the publicity it could get.

What is certain is that John Lennon, George Harrison, Yoko Ono, and Mal Evans recorded 'What's The New Mary Jane' at Abbey Road on Wednesday August 14 1968. Four takes were recorded, the final take being overdubbed with additional guitar, piano, and vocals. At the end of the session the track was mixed to mono, and that's how it remained until November 1969. On November 26, Lennon and Ono added more overdubs to a 2-track stereo master produced 15 months earlier. Once they had completed the overdubs, the tape was edited and several versions produced. The final master was selected from the many Lennon made that night.

'What's The New Mary Jane' is a darkly disturbing recording that lacks the natural humour of 'You Know My Name'. As harrowing to listen to as any of John and Yoko's avant-garde recordings, it would have been best left in Abbey Road's tape archive. However, take 4 was eventually issued in stereo on The Beatles *Anthology Vol. 3*.

An extended version of 'You Know My Name (Look Up The Number)' was issued in stereo on The Beatles *Anthology Vol. 2*. It is almost 2 minutes longer than the version issued on the b-side of 'Let It Be', but for some reason the last few seconds of Lennon's goon-inspired mutterings were edited from this version.

Above: 10-inch acetate.

Above: 12-inch acetate.

Above: 7-inch test pressing.

Above: Finally released as the B-side of 'Let It Be'.

42

PLASTIC ONO BAND – LIVE PEACE IN TORONTO 1969
PLASTIC ONO BAND

Side 1 'Blue Suede Shoes', 'Money (That's What I Want)', 'Dizzy Miss Lizzy', 'Yer Blues', 'Cold Turkey', 'Give Peace A Chance'.
Side 2 'Don't Worry Kyoko (Mummy's Only Looking For Her Hand In The Snow)', 'John John (Let's Hope For Peace)'.

UK release December 12 1969; Apple CORE 2001; failed to chart.
US release December 12 1969; LP Apple SW 3362; 8-track cartridge Apple 8XT-3362; stereo reel-to-reel tape Apple L-3362; chart high No.10.

'Blue Suede Shoes' (Perkins)
'Money (That's What I Want)' (Bradford, Gordy)
'Dizzy Miss Lizzy' (Williams)
'Yer Blues' (Lennon, McCartney)
'Cold Turkey' (Lennon)
'Give Peace A Chance' (Lennon, McCartney)
'Don't Worry Kyoko (Mummy's Only Looking For Her Hand In The Snow)' (Ono)
'John John (Let's Hope For Peace)' (Ono)

All with John Lennon (vocals, guitar), Yoko Ono (vocals), Eric Clapton (guitar, backing vocals), Klaus Voormann (bass), Alan White (drums), except 'Don't Worry Kyoko' and 'John John' with Yoko Ono (vocals), John Lennon (guitar), Eric Clapton (guitar), Klaus Voormann (bass), Alan White (drums).
All recorded live at Varsity Stadium, Toronto, Canada. All produced by John and Yoko (Bag Productions).

LIVE PEACE IN TORONTO

This is perhaps the defining moment in Lennon's career. While travelling to Toronto for this show, he decided the time was right to leave The Beatles.

The Toronto Rock'n'Roll Revival festival may have featured some of the biggest names from the 1950s playing alongside newcomers like the Doors and Chicago Transit Authority but, with only a couple of days to go, the event was far from sold-out. On the afternoon of September 12, in an act of desperation, concert promoter John Bower contacted Lennon at his London office to ask if he might consider acting as compère for the event. Lennon's reply was typically spontaneous. Not only would he attend, he would also perform. The only problem was that Plastic Ono Band existed in name only. This didn't bother Lennon. Wheels were set in motion and the trip arranged.

The next task was to assemble a band. Not that difficult a job, if you're John Lennon. George Harrison was asked if he wanted the gig, but he turned it down. Lennon's next choice was Eric Clapton. He was somewhat harder to contact and claimed to know nothing of the concert until the morning of September 13, the day of the concert. Klaus Voormann was invited to play bass and Alan White drums.

The next morning, the 13th, the Lennon entourage, which included Beatles roadie Mal Evans and Lennon's personal assistant Anthony Fawcett, convened at London Airport. There was, however, no sign of the Lennons or Clapton. It appears that no one had been able to contact Clapton, who was unaware of the plans. Fawcett made a frantic call to Tittenhurst Park, only to be told by the cook that Lennon and Ono were still in bed. When Lennon eventually made it to the telephone, he told the hapless Fawcett that the gig was off. Fawcett claims that it was he who persuaded Lennon to keep his promise, but Bower tells it differently.

Bower claims that Fawcett called him to explain that Lennon and Ono weren't coming, and that during their exchange he persuaded Fawcett to give him Eric Clapton's home phone number. Clapton had by now agreed to perform, but had been unable to get to the airport to make the first flight. Bower called Clapton and said: "Eric, you may not remember me, but I'm the promoter who lost $20,000 on your Blind Faith show last month. Please call John Lennon, and tell him he must do this or I will get on a plane, come to his house, and live with him, because I will be ruined." Clapton's call to Lennon worked. Lennon respected the guitarist and was apparently ashamed at having "pissed him off so much". The gig was back on, and the entourage eventually left England on Air Canada flight 124 for Toronto.

Lennon, Ono, and Clapton boarded the aircraft and headed for first class and something to eat. The rest of the group sat in the back and waited for Lennon and Clapton to join them for a brief rehearsal. Once in flight, the group managed a rehearsal of sorts and finalised a set-list. "Now we didn't know what to play, because we'd never played together before, the band," Lennon explained. "And on the aeroplane we're running through these oldies, so the rehearsal for the record, which turned into not a bad record, was on the plane, with electric guitars ... not even acoustic, you couldn't hear."

More importantly, it was during the flight that Lennon decided to leave The Beatles. The writing had been writ large for some time. Ringo and George had left the band, only to return, and Lennon had made his discontent known through his recent solo projects. The concert in Toronto proved beyond doubt to Lennon that he no longer needed The Beatles. "I announced it to myself and the people around me on the plane – Klein came with me – I told Allen, 'It's over.' When I got back, there were a few meetings, and Allen said, 'Well, cool it, cool it.' There was a lot to do, business-wise, you know, and it would not have been suitable at the time."

At 30,000 feet over the Atlantic, Lennon called time on the greatest band the world had ever known. By the time the Lennon entourage landed at Toronto airport, a crowd of fans had gathered to welcome them. Having cleared immigration, there was a slight problem because Ono didn't have the necessary vaccinations. The group were driven to Varsity Stadium where they holed up in the dressing room. Here they had another rehearsal before taking to the stage around midnight.

Live Peace In Toronto songs

Once on stage, the band ripped through several oldies, a track from the *White Album*, and two new Lennon compositions. Carl Perkins recorded his 'Blue Suede Shoes' for Sun Records in 1955, and it became his signature tune and a massive hit, both for Perkins and Elvis Presley, who recorded the song not long after. While Perkins' recording, issued by Sun on January 1 1956, was a hit in the USA, where it sold over a million copies, Presley's take on the song was a hit in the UK. That two of Lennon's heroes should record the song must have influenced his decision to perform it when he appeared at Toronto. That and the fact he seemed able to remember lyrics to his favourite rock'n'roll songs better than his own.

Although The Beatles recorded several Perkins songs for their early albums, they did not formally record 'Blue Suede Shoes'. They did rehearse it while filming *Let It Be* in early 1969, but this was little more than an impromptu, ragged jam.

Having decided that he would open the Toronto show with the Perkins classic, Lennon was insistent that Plastic Ono Band play the correct arrangement. Speaking to Shelley Germeaux of *Daytrippin*, drummer Alan White recalled Lennon urging the band to follow Perkins' original. "I remember one conversation in particular, because he wanted to play the Carl Perkins version, not the [Elvis Presley], of *Blue Suede Shoes*, because it's one beat shorter. 'One for the money – da-da-da – two for the show...' It was very funny because he was insistent that we stick to that version for the show."

Barrett Strong recorded 'Money (That's What I Want)' in 1958. A hit for Anna Records in America, it was issued by London-America in the UK. The Beatles first recorded the song on January 1 1962. Auditioning at Decca Records' London studio, the group, with Pete Best on drums, ran through highlights from their concert repertoire, selected for them by their manager, Brian Epstein. Their arrangement at Decca lacked the drive that made the version recorded at Abbey Road Studios on July 18 and 30 1963 eclipse Barrett's original. That version appeared on the group's second album, *With The Beatles*. They also recorded the song six times for broadcast by BBC radio. The Plastic Ono Band's performance lacks the verve of The Beatles' version; instead they produce a grungy, garage-band reading that is as loose as The Beatles' take is tight.

The Beatles also recorded a version of the Larry Williams rocker 'Dizzy Miss Lizzy', at the request of Capitol Records. The group's American label needed additional material for what would become the sixth US album, *Beatles VI*. By holding back a couple of tracks from the British albums and by including B-sides, Capitol managed to expand the group's catalogue by several albums.

Convening at Abbey Road on the evening of May 10 1965, The Beatles cut two Williams songs, 'Dizzy Miss Lizzy' and 'Bad Boy', both of which had been in the group's pre-fame concert repertoire. Mono and stereo mixes were completed at the end of the session and sent to Capitol, who issued them five weeks later. British fans had to wait until Friday August 6 before they could hear 'Dizzy Miss Lizzy', issued on *Help!* (PMC 1255/PCS 3071), and 19 months before they could hear 'Bad Boy', issued on December 9 1966 on *A Collection Of Beatles Oldies* (PMC 7067/PCS 7016).

The Beatles also recorded 'Dizzy Miss Lizzy' for the BBC at the Piccadilly Theatre, London, a little over two weeks after recording it for EMI. This version, recorded on May 26 1965, was later issued on *The Beatles At The Beeb* (8 31796 2). Finally, a live version recorded at the Hollywood Bowl on August 30 1965 was issued on *The Beatles Live At The Hollywood Bowl* (EMTV 4) on May 6 1977. The Plastic Ono Band's reading is looser than the Beatles take, but they drive Williams' moronic riff home like proto-headbangers.

A parody of the British blues boom, Lennon wrote 'Yer Blues' while studying transcendental meditation with the Maharishi Mahesh Yogi in Rishikesh, India in 1968. On their return from Rishikesh, The Beatles convened at George Harrison's house to record demos of what they had written while in India, including 'Yer Blues'. Recording proper began at Abbey Road Studios on Tuesday August 13.

In an attempt to introduce some spontaneity to the recording process (Harrison's 'Not Guilty' had gone to more than 100 takes), The Beatles moved out of their home-from-home, Studio Two, and into a small annexe to that studio's control room. Recording in what for them were cramped conditions, they set up their equipment, turned up the volume, and recorded 14 takes of the basic track. Two reduction mixes and one edit piece were then made. Finally, the beginning of take 17 was edited onto the end of take 16 – the edit is clearly audible at 3:17. This was done on the original 4-track master, an unusual and radical decision. The following evening, Lennon returned to the song, overdubbing a second vocal and mixing the track to mono. Finally, Ringo's count-in was recorded on Tuesday August 20 and edited onto the previous mono mix. The stereo mix was created on Monday October 14.

Lennon performed the song again on December 10 1968, not with The Beatles but with a spur-of-the-moment band, The Dirty Mac, which consisted of Lennon (vocals, guitar), Keith Richard (bass), Eric Clapton (guitar), and Mitch Mitchell (drums). Lennon was invited to perform for the Rolling Stones film project *Rock'n'Roll Circus*, and he chose to do so without The Beatles, an early sign of his growing dissatisfaction with the group. Lennon's performance would remain unreleased for almost 27 years (it was eventually issued in 1996). Rehearsals for the Stones film took place on December 10; filming, which took place before an invited audience, was completed the following night.

Lennon also chose to perform 'Yer Blues' at Toronto. At least two of the musicians involved knew the song from the *Circus* date, and its authentic blues shuffle made it easy for the rhythm section to fall into place. The irony of having Eric Clapton performing on a song that parodied the genre he was most associated with can't have been lost on Lennon, who gives a spirited performance.

The world premiere of 'Cold Turkey', Lennon's account of his withdrawal from heroin addiction, was a truly public event. In keeping with his manifesto of blurring the boundaries between art and life, Lennon came out of the closet to 20,000 people and admitted his addiction. No doubt his intention was to offer a warning to those in the audience who might be tempted into trying anything stronger than cannabis. Yet much of its shock value was lost. Had there been sufficient rehearsal time, Plastic Ono Band could have turned in a vicious aural assault to equal Lennon's purpose. Unfortunately, because the song was as new to the band as it was to the Toronto audience, this was little more than a fumbling, rudimentary public rehearsal for the genuinely unsettling studio recording made a little over two weeks later.

Lennon would perform the song again on December 15 at the Lyceum Ballroom in central London with an extended line-up of Plastic Ono Band. This recording, eventually issued on the double album *Some Time In New York City*, has a vicious potency that the Toronto performance lacks. Lennon also chose to perform the song when he gave two concerts at Madison Square Garden in New York City on August 30 1972.

What was by far the simplest song in Plastic Ono Band's repertoire appeared the most difficult to perform convincingly. The band struggle through 'Give Peace A Chance' as if wading through treacle. What Lennon had managed to capture with two acoustic guitars and a room full of people was simply impossible to replicate with the standard rock line-up of two guitars, bass, and drums. Ono didn't help by singing off key, but at least Lennon had the good sense to bury her deep in the mix. However, Lennon wasn't there to give a stunning performance; he was there to spread the good gospel of peace – and this was *the* peace anthem. Did it matter that he couldn't remember the verses, or that the band sound like a group of amateurs? No. In this instance it was the message rather than the medium that was important, and Lennon was determined to deliver it in whatever way he could.

After that, it was Ono's turn. Crowd reaction to her two songs was muted. The Toronto audience's reaction to Plastic Ono Band was mixed from the outset, but there were reports of booing during her performance. Lennon had chided them for being less than enthusiastic; now they were verging on hostility. On 'Don't Worry Kyoko (Mummy's Only Looking For Her Hand In The Snow)', Lennon and Clapton trade blues riffs over which Ono improvises a message of reassurance to her estranged daughter. An early version of the song had appeared on the *Aspen* flexi-disc and part of the lyric formed one of Ono's instruction pieces first published in her book *Grapefruit*. The same line-up recorded a studio version of the song a few weeks after this performance, issued as the B-side of *Cold Turkey*.

While one could at least get into the groove of 'Don't Worry Kyoko', Ono's second song of the evening was pure avant-garde noise. 'John John (Let's Hope For Peace)' first appeared on side two of *The Wedding Album*, but this 12-minute version is devoid of either melody or rhythm – the very antithesis of what the audience had come to experience. You have to be either brave or stupid to perform this kind of material in public, particularly to a festival audience. Lennon and Ono obviously thought that their audience were intelligent enough to 'get' the message they were attempting to convey. However, all the audience could do was stand and wonder. Had the song been performed at an art event, it would probably have gone down a storm. As it was, by the time this atonal, feedback-drenched attack on the senses finished, the audience were all but stunned into silence. The Plastic Ono Band left the stage to the sound of howling feedback, rather than a crowd screaming for more. They were then driven to Thor Eaton's country retreat, where they spent a relaxing weekend before returning to London.

Almost two weeks later, on September 25 1969, Lennon mixed the 8-track tapes of the Toronto concert at Abbey Road. Working from 10:00am to 1:45pm, he produced the finished stereo master. Then, on October 20, he produced a new stereo mix of Yoko's 'Don't Worry Kyoko' to replace the previous one. Thankfully, Lennon removed most of Yoko's caterwauling from his songs. A wise move, for had they remained they would have spoilt an otherwise enjoyable set. The film soundtrack reveals just how invasive Ono's vocals were. (D. A. Pennebaker's film of the concert was later released as *Sweet Toronto* both on video and DVD, the DVD claiming to have a 5.1 soundtrack created from the original two-track mix.) Some of Clapton's equally flat backing vocals were also removed. The album was cut at Apple's new cutting room at 3 Savile Row in central London and issued on December 12.

Even though this album was more mainstream than Lennon's previous solo efforts, Capitol Records were not happy about issuing the disc. Speaking to Andy Peebles in December 1980, Lennon recalled: "We tried to put it out on Capitol, and Capitol didn't want to put it out. They said, 'This is garbage, we're not going to put it out with her screaming on one side and you doing this sort of live stuff.' And they just refused to put it out. But we finally persuaded them that, you know, people might buy this. Of course, it went gold the next day. "And then, the funny thing was – this is a side story – Klein had got a deal on that record that it was a John and Yoko Plastic Ono record, not a Beatles record, so we could get a higher royalty, because the Beatles' royalties were so low – they'd been locked in '63 – and Capitol said, 'Sure you can have it,' you know. Nobody's going to buy that crap. They just threw it away and gave it us. And it came out, and it was fairly successful and it went gold. I don't know what chart position, but I've got a gold record somewhere that says … . And four years later, we go to collect the royalties, and you know what they say? 'This is a Beatle record.' So Capitol have it in my file under Beatle records. Isn't it incredible?"

Live Peace In Toronto data

In Britain, the LP was issued with a unique catalogue number, CORE 2001, that didn't follow Apple's customary APCOR/SAPCOR mono/stereo numbering system. Issued in a minimalist blue cover with a wispy white cloud bottom left, *Plastic Ono Band – Live Peace In Toronto 1969* was supplied with a 13-month John and Yoko calendar, of which three different versions were produced: stapled; wire spiral bound; or plastic comb bound. Both the wire and plastic comb styles were placed inside the LP jacket with the spines toward the opening. However, because the metal spines were found to be damaging the records, some American copies of the album were issued with a card that could be posted to Apple, who sent a copy of the calendar by return post. American pressings (SW 3362) erroneously state that the album was recorded in England.

The LP was issued with two label variants. Labels printed in Los Angeles were produced with or without SW prefixing the catalogue number and with either 'MFD. BY APPLE RECORDS' or 'MFD. BY CAPITOL RECORDS' etc. in the perimeter. Labels manufactured at Capitol's Scranton factory have an alternative layout, with the band's name on the first line and the album title *Live Peace In Toronto 1969* on the second. The album was reissued in America in 1982 with purple Capitol labels and in 1986 with black/colour-band Capitol labels. MFSL issued a half-speed mastered edition of the LP in 2006. This numbered edition (MFSL 1-283) was issued with a reproduction of the original John and Yoko calendar for 2007.

The album was also issued in America on 8-track (8XT-3362) and 7-inch reel-to-reel tape (L-3362).

When issued on CD (CDP 7904282), the album was remixed from the original 8-track tapes at Quad Recording Studios, New York. The new mix by Rob Stevens differs considerably from the original LP version, with Ono placed even lower in the mix on some songs but heard more prominently on others. This mix was issued on CD, complete with an updated version of the John and Yoko calendar, on May 1 1995.

Mfd by Apple pressing

Mfd by Capitol pressing

Los Angeles pressing

Scranton pressing

Winchester pressing

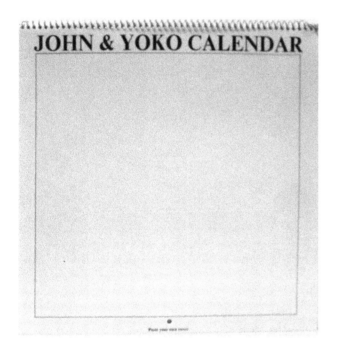

Spiral bound and stapled examples of the John & Yoko calendar

JOHN & YOKO
KLAUS VOORMANN
ALAN WHITE

ERIC CLAPTON
courtesy of Polydor
Records

With fab pics and poetry
in 1970 calendar!

PLASTIC ONO BAND–LIVE PEACE IN TORONTO APPLE RECORDS CORE 2001 OUT NOW

1970 to 1972: Power To The People

'INSTANT KARMA!' / 'WHO HAS SEEN THE WIND?'
LENNON/ONO WITH PLASTIC ONO BAND

UK release February 6 1970; Apple APPLES 1003; chart high No.5.
US release February 20 1970; Apple APPLE 1818; chart high No.3.

'Instant Karma!' (Lennon)
John Lennon (vocals, guitar, electric piano), Yoko Ono (vocals), George Harrison (guitar, piano), Klaus Voormann (bass, electric piano), Billy Preston (organ), Mal Evans (handclaps, chimes), Alan White (drums, piano), Allen Klein and unknown others (backing vocals). Recorded at Abbey Road Studios, London, England. Produced by John and Yoko and Phil Spector.
'Who Has Seen The Wind?' (Ono)
Yoko Ono (vocals, recorder), John Lennon (guitar), John Barham (harpsichord). Recorded at Trident Studios, London, England.
Produced by John Lennon.

'INSTANT KARMA!'

John Lennon wrote 'Instant Karma!' on January 27 1970, constructing the melody around a simple three-chord pattern that many have argued he borrowed from the nursery rhyme 'Three Blind Mice'. Melinde Kendall, wife of Yoko Ono's ex-husband Tony Cox, provided the lyrical theme. The Lennons had spent Christmas with the Coxes and the phrase "instant karma" had turned up in conversation.

Lennon would have been well aware of the basic concept of karma. The Beatles having studied Hinduism, largely under George Harrison's influence, with the Maharishi Mahesh Yogi. They weren't alone in developing an interest in Eastern spirituality. Hippies borrowed from Eastern religions, in an attempt to circumvent what they considered corrupt Western influences, but in doing so they trivialised the notion of karma to mean a deserved fate, good or bad. The idea that one could somehow obtain 'instant karma' was nothing more than an absurd Western contradiction.

Lennon, of course, loved the idea of 'instant karma'. Like many of us, he was hooked on instant gratification. Whether it was emotional, sexual, or creative pleasure, Lennon may not have always known what he wanted, but he knew when he wanted it. And more often than not he wanted it now. But instant satisfaction is more often than not a hollow experience, its delights fleeting. Lennon didn't trust immediate enlightenment any more than he trusted those who embraced it.

'Instant Karma!', then, is both a plea for mankind to take responsibility for its fate and a warning against the quick fix. It also finds Lennon questioning the idea of stardom and suggesting that everyone has the potential within them to achieve greatness. 'Instant Karma!' also signalled a move away from simple sloganeering to a more sophisticated political critique. This was Lennon developing his own brand of egalitarianism, an ideal he sustained throughout his solo career.

Typically, Lennon decided to record and issue the song as quickly as possible (and it was released by Apple just a few weeks before Paul McCartney called time on The Beatles). Lennon said: "I wrote it in the morning on the piano, and I went into the office and I sang it many times, and I said, 'Hell, let's do it,' and we booked the studio and Phil (Spector) came in and said, 'How do you want it?' And I said, '1950s,' and he said, 'Right,' and BOOM! I did it in about three goes: he played it back and there it was. The only argument was I said a bit more bass, that's all, and off we went. He doesn't fuss about with fucking stereo or all that bullshit, just 'does it sound all right?' then, 'Let's have it!' It doesn't matter whether something's prominent or not prominent, if it sounds good to you, as a layman, or as a human, take it – just take it, and that suits me fine."

Lennon was working so quickly that Geoff Emerick, who began engineering the session before being asked to leave as it was making Spector "edgy", claims that the song was not mixed properly. Emerick has said that 'Instant Karma!' received only a rough mix and that Spector marked the tape box "Do Not Use".

Phil Spector had been called in to salvage The Beatles' ill-fated *Let It Be* album, which had been intended to see the group return to its rock'n'roll roots. He was also working for George Harrison, producing his *All Things Must Pass* album. As Harrison recalled, he asked Spector to produce the 'Karma!' session for Lennon. "John phoned me one morning in January and said, 'I've written this tune and I'm going to record it tonight and have it pressed up and out tomorrow – that's the whole point: 'Instant Karma!', you know." So I was in. I said, 'OK, I'll see you in town.' I was in town with Phil Spector and I said to Phil, 'Why don't you come to the session?' There were just four people: John played piano, I played acoustic guitar, there was Klaus Voormann on bass, and Alan White on drums. We recorded the song and brought it out that week, mixed – instantly – by Phil Spector."

Although Spector moved the *Let It Be* project away from McCartney's original idea, adding layers of orchestration to the group's simple backing tracks to create his 'wall of sound', his grandiose production style was exactly what Lennon wanted for 'Instant Karma!'.

The eccentric American took Lennon's song and transformed it into an echo-drenched hypnotic masterpiece. Alan White's drums deliver a barrage of fills in place of lead guitar lines, and Klaus Voormann's bass supplies a thunderous bottom-end rumble over which heavily sustained keyboards hover like sheets of quicksilver. A crowd of nightclubbers, recruited by keyboardist Billy Preston from a nearby nightspot, provided the backing vocals. The finished result was startling. At last Lennon had produced a musical statement that defined him as a solo artist. (On the B-side, Ono's 'Who Has Seen The Wind?' is a gentle acoustic ballad that draws on several ideas that first appeared among her 'instruction pieces', which were like small instructional poems.)

'Instant Karma!' data

As with the Lennons' previous single, this one was issued with generic Apple labels with 'PLAY LOUD' printed in large bold type in the centre of the A-side label and 'PLAY QUIET' printed in the same bold text on the B-side.

Issued in America two weeks later than in Britain, 'Instant Karma!' was the first solo Beatle single to sell one million copies there. As Apple's American office had a few weeks rather than a few days in which to produce a picture cover, the US sleeve featured photographs of Lennon and Ono. One other difference between American and British pressings is that the US single was credited to John Ono Lennon with no mention of Plastic Ono Band.

American pressings were issued with eight label variations. The first has a dark green Apple label, with song title at 10 o'clock with composer credit below and 'STEREO' at 9 o'clock. 'PLAY' is at 12 o'clock and 'LOUD' at 6 o'clock, with the artist's name 'JOHN ONO LENNON' centre bottom.

The second has a dark green Apple label with song title on five lines at 9 o'clock and composer credit below. 'PLAY' and 'LOUD' are in slightly larger text at 12 and 6 o'clock. Artist's name 'JOHN ONO LENNON' is centre bottom.

The third variation has a medium dark green Apple label, with song title on four lines at 10 o'clock and composer credit below. A small 'PLAY' and 'LOUD' are at 12 and 6 o'clock, 'STEREO' at 2 o'clock, and artist's name 'JOHN ONO LENNON' centre bottom. Fourth has a light green Apple label, song title on four lines at 10 o'clock with composer credit and 'STEREO' below; 'PLAY' and 'LOUD' at 12 and 6 o'clock; catalogue number and producer credit on the right side of the label; artist's name 'JOHN ONO LENNON' centre bottom. Fifth has a light green Apple label, song title on four lines at 10 o'clock, with composer credit and 'STEREO' below; 'PLAY' and 'LOUD' at 12 and 6 o'clock; catalogue number and producer credit on the right side of the label; artist's name 'JOHN ONO LENNON (with the Plastic Ono Band)' centre bottom. The sixth US label variation has a light green Apple label with song title on five lines at nine o'clock and composer credit below; 'PLAY' and 'LOUD' at 12 and 6 o'clock; 'STEREO' at 2 o'clock; artist's name 'JOHN ONO LENNON' centre bottom. Seventh has a medium dark green Apple label with song title on four lines at 10 o'clock and composer credit below; small 'PLAY' and 'LOUD' at 12 and 6 o'clock; 'STEREO' at 2 o'clock; artist's name 'JOHN ONO LENNON (with the Plastic Ono Band)' centre bottom. The eighth and last variation has a medium dark green Apple label with song title on five lines at 9 o'clock with composer credit below; 'PLAY' and 'LOUD' at 12 and 6 o'clock; artist's name 'JOHN ONO LENNON' with 'Recorded in England' centre bottom.

To promote the 'Instant Karma!' single in Britain, Lennon and Ono appeared on the BBC TV chart show *Top Of The Pops*. Two different performances were filmed on February 11 for broadcast on the 12th and 19th. Lennon sang a live vocal to a pre-recorded backing track, while Alan White, Klaus Voormann, B. P. Fallon, Mal Evans, and Ono mimed with varying degrees of success. Both performances have since been issued. The 'cue card' version appeared on the John Lennon Collection video, the 'knitting' version, with an extended and remixed soundtrack, on the Lennon Legend DVD. This recording was also issued on the CD single Happy Xmas (War Is Over) (CDR 6627), released in Britain on December 8 2003.

A two-song CD single (8800492) of 'Instant Karma!' backed with 'Oh My Love' was issued in The Netherlands in July 1992. Copies were given free with initial copies of the *John Lennon Collection* video. A four-song version of the CD single, with 'Karma!' plus 'Bless You', 'Mother', and 'Oh My Love', was released in the rest of Europe (excluding Britain).

LENNON
INSTANT KARMA!

APPLES 1003

ONO
WHO HAS SEEN THE WIND?

APPLES 1003

JOHN ONO LENNON INSTANT KARMA!
(WE ALL SHINE ON)

PRODUCED BY PHIL SPECTOR

APPLE RECORDS 1818

YOKO ONO LENNON WHO HAS SEEN THE WIND?

PRODUCED BY JOHN LENNON

Manufactured by APPLE RECORDS INC. • 1700 Broadway, New York, N.Y. 10019 • Printed in U.S.A.

57

JOHN ONO LENNON
INSTANT KARMA!
(WE ALL SHINE ON)

PRODUCED BY
PHIL SPECTOR

APPLE RECORDS 1818

LENNON/ONO
with The Plastic Ono Band

INSTANT KARMA!
B/w Who has seen the wind?
Produced by Phil Spector
Ritten, Recorded, Remixed 27th Jan 1970

APPLE RECORDS   APPLES 1003

YOKO ONO LENNON
WHO HAS SEEN THE WIND?

PRODUCED BY
JOHN LENNON

APPLE RECORDS 1818

THE SHORT RAP', 'DOWN IN THE ALLEY' / 'THE LONG RAP'
JOHN LENNON ON RONNIE HAWKINS / JOHN LENNON

US release February 1970; Cotillion PR-104/105; promotional record, no commercial release.

'The Short Rap'/ 'The Long Rap' (Lennon)
John Lennon (spoken word). Recording location unknown. Producer unknown.

'THE SHORT RAP' / 'THE LONG RAP'

Lennon and Ono's second visit to Canada began on December 16 1969. The trip, part of the couple's peace campaign, included talks with John Brower (who had persuaded Lennon to perform in Toronto earlier that year) to plan a massive free peace festival. The Lennons' headquarters were at the home of singer Ronnie Hawkins, from where Lennon gave radio interviews, signed copies of his *Bag One* lithographs, and relaxed by listening to Hawkins' new album. Lennon was impressed by the record and promised to record a brief message to promote it. Back in England, he made good on his promise by recording a brief promo that was issued as the B-side of promotional copies of Hawkins' single 'Down In The Alley'.

For the 'The Long Rap', Lennon says: "This is John 'O' Lennon here just muttering about Ronnie Hawkins, and how on our last trip to Canada, somehow it was arranged that we stay at his house. I had a great time, and of course I knew him from way back on record, 'Forty Days' and all that. I didn't know anything about him but he turned out to be a great guy, and it just so happened, as it were, that he'd just made an album. He's about the only person that doesn't try and greet you, as they say, and he played us this album, but he didn't want to play it, he was shy like most musicians or artists are shy, you know. I don't like playing my record to people. I have to do it because you have that need. I hope this isn't too long for a promo? Anyway, I was signing these 20-million lithographs, and this album was going on. And I was listening to most of it and still signing, until this track came on 'Down In The Alley', and it really sort of buzzed me, you know? And it sounded like now and then, and I like that. So let's hear it."

59

JOHN LENNON/PLASTIC ONO BAND
JOHN LENNON

Side 1 'Mother', 'Hold On', 'I Found Out', 'Working Class Hero', 'Isolation'.
Side 2 'Remember', 'Love', 'Well Well Well', 'Look At Me', 'God', 'My Mummy's Dead'.

UK release December 11 1970; LP Apple PCS 7124; 8-track cartridge Apple 8X-PCS 7124; chart high No.11.
US release December 11 1970; LP Apple SW 3372; 8-track cartridge Apple 8XW-3372; stereo reel-to-reel tape Apple M-3372; chart high No.6.

'Mother' (Lennon)
John Lennon (vocals, piano), Klaus Voormann (bass), Ringo Starr (drums).
'Hold On' (Lennon)
John Lennon (vocals, guitar), Klaus Voormann (bass), Ringo Starr (drums).
'I Found Out' (Lennon)
John Lennon (vocals, guitar), Klaus Voormann (bass), Ringo Starr (drums).
'Working Class Hero' (Lennon)
John Lennon (vocals, guitar).
'Isolation' (Lennon)
John Lennon (vocals, piano), Klaus Voormann (bass), Ringo Starr (drums).
'Remember' (Lennon)
John Lennon (vocals, piano), Klaus Voormann (bass), Ringo Starr (drums).
'Love' (Lennon)
John Lennon (vocals, acoustic guitar), Phil Spector (piano).
'Well Well Well' (Lennon)
John Lennon (vocals, guitar), Klaus Voormann (bass), Ringo Starr (drums).
'Look At Me' (Lennon)
John Lennon (vocals, guitar).
'God' (Lennon)
John Lennon (vocals), Billy Preston (piano), Klaus Voormann (bass), Ringo Starr (drums).
'My Mummy's Dead' (Lennon)
John Lennon (vocals, guitar).

All recorded at Abbey Road Studios, London, England, except 'My Mummy's Dead' recorded at a house on Nimes Road, Bel Air, California. All produced by John & Yoko and Phil Spector.

JOHN LENNON/PLASTIC ONO BAND

Having spent most of 1969 preoccupied with their peace campaign, Lennon and Ono spent much of 1970 in isolation. As every action has an equal and opposite reaction, the Lennons retreated from their frantic schedule of public appearances and immersed themselves in one another. Speaking in 1980, Lennon recalled: "We stopped talking to the press, we became 'recluses'. ... I was calling myself Greta Hughes or Howard Garbo."

Locked away in their Berkshire mansion, they spent every waking minute together. However, as the weeks turned into months, they sank into a deep depression. Lennon wasn't the only ex-Beatle suffering at the group's break-up. McCartney was equally affected. However, while Paul and Linda seemed to draw strength from their troubles, John and Yoko's relationship began to flounder. Although Lennon's love for Ono remained constant, Anthony Fawcett, the couple's personal assistant, recalled the atmosphere at Tittenhurst as tense. "Living with them became harder day by day," he said. "Beside Val, the cook, I was the only person around, and I was acutely aware of the rapid deterioration of their relationship."

Salvation came in the form of a book. Dr. Arthur Janov's *The Primal Scream – Primal Therapy: The Cure for Neurosis* arrived out of the blue and had a dramatic affect on Lennon and Ono. Typically, Lennon took to the book and the promise it offered like a zealot.

Janov argues that neurosis is caused by repressed pain that divides the subject in two. "Coming close to death at birth or feeling unloved as a child are examples of such Pain," he suggests. "The Pain goes unfelt at the time because the body is not equipped to experience it fully and deal with it. When the Pain is too much, it is repressed and stored away. When enough unresolved Pain has occurred, you lose access to your feelings and become neurotic."

Janov's definition of neurosis describes perfectly Lennon's childhood and his addictive personality. He had lost his mother, Julia, not once but twice. When his parents separated, he was sent to live with his aunt and uncle. Although his mother lived only a few streets away, his contact with her was minimal. It was only as a teenager that he developed a relationship with Julia. And then, just as they were getting to know one another, Julia was killed in a road accident. He never came to terms with the pain his mother's death caused him; instead, he repressed it.

Inevitably he turned to drugs, and as the years passed the drugs became harder. By the time Janov entered their lives, Lennon and Ono had already endured heroin addiction. But heroin just dulled the pain, it didn't remove it. Lennon obviously recognised as much, as he had already warned of the pitfalls of short-sightedness ('Instant Karma!') and the pain of heroin withdrawal ('Cold Turkey'). If anyone was ripe for Janov's primal therapy, it was Lennon.

Contact was made and Janov agreed to fly to England and treat his high-profile patients in their own home. But before treatment could begin, Janov insisted that Lennon and Ono separate for 24 hours. For the first time in over two years, they were physically cut off from one another. Ono stayed in the master bedroom, while Lennon moved into his new recording studio. "We did a lot of it in the recording studio, while they were building it," recalled Janov. "That was kind of difficult. But it went very, very well. John had about as much pain as I've ever seen in my life. And he was a very dedicated patient. Very serious about it. When I said to him, 'You've got to come to LA now, I can't spend the rest of my life in England,'" he said, "'Fine,' and he came."

However, before they decamped to California, Lennon and Ono moved into separate hotels in London for further treatment. After three weeks in Janov's care, they left England in late April 1970 for the Primal Institute in California and four months of intensive therapy.

Between their sessions with Janov, John and Yoko relaxed at a rented Bel Air house, watching television and writing songs. Lennon had already started work on two compositions, 'Mother' and 'Isolation', which he completed in California. Several others were written from scratch during their stay. Not only did Janov's treatment have a powerful effect on Lennon's mental wellbeing, but also it influenced the music he was making, which reflected the pain he experienced while in therapy. When interviewed by Jann Wenner for *Rolling Stone*, both Lennon and Ono used the word mirror when describing their experiences of primal therapy. But primal therapy did more than reflect their pain, it allowed them to see beyond it. "Janov showed me how to feel my own fear and pain; therefore I can handle it better than before, that's all," said Lennon. "I'm the same, only there's a channel." Coming close to an epiphany, Lennon found that primal therapy offered him a means by which he could transform pain into creative energy. It informed his writing, and the resulting songs were raw, emotive, personal, powerful, and sometimes shocking.

The anger that surfaced in Lennon's songs was equalled by the musical settings he recorded on his return to England. He stripped the songs of any artifice by recording them as a three-piece. Employing Ringo Starr and Klaus Voormann as his rhythm section, Lennon eschewed complex arrangements and overdubs. This was primal rock'n'roll, straight from the gut. All of the songs were performed live in the studio with the emphasis on attitude rather than perfection. Voormann told *Rolling Stone* how Lennon's candid approach spilled over into the studio. "The playing itself, to him, was not that important. It was more important to capture the feeling. We did mostly one or two takes. There's a lot of mistakes on [the album] and timing changes, but it was just like a pulse, exactly what John wanted. He loved it."

Stripping the band of its finesse, Lennon created a potent, raw sound that echoed the way in which primal therapy had stripped him of his neurosis. Lennon, Starr, and Voormann cut through the flabby flesh of pop to reveal the hard, white bone of rock'n'roll. Performing a vocal with each take, Lennon had rarely sounded so commanding. Greil Marcus was moved to remark that "John's singing on the last verse of 'God' may be the finest in all of rock".

The pain that Lennon hoped to express and disavow was not solely the result of his childhood pain or Janov's therapy. It had been building in him for years. Freed of The Beatles and all they stood for, he told the world exactly how he felt about the way it had treated him. Speaking to Jann Wenner just after the album's release, Lennon revealed just how frustrated he had become with the music business. "One has to completely humiliate oneself to be what The Beatles were, and that's what I resent. ... And that's what I'm saying on this album – I remember what it's all about now, you fuckers – fuck you! That's what I'm saying, you don't get me twice."

John Lennon/Plastic Ono Band was more than invective, it was catharsis. Lennon named and laid bare his pain to free himself of it. This was Lennon scaled to the bone. Stripping away the phoney veneer that for too long he had hidden behind, he offered instead truth and honesty. With this in mind, his choice of producer seemed perverse.

Phil Spector is best known for overblown productions that bury the singer under a trademark 'wall of sound'. Spector may be credited as co-producing this album, but Lennon suggested that he had most of the sounds before he asked the producer to help complete the record. This is confirmed by the demo recordings Lennon made in California in the summer of 1970. Nevertheless, he thought that Spector brought a lot of energy to the project and taught him a lot. Ono confirmed that Lennon produced most of the album himself and that Spector was only called in to assist with technical aspects. She was, however, unhappy with Spector's exact nature; she was, after all, more interested in ambiguity than certainty. Spector worked quickly, mixing songs as they were completed. Typically, he mixed several tracks to mono (despite the label of the issued record stating that they are in stereo). Compared to his work on The Beatles' *Let It Be* or George Harrison's *All Things Must Pass*, Spector has a peripheral presence on *John Lennon/Plastic Ono Band*, audible only in the copious amounts of echo he applied to Lennon's otherwise dry mixes.

Between recording Lennon's songs, the band worked on Ono's companion album, *Yoko Ono/Plastic Ono Band*. Previously, she had been given space on the B-side of John's singles, but with these two albums, Lennon and Ono established a practice of issuing complementary solo albums – a practice that continued through to *Double Fantasy*, which would find them sharing the same album for the first time since 1972's *Some Time In New York City*.

John Lennon/Plastic Ono Band songs

As we've seen, Lennon began writing 'Mother' in England and completed it in California. While still in therapy, he recorded a number of guitar-based demos. Even at this early stage, he had developed a sound to match his mood. Plugging his pickup'd acoustic guitar into an amplifier with the tremolo turned up to ten, he produced a sound that oscillates between shimmering clean highs and dirty distorted lows. Upon entering Abbey Road Studios, he recorded a guitar-based version, later issued on the *John Lennon Anthology*. Taken at a slightly faster tempo and without the heavily sustained piano chords of the finished master, it lacks the primal quality that Lennon was searching for.

Abandoning the guitar, he turned to the piano and remade the song. The menacing piano chords are prefigured by four tolls of a church bell, slowed down to sound even more funereal. Lennon got the idea while watching a horror film on television and decided to use the tolling of bells to open the album. Speaking to Wenner, Ono said that the church bells were an allusion to Lennon's childhood, as he often spoke to her of hearing church bells on a Sunday. Lennon also implied that they were, perhaps, an attempt to evoke the loneliness he associated with Sundays. (The track was edited when issued as a single and the recording correctly designated as being in mono. The Japanese pressing, AR 2734, was issued in stereo. Lennon performed the song at both shows he gave at Madison Square Garden on August 30 1972. An outtake of the studio version was issued with the *Lennon Signature Box* in October 2010. This version sounds almost identical to the final master, except that it has an additional electric rhythm guitar part. It adds little if anything to the arrangement and Lennon was right to delete it from the final mix.)

Described by Andy Grey of *NME* as "sombre", 'Hold On' is in fact a beacon of light in what is otherwise a dark, moody album. It is a song of reassurance, both a personal epistle of hope and a plea for harmony. Addressing himself, Ono, and the world in general, Lennon has a simple message: hold on and everything is gonna be all right. As he explained to Wenner: "It's only going to be all right ... now, at this moment it's all right .... That's how we're living now, but really like that and cherishing each day, and dreading it too. I'm really beginning to cherish it when I'm cherishing it."

But stoicism alone is not the answer: individuals, communities, and countries must all come together to build the utopia that Lennon implies is within our reach. His aspiring lyric is matched by warm, shimmering guitars and minimal backing from Starr and Voormann. Between takes, the three musicians jammed on old rock'n'roll songs from the 1950s (one of which, 'Long Lost John', was later issued on the *John Lennon Anthology*). During one lull in proceedings, they tried an up-tempo take of 'Hold On', a 44-second extract of which was later issued on the *John Lennon Anthology*.

For 'I Found Out', Lennon turns up the distortion on his amplifier and the vitriol in his voice, and decries the false idols and causes he had mistakenly let into his life. If George Harrison was the great seeker of spirituality, then Lennon was the great seeker of truth. 'I Found Out' sees him rejecting the things that divert him from the truth – whatever that is. It's not clear if it took Janov's primal therapy for Lennon to discover that he had been let down by almost everyone from his parents to Paul McCartney. Like Dylan before him, Lennon suggests that we avoid following leaders. The only path to political, social, or religious enlightenment lies within, not in abstract systems devised by others. He puts himself forward not as a leader but as an example of someone who has made mistakes only to discover that enlightenment comes from within.

Before recording in the studio, Lennon made demo recordings in California. Working through the song, he made changes to the arrangement and lyric; changing the tense from the third to first person and in the last verse substituting neurosis for religion.

Although Voormann remembers Lennon breaking down while making the album, outtakes from the sessions confirm that he was often in buoyant mood and enjoying the experience. Instructing Starr and Voormann about how they should work, Lennon said: "Just play how you feel, you know, cos it is Carl Wolf," an allusion to heroes Carl Perkins and Howlin' Wolf. A slightly longer take of the song reveals Lennon's intentions. As the band play on, he breaks into Carl Perkins' 'Gone Gone Gone'.

'Working Class Hero' was influenced as much by contemporary left-wing thinking as by Janov's primal therapy. Like several left-wingers of the time, Lennon argues that the only way to overcome a system that ensures conformity through revolution of the self, and not through organised revolution. He'd already commented on the growing political unrest and student riots of 1968 with 'Revolution' and 'Revolution 9' and found them wanting. Nevertheless, his political commitment increased apace the following year with a far-reaching peace campaign.

Aligning himself with the New Left, Lennon restates their central belief in 'Working Class Hero': "the personal is the political". Like the New Left, he argues that it is what you do and not some external theory that informs your political position. What was needed was a 'new man', a working class hero, who would refuse to be co-opted by a repressive system. The song may not be couched in intellectual terms, but it expresses these beliefs more precisely than the lengthy political screeds published at the time.

Speaking to Wenner about the song, he said: "I just think its concept is revolutionary, and I hope it's for the workers. … I think it's for the people like me who are working class, whatever, upper or lower, who are supposed to be processed into the middle classes, or in through the machinery, that's all. It's my experience, and I hope it's just a warning to people." His hopes were that it might bring about the kind of revolution in the head that the New Left were dreaming of. That it would be taken up in the same way as 'Give Peace A Chance'. For him, it was a revolutionary piece of work and the ideal New Left anthem.

Speaking to Robin Blackburn and Tariq Ali less than two months after the album's release, Lennon stressed the political beliefs that he had put forward in 'Working Class Hero'. He said: "I was very conscious of class – they would say [I had] a chip on my shoulder – because I knew what happened to me and I knew about the class repression coming down on us – it was a fucking fact, but in the hurricane Beatle world it got left out, I got farther away from reality for a time." He continued: "But nothing changed except that we all dressed up a bit, leaving the same bastards running everything. The continual awareness of what was going on made me feel ashamed I wasn't saying anything. I burst out because I could no longer play the game any more, it was just too much for me."

While Lennon would be constantly chided for preaching from an ivory tower, with 'Working Class Hero' he acknowledged the limitations he laboured under and the effect it had upon him. For all his attempts to break free of the system, he concedes that he remained defined by a set of terms as narrow as his attempts to escape them were broad.

Recorded entirely solo by Lennon at Abbey Road, 'Working Class Hero' drew comparisons with early Dylan, whom he disavows in another song on the album, 'God'. "Anyone that sings with a guitar and sings about something heavy would tend to sound like Dylan," Lennon explained. "I'm bound to be influenced by that because that is the only kind of real folk music I listen to. So in that way I've been influenced, but it doesn't sound like Dylan to me."

Because of its simple arrangement, the commercial version was issued in mono. It also features an obvious edit at 1:25. Lennon admitted to Wenner that he had missed a verse, which he had to drop in later. An alternative version, issued on the *John Lennon Anthology*, features a complete, unedited take of the song. Because the lyrics include the word 'fucking', crude edits to remove the expletive were made to the song for Australian pressings of the album. The lyrics were also censored for all countries when printed on the record's inner sleeve.

'Isolation' finds Lennon caught in a moment of existential doubt. Laying open his angst, he reveals that he is as helpless and alienated as anyone else. For someone who needed to belong as much as he did, this admission of isolaphobia sees him stripping away another layer of fiction and exposing the reality behind. Despite his success and popularity, Lennon reflects on his own limitations and proffers an epistle of acceptance and forgiveness. Despite everything he has said and done, nothing has changed. The world remains as irrational as ever; the insanity we construct and inhabit results in nothing but anxiety or despair; our search for meaning within our lives remains illusive and ultimately alienating.

Lennon recorded 'Remember' on October 9, his 30th birthday, and the song finds him in a nostalgic mood. If primal therapy required the subject to confront the pain experienced in childhood, it also brought back more pleasurable memories. Lennon presents the listener with these conflicting emotions. Tinged with disappointment, at phoney heroes and the illusion of a stable family life, 'Remember' has Lennon looking through rose-tinted glasses at a youth spent without regret. He was as nostalgic as the next person, but not at the expense of ignoring the realities of the present, or the consequences of his actions. Remember the past by all means, but don't forget today.

The version presented on *Plastic Ono Band* was edited down from a much longer take. The full version lasts 8:15 and featured an organ overdub. Lennon told Wenner that the reference to the 5th of November was an ad lib, influenced by his singing sounding like Frankie Laine. Somehow this led him to sing the opening lines from a nursery rhyme about Guido Fawkes, who attempted to blow up London's Houses Of Parliament in November 1605. Having decided to keep the take, Lennon edited an explosion on the end as a joke and further reference to the celebrated event.

'Love' dispels the myth that Lennon was an angry rocker incapable of writing tender ballads. While his up-tempo songs were often written as catharsis or out of guilt, his love songs were real expressions of devotion that held their meaning long after he dismissed other songs as "self-conscious poetry". Lennon defines what love means to him and, in keeping with the rest of the material written for the album, he does so with simple, honest precision.

He recorded a version of the song while in California, backing himself with amplified acoustic guitar treated with copious amounts of tremolo. Back at Abbey Road he repeated the process, recording an equally plain acoustic version, which appeared on the *John Lennon Anthology*. With his guitar and vocal in the bag, he asked Spector to overdub a delicate piano part to complete the arrangement. In 1982, the song was remixed for release as a single, when it was issued in territories outside of the USA to promote the *John Lennon Collection*. The introduction and ending were increased in volume, in an attempt to make the song 'radio-friendly'.

On 'Well Well Well', a pounding rhythm section and piercing guitar support a penetrating Lennon vocal that shifts from tender to savage. He recalls intimate moments with Ono over a pulsing rhythm track that echoes the beating hearts of 'John And Yoko', and he contrasts this with intense screams of painful emotional release.

Spector mixed the commercial version to mono, although an early rough mix appears in stereo. When the album was remixed in 2000, the track was given a much wider stereo picture, which reveals a second guitar part that is almost inaudible on the original. Lennon's remarks about cramp at the end of the song are also clearly audible. The song would be performed live just twice, at the matinee and evening shows of the 1972 One To One charity concert in New York.

'Look At Me' was written during The Beatles' Indian sojourn and reveals that even by early 1968 Lennon was struggling to come to terms with what he'd become. The Beatles may have had the world on a plate, but they were all feeling the pressures of fame and had discovered the unsettling truth that money doesn't make things better. Influenced by George Harrison, they looked to Eastern spirituality for an answer and thought they had found it in the Maharishi Mahesh Yogi. Looking for a spiritual answer to their problems worked for Harrison but not the others. Lennon came away from India as confused and cynical as he'd always been. The many letters that Ono sent him only contributed to his sense of unease and they undermined what was left of his relationship with Cynthia.

'Look At Me' finds Lennon addressing himself, hoping to discover who he is and what it is that makes him whole. Meditating on what it is to be, Lennon concludes that only his lover can answer the question and complete him.

He recorded two demos of the song, in 1968 and 1970, played fingerpicking-style and almost identical to the finished master, but made well before he recorded it for *John Lennon/Plastic Ono Band*. An alternative studio version issued on the *John Lennon Anthology* differs from both the demos and the master recording, with Lennon strumming his guitar and presented in stereo; the commercial release is in mono. When his *Plastic Ono Band* album was remixed in 2000 for reissue on CD, 'Look At Me' was at last issued in stereo.

Back in the summer of 1966, Lennon gave an interview to Maureen Cleave of *The Evening Standard*, a London newspaper, in which he attempted to explain his views on contemporary Christianity. His line about The Beatles being "bigger than Jesus" went almost unnoticed in Europe but, taken out of context, caused a wave of anti-Beatle behaviour to unfold across America. Bowing to pressure from his manager, Brian

Epstein, Lennon apologised for having made the remark but also tried to make himself better understood. "I'm not anti-God, anti-Christ or anti-religion," he explained. "I was not saying we are greater or better. I believe in God, but not as one thing, not as an old man in the sky. I believe that what people call God is something in all of us."

His ideas didn't change much in the years that followed. For Lennon, God was something abstract that formed part of the human condition. Speaking to David Wigg in June 1969, he said: "God is a power, which we're all capable of tapping. We're all light bulbs capable of tapping energy. You can use electricity to kill people or light the room. God is that. Neither one nor the other but everything." He continued the conversation with Dr. Janov the following year. Janov recalled: "He would say, 'What about religion?' and I would say something like, 'People in pain usually seek out religion.' And he would say, 'Oh, God is a concept by which we measure our pain.'"

Combining his own beliefs with what he'd discovered while in primal therapy, Lennon constructed 'God' in three parts to illustrate his feelings. It opens with his bold statement about God, which he repeats to validate his claim. He then introduces a second musical theme, in which he presents the listener with a litany of things he no longer believes in. The list began spontaneously and developed into a disavowal of everything once held precious. "It was just going on in my head and *I Ching* and *Bible* and the first three or four just came out, whatever came out," he explained.

Developing the list, he includes several cultural and religious icons that three years earlier appeared on the cover of *Sgt. Pepper's Lonely Hearts Club Band*. It was as if the past held too many painful memories that had to be effaced. What mattered was to experience reality as it appeared now. He dismissed ideas and things that had previously defined as phoney relics from the past. The problem was: how to end the list? "I thought, where do I end? Churchill," he said. "And who have I missed out? ... It got like that, you know, and I thought I had to stop. ... I was going to leave a gap and just say fill in your own, you know, and put whoever you don't believe in."

Lennon ends the song with the biggest illusionists of them all. His disavowal of The Beatles distanced him from the group and the past, and it also announced a new beginning for all. The dream was over, the time had come to get real. Like David Bailey's book *Goodbye Baby & Amen*, 'God' was a farewell to the 1960s and everything it stood for. It was also Lennon's way of affirming what he now believed in. The closing refrain says it all: "I was the walrus but now I'm John." And as if to reinforce his belief, Lennon delivers one of the finest vocals of his career.

He recorded several versions of the song while in California. The first take finds him mumbling his way through his litany of fakes and phoneys. By the second and third takes his list was pretty much finalised. All of these early recordings end by returning to the opening refrain, as the song's closing statement had yet to be written. When he came to record the song at Abbey Road, he tried to replicate his guitar-based demo recording with help from Starr and Voormann. However, as with other songs originally written on guitar, he turned to the piano and employed the skills of Billy Preston to capture the definitive performance. Although the song received substantial radio play on some liberal American radio stations, it was not issued as a single. (It was, however, issued as a one-track promotional CD single, PE 98030, in Spain in 1998.)

Recalling the harrowing recordings that Lennon and Ono made at Queen Charlotte's Maternity Hospital, 'My Mummy's Dead' is a concise expression of Lennon's primal experience. Its simple construction, based on 'Three Blind Mice', combined with his monotone delivery, suggests an absence of emotion. The cries of pain that Lennon employed on 'Mother' are gone; all that remains is blank acceptance. The ghostly sound of the recording evokes a sense of Lennon's long-held emptiness, and this simple, childlike song of sorrow seems to emerge as if from the distant past, a spectral reminder of a long repressed event. Like many of the songs on *John Lennon/Plastic Ono Band*, 'My Mummy's Dead' is stripped of illusion. Influenced by the precision of Japanese Haiku poetry, Lennon's lyric reveals a chilling reality. Two takes of the song were recorded, the best being selected to close the album.

John Lennon/Plastic Ono Band data

The album was issued with custom Apple labels and a printed inner sleeve. British and American label designs differ. The British label offered a plain white silhouette of an apple on a black background with copyright perimeter print. American labels were based on a similar 'white apple' label, but rather than a silhouette the apple has the illusion of depth. The 'white apple' may have been an allusion to Yoko's contemporary artworks, many of which were painted white.

It was reissued by Capitol in 1978 with purple Capitol labels that had a large Capitol logo, in 1982 with black/colour band Capitol labels, and again in 1988 with purple Capitol labels. The album was reissued in Britain in June 1984 with generic Apple labels as part of EMI's budget-price Fame series.

The album was issued as an 8-track cartridge in Britain (8X-PCS 7124) and the USA (8XW-3372). In America it was also issued as a 7-inch reel-to-reel tape by Apple/Ampex (M-3372).

The album was scheduled for release on CD by EMI on July 20 1987 but delayed for several months due to problems with the original master tapes – allegedly caused by Lennon and Spector's unorthodox recording techniques. The CD was put on hold for nine months while EMI worked on improving the sound quality. It was eventually issued in Britain and the USA on April 5 1988.

John Lennon/Plastic Ono Band was remixed and remastered at Abbey Road under Ono's supervision in spring/summer 2000 and issued by EMI with two bonus tracks and a new booklet on October 9 2000. MFSL Original Master Recordings also issued the remixed version, as an Ultradisc II 24 kt. gold CD in January 2004 (UDCD-759). In February the same year, MFSL Original Master Recordings issued a 180 grams High Definition Vinyl edition (MFSL 1-280) each copy individually number on the lower back left corner.

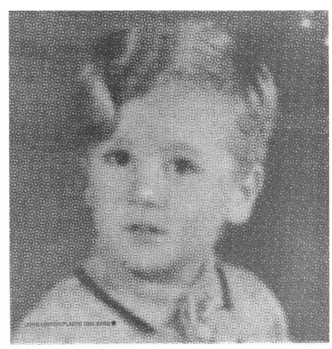

'MOTHER' / 'WHY'
JOHN LENNON / YOKO ONO PLASTIC ONO BAND

US release December 28 1970; Apple APPLE 1827; chart high No.43.
'Why' (Ono)
Yoko Ono (vocals), John Lennon (guitar), Klaus Voormann (bass), Ringo Starr (drums).
Recorded at Abbey Road Studios, London, England. Produced by John & Yoko.

'MOTHER'

Issuing 'Mother' as a single was a bold move. The recording is as harrowing to listen to as 'Cold Turkey', and it's hard to believe that many, if any, radio stations gave it primetime airplay. Nevertheless, Lennon was convinced that it was a commercial record, but conceded that if he could sell more records by singing about love than about his mother he would. So he was more interested in making a statement with this single than he was in selling records.

When issued as a single, the bells that introduce the recording were removed and the song trimmed to 3:55. Unlike the album version, which is in stereo, the single is in mono. Japanese pressings, however, use the unedited album version and are in stereo.

The antithesis of Lennon's stately A-side, Ono's 'Why', from her companion *Plastic Ono Band* album, was selected for the record's B-side. A raucous conflation of avant-gardism and rock'n'roll, it features her free-form vocalising and some of Lennon's most explosive guitar playing. He said in interviews that Ono's singing had influenced his playing, and here the two are fused perfectly. Lennon's guitar howls like a banshee, matching the vocal perfectly. Speaking to Andy Peebles in 1980, Lennon recalled the song with some pride. "The fascinating thing is, even we didn't know where Yoko's voice started and where my guitar ended on the intro."

In the late 1970s, younger musicians who formed part of the emerging punk/new wave scene were discovering Ono's work for the first time. The B-52s owed much to her vocal style, and Lennon was quick to endorse them, but later bands, such as The Pixies, must have been influenced by his extraordinary playing on this record. Jimi Hendrix may have turned guitar playing into an art form, but on this track Lennon's playing is shockingly new.

'Mother' data
The American issue had five label variations. The first has a light green Apple label; song title at 11 o'clock with composer credit below; '(From the Apple LP "John Lennon/Plastic Ono Band" SW-3372)' at 8 o'clock; 'Recorded in England' at 2 o'clock; and the artist's name 'John Lennon/Plastic Ono Band' centre bottom. The second variant has a dark green Apple label with identical text layout, and the third has the light green Apple label with identical text but a black star at 9 o'clock. The fourth US label variant has a dark green Apple label; 'Recorded in England' at 10 o'clock; '(From the Apple LP "John Lennon/Plastic Ono Band" SW-3372)' at 9 o'clock; song title at 7 o'clock with composer credit below; artist's name 'John Lennon/Plastic Ono Band YOKO ONO/PLASTIC ONO BAND' centre bottom. The fifth variant has a light green Apple label; 'MONO' at 11 o'clock; song title at 10 o'clock with composer credit below; '(From the Apple LP "John Lennon/Plastic Ono Band" SW-3372)' at 8 o'clock; artist's name 'John Lennon/Plastic Ono Band' at 2 o'clock.

The single was not issued in Britain but was released in the Republic of Ireland (DIP.517) with generic Apple labels and slip sleeve.

JOHN LENNON/PLASTIC ONO BAND ⊙
MOTHER
APPLE 1827

YOKO ONO/PLASTIC ONO BAND ⊙
WHY
APPLE 1827
Manufactured by APPLE RECORDS, INC. 1700 Broadway, New York, N.Y. 10019

MOTHER
(John Lennon)

Maclen (Music) Ltd. (U.K.) Total–3:55

1827
(45-X47426)

Produced by JOHN & YOKO & PHIL SPECTOR

Recorded in England

(From the Apple LP "JOHN LENNON/ PLASTIC ONO BAND" SW-3372)

JOHN LENNON/ PLASTIC ONO BAND

WHY
(Yoko Ono)

STEREO

Ono Music, Inc. BMI 5:30

1827
(S45-X47427)

Produced by JOHN & YOKO

From the Apple LP "Yoko Ono/ Plastic Ono Band" SW-3373)

Recorded in England

YOKO ONO / PLASTIC ONO BAND

Recorded in England

Maclen Music BMI Total–3:55

1827
(45-X47426)

Produced by JOHN & YOKO & PHIL SPECTOR

(From the Apple LP "JOHN LENNON/ PLASTIC ONO BAND" SW-3372)

MOTHER
(John Lennon)

JOHN LENNON/PLASTIC ONO BAND YOKO ONO/PLASTIC ONO BAND

WHY
(Yoko Ono)

Ono Music, Inc.-BMI
Intro.—:34 Total–5:30

1827
(S45-X47427)

Produced by JOHN & YOKO

Recorded in England

STEREO

(From the Apple LP "YOKO ONO/ PLASTIC ONO BAND" SW-3373)

YOKO ONO / PLASTIC ONO BAND

MONO

MOTHER
(John Lennon)

JOHN LENNON/ PLASTIC ONO BAND

Maclen (Music) Ltd. (U.K.) Total–3:55

1827
(X47426)

PRODUCED BY JOHN & YOKO & PHIL SPECTOR

(From the Apple LP "JOHN LENNON/ PLASTIC ONO BAND" SW-3372)

Recorded in England

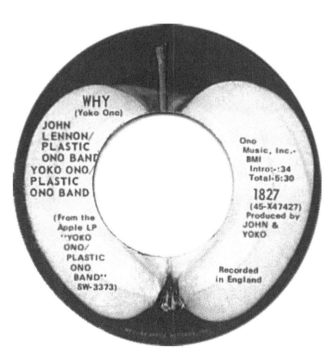

WHY
(Yoko Ono)

JOHN LENNON/ PLASTIC ONO BAND YOKO ONO/ PLASTIC ONO BAND

Ono Music, Inc.- BMI
Intro:–:34 Total–5:30

1827
(45-X47427)

Produced by JOHN & YOKO

Recorded in England

(From the Apple LP "YOKO ONO/ PLASTIC ONO BAND" SW-3373)

'POWER TO THE PEOPLE' / 'OPEN YOUR BOX'
JOHN LENNON / YOKO ONO PLASTIC ONO BAND

UK release March 12 1971; Apple R 5892; chart high No.7.

'POWER TO THE PEOPLE' / 'TOUCH ME'
JOHN LENNON / YOKO ONO PLASTIC ONO BAND

US release March 22 1971; Apple APPLE 1830; chart high No.11.

'Power To The People' (Lennon)
John Lennon (vocals, guitar, piano), Klaus Voormann (bass), Alan White (drums), Billy Preston (piano, keyboards), Bobby Keys (saxophone), Rosetta Hightower and unknown others (backing vocals).
Recorded at Abbey Road Studios, London, England. Produced by Phil Spector and John & Yoko.
'Open Your Box' (Ono)
Yoko Ono (vocals), John Lennon (guitar), Klaus Voormann (bass), Jim Gordon (drums).
Recorded at Trident Studios, London, England. Produced by John & Yoko.
'Touch Me' (Ono)
Yoko Ono (vocals), John Lennon (guitar), Klaus Voormann (bass), Ringo Starr (drums).
Recorded at Abbey Road Studios. Produced by John & Yoko.

'POWER TO THE PEOPLE'

While the McCartneys were in New York City recording *Ram*, Lennon and Ono spent much of January 1971 in Japan, only returning to England at the insistence of the lawyers dealing with McCartney's High Court action to dissolve The Beatles. Upon their return, Lennon and Ono were interviewed for *Red Mole*, a left-wing magazine edited by Tariq Ali and Robin Blackburn.

Educated at Oxford, Ali became the face of British left-wing political activism. A vigorous protester against the war in Vietnam, he helped form the Vietnam Solidarity Campaign (V.S.C.), eventually becoming its figurehead. Under his direction, the V.S.C. became a highly visible protest group. He was inspired by what had been happening in America and focused on large-scale public demonstrations to voice opposition to the war. Unlike the Lennons, who championed non-violent means of protest, Ali advocated taking to the streets and if necessary engaging in violence.

Ali wrote in *The New Revolutionaries: A Handbook Of The International Radical Left*: "The new revolutionaries were quite open about their aims: it was hypocritical to protest against violence at home while justifying it in Vietnam; we were not pacifists, and if a policeman hit us we would defend ourselves. Our violence was defensive – a response to the repressive violence of the state machine."

By the late 1960s, public demonstrations were becoming increasingly confrontational and violent. It was the V.S.C. that organised a protest on March 17 1968 that culminated outside the American Embassy in Grosvenor Square, London. It became the most violent protest to take place in Britain for years, if not decades. This was the type of protest the Lennons had spoken out against during their peace campaign. Yet two years later their whole political and philosophical outlook had changed. Now they embraced active intervention and endorsed the radical New Left.

Lennon had never fully engaged with politics, let alone thoughts of revolution. When he wrote and recorded 'Revolution' for The Beatles' *White Album* he was unable to commit to the idea. From the comfort of Abbey Road Studios, he told the world that when push came to shove they could "count me out/in". Yet by the time he was interviewed by Ali and Blackburn, his ambivalence appeared to have deserted him. But Lennon was no fool. He knew how to manipulate the media and he told Ali and Blackburn exactly what they wanted to hear, which was not necessarily what he believed. Speaking to David Sheff in 1980, Lennon confessed that 'Power To The People' was his way of gaining their acceptance. 'I felt I ought to write a song about what [Ali] was saying. That's why it didn't really come off. I was not thinking clearly about it. It was written in a state of being asleep and wanting to be loved by Tariq Ali and his ilk, you see. I have to admit to that so I won't call it hypocrisy. I couldn't write that today."

'Power To The People' openly contradicted his earlier role as peacemaker. But whether Lennon was acting hypocritically or not, he took to his new political commitments unreservedly. He donated money to worthy causes and attended several protest rallies. Yet, years later, Lennon felt troubled by his involvement with the New Left and described it as based on guilt. He told Andy Peebles in 1980: "Tariq Ali had kept coming round wanting money for the *Red Mole* or some magazine or other and I used to give anybody... money kind of out of guilt. ... I kind of wrote 'Power To The People' in a way as a guilt song, you know."

The day after his interview with *Red Mole*, Lennon set about constructing a musical manifesto that he hoped would impress Ali. As with 'Give Peace A Chance', the chorus is based on a simple slogan, ambiguous enough to be used by any group that wanted it. The verses offer nothing new or revolutionary; Lennon simply reinforces the old revolutionary war-cry by calling on the exploited to rise up and overthrow their oppressors. There is a concession to the emergent feminist movement, but despite Ono's presence, Lennon's feminism fails to convince.

Moving to the studio, Lennon began to develop the song, but it wasn't until Phil Spector intervened that it came alive. Early takes have all the basic elements in place; what Spector did was to exaggerate them. Essentially, he reworks the model he'd created for 'Instant Karma!'. The gospel-style backing vocals were developed into a full-blown choir. Bobby Keys' saxophone took the place of Alan White's dominant drumming. And with Spector's help, Lennon added an authoritative vocal, smothered in tape echo, that he'd been unable to capture on earlier takes. Spector's tour de force was to record the group's marching feet. This not only created a unique percussion effect but also evoked the sound of a street rally. If all this sounds unbearably heavy, it isn't. Spector took Lennon's rather pedestrian setting and transformed it into a funky groove, as suited to the street as it was the disco.

'Power To The People' was Lennon's first British single since 'Instant Karma!', released over a year earlier. The record should have been available in Britain on March 5 but was delayed by a week because of problems with Ono's B-side. Philip Brodie, managing Director of EMI, thought the lyrics to that song "distasteful" and requested that they be changed. For the US release, 'Open Your Box' was replaced with 'Touch Me', from *Yoko Ono/Plastic Ono Band*, which delayed the release until March 22.

With the prospect of having another song banned by their own record company, Lennon and Ono reworked 'Open Your Box' to mask Ono's apparently distasteful lyric. Although it's been suggested that she re-recorded her vocal, the offending words were simply hidden under washes of echo. Issued on her album *Fly*, where it was titled 'Hirake', the song's offending lyrics are clearly audible. EMI didn't seem too concerned about it appearing on an expensive double album – or perhaps they were fooled into believing it was a new composition. Either way, the Lennons also managed to have the offending lyrics printed on the inner sleeve, albeit backwards.

They each had their own ideas as to why the song came in for so much criticism. Lennon thought it was because of the ambiguous nature of the word 'box'. "I don't know what the hell 'box' means in America; apparently it means crotch, or whatever." Ono thought it was because the male-dominated music business simply could not accept this kind of song from a woman. "This song has been banned and I believe it is because I am a woman. One of the reasons is because the word 'box' has many different meanings, especially in America, where it refers to a certain part of a woman's body. If a man makes a statement like that, he can easily get away with it. I think the fact that it was a woman supposedly making an obscene statement [was what] really shocked people. Men sing about legs a lot. ... The song is not really that crude, and then it's banned, just like that. 'Box' is a very philosophical song, about opening everything up: minds, windows, your country, it's sort of like 'We're All Water'."

The Plastic Ono Band attempted to record 'Open Your Box' while working on the *Plastic Ono Band* albums. A slower, looser alternative seven-minute version was issued on the Rykodisc reissue of *Yoko Ono/Plastic Ono Band*. It's an early take, recorded at Abbey Road, but lacks the raw power that Plastic Ono Band captured with their remake.

Recorded at Trident Studios, the remake transformed Ono's provocative song into an avant-garde powerhouse. Lennon's guitar stutters over a tight, funky rhythm section like a needle being dragged across a record. He has disposed of the blues-based riffing that usually provided him with a musical crutch. In its place there's a freeform vortex of sound. Ricocheting frenziedly, his playing somehow locks into the rhythm track and perfectly complements the unique vocal.

'Open Your Box' would be performed at Lennon's 1972 One To One concert with Elephant's Memory during both matinee and evening shows, but live readings of the track have yet to appear commercially.

'Open Your Box' was one of several songs that Ono revisited and updated with a contemporary remix. The reworked version proved to be even more successful than the original, spending seven weeks in the *Billboard* Club Play charts. Remixed by the Vermont collective Orange Factory, it was issued in Britain by

Parlophone (CDMIND001) on June 24 2002. In the USA it was issued by Mind Train Records as a 12-inch single (MTR 001) in 2001.

The original US B-side, 'Touch Me', was taken from Ono's *Plastic Ono Band* album and finds Lennon, Starr, and Voormann exploring a jazz-rock fusion, their investigations into group dynamics producing a wave of sound to support Ono's vocal modulations. These early Plastic Ono Band compositions sound improvised – which they were. For Ono, the creative impulse is bound to the idea of reciprocity and incompleteness. It's difficult to imagine her having much time for the word 'closure'. She is more interested in openings. Improvisation was merely the first step in her creative practice. The listener is supposed to extend the process by adding to the work. Speaking to *Mojo* in July 2002, she said: "I called it Unfinished Music, which meant that you were supposed to put your own thing on, in the same way that remixers do today." This 'additional act' was intended to elicit positive reciprocity. By extending this idea to other areas of their lives, people could contribute to and improve the world for the better.

'Power To The People' data

British pressings were issued with a monochrome picture sleeve with red text. Initial pressings featured the full green Apple A-side label on both sides of the record. Two variants were issued: the first has a dark green Apple label with 'Copyright also claimed by Maclen (Music) Ltd.'; the second a light green Apple label without 'Copyright also claimed by Maclen (Music) Ltd.' Later pressings assigned the A-side label to Ono and the white sliced B-side label to Lennon.

A full-colour version of the picture cover was used for the American release and four label variations were issued. The first has a light green Apple label; song title at 11 o'clock with composer credit below; 'STEREO' at 9 o'clock with a black star below; artist's name 'JOHN LENNON PLASTIC ONO BAND' centre bottom with 'Recorded in England' below. The second has a dark green Apple label with song title top centre and composer credit below right; publisher credits at 9 o'clock and 'STEREO' below; artist's name 'JOHN LENNON PLASTIC ONO BAND' centre bottom. The third US label variant has a light green Apple label, with song title at 10 o'clock with composer credit below; 'STEREO' at 9 o'clock; artist's name 'John Lennon/Plastic Ono Band' centre bottom with 'Recorded in England' below. And the fourth variant has a light green Apple label, with song title at 11 o'clock and composer credit below; 'STEREO' at 9 o'clock; artist's name 'John Lennon/Plastic Ono Band' centre bottom with 'Recorded in England' below.

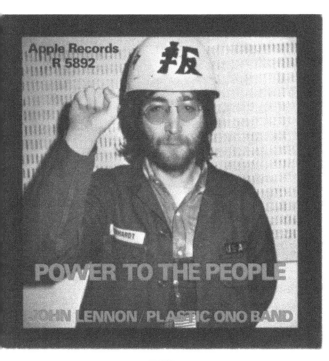

'GOD SAVE US' / 'DO THE OZ'
BILL ELLIOT & THE ELASTIC OZ BAND

UK release July 16 1971; Apple APPLE 36; failed to chart.
US release July 7 1971; Apple APPLE 1835; failed to chart.

'God Save Us' (Lennon, Ono)
Bill Elliot (vocals), John Lennon (guitar), Klaus Voormann (bass), Ringo Starr (drums), Bobby Keys (saxophone), Nicky Hopkins (electric piano). Recorded at Ascot Sound Studios, Tittenhurst Park, Sunninghill, near Ascot, England. Produced by John, Yoko, Mal Evans, and Phil Spector.
'Do The Oz' (Lennon, Ono)
John Lennon (vocals, acoustic guitar), Klaus Voormann (bass), Ringo Starr (drums), Bobby Keys (saxophone). Recorded at Ascot Sound Studios. Produced by John, Yoko, and Phil Spector.

'GOD SAVE US'

Oz magazine was a mainspring of the British underground press, along with *International Times* (which received financial assistance from McCartney). *Oz*'s mixture of satire and 'underground titbits' blossomed to take in more substantial issues such as feminism and radical politics. Under the psychedelic eye of art director Martin Sharp, who designed many of the magazine's more colourful covers, it defined the counterculture scene and its values. As the magazine's layout grew increasingly psychedelic and difficult to read, it wasn't so much what it said but how it said it that was important. Because of its alternative views, the authorities soon took an interest in the magazine, but it wasn't until issue 28, the *School Kids* issue, that the magazine felt the full weight of the Establishment bear down upon it.

The editor, Richard Neville, felt that the magazine had grown boring, so, to introduce some new blood, he placed an open invitation in issue 26 to anyone under the age of 18 interested in editing an issue of the magazine. It should be made clear that the *School Kids* issue was made by young people, not for them. Consequently, these adolescent editors, who were given the freedom to do whatever they liked, produced a magazine full of sixth-form toilet humour. The *School Kids* edition hit the streets in April 1970 with scarcely a ripple of interest from the powers that be.

However, two months later and the *Oz* offices were visited by the Obscene Publications Squad. Then, on August 18, *Oz* was served with a summons for "publishing an obscene magazine". The 'Oz Three' – Richard Neville, Jim Anderson, and Felix Dennis – were prosecuted in what became the longest obscenity trial to be held in Britain. The three editors were found guilty on four charges, fined, and given prison sentences of varying lengths. However, they spent little time in prison before being granted bail. Their convictions were overturned on appeal, but the Establishment won the day. Although *Oz* limped on for another two years, by prosecuting the magazine the government had effectively hammered another nail in the counterculture coffin.

To help pay its legal costs, the magazine organised the Friends Of *Oz* to create press kits, organize benefits, and raise money. Stan Demidjuk was one of those entrusted with running the fund, and he knew John Lennon. Like Tariq Ali and Robin Blackburn before him, Demidjuk approached Lennon for help. Typically, Lennon's support was generous, and he agreed to write and record a song, donating all royalties to *Oz*, as well as attending a march in support of the 'Oz Three' and recording a special message of encouragement.

Lennon told *Sounds*: "Stan and some people from *Oz* rang up and said, 'Will you make us a record?' and I thought, 'Well, I can't' because I'm all tied up contractually and I didn't know how to do it. So then we got down to would I write a song for them? I think [Yoko and I] wrote it the same night, didn't we? We wrote it together and the B-side. First of all we wrote it as 'God Save Oz', you know 'God Save Oz from it all', but then we decided they wouldn't really know what we were talking about in America so we changed it back to 'us'."

Lennon fashioned a song that, lyrically at least, reiterated much of what he'd said with 'Power To The People'. He began by recording a rough demo, fleshing out his unfinished lyric with ad libs. Having completed the song, he set about recording both sides of the record at his newly built recording studio, jokingly named Ascot Sound Studios (ASS), in his Tittenhurst Park home near Ascot.

Lennon began by recording a demo, performing the song on acoustic guitar with Steve Brendell on congas. Next Lennon recorded a studio version of the song that featured himself, Ono and members of *Oz* magazine. This rather plodding, ragged version features a different arrangement that borrows from The Ronettes 'Be My Baby' and a different set of lyrics. It features prominent acoustic guitars, which suggests that it's this version that Charles Shaar Murray played on along with the individuals he named when writing about the session. These include Magic Michael (vocal), John Lennon (acoustic guitar and vocal), Yoko Ono (vocal), Charles Shaar Murray (acoustic guitar), Michele (acoustic guitar), Diane (piano), Klaus Voormann (bass), Ringo Starr (drums) and Steve Brendell (percussion). Other members of *Oz* Magazine may have also contributed percussion.

Unsatisfied with this version, Lennon re-recorded the song. As usual, he recorded the basic track live in the studio, laying down a guide vocal with each take before it was replaced by Bill Elliot. Lennon explained, "We got one singer in, and he was all right but he'd never had much experience recording — or singing actually, because he needed some experience singing and holding vaguely round the note. I can't hold a note – all my songs are all sung out of tune, but I can get fairly near it sometimes. This guy was way off, but it didn't work, so then I sang it just to show him how to sing it, how it should go, and we got this guy that Mal [Evans] had found in a group called Half-breed or something, and he sounded like Paul. So I thought, 'That's a commercial sound,' – it would have been nice to have Paul's voice singing 'God Save Us' – but the guy imitated more my demo, so he sounds like himself because he doesn't sound like me really, but he doesn't sound like Paul either."

Close inspection of the two versions of the remake suggest that Elliot added his vocal to a different take to the one with Lennon's vocals. Lennon's guide-vocal version was later released on the *John Lennon Anthology*.

The record's B-side, 'Do The Oz' is a lazy remake of the old 'Hokey Cokey' dancing song. Lennon may have based his song on this party favourite as a sly reference to the *School Kids* edition of *Oz*. But like the *School Kids* issue, 'Do The Oz' was not intended for kiddies. The 'Hokey Cokey' never sounded like this. Lennon changed the original lyric, but only slightly. Besides instructing the listener to put their left arm in and right arm out, he urges the listener to vote the left-wing in and take the right-wing out.

Lennon's nightmarish B-side is as dark and menacing as the A-side is bright and unthreatening. This was music for a new, disturbing dance craze, a counterculture remake of the original party favourite, intended to freak-out the Establishment. Speaking to *Rolling Stone*, Ono recalled: "John and I actually once were thinking, 'Why don't we create a dance, you know, a dance movement, and put the instructions of how to do this new dance on the back of an album.' And he started to roll on the floor, trying to find a unique kind of action. But it just didn't happen. It was a bit difficult." 'Do The Oz' was included as a bonus track on the CD reissue of *John Lennon/Plastic Ono Band* released in 2000.

'God Save Us' data

Although this was Lennon's project, to avoid the impression that it was his official follow-up to 'Power To The People', the record was credited to Bill Elliot & The Elastic Oz Band. Singer Bill Elliot not only received top billing but appeared on the front cover of the picture sleeve. The group photograph on the reverse is of individuals associated with *Oz* magazine. They are (left to right) back row: Sue Miles, Jim Anderson, Stan Demidjuk, Felix Dennis; front row: Debbie Knight, Bill Elliot.

Unlike previous singles, there is little difference between British and American releases. However, American pressings were issued with three label variations. The first has a dark green Apple label; song title at 10 o'clock on three lines with composer credit below; 'STEREO' at 8 o'clock; artist's name 'BILL ELLIOT AND ELASTIC OZ BAND' centre bottom in small upper case text. The second variant has a dark green Apple label with song title in bold at 11 o'clock with composer credit below; 'STEREO' at 9 o'clock; artist's name 'BILL ELLIOT AND ELASTIC OZ BAND' in bold centre bottom. And the third label variant has a light green Apple label with 'STEREO' at 9 o'clock; song title with composer credit below and artist's name 'BILL ELLIOT AND ELASTIC OZ BAND' centre bottom.

In the USA, Apple issued promotional copies with light green Apple labels with 'NOT FOR SALE' at 10 o'clock; 'STEREO' at 9 o'clock; 'PROMOTIONAL RECORD' at 7 o'clock; a black star appears at 2 o'clock; and the song title with composer credit below and artist's name 'BILL ELLIOT AND ELASTIC OZ BAND' centre bottom.

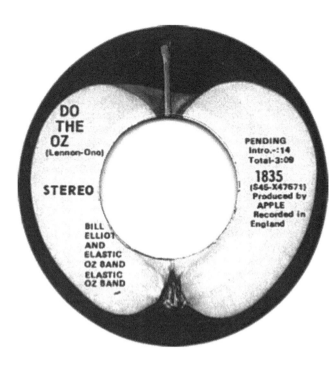

IMAGINE
JOHN LENNON AND PLASTIC ONO BAND (WITH THE FLUX FIDDLERS)

Side 1 'Imagine', 'Crippled Inside', 'Jealous Guy', 'It's So Hard', 'I Don't Want To Be A Soldier'.
Side 2 'Give Me Some Truth', 'Oh My Love', 'How Do You Sleep?', 'How?', 'Oh Yoko!'.

UK release October 7 1971; LP Apple PAS 10004; quadraphonic LP Apple Q4PAS 10004 released June 1972; 8-track cartridge Apple 8X-PAS 10004 released November 1971; quadraphonic 8-track cartridge Apple Q8-PAS 10004 released March 1972; chart high No.1.
US release September 9 1971; LP Apple SW 3379; stereo reel-to-reel tape Apple L-3379; 8-track cartridge Apple 8XW-3379; quadraphonic 8-track cartridge Apple Q8W-3379; chart high No.1.

'Imagine' (Lennon)
John Lennon (vocals, piano), Klaus Voormann (bass), Alan White (drums), The Flux Fiddlers (strings).

'Crippled Inside' (Lennon)
John Lennon (vocals, electric guitar), George Harrison (dobro), Nicky Hopkins (piano), Ted Turner (acoustic guitar), Rod Lincon (acoustic guitar), John Tout (acoustic guitar), Klaus Voormann (bass), Steve Brendell (upright bass), Alan White (drums).

'Jealous Guy' (Lennon)
John Lennon (vocals, acoustic guitar), John Barham (harmonium), Alan White (vibraphone), Joey Molland (acoustic guitar), Tom Evans (acoustic guitar), Mike Pinder (tambourine), Klaus Voormann (bass), Jim Keltner (drums), The Flux Fiddlers (strings).

'It's So Hard' (John Lennon)
John Lennon (vocals, guitar), Klaus Voormann (bass), Jim Gordon (drums), King Curtis (saxophone), The Flux Fiddlers (strings).

'I Don't Want To Be A Soldier' (Lennon)
John Lennon (vocals, guitar), George Harrison (slide guitar), Nicky Hopkins (piano), Joey Molland (acoustic guitar), Tom Evans (acoustic guitar), Klaus Voormann (bass), Jim Keltner (drums), Mike Pinder (tambourine), Steve Brendell (maracas), The Flux Fiddlers (strings).

'Give Me Some Truth' (Lennon)
John Lennon (vocals, guitar), George Harrison (lead guitar), Nicky Hopkins (piano), Rod Linton (acoustic guitar), Andy Davis (acoustic guitar), Klaus Voormann (basses), Alan White (drums).

'Oh My Love' (Lennon, Ono)
John Lennon (vocals, piano), George Harrison (guitar), Nicky Hopkins (electric piano), Klaus Voormann (bass), Alan White (drums, Tibetan cymbals).

'How Do You Sleep?' (Lennon)
John Lennon (vocals, piano), George Harrison (slide guitar), Nicky Hopkins (piano), John Tout (piano), Ted Turner (acoustic guitar), Rod Linton (acoustic guitar), Andy Davis (acoustic guitar), Klaus Voormann (bass), Alan White (drums).

'How?' (John Lennon)
John Lennon (vocals, piano), Nicky Hopkins (piano), John Barham (vibraphone), Klaus Voormann (bass), Alan White (drums), The Flux Fiddlers (strings).

'Oh Yoko!' (Lennon)
John Lennon (vocals, guitar, mouth organ), Phil Spector (backing vocals), Nicky Hopkins (piano), Rod Linton (acoustic guitar), Andy (acoustic guitar), Klaus Voormann (bass), Alan White (drums), The Flux Fiddlers (strings).

All recorded at Ascot Sound Studios, Tittenhurst Park, Sunninghill, near Ascot, England, except 'Imagine', 'Jealous Guy', 'It's So Hard', 'I Don't Want To Be A Soldier', and 'How?' recorded at Ascot Sound Studios and at The Record Plant East, New York City, NY, USA. All produced by John & Yoko and Phil Spector.

IMAGINE

Unlike Lennon's previous album, *John Lennon/Plastic Ono Band*, which was written quickly to capture the experience of primal therapy, *Imagine* was a considered collection of songs and themes that had occupied

Lennon for some time. From sweeping utopian anthems to scathing attacks on his former songwriting partner, from confessions of self-doubt to songs of devotion, *Imagine* was a richly textured collection that showed how little and how much he had changed.

The album mixed personal introspection with the political in equal measures. Lennon claimed that the album was every bit as political as anything he'd produced. However, this time the edge was missing. He'd learnt the art of subversion and hid his radicalism under Phil Spector's lush production and sugar-coating.

According to contemporary accounts, Lennon was in awe of the American producer, but not to the point of sycophancy. His working relationship with Spector may have developed to the extent that he allowed him to sweeten certain songs with the addition of strings, but he was careful to keep the producer's excesses in check. Explaining how they worked together, Lennon said: "Phil doesn't arrange or anything like that – and [Ono] and Phil will just sit in the other room and shout comments like, 'Why don't you try this sound,' or 'You're not playing the piano too well, try that,' something like that. I'll get the initial idea and say, 'Nicky [Hopkins], you get on piano, and someone else get on that,' and then Phil will suggest three acoustic guitars strumming somewhere, and we'll just find a sound from it. It's quite easy working with him."

While he was content to defer some production duties to Spector, Lennon frequently relied on Ono for advice. He may have admired Spector, but he trusted Ono, whom he depended on to 'A&R' his songs. However, despite her intervention, Alan White claimed that no one, apart from perhaps Lennon, took much notice of her. One example caught on film found Ono complaining to Lennon that the band were improvising. He tells the band to "stop jamming", but as White explained: "We didn't take notice of that, cos you know what? We'd do it again, and do it the same way, and she didn't know the difference. He knew that we knew what she was doing, and he'd just get on with it. He knew we were doing the right thing, but it's just the wife, doing her thing. We knew the music."

Basic tracks were recorded at the new 8-track studio Lennon had installed at his Tittenhurst Park home. Sessions appear to have begun in late May, as Steve Peacock, who interviewed Lennon at Tittenhurst for *Sounds* on May 22, reported that recording was well underway at the time of his visit. In the same interview, Lennon suggested that all of the backing tracks were completed over a nine-day period.

The sessions were relaxed affairs. Recording usually began in the late morning and ended in the early evening. White recalled: "We used to start warming up around 11 in the morning, and we'd go have lunch at 1 or 2 in the afternoon, and then see if we could get something down, or at least get to a point where it was sounding good. Sometimes we'd record things late in the evening. But mostly we recorded in the afternoon – we usually recorded [then], if we got a really good take, [and] we'd finish and have dinner around 6:30, 7:00."

Gathering the musicians around him, Lennon would rehearse the song they were about to record, teaching them the chords and working on a rough arrangement. They would then play through the song until Lennon, Ono, or Phil Spector was happy with it. Lennon always sang a guide vocal with each take, which he replaced later.

For this album, Plastic Ono Band was augmented by a number of seasoned professionals, who were drafted in to assist with the recording. George Harrison turned in some stunning performances, as did Nicky Hopkins, who played piano alongside Lennon on the album's title track. Guitarists Joey Molland and Tom Evans from Badfinger contributed to the album, as did keyboard player and arranger John Barham, who had recently worked on George Harrison's *All Things Must Pass* album.

Overdub sessions took place at the Record Plant East, New York City, in early July. Torrie Zito, who had worked with Frank Sinatra and Quincy Jones, wrote the album's dramatic string arrangements, which were recorded there by "some Philharmonic people", whom Lennon dubbed The Flux Fiddlers. The reference to the Fluxus group alluded to the use of toy violins, supplied by Joe Jones, that were employed for the string section. It was also during these NYC sessions that King Curtis added his saxophone to the multi-track tape.

The album produced three outtakes: a studio version of 'Well (Baby Please Don't Go)', 'I'm The Greatest', later given to Ringo Starr for his *Ringo* album, and a spontaneous rendition of 'San Francisco Bay Blues'. The sessions also produced several tracks used for Ono's companion album, *Fly*.

The Tittenhurst sessions were filmed for a feature-length documentary, *Imagine*, that was first screened on American television on December 23 1972. An edited version of this film was issued on video in 1985 and a revamped version, which paid greater attention to the recording sessions, was issued on DVD as *Gimme Some Truth* in 2000.

Imagine songs

Lennon had signed off *John Lennon/Plastic Ono Band* by stating that the dream was over. *Imagine* opens with a new dream, every bit as idealistic as the one he previously condemned. Inspired by Ono's book *Grapefruit*, which the couple were promoting while recording the *Imagine* album, Lennon composed 'Imagine'. Years later, he admitted his debt to Ono. Speaking to Andy Peebles about the song, he said: "Well, actually that should be credited as a Lennon/Ono song. A lot if it – the lyric and the concept – came from Yoko, but in those days I was a bit more selfish, a bit more macho, and I sort of omitted her contribution, but it was right out of *Grapefruit*."

Grapefruit was a collection of Ono's instruction pieces, many of which encouraged the reader to 'imagine' certain events they could hold in their memory. For her, the book wasn't important. In fact, she suggested that it be burnt once it had been read. The important part was the visualisation of ideas that could be stored in the reader's imagination. At around the same time as they were promoting *Grapefruit*, Lennon received a prayer book from Dick Gregory which, also championed the power of imagination. Combining ideas from both, he wrote a humanistic paean for the people.

Recalling Ono's early Fluxus scores and instruction pieces, Lennon's lyric asks us to imagine a world without the three main concepts that give our lives meaning – religion, nationhood, and possessions. Responding to real anxieties caused by the failure of these systems, he asks us to imagine a world without them, encouraging us to think of ourselves as citizens of the world, not as individuals defined by abstract systems. (Lennon would embrace this idea to the end – original pressings of *Double Fantasy* were inscribed "One World, One People".)

Lennon contends that global harmony is within our reach, but only if we reject the mechanisms of social control that restrict human potential. What he hoped to do was raise self-awareness, emphasise self-creation, and compel individuals to question their own abstract relationship with the institutions that order our lives. However, he offers no answers, only hypotheses. All Lennon offered was a world of possibilities that exist within us should we want them strongly enough.

Although Lennon argues for a world without grand, all-encompassing themes, when asked about the song in 1971, he stressed what he thought was the song's overriding left-wing ideology. "'Imagine', which says: 'Imagine that there was no more religion, no more country, no more politics,' is virtually the Communist manifesto, even though I'm not particularly a Communist and I do not belong to any movement."

Lennon's thinking seems a little nebulous and at odds with the songs humanist theme. Somehow his form of Communism was as nice and fluffy as the real thing was unpleasant and brutal. Speaking to the *NME*, he said: "It might be like Communism, but I don't really know what real Communism is. There is no real Communist state in the world; you must realise that. The socialism I speak about is a British Socialism, not the way some daft Russian might do it. Or the Chinese might do it. That might suit them. Us, we should have a nice Socialism here. A British Socialism."

Not only does this sound very isolationist, and not at all in keeping with the inclusive global oneness he envisions with 'Imagine', but Lennon seems more than a little confused. Indeed, the song seems riddled with contradictions. Its hymn-like setting sits uncomfortably alongside its author's plea for us to picture a world without religion. And how could a millionaire pop star's appeal for us to imagine a world without possessions be taken seriously? But that is to miss the point. Lennon knew he had nothing concrete to offer, so instead he offers a dream, a concept to be built upon.

Melodically, Lennon hints at the possibilities on offer with a simple motif that cries out to be developed and extended. The sense of indeterminacy that's evoked by his melodic sketch offers a number of possible interventions and interpretations for the listener to complete. Like many Fluxus artists, Lennon encourages the listener to add to the piece, if only in their imagination. By offering the listener the opportunity to add to his composition in this way, he hints at the sense of global progress and change that his lyric calls for. The Fluxus credo of reciprocity and participation made itself felt even here, the most unlikely Fluxus manifestation in Lennon's canon.

At the time of writing, no demo recordings of 'Imagine' have come to light. What has been issued are numerous alternative takes. Before recording 'Imagine', Lennon gathered the musicians around an upright piano to play them his new song. This rehearsal recording was issued on *Imagine: John Lennon* (CDP 7 90803 2). At the end of this rehearsal take, Klaus Voormann suggested using the white baby grand piano situated in the Lennons' 'white room'. Several takes were attempted there but, because Spector was unhappy with the room's acoustics, the session was abandoned.

When work on the song continued, the main concern was how best to capture the piano sound that Lennon had in mind. Some takes featured him and Nicky Hopkins playing the same piano in different registers. Others were augmented by harmonium, played by John Barham. Take one, which features Barham's harmonium, was issued on the *John Lennon Anthology*. The final master features Lennon on piano and a string overdub recorded in New York.

Several live versions of the title track, 'Imagine', have appeared over the years, the earliest taped not long after the *Imagine* album had been issued. On December 17 1971, Lennon and Ono appeared at the Apollo Theatre, New York City. Backed by a hastily-formed band, Lennon performed the song with acoustic guitar rather than piano. This recording was eventually issued on the *John Lennon Anthology*. A version recorded with Elephant's Memory on January 27 1972 for US TV's *The Mike Douglas Show* was issued in mono on *Lennon In His Own Words* (no catalogue number), a CD included with copies of James Henke's book *Lennon Legend*. The One To One concert on August 30 1972 produced another live version, which was issued on *John Lennon Live In New York City*. Capitol issued this recording as a 12-inch promotional record (SPRO-9575). Finally, an instrumental version of 'Imagine' found its way onto the *Lennon Legend* DVD and was issued on the *Happy Christmas (War Is Over)* CD single (CDR 6627) in 2003.

Next on the album comes 'Crippled Inside'. Blending idioms borrowed from American popular music, it swings like the goodtime music that inspired it. But behind the vitality of Nicky Hopkins's honky-tonk piano and the fluidity of George Harrison's down-home dobro lurks a lyric dripping with cynicism. The song seems to attack 'straight' society for creating falsehoods. Outwardly, Lennon's acutely observed lyric appears to attack many of the social conventions we hide behind to mask our inadequacies. However, it's as self-critical as anything from *John Lennon/Plastic Ono Band* and could easily be an expression of the guilt he felt at the fiction he himself propagated. Lennon had addressed similar issues with 'I'm A Loser', but having matured considerably and with the experience of primal therapy behind him, he wrote a song that recalls but also pokes fun at the seriousness of his previous attempts at self-analysis.

Lennon wrote the melody for 'Jealous Guy' in India in 1968. At that time, the song was called 'Child Of Nature' and reflected the hippie ethos The Beatles were then enjoying. On their return to England, The Beatles recorded 'Child Of Nature' in demo form at George Harrison's house before Lennon abandoned it. By 1971, he had rewritten the lyrics to express his growing desire to become more trusting.

Lennon's attitude to women changed little over the years, as he explained to *Playboy*. "I was a very jealous, possessive guy. Toward everything. A very insecure male. A guy who wants to put his woman in a little box, lock her up, and just bring her out when he feels like playing with her." Although 'Jealous Guy' finds Lennon expressing a desire to reject the male chauvinist values he had grown up with, in reality little had changed. As footage from the *Imagine* film reveals, Lennon relied on Ono for more than inspiration and creative advice. Despite her independence and professed feminism, she still served his meals and mended his clothes.

During the making of the *Imagine* album, Lennon and Ono were interviewed for the BBC radio programme *Woman's Hour* about attitudes to love and sex, and Lennon revealed how possessive he was. "When you actually are in love with somebody, you tend to be jealous and want to own them and possess them 100 percent, which I do. But intellectually, before that, I thought right, owning a person is rubbish, but I love Yoko, I want to possess her completely. I don't want to stifle her, you know? That's the danger, that you want to possess them to death. But that's a personal problem, you know?"

'Jealous Guy' finds Lennon acknowledging that he had a problem and attempting to do something about it, even if it were only to write a song about it. It wasn't the first time that he'd written on the subject and it wouldn't be the last. At around the time he wrote the lyrics for 'Jealous Guy', he wrote a song titled 'Call Your Name', which formed the basis of 'Aisumasen (I'm Sorry)' on 1973's *Mind Games* album. Both songs point to a shift in Lennon's songwriting, documenting a transition from arrogant bravado to a passive acceptance of his own shortcomings.

Joey Molland from Badfinger helped record 'Jealous Guy' with bandmate Tom Evans. Molland was somewhat star-struck at meeting Lennon, but also a little surprised at his no-nonsense attitude. As usual, Lennon played the song to the group before moving to the studio and was obviously keen to get the session started. As Molland recalled: "He was really brusque with us, really almost rude, but not rude. ... Then he sits down on the stool and starts playing 'Jealous Guy'. ... So we recorded acoustic guitars on that and John said, 'You can fuck off now if you'd like.' Of course, he wasn't being like, 'Fuck off.' It was like, 'Do what you like.' So they started playing 'I Don't Wanna Be A Soldier' and me and Tommy were just hanging out. We just started to play along because we weren't about to move and let somebody throw us out. We didn't play it, we just started this 'doodley-do' kind of Bo Diddley strumming, because the song didn't seem to settle into any particular rhythm. And it ended up on the record. One of the most exciting nights of me life."

Rough mixes of 'Jealous Guy' placed Molland and Evans's acoustic guitars high in the mix, but by the time Spector had finished work on the song, he'd buried them well down in the mix. Their playing is more audible on 'I Don't Want To Be A Soldier', where Spector placed them much higher in the balance. Alan White also played on the track, but because the studio was small, he found himself playing in a bathroom next to the studio. He said: "I was playing vibraphone in the bathroom. There was a door in the corner, with a bathroom back there, and we couldn't have the vibes out in the room where the drums were, cos it would go all over the mics, so they put me in the bathroom."

'It's So Hard' summarises Lennon's daily struggle with life and the problems it put in his way. Respite from his troubles wasn't far from hand. Unsurprisingly, he finds comfort in Ono's presence.

To test his new studio, Lennon gathered a small band around him and recorded a stomping, gritty rocker. He claimed that at the time his studio was so new that certain pieces of equipment – limiters and equalisers – hadn't even been installed. With only three musicians involved in recording the basic track, little could go wrong and, despite the lack of equipment, the basic track of 'It's So Hard' was captured successfully.

What in other hands could have been a maudlin song of self-pity was lifted by a bouncy arrangement that features some snappy rhythm/lead guitar, played by Lennon. Basic tracks completed, the song was set aside while the rest of the album was recorded. It was not worked on again until Lennon and Spector supervised overdub sessions at the Record Plant East in New York City. First they added strings and then, on July 4, Lennon called on the services of saxophonist King Curtis, who added his masterly playing to the track.

Curtis played on some of the greatest R&B records to come out of America and supported The Beatles on their 1965 American tour. Lennon was thrilled to have him on the track, so much so that he recorded the overdub session for posterity. Lennon's instructions to Curtis were vague; his only suggestion was that he wanted something like 'Honky Tonk', a 1956 hit for The Bill Doggett Combo. Lennon played through his song a few times, ad-libbing the melody he wanted Curtis to play. A few takes later and Curtis had the overdub in the bag.

'It's so Hard' was performed at the matinee and evening performances of the 1972 One To One concert. Both performances have since been issued: the matinee recording is available on *John Lennon In New York City*; the evening recording on the *John Lennon Anthology*.

On *John Lennon/Plastic Ono Band*, 'God' had found Lennon listing the things he no longer believed in. A little over a year later, 'I Don't Want To Be A Soldier' saw him reworking his litany to include the things he didn't want to be. He was constantly repositioning himself, changing his identity and beliefs to suit his circumstances. 'Soldier' was Lennon's way of acknowledging how precarious a grip he had on his own identity. For him to sustain acceptability within his social circle, he had to expel all that was considered inappropriate and 'straight'. By disavowing the things that rigidly define individuals in 'straight' society, he establishes a claim for authenticity. Instead of using the power of imagination to rid himself of these things, he performs a symbolic exorcism to unburden himself of their influence. By symbolically disowning the things that threaten to de-centre him, Lennon was able to define and control them. Yet, by articulating his fears, he drew himself further into the world he abhorred. He may not have wanted to be a soldier, but a few months after recording the song he was dressing in army fatigues. True, he was fighting for the 'people', but by adopting the image of a soldier he had become the very thing he abhorred.

Musically, 'I Don't Want To Be A Soldier' is unadventurous. Lennon indulged in this kind of improvisation while filming *Let It Be*. Little more than an extended jam, it would have been dull indeed without Spector's magic touch. An early version issued with the *Lennon Signature Box*, presents the song in an acoustic setting with Lennon on acoustic guitar and vocals, Andy White (?) on drums and Nicky Hopkins on piano. Presented in this rough early take, it sounds like a Phil Ochs outtake. However, by the time Lennon switched to electric guitar and got Spector to transform the song with layers of echo, it developed an eerie, unsettling texture. The track also benefits from King Curtis's playing, which adds to the recording immeasurably.

Described by Lennon as "one of those moany songs", 'Give Me Some Truth' was started while in India in early 1968. A year later, The Beatles attempted some half-hearted attempts of the song while filming *Let It Be*, but no proper recordings were made. In this context, Lennon's pleas for truth may have been directed at his fellow bandmates.

Relations within The Beatles had disintegrated to the point where each felt alienated from the others. Ringo Starr recalled for the later *Anthology* project how troubled everyone felt at the time. "I left the group because I felt two things: I felt I wasn't playing great; and I also felt that the other three were really happy and I was an outsider. I went to see John, who had been living in my apartment in Montagu Square with Yoko since he moved out of Kenwood. I said, 'I'm leaving the group because I'm not playing well and I feel unloved and out of it, and you three are really close.' And John said, 'I thought it was *you three*!'" Lennon felt just as anxious, but rather than leave the group he turned to heroin to mask his feelings. The Beatles were in trouble, but rather than face the truth, they took to hiding behind a masquerade of deceit. The truth was there, but no one wanted to face it.

By the time he came to record 'Give Me Some Truth' for *Imagine*, Lennon had rewritten some of the lyrics to include references to US President Richard Nixon. 'Tricky Dicky' Nixon became the bane of Lennon's life. It was Nixon's government who tapped his phone, watched his every move, and tried to deport him from America. But Lennon had it in for Nixon long before Nixon had it in for him. With the escalating war in Vietnam, Nixon was marked by most as Public Enemy Number One. After years of campaigning for peace, Lennon was growing tired of the lack of progress. If anything, the situation had grown worse. Thanks to Nixon's intervention, the war in Vietnam had intensified and the prospect of a world at peace seemed as remote as ever. Although 'Give Me Some Truth' appears to signal despair at the lack of political progress and the intransigence of world leaders, Lennon remained committed to politics and increased his political activity.

The next song on *Imagine* also dates from 1968. 'Oh My Love' is a tender love song that Lennon wrote at the start of his relationship with Ono. It's an intense expression of affection that finds him in the grip of infatuation, experiencing the world anew. If 'Give Me Some Truth' suggested a mind clouded by untruths, here Lennon confesses to a clarity of vision restored by the purity of his love. Fittingly, Ono received a co-author credit, and her influence can be clearly heard in the song's lyric. The allusions to natural elements such as the wind and clouds are typical of her instruction pieces.

Lennon's innocent lyric is supported by the most delicate of melodies, performed with a lightness of touch as gentle as his expression of devotion is honest. George Harrison's hauntingly beautiful guitar figure offers the perfect complement to Lennon's vaguely Oriental sounding melody. Harrison started the session on dobro but quickly moved to his Gibson Les Paul, its rich, warm tones complementing the intimate nature of the recording perfectly. Lennon's own playing is enhanced by Nicky Hopkins's delicate piano motif, which adds a rococo sparkle to the arrangement.

Not content with calling each other names over the boardroom table and in the pages of the British music press, John Lennon and Paul McCartney had turned to songwriting to badmouth one another. McCartney's *Ram* album was littered with snipes at his former partner. Songs like 'Too Many People' and 'The Back Seat Of My Car', with its refrain "We believe that we can't be wrong", really galled Lennon.

"I heard Paul's messages in *Ram* – yes there are dear reader!" Lennon told *Crawdaddy*. "Too many people going where? Missed our lucky what? What was our first mistake? Can't be wrong? Huh! I mean Yoko, me, and other friends can't all be hearing things. So to have some fun, I must thank Allen Klein publicly for the line 'just another day'. A real poet! Some people don't see the funny side of it. Too bad. What am I supposed to do, make you laugh? It's what you might call an 'angry letter', sung – get it?"

When Lennon and McCartney channelled their rivalry in a common cause, it was a positive power for good. When channelled at one another, it was only destructive. Never one to take things lying down, Lennon couldn't resist replying to McCartney's jibes. On 'How Do You Sleep?' he attacks McCartney for breaking up The Beatles and claims that he's a spent force. Alluding to the myth that McCartney had died in 1966 and been replaced with a double, Lennon suggests that the "freaks" who promulgated these fictions were right and that McCartney had died, at least creatively.

Although Lennon took sole credit for writing the song, at least two others contributed to the lyrics. When Lennon first played the song to Harrison, the lyrics appeared finished. But as Spector noted at the time, Lennon was apt to change lyrics right up to the last take. Felix Denis of *Oz* magazine recalled that Ono contributed to the song. "Yoko wrote many of the lyrics. I watched her racing into the studio to show John, and they'd burst out laughing. The mood there wasn't totally vindictive – they were taking the piss out of the headmaster."

Allen Klein told *Playboy* that he got Lennon to change a potentially libellous line about McCartney plagiarising his song 'Yesterday'. Klein said the original couplet was "The only thing you done was yesterday / You probably pinched that bitch anyway" and that he thought it too strong, offering "Since you've gone you're just another day" as an alternative for that second line.

The song was obviously written in the heat of the moment and intended to irk McCartney, but Lennon claimed that he simply used his former partner as a catalyst. "It was like Dylan doing 'Like A Rolling Stone', one of his nasty songs," said Lennon. "It's using somebody as an object to create something. I wasn't really feeling that vicious at the time, but I was using my resentment towards Paul to create a song. Let's put it that way. It was just a mood. Paul took it the way he did because it, obviously, pointedly refers to him, and people just hounded him about it, asking, 'How do ya feel about it?' But there were a few little digs on *his* album, which he kept so obscure that other people didn't notice 'em, you know? But I heard them. So, I thought, 'Well, hang up being obscure! I'll just get right down to the nitty-gritty.'" Lennon was clearly out to get McCartney, but also intent on having fun. He may have been enjoying himself but at least one ex-Beatle thought he was going too far. Ringo Starr, who was visiting the studio at the time, was upset by the song and reportedly told Lennon, "That's enough, John."

Starr was right: Lennon had gone far enough. 'How Do You Sleep?' effectively ended Lennon and McCartney's public squabbling. As a form of catharsis it allowed Lennon to rid himself of the anger and frustration he experienced at the break-up of The Beatles, and it was shocking enough to silence McCartney, whose follow-up to *Ram*, *Wild Life*, all but ignored the situation. Instead, McCartney turned in 'Dear Friend', a ballad that pointed to the reconciliation that was to come. Similarly, Lennon never directly attacked McCartney through song again. Ironically, within a few years Lennon and Ono were engaged in and relishing the kind of cosy domesticity they'd lambasted the McCartneys for enjoying. By the mid 1970s, Lennon had become a 'house husband', besotted with his son Sean and, like McCartney before him, writing cosy pop songs about his newly found joy.

'How?' finds Lennon staring into an existential void and attempting to make sense of who he was becoming. He sees no meaning to his life, only choices that fill him with anxiety. Caught in abeyance, Lennon had reached a defining moment where the choices he made would shape his future in countless ways. The closing verse, sung in the third person, suggests that all of us share similar feelings and fates, but are unwilling to face them. Like 'Imagine', 'How?' asks listeners to take control of their life and consider a future better than the one they inhabit.

As a confession of insecurity, 'How?' could have sat comfortably alongside anything on *John Lennon/Plastic Ono Band*. Its hesitant pauses underline a mood of uncertainty, but the glorious middle eight and Zito's string arrangement lift it from the slough of despair. Lennon took several takes to capture his vocal, but the effort paid off and he delivered one of his best.

Imagine closes with the jubilant 'Oh Yoko!'. The song has little more to say than I love you, but Lennon's tender-heartedness was also a plea for reassurance. Speaking in 1980, he said: "It's a message to Yoko. Because I couldn't say it in real life. Maybe, I don't know." Lennon's ambivalence was reflected in the different approaches he took to the song before recording it properly. An early version, recorded in June 1969 while Lennon and Ono were very much a love-struck couple, has the same buoyant mood as the album version. However, when Lennon returned to the song a little over a year later, in November 1970, it had taken on a melancholy air. Performed on piano, the demo recording reveals just how primal therapy had affected Lennon. Recorded a few weeks after completing *John Lennon/Plastic Ono Band*, it finds him reeling from its effects and close to the edge of an emotional abyss. When it came time to record 'Oh Yoko!' for the *Imagine* album, Lennon reverted to its original up-beat arrangement.

Imagine data
Imagine was the first Apple album issued in quadraphonic, a shortlived four-channel system that provided an early form of surround-sound. In Britain, the quadraphonic mix was issued on LP (Q4PAS 10004) and 8-track cartridge (Q8-PAS 10004) but in the USA was available only on 8-track (Q8W-3379). The quadraphonic mix produced only one noticeable anomaly: the sound of the orchestra warming up was removed from the beginning of 'How Do You Sleep?'. In America, the album was issued on reel-to-reel tape (L 3379) by Apple/Ampex.

Bespoke Apple labels were used for both British and American editions, which were issued with a printed inner sleeve, poster, and postcard. Ono took the cover photograph, after the original design – a photograph of Lennon with his eyes replaced by clouds – was abandoned. George Maciunas, a central figure within the Fluxus movement, was commissioned to design the inner sleeve and the typography used on the front cover.

The most commercially successful of Lennon's albums, *Imagine* has been reissued several times. EMI reissued it on November 17 1997 (LPCENT27) as a special limited-edition release to celebrate the company's centenary. The album featured original packaging, 180-gram virgin vinyl, analogue cutting from analogue tape, and heavy quality cover. The LP was reissued again in 2000 when it was remixed and remastered by EMI/Parlophone (5248571) on February 14 2000. This pressing featured generic Apple labels with slightly altered credits: 'I Don't Want To Be A Soldier' was suffixed with 'Mama'. Unlike original pressings, it was issued with a gatefold cover and card inner sleeve.

When Capitol reissued *Imagine* in 1978, it replaced the custom Apple labels with purple Capitol labels with a large Capitol logo. Capitol issued the LP again in 1986, this time with black/colour band labels. In 1987, Capitol issued the album with black/colour band labels; this version has 'Digitally Remastered' printed at the top of the front cover. In 1988, Capitol issued the album with purple Capitol labels with a small Capitol logo.

The album was remastered in 1984 by MFSL Original Master Recordings, which issued a half speed master version of the album (MFSL-1-153). In February 2000, MFSL issued a 180-gram GAIN 2 Ultra Analog half speed master vinyl pressing of the 2000 remix (MFSL 1-277).

The album was issued on coloured vinyl in two countries. Original Japanese pressings of the LP (AP-80370) were issued on red vinyl, and in France the LP was issued on blue vinyl (2C 064-4914).

Imagine was issued on 8-track in Britain (8X-PAS 10004) and America (8XW-3379). A quadraphonic mix was also issued on 8-track: Q8-PAS 10004 in the UK and Q8W-3379 in the USA.

Imagine was first issued on CD by EMI in Britain on May 26 1987 (CDP 7 46641 2). As was the practice at the time, EMI manufactured the CDs in Japan and matched them with covers made in Britain. In America, Capitol issued the CD on March 17 1988. The Japanese CD (CP32-5451) featured a mono version of 'How Do You Sleep?'. On February 14 2000, EMI/Capitol issued a remixed and remastered edition of *Imagine* on CD (524 8582). It was also issued on August 22 2003 by MFSL Original Master Recordings as an Ultradisc II 24 kt. gold CD (UDCD-758).

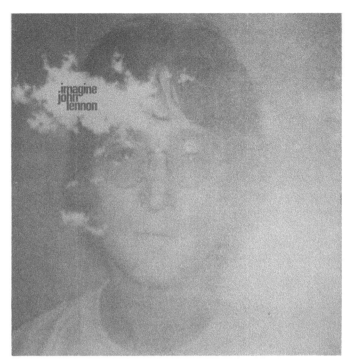

IMAGINE
JOHN LENNON
PLASTIC ONO BAND
(with The Flux Fiddlers)

All Songs Published by
Northern Songs. NCB

("An EMI
Recording")

33⅓

Mfd. In U.K.

Stereo
PAS 10004
(YEX.865)

Side One

℗ 1971

1. IMAGINE
   (Lennon) 2:59
2. CRIPPLED INSIDE
   (Lennon) 3:43
3. JEALOUS GUY
   (Lennon) 4:10
4. IT'S SO HARD
   (Lennon) 2:22
5. I DON'T WANT TO BE A SOLDIER
   (Lennon) 6:01

Produced By: JOHN & YOKO
and PHIL SPECTOR

IMAGINE
JOHN LENNON
PLASTIC ONO BAND
(with The Flux Fiddlers)

("An EMI
Recording")

33⅓

Mfd. In U.K.

Stereo
PAS 10004
(YEX.866)

Side Two

All Songs Published by
Northern Songs. NCB

* Joint copyright
  claimed by
  Ono Music Ltd.

℗ 1971

1. GIVE ME SOME TRUTH
   (Lennon) 3:11
2. OH MY LOVE *
   (Lennon/Ono) 2:40
3. HOW DO YOU SLEEP?
   (Lennon) 5:29
4. HOW?
   (Lennon) 3:37
5. OH YOKO!
   (Lennon) 4:18

Produced By: JOHN & YOKO
and PHIL SPECTOR

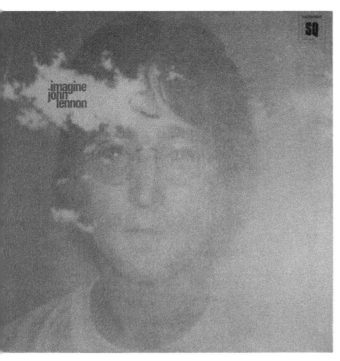

Without 'All Rights Reserved' text

With 'All Rights Reserved' text

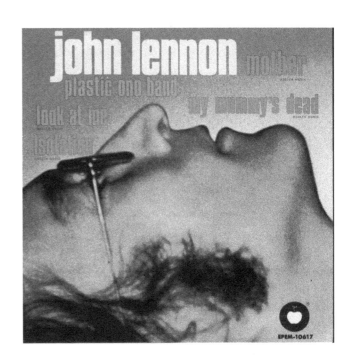

'IMAGINE' / 'IT'S SO HARD'
JOHN LENNON AND PLASTIC ONO BAND (WITH THE FLUX FIDDLERS)

US release October 11 1971; Apple APPLE 1840; chart high No.3.

'IMAGINE'

Issued as a single two days after Lennon's 31st birthday, 'Imagine' was his first solo single not to feature one of Ono's songs on its B-side.

The single was issued with a white Apple label, similar to those used for the *John Lennon/Plastic Ono Band* LP, and generic Apple sleeve. Two label variations were issued. Both have identical text layout, but one has 'MFD. BY APPLE, RECORDS INC', the other 'MFD. BY APPLE, RECORDS INC UNAUTHORISED DUPLICATION IS A VIOLATION OF APPLICABLE LAWS'. The single was reissued with purple Capitol labels in 1978 and with black/colour band Capitol labels in 1983. It was reissued in 1988 with purple Capitol labels.

In 1992, Capitol's Special Markets Division issued the record with a new catalogue number (S7-17688). This edition was intended to be gold-plated for presentation sets, but approximately 1,000 copies escaped the electro-plating process and found their way onto the open market.

'HAPPY XMAS (WAR IS OVER)' / 'LISTEN THE SNOW IS FALLING'
JOHN LENNON & YOKO ONO/PLASTIC ONO BAND WITH THE HARLEM
COMMUNITY CHOIR / YOKO ONO AND PLASTIC ONO BAND

UK release November 24 1972; Apple R 5870; chart high No.4 (re-enters January 4 1975, chart high No.48; re-enters December 20 1980 chart high No.2; re-enters December 19 1981 chart high No.28; re-enters December 25 1982 chart high No.56; re-enters December 24 1983 chart high No.92; re-enters December 22 1984 chart high No.92; as R 6627 re-enters December 20 2003 chart high No.33).
US release December 1 1971; Apple APPLE 1842; failed to chart.

'Happy Xmas (War Is Over)' (Ono, Lennon)
John Lennon (vocals, guitar), Yoko Ono (vocals), Hugh McCracken (guitar), Chris Osbourne (guitar), Teddy Irwin (guitar), Stuart Scharf (guitar), Nicky Hopkins (piano, chimes, glockenspiel), Jim Keltner (drums, sleigh bells), The Harlem Community Choir (backing vocals).
'Listen, The Snow Is Falling' (Ono)
Yoko Ono (vocals), John Lennon (guitar), Hugh McCracken (guitar), Nicky Hopkins (piano, chimes), Klaus Voormann (bass), Jim Keltner (drums).

Both recorded at The Record Plant East, New York City, NY, USA. Both produced by John & Yoko and Phil Spector.

'HAPPY XMAS (WAR IS OVER)'

The origins of 'Happy Xmas (War Is Over)' stretched back to Lennon and Ono's 'War Is Over' poster campaign, launched on December 15 1969 in 12 cities around the world. The simple white posters proclaimed: "War Is Over! If You Want It. Happy Christmas from John & Yoko." With this germ of an idea in place, the pair wrote a seasonal song, developing the theme of peaceful revolution that Lennon had argued for with 'Imagine'.

Lennon often 'borrowed' motifs from other songs to kick-start his own. He'd based 'Come Together' on Chuck Berry's 'You Can't Catch Me', but the first few bars of 'Happy Xmas (War Is Over)' were appropriated from The Paris Sisters' 'I Love How You Love Me' – at least, that's what Phil Spector claimed. Spector had produced the Paris Sisters record, so he should have known. Also, Lennon instructed the producer that he wanted the record to sound like the one he'd just produced for his wife, Ronnie Spector, 'Try Some, Buy Some'. Spector obliged by having the assembled guitarists play a mandolin-like riff to complement the song's main musical motif.

Klaus Voormann was to have played bass on the record, but his flight to New York was delayed, with the result that one of the guitarists was called on to play bass on the track. Basic tracks and instrumental overdubs were completed in one evening, at the end of which a rough mix, perhaps the one that appears on the *John Lennon Anthology*, was taken away by the Lennons. The Harlem Community Choir added its contribution to the record two days later, on October 31.

A Christmas classic with a timeless melody and poignant lyrics, 'Happy Xmas (War Is Over)' was produced to perfection by Phil Spector. Sadly, it is as relevant today as when it was written.

Ono's 'Listen, The Snow Is Falling' predated by almost a year the 'War Is Over!' poster campaign that influenced Lennon's A-side. Her song first surfaced as 'Snow Is Falling All The Time' on the Aspen flexi-disc recorded in late 1968. It restates an idea used for another B-side, 'Who Has Seen The Wind?'. For Ono, natural elements have the power to connect people. 'Listen, The Snow Is Falling' combines her fascination with natural elements, such as wind and water, with her desire for global harmony and unity.

Recording the song should have been simple, but Ono grew increasingly frustrated with the musicians, who she thought weren't taking her work seriously. First she couldn't agree with Lennon on the song's tempo. She wanted it fast, but all that happened was that the band started to rock out, which wasn't what she wanted. Nicky Hopkins' playing came in for criticism, and when Klaus Voormann and Hugh McCracken began to develop some riffs to enhance the melody, she got into a shouting match with Voormann over where they should go. It was only Lennon's intervention that stopped the bass player from walking out of the session. The studio atmosphere may have been tense, but the recording sounded as relaxed and graceful as her earlier recordings had sounded tense and feral.

Apple issued 'Happy Xmas (War Is Over)' in the USA on December 1 1971, but the British release was held up by almost a year because of Ono's claim as co-author. The Lennons, like the McCartneys, were having problems with their music publishers, who were unhappy at Lennon's claim that he was writing with his wife. Lennon's British publishers, Northern Songs, were refusing to accept the fact that Ono had contributed to the composition. Consequently, the British single was not released until the dispute was resolved.

'Happy Xmas (War Is Over)' data

American pressings were issued on green or black vinyl with a picture cover and two label variations. Copies were issued with a bespoke 'merging heads' label, based on photographs of Lennon and Ono taken by Ian Macmillan, or generic Apple labels.

The American Apple label variant was issued with three typographical variations. The first has a light green Apple label with song title on three lines at 11 o'clock and composer credit below; 'STEREO' at 9 o'clock; publisher credits at 2 o'clock; artist's name 'JOHN & YOKO and the LENNON PLASTIC ONO BAND with THE HARLEM COMMUNITY CHOIR' centre bottom. The second variant has a light green Apple label with song title on four lines at 11 o'clock and composer credit below; 'STEREO' at 9 o'clock; artist's name 'JOHN & YOKO and the LENNON PLASTIC ONO BAND with THE HARLEM COMMUNITY CHOIR' bottom left. And the third has a light green Apple label with song title on two lines at 11 o'clock and composer credit below; 'STEREO' at 9 o'clock; artist's name 'JOHN & YOKO and the LENNON PLASTIC ONO BAND with THE HARLEM COMMUNITY CHOIR' centre bottom.

Seven-inch white-label promotional copies of the single (S-45X-47663) were manufactured in very limited numbers for US radio stations.

By the mid 1980s, Capitol had manufactured the single with several label variations. They reissued the single in 1976 with orange Capitol labels; in 1978 with purple Capitol labels; in 1983 with black/colour band labels (these can be found with or without 'Under License From ATV Music'); and in 1988 with purple Capitol labels with the publishing credited to 'Ono Music / Blackwood Music Inc. Under License From ATV Music (Maclen)-BMI.'

In 1986 Capitol produced two different white vinyl 12-inch pressings for promotional use. The first of these (SPRO-9929) was limited to 2,500. Pressed with a silver and white variant of the 'merging heads' label, it was packaged in a transparent vinyl sleeve with a large silver sticker depicting one of Lennon's drawings. The second white vinyl 12-inch (SPRO-9894) was issued with black/colour band labels and a custom cover. The record featured 'Happy Xmas (War Is Over)' on both sides of the disc and was issued in a picture cover, which was hand numbered. Released in an edition of 2,000, this promotional record was produced to benefit the Central Virginia Foodbank charity.

In 1996, Capitol's Special Markets Division reissued 'Happy Xmas (War Is Over)' as a jukebox single (S7-17644) on green vinyl with purple Capitol labels. Between 20,000 and 22,000 copies of this edition of the single were manufactured and distributed.

Geffen Records reissued the single in November 1982, to promote the *John Lennon Collection*. The commercial 7-inch single (7-29855) was issued with a new picture cover and B-side, 'Beautiful Boy (Darling Boy)' from *Double Fantasy*. Geffen also produced a 12-inch promotional single (PRO-A-1079) issued to radio stations.

British pressings of 'Happy Xmas (War Is Over)' were only issued with the 'merging heads' label. Initial copies were pressed on opaque green vinyl (American pressings use transparent green vinyl). Because of the single's success in Britain, the initial batch of green vinyl pressings was quickly exhausted and the record was re-pressed on black vinyl.

In Britain the single was re-promoted almost every year after its original release, but it was not until 1980, when the record was re-promoted in the wake of Lennon's murder, that the picture cover was reinstated. The only difference between original 1972 covers and the 1980 reissue is that originals are made from heavier card.

The single was reissued, rather than re-promoted, in 2003 with a new B-side, 'Imagine'. That issue (R 6627) used a newly remastered version of 'Happy Xmas (War Is Over)' produced for the *John Lennon Legend* DVD. This single was also issued on green vinyl with a black Parlophone label in a revised picture cover with additional information about the *John Lennon Legend* DVD and CD. An enhanced CD single (CDR 6227) accompanied the vinyl release.

Promotional CD singles were issued to promote both the *Lennon Legend* and *Anthology* albums. A one-track CD single (IMAGINE 002) was manufactured by Parlophone/EMI for British radio stations to promote *Lennon Legend*. A two-track CD single (LENNON 002) of the rough mix of 'Happy Xmas (War Is

Over)' backed with 'Be-Bop-A-Lula' was produced by Capitol to promote the *Anthology/Wonsaponatime* albums.

Ono also used 'Happy Xmas (War Is Over)' to promote the reissue of her back catalogue by Rykodisc. Issued as a CD single (VRCD-ONO) in 1991 with a Christmas message from her, the single was issued with a custom sleeve in a PVC wallet. In 1997, she had a limited number of CD singles of 'Listen The Snow Is Falling' / 'Happy Xmas (War Is Over)' produced as Christmas presents for friends. These privately produced CDs came with a picture cover depicting a burning match and instructions for her *Lighting Piece*.

WAR IS OVER!

IF YOU WANT IT

Happy Christmas from John & Yoko

www.IMAGINEPEACE.com

99

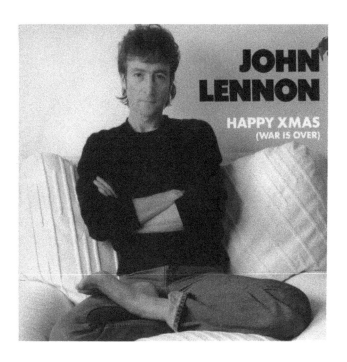

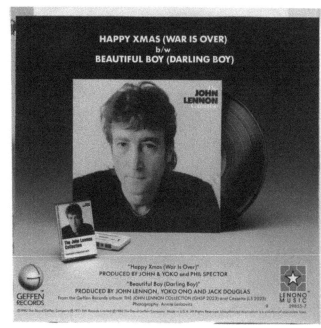

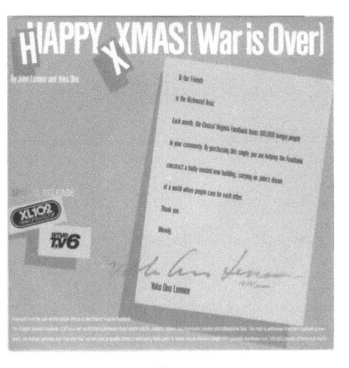

GEFFEN RECORDS

Geffen Records, 9126 Sunset Blvd., Los Angeles, Calif. 90069 • Manufactured exclusively by Warner Bros. Records Inc. • A Warner Communications Company • Made in U.S.A.

LENONO MUSIC

PRO-A-1079
PROMOTIONAL COPY
NOT FOR SALE

SIDE 1

33 1/3 RPM

JOHN LENNON

PRODUCED BY JOHN & YOKO AND PHIL SPECTOR
From the Geffen Records cassette
THE JOHN LENNON COLLECTION (M5 2023)

HAPPY XMAS (War Is Over) 3:32
(Yoko Ono/John Lennon)

Ono Music, Inc./Maclen Music, Inc. BMI
℗ 1971 EMI Records Limited

Capitol
REG. U.S. PAT. OFF.

MANUFACTURED BY CAPITOL RECORDS, INC. • A SUBSIDIARY OF CAPITOL INDUSTRIES-EMI, INC. U.S.A.

UNAUTHORIZED DUPLICATION IS A VIOLATION OF APPLICABLE LAWS

FOR
JUKEBOXES
ONLY!

S7-17644-A

Cema
SPECIAL
MARKETS

3:32

HAPPY XMAS (WAR IS OVER)
(J. Lennon-Y. Ono)
JOHN & YOKO/
THE PLASTIC ONO BAND
WITH THE HARLEM CHOIR

Capitol MARCA REG. ALL RIGHTS RESERVED.

happy xmas
yoko
1991

happy xmas (war is over) (Lennon/Ono)

FOR PROMOTION ONLY
NOT FOR SALE
this release
© & ℗ 1991 yoko ono
VRCD ONO

℗1971 Lenono Music BMI courtesy of Capitol Records, Inc., by arrangement with CEMA Special Markets

an xmas message from yoko
1991

HAPPYXMAS
JOHNLENNON
from The John Lennon Anthology

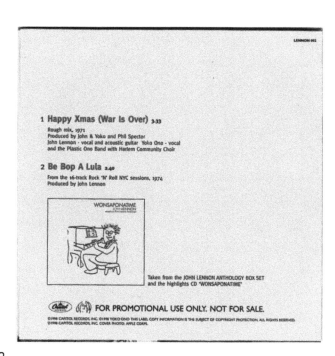

LENNON 002

1 Happy Xmas (War Is Over) 3:33
Rough mix, 1971
Produced by John & Yoko and Phil Spector
John Lennon - vocal and acoustic guitar Yoko Ono - vocal
and the Plastic Ono Band with Harlem Community Choir

2 Be Bop A Lula 2:40
From the 16-track Rock 'N' Roll NYC sessions, 1974
Produced by John Lennon

WONSAPONATIME
JOHN LENNON

Taken from the JOHN LENNON ANTHOLOGY BOX SET
and the highlights CD "WONSAPONATIME"

FOR PROMOTIONAL USE ONLY. NOT FOR SALE.

©1998 CAPITOL RECORDS, INC. ©1998 YOKO ONO THIS LABEL COPY INFORMATION IS THE SUBJECT OF COPYRIGHT PROTECTION. ALL RIGHTS RESERVED.
©1998 CAPITOL RECORDS, INC. COVER PHOTO: APPLE CORPS.

HAPPY XMAS
(War Is Over)

JOHN & YOKO
THE PLASTIC ONO BAND
With The Harlem Community Choir

R 5970

LISTEN, THE SNOW IS FALLING

YOKO ONO
THE PLASTIC ONO BAND

R 5970

HAPPY XMAS
(War Is Over)

Digital re-master ℗ 2003 The copyright in this sound recording is owned by EMI Records Ltd.
© 2003 EMI Records Ltd.

7243 5 53674 7 1
R 6627

Parlophone

JOHN & YOKO
THE PLASTIC ONO BAND
With The Harlem Community Choir

A SIDE

IMAGINE

Digital re-master ℗ 2000 This copyright in this sound recording is owned by EMI Records Ltd.
© 2003 EMI Records Ltd.

7243 5 53674 7 1
R 6627
Made in EU

Parlophone

JOHN LENNON

B SIDE

'WOMAN IS THE NIGGER OF THE WORLD' / 'SISTERS, O SISTERS'
JOHN LENNON/PLASTIC ONO BAND WITH ELEPHANT'S MEMORY AND THE INVISIBLE STRINGS / YOKO ONO/PLASTIC ONO BAND WITH ELEPHANT'S MEMORY AND THE INVISIBLE STRINGS

UK release December 5 1972; Apple R 5853; withdrawn.
US release April 24 1972; Apple APPLE 1848; chart high No. 57.

'Woman Is The Nigger Of The World' (Lennon, Ono)
John Lennon (vocals, guitar), Stan Bronstein (saxophone), Gary Van Scyoc (bass), Adam Ippolito (piano, organ), Wayne 'Tex' Gabriel (guitar), Richard Frank Jr. (drums, percussion), Jim Keltner (drums).

'Sisters, O Sisters' (Ono)
Yoko Ono (vocals), John Lennon (guitar), Stan Bronstein (saxophone), Gary Van Scyoc (bass), Adam Ippolito (piano, organ), Richard Frank Jr. (drums, percussion), Jim Keltner (drums).

Both recorded at The Record Plant East, New York City, NY, USA. Both produced by John & Yoko and Phil Spector.

'WOMAN IS THE NIGGER OF THE WORLD'

Lennon the dreamer. Lennon the peacemaker. Lennon the activist. All these facets of his persona were believable. But Lennon the feminist? By the time 'Woman Is The Nigger Of The World' was issued, his sloganeering was wearing thin. When he wrote from the heart, there were few who could match him. But when he let his head rule his heart, as he did here, the result was hollow at best.

Where once he led, now he followed. This song stretched the theme of revolutionary change to breaking point. It wasn't as if the subject hadn't been tackled before. Loretta Lynn composed several proto-feminist songs, including 'Don't Come Home A' Drinkin' (With Lovin' On Your Mind)' and 'The Pill'. Even Helen Reddy wrote 'I Am Woman', for which she received a Grammy in 1972. Even if Lennon wasn't the first songwriter to tackle feminism, he was probably among the first male songwriters to do so.

Of course, the idea was Ono's. Lennon's feminist anthem was inspired by something she said in a *Nova* magazine interview in 1969. Although he was keen to promote the idea that the two of them were equals, he was the typical male artist. Speaking with Robert Enright in 1994, Ono recalled how the London music scene drove her to make the remark. "When I went to London and got together with John that was the biggest macho scene imaginable. That's when I made the statement 'woman is the nigger of the world'." Ono's remark was more a cry of frustration than a considered feminist statement. While speaking to Enright, she confirmed that when she said it, she had "no notion of feminism". But when the Lennons transformed themselves into hip New York activists, her comment on rock's macho posturing was recycled and used as a feminist slogan, intended to change the 'heads' of people like her husband.

Lennon, of course, was a typical male chauvinist. But Ono is a strong woman and her impact on him was considerable. Without her, it's doubtful that he would have written a song like 'Woman Is The Nigger Of The World'. Talking to Roy Carr in 1972, he admitted her influence. "She changed my life completely. Not just physically … the only way I can describe it is that Yoko was like an acid trip or the first time you got drunk. It was that big a change, and that's just about it. I can't really describe it to this day."

Ono opened his eyes to a world of possibilities, not least of which was personal freedom. By the early 1970s, the Lennons' plea for global harmony had become more focused. The only way to achieve revolution on a global scale was through a revolution of the self that included equality of the sexes. Speaking to *Red Mole*, Lennon suggested that his attitude to women was changing. "The women are very important too, we can't have a revolution that doesn't involve and liberate women. It's so subtle the way you're taught male superiority. It took me quite a long time to realise that my maleness was cutting off certain areas for Yoko. She's a red hot liberationist and was quick to show me where I was going wrong, even though it seemed to me that I was just acting naturally. That's why I'm always interested to know how people who claim to be radical treat women."

Lennon was right. A lot of Ono's work was about liberation and freedom from sexual oppression. But despite what he said to *Red Mole*, in reality he and his fellow male activists had changed their ways much. Lennon was hip to this, and 'Woman Is The Nigger Of The World' was his way of criticising the macho attitudes that male left-wing activists were perpetuating. Activists Jerry Rubin and Abbie Hoffman may have had 'radical' ideas, but what of their attitude to women? The truth was that, like Lennon, they were typical male chauvinists.

Besides borrowing the title of his song from Ono, Lennon appropriated the chord sequence from The Platters' 'Only You' to kick-start the writing process. He recorded solo acoustic demos in late 1971 before recording with Elephant's Memory in February '72. Phil Spector was called in to work his magic on the track, but even he struggled to breathe life into what was one of Lennon's weaker songs. Stan Bronstein's sax fills echo those on 'Power To The People', and Lennon delivered another electrifying vocal that outstrips Spector's echo-laden backing with confident ease – even if he wasn't a full-blown feminist, his performance just might convince you that he was. Yet despite everyone's best efforts the track failed to convince.

'Woman Is The Nigger Of The World' received its live debut on US TV's *The Dick Calvett Show* on May 11 1972, as did Ono's B-side – but it made little difference to the record's chart placing. One reason the record didn't sell was because radio stations refused to play it. The 'N' word was a big turn-off, but the record's chances weren't helped by Apple's failure to promote the single.

Pete Bennett, Apple's American promotion manager, hated the record and refused to promote it. Although Lennon and Ono thought they had a sure fire Number 1, Bennett knew better. "I told [Lennon] that I wouldn't promote it. So John says to me, 'Well, you're our promotions man, you have to listen to us, we pay you … I'm the President of Apple.' I said, 'John, I don't care what the story is. I don't want the record – I'm not going to promote it. If I don't like it I won't promote it.' So John says, 'I'll tell you what – I'll promote it, and if I make this record Number 1, that means you're not the number one promotions man in the business.' I said, 'John, you got a deal … but if the record doesn't happen, I want you to kiss my butt and double my salary and expenses.' So he says, 'You got a deal … but I'm gonna make it Number 1.'

Bennett continued: "But without John knowing, I checked out all the radio stations and they said they weren't going to play it. So John called all of the stations himself and he tried to do a promo job. He was so happy and he came back to me and said, 'We still got that bet?' and I said, 'John, God bless you, we still have that bet and you better kiss my butt if you lose, and if you win, you can tell me, Peter, you're shit, and if you don't want me to work with you any more, that's it.' 'Well, you're gonna lose,' he told me, because he had called Chicago, he called San Francisco, and he talked to the Program Directors, and they were so nice to him, they took interviews with him. The thing was, the stations put him on tape, and while they played the record in the studio, they never put it on the air. What happened was that a few idiots played it on FM – but at that time FM was nothing, it couldn't sell two records – and all the top stations wouldn't play it. Apple sent out 30,000 records and about 15,000 came back."

'Sisters, O Sisters', Ono's open letter to her oppressed sisters, marked a dramatic change in her work. Previously, she and Lennon had encouraged their listeners to use the power of positive projection to bring about radical change. Here, she encourages direct intervention. As praiseworthy as her message was, if she'd couched it as a metaphor it would have had considerably more weight. As it stood, 'Sisters, O Sisters' had all the power of second-hand political dogma.

It also reveals the effect that Lennon was having on her work. 'Sisters, O Sisters' was a conventional rock song with a 'reggae' twist. Musically, at least, she was moving away from the avant-garde into the mainstream. Her next album, *Approximately Infinite Universe*, a two-record set, contained no avant-garde music at all. Speaking to Roy Carr in 1972, she said: "Rock is a whole new field for me, and I get inspired so much that I find that now a lot of songs are coming out of me. Also, I think I was getting to a point where I didn't have too much competition. John was always with boys who were working together and therefore in direct competition." Ironically, Yoko was writing more, and better songs, than her husband.

Working with Elephant's Memory had its limitations. Lennon, like McCartney, was greatly influenced by reggae and wanted to record 'Sisters, O Sisters' in that idiom. The problem was that these musicians hadn't a clue, and the only reggae lick Lennon had to teach them with was Desmond Dekker's 'Israelites'. Talking to Andy Peebles in 1980, Lennon described how difficult it was to get them to play what he wanted. "I remember that session, Elephant's Memory, all New York kids, you know, saying they don't know what reggae was, I'm trying to explain to them all … so if you listen to it you'll hear me trying to get them to reggae." He never did get them 'to reggae', and all the attempt produced was an uncomfortable juxtaposition of two contrasting styles. Better to have let them rock out and pretend to be the MC5, which is probably what they wanted.

'Woman Is The Nigger Of The World' data

Issued with the Lennon and Ono 'merging heads' label and in a picture sleeve, 'Woman Is The Nigger Of The World' was the first and only single lifted from the Lennons' forthcoming album, *Some Time In New*

York City. Despite Lennon's claims that the record was "banned" because it featured the word nigger, it was more successful than the Lennons' previous single, but still failed to enter the Top 40.

'Woman Is The Nigger Of The World' was due to be issued as a single in Britain on December 5 1972 but was withdrawn. White-label test pressings were made, but commercial copies of the record were not produced. The record may have suffered the same fate as 'Happy Xmas (War Is Over)', which was postponed because of a dispute with Northern Songs over Ono's claim as co-author. By the time 'Woman Is The Nigger Of The World' had been cleared for release, the album it was intended to promote had already been issued and had flopped. Rather than issued a challenging single that would have been difficult to market and sell, it made more commercial sense to go with that seasonal 'Happy Xmas (War Is Over)'.

SOME TIME IN NEW YORK CITY
JOHN & YOKO/PLASTIC ONO BAND WITH ELEPHANT'S MEMORY AND INVISIBLE STRINGS

Side 1 'Woman Is The Nigger Of The World', 'Sisters, O Sisters', 'Attica State', 'Born In A Prison', 'New York City'.
Side 2 'Sunday Bloody Sunday', 'The Luck Of The Irish', 'John Sinclair', 'Angela', 'We're All Water'.

Live Jam: John & Yoko/Plastic Ono Band
Side 3: 'Cold Turkey', 'Don't Worry Kyoko'.
Side 4: 'Well (Baby Please Don't Go)', 'Jamrag', 'Scumbag', 'Aü'.

UK release September 15 1972; LP Apple PCSP 716; 8-track cartridge Apple 8X-PCSP 716; chart high No. 11.
US release June 12 1972; LP Apple SVBB 3392; 8-track cartridge Apple 8XW 3393 and 8XW 3394; chart high No. 48.

'Attica State' (Lennon, Ono)
Yoko Ono (vocals), John Lennon (vocals, guitar), Stan Bronstein (saxophone), Gary Van Scyoc (bass), Adam Ippolito (piano, organ), Richard Frank Jr. (drums, percussion), Jim Keltner (drums).
'Born In A Prison' (Ono)
Yoko Ono (vocals), John Lennon (vocals, guitar), Stan Bronstein (saxophone), Gary Van Scyoc (bass), John La Bosca (piano), Richard Frank Jr. (drums, percussion), Jim Keltner (drums).
'New York City' (Lennon)
John Lennon (guitar), Stan Bronstein (saxophone), Gary Van Scyoc (bass), Adam Ippolito (piano, organ), Richard Frank Jr. (drums, percussion), Jim Keltner (drums).
'Sunday Bloody Sunday' (Lennon, Ono)
John Lennon (guitar), Stan Bronstein (saxophone), Gary Van Scyoc (bass), Adam Ippolito (piano, organ), Richard Frank Jr. (drums, percussion), Jim Keltner (drums).
'The Luck Of The Irish' (Lennon, Ono)
John Lennon (vocals, guitar), Stan Bronstein (flute), Gary Van Scyoc (bass), Adam Ippolito (piano, organ), Richard Frank Jr. (drums, percussion), Jim Keltner (drums).
'John Sinclair' (Lennon)
John Lennon (vocals, guitar), Gary Van Scyoc (bass), Adam Ippolito (piano, organ), Richard Frank Jr. (drums, percussion), Jim Keltner (drums).
'Angela' (Lennon, Ono)
John Lennon (vocals, guitar), Stan Bronstein (saxophone), Gary Van Scyoc (bass), Adam Ippolito (piano, organ), Richard Frank Jr. (drums, percussion), Jim Keltner (drums).
'We're All Water' (Ono)
Yoko Ono (vocals), John Lennon (guitar), Stan Bronstein (saxophone), Gary Van Scyoc (bass), Adam Ippolito (piano, organ), Richard Frank Jr. (drums, percussion), Jim Keltner (drums).
'Cold Turkey' (Lennon)
John Lennon (vocals, guitar), Yoko Ono (vocals, bag), George Harrison (guitar), Eric Clapton (guitar), Klaus Voormann (bass), Billy Preston (organ), Delaney Bramlett (guitar), Bonnie Bramlett (percussion), Bobby Keys (saxophone), Jim Price (trumpet), Andy White (drums), Jim Gordon (drums), Keith Moon (drums), Nicky Hopkins (piano overdub).
'Don't Worry Kyoko' (Yoko Ono)
Yoko Ono (vocals, bag), John Lennon (guitar), rest as 'Cold Turkey'.
'Well (Baby Please Don't Go)' (Ward)
John Lennon (vocals, guitar), Yoko Ono (vocals), Frank Zappa (vocals, guitar), Mark Volman (vocals), Howard Kaylan (vocals), Ian Underwood (woodwind, keyboard, vocals), Aynsley Dunbar (drums), Jim Pons (bass, vocals), Bob Harris (keyboard, vocals), Don Preston (Minimoog).
'Jamrag' (Lennon, Ono)
Personnel as 'Well (Baby Please Don't Go)'.
'Scumbag' (Lennon, Ono, Zappa)
Personnel as 'Well (Baby Please Don't Go)'.

'Aü' (Lennon, Ono)
Personnel as 'Well (Baby Please Don't Go)'.

All recorded at The Record Plant East, New York City, NY, USA and produced by John & Yoko and Phil Spector, except: 'Cold Turkey' and 'Don't Worry Kyoko' recorded live at Lyceum Ballroom, London, England and produced by John & Yoko; 'Well', 'Jamrag', 'Scumbag' and 'Aü' recorded live at Filmore East, New York City, NY, USA and produced by John & Yoko and Phil Spector.

SOME TIME IN NEW YORK CITY

If you want to know what John Lennon and Yoko Ono were doing and thinking in late 1971/'72, listen to *Some Time In New York City*. Although they were based in England for most of '71, they were frequent visitors to New York City. They were there in June that year, attempting to gain custody of Ono's daughter Kyoko. During that trip, they joined Frank Zappa on stage on June 6, and they issued the joint performance on *Some Time In New York City*. They returned again in July to record overdubs for *Imagine*. During that visit, Lennon and Ono made contact with political activist Jerry Rubin, before returning to England on July 14 to continue work on *Imagine* and promote Ono's book, *Grapefruit*. And on August 31, in another attempt to obtain custody of Kyoko, they returned to New York City; this time to stay.

Besides moving to America to continue their quest to regain custody of Yoko's daughter, Lennon told Ray Coleman he wanted to live there because: "It's the Rome of today, a bit like a together Liverpool. I always like to be where the action is. In olden times I'd like to have lived in Rome or Paris or the East. The 1970s are going to be America's."

The 1960s had certainly belong to Britain. The Beatles had seen to that. Although the 1970s had barely started, it was obvious that Britain was changing and not for the better. Lennon had grown dissatisfied with the offhand way the British press treated the work that he and Ono did and thought, mistakenly as it happened, that America would embrace him with open arms. "It's Yoko's old stamping ground," he explained, "and she felt the country would be more receptive to what we were up to." Ironically, America, or more precisely the Nixon led American government, was far from welcoming.

Lennon's desire to play an active role in what was already an ebbing counterculture brought him into conflict with the authorities in ways that would never have happened had he remained in Britain.

By the time he moved to New York City, he had already committed himself to political activism. He'd spoken of 'British socialism', supported the Oz Three and namechecked the Yippies in 'Give Peace A Chance' and issued 'Power To The People', 'Imagine' and 'Happy Xmas (War Is Over)'. The 'radical' views that Lennon put so much effort into promulgating were tolerated in Britain, but proved too much for Nixon's paranoid administration.

The Nixon administration attempted to deport Lennon by using his criminal record as their main objection to his US residency. In reality, the US government considered Lennon – who was freely associating with members of the radical New Left – a potential threat to political stability. A memo in official government files stated that "radical New Left leaders plan to use Mr Lennon as a drawing card to promote the success of rock festivals, to obtain funds for a 'dump Nixon' campaign".

Senator Strom Thurmond suggested to Attorney General John Mitchell that if rapid action were taken against Lennon they would avoid "many headaches". The FBI began tapping Lennon's telephone, attending his concerts, and studying his lyrics in an attempt to gather enough evidence to deport him. However, the US authorities could not deport him for his beliefs, no matter how 'radical' they were. Instead, it was suggested that he "be arrested, if at all possible, on a possession of narcotics charge". Lennon's US visa expired on February 29 1972, an extension was granted that led to an appeal against deportation, and so began his long struggle to remain in the USA.

If the American authorities didn't welcomed the Lennons with open arms, the counterculture did. David Peel, a fervent campaigner for the legalisation of cannabis, made a big impression on Lennon, who loved his irreverent songs and unique brand of street politics. Lennon was so infatuated with Peel that they shared a stage and band at the John Sinclair Freedom Rally. They appeared together again when the Lennons recorded a TV appearance for *The David Frost Show* on December 16. Lennon went on to name-check Peel in *New York City*, produce Peel's third album, *The Pope Smokes Dope*, and invite him to take part in the 'Give Peace A Chance' encore at the One To One concert.

More important, but more damaging for Lennon, was his association with Jerry Rubin. Rubin had spent much of his adult life harassing the Establishment. He was instrumental in organising sophisticated, theatrical and media-orientated protests against the Vietnam War. Along with Abbie Hoffman, Rubin founded the Youth International Party, the 'Yippies', who were vehemently anti-Establishment and trouble bound.

The apotheosis of Yippie activity took place in Chicago in 1968, when they organised a massive rally, the Festival Of Life, in opposition to the National Democratic Convention, also being held there. The Festival Of Life was intended to give those opposed to the Establishment a voice. A Yippie announcement proclaimed that the event would "be a contrast in lifestyles. Ours will be an affirmation of life; theirs is d-e-a-t-h". Thanks to heavy-handed policing, the festival turned violent, and when Rubin and several others, including the singer and fellow Yippie activist Phil Ochs, attempted to nominate a pig for President, Rubin was arrested. He was prosecuted for conspiracy and intent to encourage a riot.

The trial of the Chicago Seven became one of the most infamous in American legal history. The Establishment were out to destroy the counterculture and would have done so had it not been for the high-handed attitude taken by Judge Julius Hoffman, who caused outrage with his treatment of Bobby Seale, an American civil rights activist, co-founder, chairman, and national organiser of the Black Panther Party, whom he ordered gagged and bound. Although Hoffman found them guilty, the Chicago Seven had their convictions overturned by the Supreme Court, who found that the Judge had used unscrupulous tactics in handling the case.

The experience left Rubin depressed and disillusioned with the interventionist style of politics he'd helped to spearhead. But salvation, came in the form of a song from the *John Lennon/Plastic Ono Band* album. When Rubin heard 'Working Class Hero' it turned his life around. On discovering that the Lennons were in New York, all it took was a phone call to secure a meeting with them. Rubin arranged to meet them at Washington Square Park, from where they moved to Abbie Hoffman's apartment to discuss business. Both parties hit it off immediately, and Rubin was made the Lennons' 'political advisor' and a member of their ad hoc band.

It's no surprise that Rubin and Hoffman felt an affinity with Lennon. Lennon informed them that he planned to tour America with a political travelling circus and give the money generated to good causes. "We want to go around from town to town, doing a concert every other night for a month, at least," said Lennon. The funds he hoped to raise with his tour would be used for "disruptive activities". The final concert was planned to take place in San Diego, California, and coincide with the Republican National Congress. It would be Chicago all over again, with Lennon in the lead. What self-respecting activist wouldn't be impressed by such a generous patron?

The Lennon-Rubin partnership was made in heaven. Lennon's desire to be recognised as a bona fide political activist was complete and Rubin acquired a readymade spokesman whom he could manipulate for his own political gain. There was, however, one small problem. The Lennons could not obtain work permits, which limited their plans to tour and promote their work and political views. But Rubin had a cunning plan. Where no payment was made to the artist, work permits were not required. The Lennons were only too pleased to give their services for free, particularly when it was in the name of radicalism.

The first charity event they attended was the John Sinclair Freedom Rally, a star-studded event held at the Crisler Arena in Ann Arbor, Michigan. Sinclair had managed the MC5 and was minister of information for the White Panther Party, whose war cry was 'Everything free for everybody!' At the time, Sinclair was serving a ten-year prison sentence for selling a couple of joints to some undercover cops. The concert was part of a Yippie-led campaign to free him.

The audience waited hours to see Lennon and anticipation was running high. But when Lennon and Ono eventually ambled onto the stage in the early hours of the morning of December 11, their four-song performance was a heroic anticlimax. New York's *Village Voice* expressed an opinion that many in the crowd must have shared: "The audience was slightly stunned. John and Yoko had performed for 15 minutes, urged political activism and support for John Sinclair, and split. … It was depressing."

His appearance at the Sinclair rally hadn't impressed, but Lennon had filmed and recorded the event and planned to issue his four-song performance as an EP. However, as Sinclair was released from prison early, plans to issue the record were scrapped. Two songs from the show, 'The Luck Of The Irish' and 'John Sinclair', were later issued on the *John Lennon Anthology*.

Lennon and Ono's next appearance was at the Apollo Theatre on December 17. The Attica State Benefit was intended to raise money for the families of prisoners who had been killed during the riot at the Attica Correctional Facility. Lennon appeared with a stripped-down acoustic band, performing two songs, 'Attica State' and 'Imagine', both issued later on the *John Lennon Anthology*. The rough and ready Sinclair and Attica State live recordings are of historical interest and not comparable to the studio versions – while they are of interest to the completist, the casual listener may find them wanting.

Lennon's ad hoc group were adequate enough for the kind of low-key hit-and-run performances he gave in late '71, but if he wanted to record and tour, which is what he was planning to do, something more professional was required. Once again, Rubin provided the solution by suggesting that Lennon check out a group of hairy rockers. Although Rubin played a part in bringing the two parties together, Rick Frank, drummer with the band, recalled that Lennon first heard Elephant's Memory on the radio, when they played a live show for a Long Island radio station, WLIR. Lennon liked what he heard and invited Frank to audition for him. Frank: "He had me play on material that had no drum tracks recorded. … I walked into the Record Plant and I saw an engineer we had worked with, so I connected with him right away. I was never a Beatles fan, so the awe-struck aspect of it … it was there, but it was not like I had some fanatical desire to meet John Lennon, or his lovely wife. But I connected with Lennon and he asked me to put drums on these songs." Lennon made his mind up there and then to offer Frank and his bandmates the gig and a contract with Apple records. Rehearsals began almost immediately. Within weeks Lennon had dropped the acoustic folk style and adopted a harder edge with Elephant's Memory.

Stan Bronstein and Rick Frank had formed Elephant's Memory in 1967, developing an outrageous stage routine along the lines of The Who and The Move's loud, destructive performances. The group's first album was issued in 1969 and included two songs that later featured on the soundtrack of *Midnight Cowboy*, but their next record marked a change in direction. Influenced by Detroit-area bands such as MC5 and The Stooges, the Elephants were now producing in-your-face rock. Their second album also revealed a radical political bent. *Take It To The Streets* saw the band engage in Yippie sloganeering.

Danny Adler, who played guitar with the band for a while in the early '70s, recalled that they were "laying the revolution stuff on with a shovel". Their songs were, he continued, "very standard hippie/Yippie anthems and sloganeering, expensively produced, blindingly loud, and ridiculously extravagant," which is exactly what Lennon wanted. Lennon made only one change to the band: he added a second drummer. Jim Keltner, who had played on *Imagine*, was drafted in to add extra weight to the rhythm section.

Despite the fact that they were backed by big money, Elephant's Memory were committed to overthrowing the very system that supported them. They were, then, the perfect complement to Lennon's own mixed-up political programme. The band was also under FBI surveillance, which gave it real street credibility but did little to help Lennon and his plan to stay in America. Re-christened Plastic Ono Elephant's Memory Band, their first job was to back the Lennons during their week-long residency on *The Mike Douglas Show*. Their performance of 'Imagine' was later issued on a CD that accompanied the *Lennon Legend* book.

The Lennons' appearance on the *Douglas* show was part of a concerted campaign to establish themselves as serious artists and political activists. Besides promoting Ono's art, they premiered clips from the *Imagine* film and performed material destined for their soon-to-be-released *Some Time In New York City* album. They made their political views known by inviting various activists onto the show, giving them unprecedented primetime exposure on American television. Naturally, Rubin was interviewed to explain himself. He also performed with Plastic Ono Elephant's Memory Band, as did actress and film director Barbara Loden.

Now that Lennon had a new band, recording began in earnest. Studio time was booked at the Record Plant East, with Phil Spector co-producing. Sessions began in February and continued into March. The album was completed on March 20, the Lennons' third wedding anniversary. However, two weeks before that, their visas expired. They were both granted extensions, but on March 6 their visas were suddenly cancelled. Lennon and Ono had officially outstayed their welcome.

When it was released, *Some Time In New York City* was universally slammed. Stephen Holden's review for *Rolling Stone* summed up critical reaction to the album. "Throughout their artistic careers, separately and together, the Lennons have been committed avant-gardists. Such commitment takes guts. It takes even more guts when you've made it so big that you don't need to take chances to stay on top: the Lennons should be commended for their daring. What is deplorable, however, is the egotistical laziness (and the sycophantic milieu in which it thrives) that allows artists of such proven stature, who claim to identify with the 'working class hero', to think they can patronise all whom they would call sisters and brothers."

British critics were equally perturbed by what they saw as Lennon's patronising tone. Tony Tyler's review for the *Melody Maker* criticised Lennon for the way he presented his songs, as well as the songs themselves. Although Tyler praised the musicianship, he singled out the lyrics, describing them as "Insulting, Arrogant, Rigid, Dogmatic … in short, the effect achieved was the opposite of the effect desired (I hope)".

Perhaps one reason *Some Time In New York City* fails to satisfy is because it features just two songs written by Lennon. Everything else was either co-written with Ono or an Ono solo composition. Ono's earlier avant-garde work had forced Lennon to explore new forms of self-expression. But as she moved closer to the mainstream, her music became more influenced by his. Their relationship was changing, and it wouldn't be long before they separated.

Both Lennon and Ono's work was at its best when it remained unresolved, ambiguous and open to multiple interpretations. For all its apparent opaqueness, *Two Virgins* was more radical and potentially life-changing than all the sloganeering on *Some Time In New York City*. When Lennon asked the world to "imagine", anything was possible. By simply repeating hackneyed slogans, he limited the number of possibilities to those prescribed by a handful of left-wing political activists, thereby alienating anyone who didn't share his view. Furthermore, as politically correct as Lennon's songs were, they only addressed those who shared or were convinced by his view. The songs on *Some Time In New York City* did little to make people think or persuade anyone to change their position.

Critical reaction to the album hit Lennon hard. Perhaps he never fully recovered from it. From now on he would always doubt the quality of his work. None of the albums he recorded in the wake of *New York City* captured the brilliance of his first two solo records. That's not to say that they were artistic failures, it's just that the magic that permeated *Plastic Ono Band* and *Imagine* had disappeared.

Some Time In New York City songs

The album opens with 'Woman Is The Nigger Of The World' and 'Sisters, O Sisters', both issued as the first single from the album and discussed earlier. The third song on *Some Time In New York City* had its roots in an event on September 13 1971, when a riot broke out at Attica Correctional Facility in upstate New York, up towards Lake Ontario. Around 1,200 prisoners, mostly African-Americans, took control of the prison and took 50 hostages. Their demands were simple – better conditions and terms for amnesty. Rather than give in to the prisoners' demands, the police and army moved in and shot 32 prisoners and 11 guards.

A few weeks after the riot, Lennon started to fashion his response. On the night of October 9, he celebrated his 31st birthday at the Syracuse hotel with an impromptu singalong with some friends. During the party, he sang what he had of 'Attica State', which was little more than a chanted chorus. He finished the song a few weeks later, fleshing out his idea and recording a rough demo with Ono on percussion. The song received its world premiere on December 10 at the John Sinclair Freedom Rally. Lennon performed it again six days later on *The David Frost Show*.

During the *Frost Show*, Lennon was criticised by members of the audience, who argued that he was glorifying prisoners. He responded by quoting his own lyrics: "The song says, '43 widowed wives.' That means guards' wives as well as prisoners' wives." He repeated his belief that all that the prisoners needed was "love and care". What he didn't mention was his and Ono's desire to "free all prisoners everywhere", something they were actively planning to do with funds from their proposed tour. Although Lennon and Ono managed to avoid explicit support for the prisoners during the TV show, their appearance at the Attica State Benefit at the Apollo Theatre the following day, December 17, confirmed it (the live recording made at the Apollo was issued years later on the *John Lennon Anthology*).

Recorded for *Some Time In New York City*, 'Attica State' featured honking saxophone and aggressive slide guitar. It also took on a thuggish backbeat that made it particularly suited for use on protest marches. And as if to prove that they were equally committed to the cause, Lennon and Ono share the lead vocal.

Ono's 'Born In A Prison' comes next, reworking earlier pleas for personal freedom she abandons abstract metaphors and replaces them with simple leftist dogma. If Ono had once been able to imagine a better world, here she seems weighed down by the meaninglessness of human existence and broken on a wheel of despair. She offers some hope of liberation, but the allusions to change she offers fail to counterbalance the engulfing darkness of the verses. All the positive vibrations that the Lennons had attempted to share with the world were erased with this negative commentary on the human condition. (The song was performed at the One To One concert, and featured on the video *John Lennon Live In New York City*, but it did not appear on the 1986 album of the same name.)

The move to New York City energised Lennon in many ways, one of which was his return to gutsy rock'n'roll. Speaking to Ron Skoler in September '71, he explained how the city had influenced him. "It's the hippest place on earth, and that's why it's really inspiring to be here, and it just makes you wanna rock like crazy." Influenced by the place and the people he encountered there, Lennon wrote 'New York City', a rough and tumble rocker to record what had happened to him since setting foot in the Big Apple.

Within a few weeks of establishing himself in New York City, Lennon had written the bare bones of the song but had yet to complete more the first verse. An early version featured in the soundtrack of Lennon and Ono's film *Clock*, filmed in September '71. Further demo recordings followed, with Lennon fleshing out his lyric with more recent experiences. An acoustic demo recorded late in '71 appears on the *John Lennon Anthology*. Lennon eventually cut a dense, exciting street rocker that was the highlight of the album.

Unsurprisingly, he chose to open his One To One concert with the song (and the matinee performance of the song appears on the *John Lennon In New York City* album).

Like many, including Paul McCartney, Lennon was appalled by the Bloody Sunday Massacre that took place in Northern Ireland on January 30 1972. And like his former partner he decided to express his feelings in song. "Most other people express themselves by shouting or playing football at the weekend," he explained. "But me, here I am in New York and I hear about the 13 people shot dead in Ireland, and I react immediately. And being what I am, I react in four-to-the-bar with a guitar break in the middle. I don't say, 'My God, what's happening? ... We should do something.'"

'Sunday Bloody Sunday' was, like much of what appeared on *Some Time In New York City*, a visceral response to a politically charged event, and typically partisan. Lennon may have felt compelled to set down in song his feelings about the killings, but his song was also a piece of pro-Republican propaganda that ignored the historical facts in favour of emotional blackmail. The 'Irish problem' was a political issue that encompassed state oppression, sectarianism, violent conflict, and terrible killings. In short, everything the Lennons had campaigned against. Lennon's pro-Republican agenda did little to bring either side together and was somewhat hypocritical. Hadn't he spent many, many hours preaching pacifism and peaceful revolution? The Irish Republican movement that Lennon supported had a long history of violent protest, something he was well aware of.

Speaking in September '71 about his apparent hypocrisy, he said: "I understand why [these people are] doing it, and if it's a choice between the IRA or the British army, I'm with the IRA. But if it's a choice between violence and non-violence, I'm with non-violence. So it's a very delicate line ... . Our backing of the Irish people is done, really, through the Irish Civil Rights, which is not the IRA. Although I condemn violence, if two people are fighting, I'm probably gonna be on one side or the other, even though I'm against violence."

Lennon's disgust merged with an awareness of his own Irish roots. Liverpool had a large Irish population and both Lennon and McCartney had family ties with the country. Speaking with Ron Skoler, again in September '71, Lennon spoke of his link to Ireland. "I'm a quarter Irish or half Irish or something, and long, long before the trouble started, I told Yoko that's where we're going to retire, and I took her to Ireland. We went around Ireland a bit and we stayed in Ireland and we had a sort of second honeymoon there. So I was completely involved in Ireland."

When he came to write 'Sunday Bloody Sunday', Lennon made his bond with Ireland all the more personal by aligning himself with the oppressed. Singing "When Stormont bans *our* marches" he associates himself with the Irish people and their struggle. Not only did he give the Civil Rights Movement the oxygen of publicity, he donated his songwriting royalties to it as well. "On the *Some Time In New York City* LP, the royalties of 'Sunday Bloody Sunday' and 'The Luck Of The Irish' are supposed to go to the Civil Rights Movement in Ireland and New York," he explained.

Lennon was obviously thinking about his roots and the political situation in Ireland long before the events of January 30 1972. He wrote 'The Luck Of The Irish' in the autumn of '71. He began by recording two demos of the unfinished song, which reveal he had yet to complete either the melody or lyric. He returned to the song on November 12 '71, recording more acoustic guitar demos for a film by John Reily, also called *The Luck Of The Irish*. A month later, Lennon performed the song at the John Sinclair Freedom Rally, and four days later he gave it a brief reading on *The David Frost Show*. He performed it again on television, in full, on *The Mike Douglas Show* on January 28 '72.

Lennon's referencing of traditional folk music may have been an attempt to allude to Republican protest songs; it may also have been a way of connecting the melody with the subject matter. He was certainly familiar with traditional music, and both he and Ono considered themselves 'folk' artists who were writing songs that could be taken up by 'the people' and used to political ends.

When they were criticised for performing overtly simplistic music at the John Sinclair Freedom Rally, Ono replied with a considered defence. Arguing that they were writing to encourage audience participation, she said: "Both in the West and the East, music was once separated into two forms. One was court music, to entertain the aristocrats. The other was folk songs, sung by the people to express their emotions and their political opinions. But lately, folk songs of this age, pop song, is becoming intellectualised and is starting to lose the original meaning and function. Aristocrats of our age, critics, reviewed the Ann Arbor rally and criticised the musical quality for not coming up to their expectations. That was because they lost the ears to understand the type of music that was played there. That was not artsy-craftsy music. It was music alongside the idea of: message is the music. We went back to the original concept of folk song, like a newspaper," Ono continued. "The function was to present the message accurately and quickly. And in that sense, it was funky music, just as newspaper layout could be called funky. Also, it is supposed to stimulate people among the audience and … make them think, 'Oh, it's so simple, even I could do it.' It should not alienate the audience with its professionalism but … communicate to the audience the fact that they, the audience, can be just as creative as the performers on the stage, and encourage them to make their own music with the performers rather than to just sit back and applaud."

Lennon and Ono had been trying to engage people in the creative process from the very start of their partnership. Their early avant-garde albums were attempts to establish a reciprocal creative relationship with their audience. But by abandoning avant-gardism in favour of sloganeering, they were no nearer to reaching their goal. After the euphoria of their protests had worn off, Lennon and Ono quickly realised that their activism had been in vain. Speaking to Peter Hamil in 1975, Lennon revealed how disillusioned he had become with writing protest songs. "It became journalism and not poetry. And I basically feel that I'm a poet. … I'm not a formalised poet, I have no education, so I have to write in the simplest forms, usually. And I realised that over a period of time – and not just cos I met Jerry Rubin off the plane, but that was like a culmination. I realised that we were poets but we were really folk poets, and rock'n'roll was folk poetry – I've always felt that. Rock'n'roll *was* folk music. Then I began to take it seriously on another level, saying, 'Well, I am reflecting what is going on, right?'" Lennon continued. "And then I was making an effort to reflect what was going on. Well, it doesn't work like that. It doesn't work as pop music or what I want to do. It just doesn't make sense. You get into that bit where you can't talk about trees, cos, y'know, y'gotta talk about 'corruption on 54ᵗʰ Street!'. It's nothing to do with that. It's a bit *larger* than that. It's the usual lesson that I've learned in me little 34 years: as soon as you've clutched onto something, you think – you're always clutchin' at straws – *this is what life is all about.*"

'The Luck Of The Irish' was planned as the lead single from the album, backed with 'Attica State' (Apple 1846). It may have been well intentioned, but it was fundamentally flawed and ultimately impotent. Its plodding metre, rose-tinted lyric, and uninspired vocal (Lennon's and Ono's) make it an unwelcome aberration in Lennon's oeuvre.

John Lennon and John Sinclair had more in common than a forename: both shared an interest in political activism and each had convictions for possessing cannabis. Lennon's drug bust was causing him problems with American immigration, but compared with Sinclair he'd got off lightly. Sinclair's ten-year prison sentence might have seemed harsh, but he did have a history of drug-related convictions. He was arrested for possessing marijuana in late 1964. A second arrest took place in 1965, when Sinclair was sentenced to six months in the Detroit House of Correction for "sales and possession of marijuana". Four years later, in July 1969, he was sentenced to prison for nine to ten years for possession of two reefers. Convinced that Sinclair's prison sentence was further evidence of the Establishment's draconian use of drug laws to silence the counterculture, Lennon wrote an impassioned song of protest to be performed at the John Sinclair Freedom Rally.

Lennon wrote 'John Sinclair' in late 1971 and recorded a demo accompanying himself on dobro at about the same time as he recorded demos of 'Luck Of The Irish' and 'Attica State'. The song was finished in time for the John Sinclair Freedom Rally on December 10. By the time Lennon performed the song again, on *The David Frost Show* on December 16, Sinclair had been released from prison and the song made redundant. Rather than abandon the song, as they abandoned Sinclair, Lennon decided to record it for *Some Time In New York City*. Once they realised that associating with leftist radicals was jeopardising their chances of remaining in the USA, they sidelined Sinclair and his contemporaries and dropped their radical crusading as quickly as they had adopted it.

'Angela' was written by Lennon while staying at the St. Regis Hotel in November 1971. Recorded there along with several others intended for *Some Time In New York City,* the song began as an unfinished ballad, 'JJ', that evolved into another political tirade.

Angela Davis was a talented academic and a member of the Student Non-violent Co-ordinating Committee (SNCC), the Black Panther Party, and the American Communist Party. Removed from her teaching position at UCLA as a result of her social activism, she made national headlines when guns allegedly registered in her name were used in an attempted prison escape, during which four people were killed. Even though she was nowhere near the scene, Davis was placed on the FBI's Ten Most Wanted list and driven underground. An articulate speaker, Davis had argued that the state used the threat of prison to control politically active African-Americans. Ironically, when she was arrested and charged with kidnap, conspiracy, and murder, that is exactly where she found herself.

When asked to contribute to the 'Free Angela Davis' campaign, Lennon returned to the unfinished 'JJ' and with Ono wrote a new set of lyrics. The song had already been re-worked as 'People', but the third set of lyrics were obviously influenced by Ono, as her aphorisms are scattered throughout. Lines like "Angela, there's a wind that never dies" leads one to suspect that it was Ono who wrote most of the words. The fact that she takes the lead vocal, with Lennon adding harmonies on the chorus, confirms this.

Water fascinates Ono and featured in some of her earliest work. For her, water has magical properties and subversive qualities that potentially can bring about physical change or social unity – a consistent theme that runs throughout her work. For her *This Is Not Here* exhibition at the Everson Museum in Syracuse, New York, in October 1971, the audience was encouraged to submit a water sculpture to which Ono would contribute. The water event was intended to promote unity by symbolically establishing a relationship between the artist and audience. With this event foremost in her mind, Ono revisited the notes she wrote to accompany her *half-A-wind* exhibition at the Lisson Gallery, London. Reworking a piece called *Water Talk*, Yoko fashioned a lyric for 'We're All Water' that emphasised similarities rather than differences. (Backed by Elephant's Memory, she performed the song at 1972's One To One concert, but it does not appear on either the album or video of that event.)

Lennon has intended to issue sides three and four of *Some Time In New York City* as a budget price album titled *Live Jam*. Issued as a 'bonus' with *Some Time* it featured live recordings made in London and New York City. The London concert took place at the Lyceum Ballroom, London, on December 15 1969 in aid of the United Nations Children's Fund. Alan White, who played drums with the band that night, has suggested that Lennon was initially unhappy about playing the concert. "I remember going to Apple first, and [Lennon was saying to] Allen Klein: 'Why are you making me do this?' It was something contractually that he signed up for, or something like that, without knowing, and he had to do it. But in the end it became a really great evening, and he enjoyed it," White explained.

Lennon originally intended to perform with the same line-up that had backed him in Toronto a few months earlier, with the addition of Billy Preston on keyboards. But in keeping with the fluid nature of Plastic Ono Band, it was a much larger 'supergroup' that took to the stage. Eric Clapton and George Harrison arrived with Delaney & Bonnie Bramlett's band in tow, some of whom were invited to join Plastic Ono Band for the night.

The band walked on stage at midnight to a less than capacity crowd. According to contemporary reports, the 2,000-capacity ballroom was only half full. Most of the audience sat on the floor for the performance, which lasted a little under 30 minutes.

Plugging in their instruments, the band ripped through the first number of the night, 'Cold Turkey'. For a band that had barely rehearsed, Plastic Ono Supergroup delivered a stunning reading of Lennon's anti-drug anthem. However, because the ensemble had grown to twice its original size, the 4-track tape machine booked to record the concert was unable to capture all the musicians assembled on stage. Billy Preston's performance was lost, so Nicky Hopkins was called on to overdub electric piano to replace the lost organ part.

Although 'Cold Turkey' had been a sizeable hit, some in the audience were a little disappointed with Lennon's choice of material. One concert-goer said: "Why couldn't they have done stuff like 'Blue Suede Shoes', 'Dizzy Miss Lizzy', or 'Roll Over Beethoven'? Music is supposed to release the emotions. All I felt was depressed." Lennon was moving faster than his audience, many of whom still thought of The Beatles as cute mop-tops. Speaking after the show, Lennon took another step towards distancing himself from The Beatles as he explained how he saw Plastic Ono Band developing. "I'm sorry people get disappointed – but that's rock'n'roll! I'm not The Beatles anymore. The Plastic Ono Band is an impromptu thing. We could play 'Blue Suede Shoes' or Beethoven's 9th. It depends on how we feel."

Following the six-minute reading of 'Cold Turkey', Ono led the band through a 15-minute rendition of 'Don't Worry Kyoko'. With everyone locked into the song's hypnotic riff, the problem was how to bring the song to a close. Alan White had the solution. White recalled: "One thing I had learned at a very early age is when something's just going on and on and on, how do you get out of the song? Because nobody knows who's doing what. So I taught myself to just start speeding the song up. So I started speeding the song up, and everybody went with me. [Then you] speed it up so fast that nobody [can] play any more," White laughed. "It was so fast, so it was like *nee-nee-nee*, and it becomes one note, and then you slow it down, and go bomp and finish it. … It's going faster and faster and faster, and it gets so fast, nobody can play that fast any more, and then you can slow it down and – oh, it's finished."

While in New York to overdub strings on the *Imagine* album, Lennon and Ono were introduced to Frank Zappa by journalist Howard Smith. The introductions took place at Zappa's hotel, and Smith suggested that the Lennons might join Zappa on stage. Zappa recalled the meeting with casual indifference. "The day before the show, a journalist in New York City woke me up – knocked on the door and is standing there with a tape recorder, and goes: 'Frank, I'd like to introduce you to John Lennon,' you know, waiting for me to gasp and fall on the floor. And I said, 'Well, OK, come on in.' And we sat around and talked, and I think the first thing [Lennon] said to me was, 'You're not as ugly as I thought you would be.' So anyway, I thought he had a pretty good sense of humour, so I invited him to come down and jam with us at the Filmore East. We had already booked in a recording truck because we were making the *Live At The Filmore* album at the time. After they had sat in with us, an arrangement was made that we would both have access to the tapes. He wanted to release it with his mix and I had the right to release it with my mix – so that's how that one section came about."

The Lennons joined Zappa on stage at about 2:00am for the band's final encore. After a brief introduction, Lennon backed by The Mothers Of Invention turned in a convincing performance of The Olympics' 'Well (Baby Please Don't Go)'. It was marred only by the band's inability to bring the song to a proper conclusion. (If only Alan White had been available.) Consequently, the sloppy ending was edited from the record. While Lennon alluded to the fact that he hadn't sung the song since his days at the Cavern, he had in fact only recently recorded it. He cut a version while making *Imagine* that didn't make that album but would later be made available on the *John Lennon Anthology*. (The Zappa event was also filmed, and although it has yet to be commercially released, it does circulate among video collectors.)

Having got things rolling with a blast from the past, Lennon, Ono, and Zappa set about confounding the audience with some reworked and improvised 'music'. 'Jamrag' was in fact a revised take of Zappa's composition 'King Kong'. Lennon and Ono contributed nothing to the piece, but, nevertheless, claimed the song as their own. Zappa, naturally, was less than happy. "The bad part is," he explained, "there's a song that I wrote called 'King Kong' which we played that night, and I don't know whether it was Yoko's idea or John's idea, but they changed the name of the song to 'Jamrag', gave themselves writing and publishing credit on it, stuck it on an album, and never paid me. It was obviously not a jam-session song – it's got a melody, it's got a bassline, it's obviously an organised song. [That was a] little bit disappointing."

There are two more live cuts from the Zappa concert. 'Scumbag', an improvised song consisting of the title sung over and over again, is marginally better than what follows. On 'Aü', Ono wails, guitars feed back, and another evening with Lennon and Ono comes to an anticlimactic end. Lennon was so bored that he left the stage and Ono trapped in her ever-present bag.

Some Time In New York City data

The album was issued in America by Apple on June 12 1972. Released as a two-record set in a gatefold jacket, it included printed inner sleeves, a postcard, and a petition. Initial pressings have a hand-etched message in the dead wax: "John and Yoko forever, peace on earth and good will to men 72" and carry 'merging heads' labels.

The LP was reissued by Capitol records in the late 1970s with purple labels with a large Capitol logo. This variant of the album was issued with both records placed in the rear pocket of the gatefold cover, the front pocket being glued shut.

British pressings were similar to those issued in the USA, but did not include the petition. Like the previous two singles, the British release of *Some Time In New York City* was held up because of the Lennons' dispute with Northern Songs. Despite the fact that the British release date was delayed by three months, it made a better impression on the charts there than it had in America.

The album was issued as a double 8-track in Britain (8X-PCSP) and the USA (8XW 3393/94), with both cartridges fitting into a card sleeve.

Some Time In New York City was issued as a two-CD set in Britain and America on August 10 1987 (CDS 7 46782 8). The album was remixed, remastered, and reissued in November 2005 as a single CD (0946 3 40976 2 8) with several of the 'Live Jam' cuts and the studio versions of 'Listen, The Snow Is Falling' and 'Happy Xmas (War Is Over)'.

Side One
SOMETIME IN NEW YORK CITY
JOHN & YOKO/PLASTIC ONO BAND
with ELEPHANTS MEMORY and
INVISIBLE STRINGS
(a)℗1972 The Gramophone Company Limited

(b)℗1972
Apple Records, Inc.

SVBB 3392
SVBB-1-3392

WOMAN IS THE NIGGER OF THE WORLD(a)
Lennon/Ono 5:15
Ono Music Inc.* (BMI)
SISTERS, O SISTERS(b)
Ono 3:46
Ono Music Inc.* (BMI)
ATTICA STATE(a)
Lennon/Ono 2:52
Ono Music Inc.* (BMI)
BORN IN A PRISON(a)
Ono 4:04
Ono Music Inc.* (BMI)
NEW YORK CITY(a)
Lennon 4:32
Maclen Music Inc. (BMI)
*also claimed by Maclen Music/Northern Songs

Produced by: John & Yoko and
Phil Spector
Manufactured by Apple Records, Inc.

Side Two
SOMETIME IN NEW YORK CITY
JOHN & YOKO/PLASTIC ONO BAND
with ELEPHANTS MEMORY and
INVISIBLE STRINGS
(a)℗1972 The Gramophone Company Limited

(b)℗1972
Apple Records, Inc.

SVBB 3392
SVBB-2-3392

SUNDAY BLOODY SUNDAY(a)
Lennon/Ono 5:00
Ono Music Inc.* (BMI)
LUCK OF THE IRISH(b)
Lennon/Ono 2:54
Ono Music Inc.* (BMI)
JOHN SINCLAIR(a)
Lennon 3:28
Maclen Music Inc. (BMI)
ANGELA(a)
Lennon/Ono 4:08
Ono Music Inc.* (BMI)
WE'RE ALL WATER(b)
Ono 7:15
Ono Music Inc. (BMI)
*also claimed by Maclen Music/Northern Songs

Produced by: John & Yoko and
Phil Spector
Manufactured by Apple Records, Inc.

Side One
LIVE JAM
JOHN & YOKO/PLASTIC ONO BAND
with a cast of 1000's

COLD TURKEY
Lennon
Maclen Music Inc. (BMI)
DON'T WORRY KYOKO
Ono
Ono Music Inc. (BMI)

SVBB 3392
SVBB-3-3392

Total Time: 24:46

Produced by: John & Yoko and
Phil Spector
Manufactured by Apple Records, Inc.

Side Two
LIVE JAM
JOHN & YOKO/PLASTIC ONO BAND
with FRANK ZAPPA
AND THE MOTHERS OF INVENTION

WELL (Baby Please Don't Go)
Walter Ward
Elizabeth Music/Aires Co. (BMI)
JAMRAG
Lennon/Ono
Ono Music Inc.* (BMI)
SCUMBAG
Lennon/Ono/Zappa
Ono Music Inc.* (BMI)
AU
Lennon/Ono

SVBB 3392
SVBB-4-3392

Total Time: 22:58
*also claimed by Maclen Music/Northern Songs

Produced by: John & Yoko and
Phil Spector
Manufactured by Apple Records, Inc.

Sometime in New York City '72.

1973 to 1975: The Lost Weekend Starts Here

'MIND GAMES' / 'MEAT CITY'
JOHN LENNON

UK release November 16 1973; Apple R 5894; chart high No.26.
US release October 29 1973; Apple APPLE 1868; chart high No.18.

'Mind Games' (Lennon)
'Meat City' (Lennon)
Both with John Lennon (vocals, guitar), Ken Ascher (keyboards), David Spinozza (guitar), Gordon Edwards (bass), Jim Keltner (drums), except add Rick Marotta (drums) on 'Meat City'. Both recorded at Record Plant East, New York City, NY, USA.
Both produced by John Lennon.

'MIND GAMES'

As 1972 slipped into '73, Lennon began to distance himself from the radical politics he'd spent much of the previous eighteen months engaged in. The Army fatigues of the radical activist cum street fighter were exchanged for less militant garb. Growing tired of the lack of political success, he transformed himself into the very thing he'd once despised, a safe middle-of-the-road pop star. His reasons for leaving the Yippies were personal rather than political. Lennon wanted to make America his home and the only way he could do that was to appease the US Immigration and Naturalisation Service and, of course, the FBI, by rejecting activism and the radical Left. He had already been instructed to leave the country and successfully appealed against the order. Then, on 23 March 1973, he was told to leave the country within sixty days. Again, he appealed. The US government were still out to get him, but he wouldn't give up without a fight. His battle with the US authorities dragged on until July 1976, by which time they relented and granted him a green card.

Although it lacked the obvious political tendency of Lennon's previous singles, he originally conceived 'Mind Games' as a protest song in the same vein as 'Give Peace A Chance'. Lennon began work on the song as early as 1969, completing a working version titled 'Make Love, Not War' in 1970. Never one to waste a good tune, he used the melody as the basis for another song he was working on at the time, 'I Promise'. Demos of both songs were recorded at his Tittenhurst home in 1970, and examples of each appear on the *John Lennon Anthology*.

'Mind Games' remained unfinished until Lennon began work on the follow-up album to 1972's *Some Time In New York City*. Aware that the aphorism 'make love, not war' was well past its sell-by date, he found the inspiration he needed to finish the song in a book. *Mind Games: The Guide To Inner Space* by Robert Masters and Jean Houston was about consciousness-raising – something the Lennons had been preaching for years. Their desire for revolutionary change was still present, only now it was tempered with a yearning for something more spiritual and lasting. The avant-gardism and in-your-face sloganeering of earlier works was replaced by an ambiguous mysticism.

Lennon's return to 'pop' confirmed his earlier acknowledgement that the public would only accept radical ideas if they were sugar-coated. Having ditched Elephant's Memory, Lennon found himself solo again and employing top New York musicians to create the lush pop soundscapes he now desired. However, he was still struggling to have the musicians he employed play what he heard in his head. Talking to Andy Peebles about the song in 1980, he said: "The seeming orchestra on it is just me playing three notes on a slide guitar. And the middle eight is reggae. Trying to explain to American musicians what reggae was in 1973 was pretty hard, but it's basically a reggae middle eight if you listen to it."

Lennon chose to produce the record himself, breaking his two-year partnership with Phil Spector. This wasn't the end of the Lennon/Spector relationship – but Lennon's next project with the eccentric producer would be doomed from the start. Even without Spector, Lennon managed to create a dense sonic soup that echoed the commercial sophistication of *Imagine* but masked some of the song's subtleties. 'Mind Games' was a positive, upbeat return to pop and a welcome respite from Lennon's political sloganeering of the pervious year.

Lennon wrote 'Meat City' soon after he and Ono moved to New York, and it chronicled a fascination with the city and his life-long love affair with rock'n'roll. The song began to take shape in late 1971 with the basic idea that rock'n'roll could either liberate or imperil. His first attempt had more than its fair share of improvised lyrics, but the melody was clearly taking shape. Just over a year later, he returned to the song, rewriting the lyrics and completing the melody.

'Meat City' reveals that Lennon was both fascinated and horrified by the events he describes. The total abandonment of reason that rock'n'roll could elicit from its audience – the hysteria that surrounded Beatlemania, for example – could be both exciting and disturbing. It created a culture of 'freaks' who played out a wild rock'n'roll fantasy of Lennon's making. Although he experienced the fantasy firsthand and still desired it, total abandonment appeared to disturb him. He may have poked and prodded at the boundaries of convention and indulged in sex and drugs, but unlike some of his contemporaries, complete abandonment to hedonism was never his scene.

Lennon develops the fantasy to take in China, which at this time still rejected Western values. China remained a distant, exotic land, which Lennon hoped to visit one day. His desire to bring rock'n'roll to the Chinese was perhaps fuelled by the hope that it would emancipate the East in the same way it liberated the West. But it wasn't to be.

Two versions of 'Meat City' were issued, each with a unique backwards message. The single urges the listener to "check the album". The album version has a more explicit message; referring to the song's backing vocals, the mystery voice intones: "Fuck a pig."

'Mind Games' data

Apple issued 'Mind Games' in Britain with generic Apple labels and a picture cover. In America, the single also came with generic Apple labels and in a picture cover identical to the British release.

American pressings were issued with two label variations. The first has a dark green Apple label; 'from the LP MIND GAMES SW-3414' on four lines at 11 o'clock; 'STEREO' at nine o'clock; song title, composer credit, and artist's name 'JOHN LENNON' centre bottom. The other variant has a medium dark green Apple label; 'from the LP MIND GAMES SW-3414' on three lines at 11 o'clock; 'STEREO' at 9 o'clock; song title, composer credit, and artist's name 'JOHN LENNON' and '(P) 1973 EMI Records Limited' centre bottom.

In the USA, Apple issued mono/stereo promotional copies (P-1868/PRO-6768) with light green Apple labels with a black star at 7 o'clock. 'Mind Games' was reissued by Capitol in 1978 with purple labels, and again in 1983 with black/colour band labels.

While the rest of the world issued 'Mind Games' as a single, Venezuela went with 'Bring On The Lucie (Freeda Peeple)' backed with 'You Are Here' (4AP 1844).

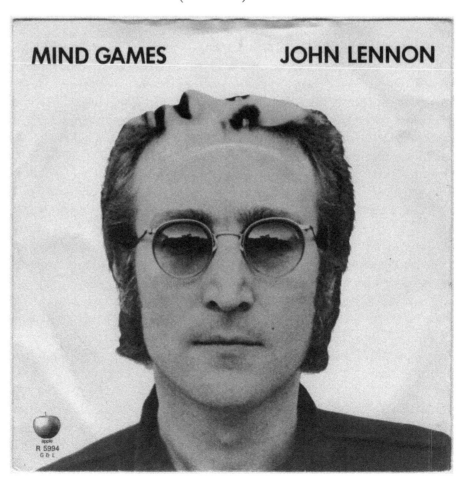

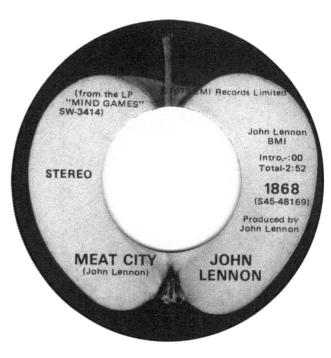

126

Below: Uruguayan and Canadian editions

MIND GAMES
JOHN LENNON (WITH THE PLASTIC U.F.ONO BAND)

Side 1 'Mind Games', 'Tight A$', 'Aisumasen (I'm Sorry)', 'One Day (At A Time)', 'Bring On The Lucie (Freda Peeple)', 'Nutopian International Anthem'.
Side 2 'Intuition', 'Out The Blue', 'Only People', 'I Know (I Know)', 'You Are Here', 'Meat City'.
UK release November 16 1973; LP Apple PCS 7165; 8-track cartridge Apple 8X-PCS 7165 released January 1974; chart high No. 13.
US release November 2 1973; LP Apple SW 3414; 8-track cartridge Apple 8XW-3414; chart high No. 9.

'Tight A$' (Lennon)
John Lennon (vocals, guitar), Ken Ascher (keyboards), David Spinozza (guitar), Gordon Edwards (bass), Jim Keltner (drums).
'Aisumasen (I'm Sorry)' (Lennon)
John Lennon (vocals, guitar), Ken Ascher (keyboards), David Spinozza (guitar), Sneaky Pete (pedal steel), Gordon Edwards (bass), Jim Keltner (drums).
'One Day (At A Time)' (Lennon)
John Lennon (vocals, guitar), Ken Ascher (keyboards), David Spinozza (guitar), Gordon Edwards (bass), Sneaky Pete (pedal steel), Michael Brecker (saxophone), Something Different (female backing vocals), Jim Keltner (drums).
'Bring On The Lucie (Freeda Peeple)' (Lennon)
John Lennon (vocals, guitar), Ken Ascher (keyboards), David Spinozza (guitar), Gordon Edwards (bass), Sneaky Pete (pedal steel), Something Different (backing vocals), Jim Keltner (drums), Rick Marotta (drums).
'Nutopian International Anthem' (Lennon)
No personnel.
'Intuition' (Lennon)
John Lennon (vocals), Ken Ascher (keyboards), David Spinozza (guitar), Gordon Edwards (bass), Sneaky Pete (pedal steel), Michael Brecker (saxophone), Jim Keltner (drums).
'Out The Blue' (Lennon)
John Lennon (vocals, guitar), Ken Ascher (keyboards), David Spinozza (guitar), Gordon Edwards (bass), Sneaky Pete (pedal steel), Something Different (backing vocals), Jim Keltner (drums).
'Only People' (Lennon)
John Lennon (vocals, guitar), Ken Ascher (keyboards), David Spinozza (guitar), Gordon Edwards (bass), Michael Brecker (saxophone), Something Different (backing vocals), Jim Keltner (drums).
'I Know (I Know)' (Lennon)
John Lennon (vocals, guitar), Ken Ascher (keyboards), David Spinozza (guitar), Gordon Edwards (bass), Jim Keltner (drums).
'You Are Here' (Lennon)
John Lennon (vocals, guitar), Ken Ascher (keyboards), David Spinozza (guitar), Gordon Edwards (bass), Sneaky Pete (pedal steel), Something Different (backing vocals), Jim Keltner (drums).
All recorded at Record Plant East, New York City, NY, USA. All produced by John Lennon.

MIND GAMES

As if to further distance themselves from the radical left-wing politics of the previous year, in early May 1973 the Lennons made another symbolic move: leaving the Village, they relocated to a 12-room apartment in the Dakota building overlooking Central Park. Lennon had done little since *Some Time In New York City* other than write and demo a few songs for his next album, *Mind Games*. Ono, however, had busied herself with a number of recording and performance projects. They were growing apart and their marriage was going through a rough patch. "Now she knows how to produce records and everything about it, I think the best thing I can do is keep out of her hair," Lennon told Chris Charlesworth of *Melody Maker*.

According to Ono, Lennon was going through a phase of soul-searching that led him to give her more space – to the extent that he was happy to sit in the wings while she took centre stage. When she began recording her follow-up to *Approximately Infinite Universe*, she took complete control of the project. He turned up to a few sessions, playing guitar on 'Woman Power' and 'She Hits Back', but *Feeling The Space* was Ono's album from start to finish. Although he had little to do with the record, Lennon was impressed by the New York musicians she'd hired. So much so that he decided to use them for his own album.

Lennon knew he had to produce something to surpass the disappointing *Some Time In New York City*. Adverse criticism had shattered his confidence and his battle to stay in America was also weighing him down. The constant court appearances and FBI surveillance were also affecting his work. "I just couldn't function, you know? I was so paranoid from them tappin' the phone and followin' me." As his relationship with Ono disintegrated, he found himself adrift from everything that had grounded him. Where previously he'd used his pain to drive his songwriting, now he eschewed it. Instead of channelling his pain, he put it to one side and wrote an album of well-crafted but anodyne songs.

Lennon's disappointment at being treated like property had turned to anger on more than one occasion. Speaking in 1970, he had been adamant that he would never allow the music business to have the upper hand again. Now here he was producing an album simply to fulfil contractual obligations. Big business had beaten him, again. That Lennon should take an extended sabbatical as soon as his contract ended says much about his desire to escape an industry to which he felt shackled.

Faced with similar uncertainties, Paul McCartney forged *Band On The Run*, an album that many still argue is among his best. Even Ringo Starr, admittedly with the help of Lennon, McCartney, and Harrison, turned in a confident album packed full of classy pop songs. *Mind Games*, however, was downbeat album of mixed themes and emotions. From the cover depicting Lennon, bag in hand, walking away from Ono, to its syrupy over-production, *Mind Games* saw Lennon retreating into his own world of thoughts and dreams. Circumventing the passion he'd employed previously, Lennon played it safe. *Mind Games* was an album that he or, more likely, his record company thought he should make. Ironically, the record was Lennon's first not to play mind games with his audience. Rather, it presented a picture of the artist as a conformist rather than a rebel.

Tony King, who was working for Apple in Los Angeles, suggested to Lennon that he play up this image. King encouraged him to get out and promote the record by arranging for him to be interviewed by trade magazines *Record World* and *Billboard*. "I started working on the *Mind Games* album," said King, "the promotion, fixing John up to do interviews, … getting him to do stuff I thought he should be doing because he hadn't been doing these things. While he had been with Yoko he had been involved with all these semi-subversive activities, which had not given him a great reputation in America. He said to me at the time, 'Look, I've got this album, what do you think I should do?' I said, 'Honestly, you've just got to go out and make a few friends, because you've lost a bit of support because you've been involved with things of a controversial nature.' So he said, 'Fine, you organise it, I'll do it.' And he did."

Recording began in July and continued through August. As usual, Lennon recorded quickly, perhaps a little too quickly. The album was mixed over a two-week period, which left many of the production subtleties buried in his dense mix. The rough mixes that have surfaced on bootlegs and the *John Lennon Anthology* offer a glimpse of what the album might have sounded like had Lennon the confidence to let the songs stand on their own merits. The album was remixed at Abbey Road in 2002 and reveals much that had been hidden by Lennon's rushed job. The album produced just one outtake. 'Rock And Roll People' had been in a work in progress for some time, and still needed a lot of work doing to it. It was left in the can and eventually issued on the patchy *Menlove Ave.* album.

Mind Games songs

The album opens with 'Mind Games', discussed earlier, and continues with 'Tight A\$', the first John Lennon song in some time that really had little to say. Gone are the visions and diatribes; in their place: sex and drugs. And that's about as deep as it gets. The return to jokey wordplay was a timely reminder of Lennon's talent, but only served to reveal how sterile his work had become.

An early demo begins with the guitar riff that would, with a little more work, become the instrumental 'Beef Jerky'. Holed up in Record Plant East, Lennon led his team of crack session musicians through several extended takes of the song. Take four was deemed best and edited for use as the master.

'Aisumasen (I'm Sorry)' introduces a dramatic change in mood. Whereas Ono had once brought Lennon unbounded joy, which had inspired him to write some of his most beautiful and moving love songs, here she is the root of deep-seated depression. By the time Lennon came to record *Mind Games* he was no longer a living with Ono. Like most men, Lennon had a roving eye. But unlike most men, he was in the unique position of being able to draw on his fame, wealth, and status to seduce whomsoever he fancied. Lennon was also capable of gross insensitivity. One particular incident found him seducing another woman within Ono's earshot, and became a source of much regret.

'Aisumasen (I'm Sorry)' was a very public apology, but like several other songs recorded for *Mind Games* it had a long gestation period. It began to take shape in 1971. Originally titled 'Call My Name', it featured Lennon in the role of comforter, but by the time he recorded it properly, the tables had turned. It was Lennon who now found himself in need of comfort but, despite his pleas, he wasn't about to get any from Ono. The break-up hit Lennon hardest, and 'Aisumasen (I'm Sorry)' reveals just how much he relied on Ono for support. Without her, he was incomplete and adrift. He quickly returned to his old ways. Drinking to obliterate his pain, he became the archetypical hedonistic rock star, a figure every bit as pathetic as the one in this song.

'One Day (At A Time)' is a good song spoilt by an uncharacteristic falsetto vocal, suggested by Ono. While recording the track, Lennon sang his guide vocals in his usual register, only adopting his falsetto when he came to deliver the vocal overdub. In its rough form, without Something Different's backing vocals (described by one journalist as sounding like "a dozen school girls from a church choir"), the song has a genuine honesty that was masked by Lennon's saccharine production. In its naked form, it reveals exactly how Lennon felt about Ono, but when he dressed the song with layers of unnecessary overdubs, it became impossibly idealistic. He had sung about his devotion to Ono on several occasions, but never had he made his feelings for her appear this tired.

Dating from late 1971, 'Bring On The Lucie (Freeda Peeple)' saw Lennon return briefly to the kind of political commentary that, until *Mind Games*, had been his post-Beatle stock in trade. Written while he was fully engaged with radical politics, the song has more humour than anything that found its way onto *Some Time In New York City*, yet it retains real bite. Unfortunately, Lennon's band of super-slick New York session players were incapable of producing a musical setting to match his pungent lyrics. Despite Lennon's opening war cry, the band settle into a comfortable groove that misrepresents its author's original intent. Even Lennon manages to conceal his real feelings. Far from sounding angry, he gives the impression of weary resignation, an emotion that only months earlier he wouldn't have dared to contemplate.

The song began life as little more than a chorus, played on a newly acquired National guitar (a fragment from Lennon's composing tape would be included as a bonus track on the remastered CD of *Mind Games*). Working on his lyric, Lennon developed its simple political sloganeering into a well observed, even prophetic, lyric full of revolutionary zeal that echoes earlier pleas for social, political, and personal change, which he'd championed with 'Imagine' and 'Power To The People'.

Even though he was under FBI surveillance and threatened with deportation, Lennon sailed close to the wind with a personal attack on Nixon and his government. He was never one to pull his punches, and his critique of Nixon and his administration was as libellous as his remark about Mr. Justice Argyle, whom he called an "old wanker" when recording his message of support for *Oz* magazine.

The song closes with Lennon citing further evidence of state-sanctioned violence against both Americans and Vietnamese. Despite the fact that Henry Kissinger and Le Duc Tho had signed a ceasefire agreement, the Vietnam War still raged. Lennon's demand that they "stop the killing now" fell on deaf ears, but by early 1974 Richard Nixon had been impeached and his days as President were rapidly coming to an end, as was the war.

Some more Cage-like high jinx follow, with the six seconds of silence intended as the national anthem for a new country, Nutopia. In the spirit of Fluxus, the Lennons announced at a bizarre press conference on April 1 1973 the birth of their conceptual country and their citizenship of it. They based the concept for their imaginary country on an idea first proposed by Thomas Moore in 1516. His book *Utopia* took its name from a word that has its origins in modern Latin and means literally 'not place'. It was fitting, then, that Lennon's national anthem should consist of 'not sound' and that the country's flag should be plain white.

The theme was extended to the album's inner sleeve which carried a 'Declaration of Nutopia' that offered citizenship to anyone who could declare their awareness of Nutopia. Like the song 'Imagine', Nutopia offered boundless possibilities and freedoms that flew in the face of state-sanctioned laws concerning citizenship and national identity. While poking fun at the American authorities, it also raised public awareness of the Lennons' plight.

Lennon was often at his best when exploring the darker side of life. Whenever he addressed his addictions, neurosis, or paranoia, he had a knack of writing insightful and enlightening songs. However, when it came to celebrating his own genius and the miracle of life, he was less successful. Set to a bouncy cadence that underscores a self-congratulatory lyric, 'Intuition' seems somehow ill-fitting on an album that appears to celebrate the darker side of personal relationships. Given what he was going through, the line "It's good to be alive" seems as out of place as the song's contrived cheeriness, more readily associated with Tin Pan Alley than an artist of Lennon's calibre.

Lennon wrote the song on piano, recording rough demos on the instrument in early 1973. With the lyrics still unfinished, he included a few lines from two earlier songs, 'How?' and 'God', to fill in the gaps.

The next song on *Mind Games*, 'Out The Blue', is an exquisite ballad that ranks among Lennon's finest. From the graceful acoustic guitar introduction to the majestic piano motif and inventive McCartneyesque bass lines, it reveals more than a glimpse of Lennon's genius.

Not for the first or last time, he acknowledges the debt he owed Ono. Like many songs in his canon, it was driven by a powerful devotion that was often stretched but never broken. Lennon was the hardest hit by the trial separation. While Ono remained focused and controlled, he slipped into a drunken twilight zone of his own making. If previously he had written love songs to express his security, now he wrote them to remind Ono how insecure he was without her.

'Out The Blue' formed part of a very personal musical dialogue between two remarkably mercurial individuals. Although Lennon and Ono were happy to present themselves as the perfect couple, they were never afraid to admit their failures. Lennon's acknowledgement of emotional insecurity may have been an attempt to rebuild the bond with Ono that he'd temporarily lost. It was also an honest expression of self-doubt, the like of which he hadn't committed to tape since *John Lennon/Plastic Ono Band*.

'Only People' found Lennon reworking a theme that lay at the heart of his and Ono's personal philosophy. They both believed that collective change through self-realisation would beneficially transform the world. Speaking on *The Mike Douglas Show*, John had prefigured the song's message when he said: "Only people can save the world." Ono's rephrased statement, "Only people can change the world," which was more in line with their intended goal, was printed on the inner sleeve of *Mind Games*.

The pair had addressed many times the notion that socio-political change could be obtained through collective potential. Unlike their early avant-garde recordings, which proffered genuine alternatives to conventional models of being, their orthodox protest songs were less successful. Despite their immediacy, songs like 'Give Peace A Chance', 'Instant Karma!', and 'Imagine' all worked within the system that they wanted people to transcend. These songs may have aroused debate, but they failed to threaten the system of order and control that the Lennons seemed determined to undermine. Like the politically correct songs written for *Some Time In New York City*, 'Only People' merely appeals to those already swayed by Lennon's argument.

Lennon recognised that 'Only People' failed as a song. Talking to *Playboy* magazine, he said: "It was a good lick, but I couldn't get the words to make sense." Even if he'd managed to write a more considered lyric, it's difficult to believe that the song would have been taken up in the same way as 'Give Peace A Chance'. Its happy-clappy gospel feel may have been great to sing along to, but the track lacks the bite of 'Instant Karma!' or the pseudo religiosity of 'Imagine', which are the qualities that made those songs so appealing.

The couple had travelled a long way in their short marriage, and much of the journey was recounted in song. *Imagine* featured some of Lennon's most heartfelt and joyous love songs. It also had songs of self-doubt, but nothing as emotionally irresolute as 'I Know (I Know)'. A mere two years had passed since the *Imagine* album, and his love for Ono was as strong as ever – but how the tone had changed. 'I Know (I Know)' suggests that Lennon was no more emotionally stable post-primal therapy than before. If he had learnt anything, it was to forgive and recognise his shortcomings. For 'I Know (I Know)' finds him in conciliatory mood, apologising, again, for his thoughtlessness. He acknowledges that he still has a lot to learn, but more importantly that he knows the cause of his insecurity.

The song features a delicate guitar figure that echoes the fingerpicking folk style that Lennon learnt from Donavan while in Rishikesh, India, in 1968. Employed sparingly throughout, it gives 'I Know (I Know)' an honesty that enhances his plea for his lover's absolution. However, its considered, reflective mood balances Lennon's feelings of angst with those of unbridled optimism. Working with a small band, he fashioned a musical setting that was the match for anything on *Imagine*. The rough mixes that have surfaced on bootlegs reveal the painstaking overdubbing process he employed to develop his arrangement.

The phrase "you are here" had haunted Lennon for some time. It first appeared as the title for his debut one-man show at the Robert Frazer Gallery, London. The show, which opened on July 1 1968, was obviously influenced by Ono and Fluxus. Visitors were invited to contribute to the event, either by placing money in a hat, inscribed by Lennon "for the artist thank you", or by returning cards attached to helium-filled white balloons, which Lennon and Ono had released into the sky. Lennon intended to publish a book based of the replies he received; typically, he never got around to it. At the heart of the exhibition was a white circular canvas upon which he'd written "you are here". Lennon next had the words printed on T-shirts, which he and members of Elephant's Memory sported during the early 1970s.

By the time he came to shape the song, his original concept had taken on many different forms and meanings. From conceptual joke to installation art, from fashion statement to love song, it occupied him for over five years.

As a song, 'You Are Here' combined two themes close to Lennon's heart – love and peace. While it was obviously a love song written for Ono, it was also about the coming together of individuals, countries, and cultures. Lennon imagines a world without differences, modelled on his own relationship with Ono. The global harmony he envisions is as graceful and beatific as the melody he fashioned to support his words. The song originally had an extra verse, edited from the completed master, that made further references to the differences and similarities between Japan and England. A version with the extra verse was issued on the *John Lennon Anthology*.

Mind Games data

Apple issued the album in the USA with generic Apple labels and in a printed inner sleeve. The album was reissued by Capitol in 1978 with purple labels with a large Capitol logo. In 1980, Capitol issued a budget-price version with a new catalogue number, SN-15968.

Apple issued the album in Britain with the same packaging as the American release. The album was reissued on November 27 1980 on EMI's budget MFP label (MFP 5058) with a new cover and generic MFP labels.

Mind Games was issued on 8-track in Britain (8X-PCS 7165) and America (8XW-3414).

EMI issued the album on CD in Britain on August 3 1987 (CDP 7 46769 2), and Capitol issued the CD in America seven months later, on March 22 1988. The album was remixed, remastered and reissued on CD with three bonus tracks on October 7 2002 (UK) and November 5 2002 (USA). MFSL Original Master Recordings issued the remastered CD on November 22 2004 and a vinyl edition (MFSL-1-293) in 2005.

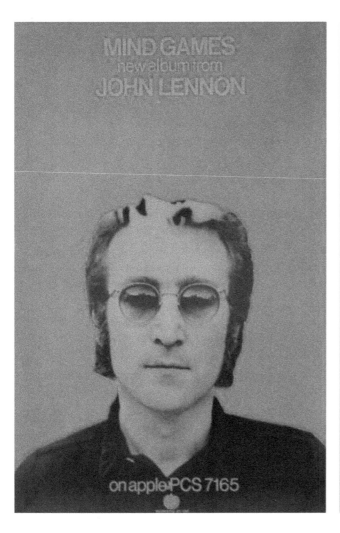 

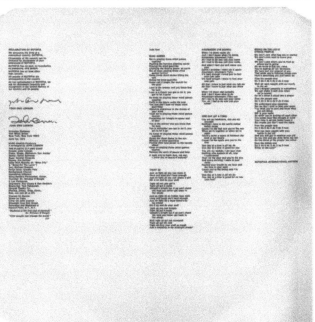

134

'WHATEVER GETS YOU THRU THE NIGHT' / 'BEEF JERKY'
JOHN LENNON

UK release October 4 1974; Apple R 5898; chart high No.36.
US release September 23 1974; Apple APPLE 1874; chart high No.1.

'Whatever Gets You Thru The Night' (Lennon)

John Lennon (vocals, guitar), Elton John (piano, organ, vocal harmony), Jesse Ed Davis (guitar), Eddie Mottau (acoustic guitar), Ken Ascher (clavinet), Bobby Keys (saxophone), Klaus Voormann (bass), Arthur Jenkins (percussion), Jim Keltner (drums).

'Beef Jerky' (Lennon)

John Lennon (guitar), Jesse Ed Davis (guitar), Klaus Voormann (bass), Arthur Jenkins (percussion), Little Big Horns: Bobby Keys, Steve Madaio, Howard Johnson, Ron Aprea, Frank Vicari (horns), Jim Keltner (drums).

Both recorded at Record Plant East, New York City, NY, USA. Both produced by John Lennon.

'WHATEVER GETS YOU THRU THE NIGHT'

Strange how Lennon and McCartney's solo careers seem to mirror one another. McCartney had just had a Number 1 single with 'Band On The Run', and now it was Lennon's turn with 'Whatever Gets You Thru The Night'.

Lennon's first solo chart-topper had little to say that was profound but got those toes tapping. At the time he wrote the song, he was in the grip of what he called his 'lost weekend'. Emerging from an extended period of over indulgence and self-destructive chaos, Lennon wrote a lyric that was both permissive and a eulogy to self-preservation.

Despite his recent bout of hedonism, 'Whatever Gets You Thru The Night' represents a more balanced attitude to life and marked a change in mood. The prescriptive tone of old was gone. If he still wanted change, it was with a more relaxed live-and-let-live attitude. Better to let people think and act for themselves rather than bludgeon them with radicalism. But just as importantly, 'Whatever Gets You Thru The Night' marked a return to form, propelling Lennon to the top of the American charts for the first and only time in his lifetime. Its pop-disco fusion made it the perfect antidote to the self-inflicted pity he had recently experienced.

The song was inspired by two sources: George McRae's 'Rock Your Baby', and a phrase heard on a late-night radio phone-in. "I heard someone saying it on the radio, on a late night talk show, talking to someone on a phone, saying, 'Well, whatever gets you through the night.' And there it was, the whole tune came to me in my head," Lennon explained.

The phrase may have inspired him, but demo recordings reveal that a considerable amount of effort went into shaping the song (a fragment from Lennon's composing tape would turn up later on the *John Lennon Anthology*). Early attempts found him experimenting with different chord changes and lyrics. His early demos also have a downbeat feel that Lennon took with him when he entered the Record Plant to rehearse the song with a band.

Speaking to Lisa Robinson of the *NME*, he confirmed that he'd been under considerable pressure of late: "I would say that I was under emotional stress – a manic depression, I would call it." Rather than retain the mood, Lennon rejected his original pessimistic arrangement and dramatically rearranged the song, transforming it into an upbeat rocker that caught the ear instantly. "It was going to be like 'Rock Your Baby', but I often have an idea what it is going to be like but it never turns out anything like it. It's a very loose track," Lennon said. "I call it the 'Crippled Inside' of the album, you know, or the 'Oh Yoko!' of the album, which are tracks I made which people say I should put out as a single, and I always fought it. But this time I swayed with the people who told me to put it out. I think they were right. It's almost the first or second take, and the musicians are ragged but swinging. We tried to cut it a few times again but it never got that feel."

Elton John helped record the song with the addition of piano, organ and harmony vocal overdubs. "How the record came about was that Elton was in town and I was doing it and needed a harmony," Lennon explained. "He did the harmony on that and a couple more, and played beautiful piano on it." Despite Elton's powerful presence on the record, Lennon was never completely happy with the song. However, Elton was convinced that it was going to be a hit and asked Lennon to return the favour by joining him on stage should it make Number 1. Not thinking that it would ever be a hit, Lennon agreed. Within weeks of 'Whatever Gets

You Thru The Night' being issued, it was sitting at the top of the US charts and Lennon was committed to performing with Elton John at Madison Square Garden in New York City.

He joined Elton John on November 28 1974 for the first of two shows the pianist gave there. The two Johns performed 'Whatever Gets You Thru The Night', 'Lucy In The Sky With Diamonds', and 'I Saw Her Standing There'. Lennon returned to play tambourine on 'The Bitch Is Back'. The show was recorded, and 'I Saw Her Standing There' issued as the B-side of Elton John's 'Philadelphia Freedom' (DJM DJS 10354). All three tracks were issued as an EP in 1981 (DJM DJS 10965).

'Beef Jerky' was modelled on the R&B records that Lennon had grown up with. The riff-heavy instrumental was recorded in July and August 1974, helped by a snappy brass arrangement and clever production touches. Lennon used every trick in the book to instil some verve in this otherwise pedestrian instrumental. However, his decision to place the rhythm section well down in the mix effectively prevented it from really taking off. Although Lennon never claimed to be a great guitarist, his playing on this track was more than a match for guitar virtuoso Jesse Ed Davis.

'Whatever Gets You Thru The Night' data

Apple issued 'Whatever Gets You Thru The Night' in Britain with generic Apple labels and paper sleeve.

American pressings were issued with three label variants. The first has a dark green Apple label; song title with composer credit and artist's name 'JOHN LENNON WITH THE PLASTIC ONO NUCLEAR BAND' centre bottom; 'STEREO' at 9 o'clock; publisher, intro and total playing time, catalogue number, and producer credit on the right side of the label.

The second variant has a dark green Apple label with artist's name offset right centre top; song title in bold with composer credit centre bottom; 'STEREO' at 9 o'clock with intro and total playing time and publisher credit below; catalogue number at 3 o'clock; producer credit at four o'clock.

The third US variant has a medium green Apple label with song title and composer credit at 11 o'clock; 'STEREO' at 9 o'clock; artist's name centre bottom; publisher, intro and total playing time, catalogue number, and producer credit on right side of label.

American promotional copies of the single (P-1874) were issued with light green Apple labels with the song title and composer credit centre bottom, plus a black star and 'NOT FOR SALE' at 10 o'clock. The A-side was issued in mono, the B-side in stereo. British promotional copies replicate the commercial pressing with the addition of a large 'A' at 11 o'clock, 'DEMO RECORD NOT FOR SALE' in the centre of the label, and '(4.10.74)' at 3 o'clock.

137

JOHN LENNON (WITH PLASTIC ONO NUCLEAR BAND/LITTLE BIG HORNS/AND THE PHILHARMONIC ORCHESTRANGE)

Side 1 'Going Down On Love', 'Whatever Gets You Thru The Night', 'Old Dirt Road', 'What You Got', 'Bless You', 'Scared'.
Side 2 '#9 Dream', 'Surprise, Surprise (Sweet Bird Of Paradox)', 'Steel And Glass', 'Beef Jerky', 'Nobody Loves You When You're Down And Out', 'Ya Ya'.

UK release October 4 1974; LP Apple PCTC 253; 8-track cartridge Apple 8X-PCTC 253; chart high No.6.
US release September 26 1974; LP Apple SW 3416; 8-track cartridge Apple 8XW-3416; quadraphonic 8-track cartridge Apple Q8W-3416; chart high No.1.

'Going Down On Love' (Lennon)
Personnel as 'What You Got' except Ken Ascher (electric piano).
'Old Dirt Road' (Lennon, Nilsson)
John Lennon (vocals, piano), Jesse Ed Davis (guitar), Eddie Mottau (acoustic guitar), Ken Ascher (electric piano), Nicky Hopkins (piano), Klaus Voormann (bass), Harry Nilsson (backing vocal), Jim Keltner (drums).
'What You Got' (Lennon)
John Lennon (vocals, guitar), Jesse Ed Davis (guitar), Eddie Mottau (acoustic guitar), Ken Ascher (Clavinet), Nicky Hopkins (piano), Klaus Voormann (bass), Arthur Jenkins (percussion), Little Big Horns: Bobby Keys, Steve Madaio, Howard Johnson, Ron Aprea, Frank Vicari (horns), Jim Keltner (drums).
'Bless You' (Lennon)
John Lennon (vocals, acoustic guitar), Jesse Ed Davis (guitar), Eddie Mottau (acoustic guitar), Ken Ascher (piano, Mellotron), Klaus Voormann (bass), Arthur Jenkins (percussion), Jim Keltner (drums).
'Scared' (Lennon)
Personnel as 'What You Got' except Ken Ascher (electric piano).
'#9 Dream' (Lennon)
John Lennon (vocals, acoustic guitar), Jesse Ed Davis (guitar), Eddie Mottau (acoustic guitar), Ken Ascher (Clavinet), Nicky Hopkins (electric piano), Bobby Keys (saxophone), Klaus Voormann (bass), Arthur Jenkins (percussion), The 44th Street Fairies: May Pang, Lori Burton, Joey Dambra (backing vocals), Jim Keltner (drums).
'Surprise, Surprise (Sweet Bird Of Paradox)' (Lennon)
John Lennon (vocals, acoustic guitar), Elton John (vocal harmony), rest as 'What You Got'.
'Steel And Glass' (Lennon)
John Lennon (vocals, acoustic guitar), rest as 'What You Got'.
'Nobody Loves You (When You're Down And Out)' (Lennon)
John Lennon (vocals, acoustic guitar), Jesse Ed Davis (guitar), Klaus Voormann (bass), Little Big Horns: Bobby Keys, Steve Madaio, Howard Johnson, Ron Aprea, Frank Vicari (horns), Jim Keltner (drums).
'Ya Ya' (Robinson, Lewis, Dorsey)
John Lennon (vocals, piano), Julian Lennon (drums).
All recorded at Record Plant East, New York City, NY, USA. All produced by John Lennon.

WALLS AND BRIDGES

On completing *Mind Games*, Lennon and Ono separated. Ono stayed in New York City while Lennon headed west for Los Angeles with his personal assistant and new girlfriend, May Pang. No longer able to live together, Lennon and Ono found that they couldn't live apart either. While they were no longer collaborating, they nevertheless remained in constant communication. Neither it seems were capable of making a clean break.

However, once he was out of Ono's immediate control, Lennon reverted to type. Having moved from pop star to peacenik to activist, he now made the move back to wild rocker. Determined to enjoy his new-found freedom, he reacquainted himself with the old London Ad Lib club crowd. Keith Moon, drummer with The Who and all round wild man of rock, was in town, as were Ringo Starr and Harry Nilsson. With nothing better to do, this boorish 'wild bunch' hit the town and painted it red. Their drunken antics were legion and legendary. Suffice to say, Lennon was making headline news, but for all the wrong reasons.

In a vain attempt to bring some order back into his life, Lennon decided the time was right to return to the studio. Unfortunately, all that happened was that the madness moved with him. The first thing he did was to reunite with Phil Spector for an album of rock'n'roll oldies. With no one prepared to control either Lennon or Spector's ego, the sessions quickly degenerated into chaos. John and Phil's 'Back To Mono' sessions became the biggest, wildest, and most expensive party in rock's history. Everyone indulged Lennon, who, more often than not, was drunk. The sessions didn't fizzle out as one might have expected, but came to an abrupt halt when Spector disappeared with the tapes.

Faced with a lengthy delay, in March 1974 Lennon turned to producing an album for Harry Nilsson. Recording with many of the musicians who'd worked on the *Rock 'N' Roll* project wasn't a good idea. Sessions for Nilsson's *Pussy Cats* album quickly became as chaotic as those abandoned a few months earlier.

Paul and Linda McCartney also happened to be in Los Angeles and decided the time was right to meet up with Lennon and dropped by the studio for a jam. Relations between Lennon and McCartney had been improving for some time, and while the pair were nowhere as close as they had been, relations had obviously improved to the extent that McCartney felt comfortable enough to visit Lennon and even record with him in the studio. Speaking to Denis Elsas on September 28 1974, Lennon said: "Paul was here about a month ago and I spent a couple of Beaujolais evenings with him." Lennon described their relationship as "very warm". Interviewed in 1997, McCartney too recalled the informal session. "The main thing that I recall, apart from the fact that Stevie Wonder was there, is that someone said, 'What songs shall we do?' and John said, 'Anything before '63; I don't know anything after '63!' Which I understood, because the songs from your formative years are the ones that you tend to use to jam."

Although the session involved two ex-Beatles, Harry Nilsson, Stevie Wonder, Jesse Ed Davis, and Bobby Keys, the results were ramshackle, marred by the consumption of certain illegal stimulants. It may have been uninspired, but this turned out to be the only post-Beatles recording that Lennon and McCartney made together. More importantly, it indicated that they were well on the way to resolving their differences.

While working on Nilsson's *Pussy Cats* album, Lennon also recorded a demo of '(It's All Down To) Goodnight Vienna' for Ringo Starr and produced a proposed single for Mick Jagger ('Too Many Cooks'). He also managed to write a batch of new songs for his next solo album. Not bad for a self-confessed drunken fool.

The non-stop party atmosphere he experienced in Los Angeles was beginning to take its toll, and Lennon realised that for his own health and sanity he had to leave it behind. "In LA you either have to be down by the beach or you become part of that never-ending show-business party circuit," he explained. "That scene makes me nervous, and when I get nervous I have to have a drink, and when I drink I get aggressive. So I prefer to stay in New York. I try not to drink at all here."

Back in New York City, Lennon finished Nilsson's album and began writing. As usual, he recorded a number of simple home demos, fleshing out ideas, melodies, and lyrics as the songs progressed. He would later dismiss these songs as the uninspired work of a "semi-sick craftsman". Nevertheless, he gained some benefit from the work; unpacking his bundle of emotional baggage was cathartic. Speaking just after the album's release, Lennon appeared relieved but also disappointed. "Let's say this last year has been an extraordinary year for me personally," he said. "And I'm almost amazed that I could get anything out. But I enjoyed doing *Walls And Bridges*, and it wasn't hard when I had the whole thing to go into the studio and do it. I'm surprised it wasn't just all blanunugggggghhhh. I had the most peculiar year. And … I'm just glad that something came out. It's describing the year, in a way, but it's not as sort of schizophrenic as the year really was. I think I got such a shock during that year that the impact hasn't come through. It isn't all on *Walls And Bridges*, though. There's a hint of it there. It has to do with age and god knows what else. But only the surface has been touched on *Walls And Bridges*, you know?"

Although he thought the work lacked originality, the record had continuity and confidence – which couldn't be said for the last album, *Mind Games*. In the light of what had been happening to him, *Walls And Bridges* was a solid album and proof that he was still capable of flashes of greatness, even if he was growing tired of the music industry's demands.

Writing *Walls And Bridges* may not have been as cathartic an experience for Lennon as writing *John Lennon/Plastic Ono Band*, but at least he came through the episode with a better understanding of who he was and what he wanted from life. He remained a seeker, but what he sought now was not political change, global harmony, or an unobtainable utopia, but personal fulfilment. The quest to bring meaning to his life was slowly becoming a reality. *Walls And Bridges* points the way to Lennon's final musical statement, *Double Fantasy*. That, however, was six years away; for the moment, he had more pressing matters to deal with.

Once he was ready to record, Lennon called upon his usual pool of musicians and, to familiarise them with the new material, began rehearsing at New York City's Record Plant studio in early July. Typically, these sessions were recorded – and several songs taped at these rehearsals would later appear on the *Menlove Ave.* album and the *John Lennon Anthology* boxed set. Because the musicians had rehearsed the material Lennon wanted to record, working out their own 'head' arrangements, the recording progressed quickly. Unlike the Spector 'Back To Mono' sessions, these were a model of professionalism. Regular work hours were established and all stimulants banned from the studio.

Jimmy Iovine, who acted as overdub engineer on *Walls And Bridges*, confirmed that Lennon was a consummate professional. "The *Walls And Bridges* sessions were *the* most professional I have been on," he recalled. "He was [there] every day, 12 o'clock to 10 o'clock; go home; off [at] the weekends; eight weeks; done. John knew what he wanted, he knew how to get what he was going after: he was going after a noise and he knew how to get it. And for the most part he got it. What he explained, we used to get. … His solo thing had an incredible sound to it. And he really had his own sound."

With the basic tracks in the can, Lennon started the process of adding overdubs. Ron Aprea, saxophonist with the newly recruited Little Big Horns, recalled that the brass section was added over a frantic two-week period. Although he was astonished to discover that none of the songs had formal arrangements written for them, he was pleasantly surprised to discover just how accommodating Lennon could be. "Since he had no formal training in arranging, he would sit in the control room and let us make up our own parts," said Aprea. "If he liked what we played, he would let us know and then ask us for our opinion. He would also ask if there were any 'secrets' [mistakes]. If we thought we could get it better, he would say 'go for it'."

Although the Record Plant was one of the most advanced and sophisticated recording studios in New York, Lennon's vocal overdubs were recorded with an old stage microphone. Iovine: "[It] was an old beat-up one that was in a bass drum for years, so it was dull in a way, but John's voice was so bright that it sounded incredible on it. It turned out to be a great vocal sound, like on '#9 Dream'."

Days before Lennon was due to start recording what would become *Walls And Bridges*, Capitol Records executive Al Coury recovered the Spector 'Back To Mono' tapes. At roughly the same time, the US authorities gave Lennon 60 days to leave the country. Once again, he appealed against the decision. In light of these problems, the album's title was an apt one. Lennon was facing numerous barriers and the title, *Walls And Bridges*, taken from a public service announcement, summed up his situation perfectly.

Walls And Bridges turned out to be Lennon's last album of original material until *Double Fantasy* in 1980 – but a follow-up was planned for late 1975. Apple executive Tony King has suggested that Lennon planned to follow *Walls And Bridges* with an album called *Between The Lines*. King also suggested that guitarist Carlos Alomar had been hired to recruit a band of Afro-American musicians and that Lennon had already written 'Tennessee' and 'Nobody Told Me' for the album. When interviewed by Bob Harris for BBC TV's *Old Grey Whistle Test* in 1975, Lennon confirmed that he was planning a new album and a one-off television show, but neither surfaced.

Walls And Bridges songs

Hardly the most auspicious way to start an album, 'Going Down On Love' set the tone for most of what followed. Its sexual innuendo apart, the song is a bleak confession of despair. The 'lost weekend' may have looked like fun from the outside, but from Lennon's perspective things could not have been worse. He really had hit the bottom, and with no end in sight and no evident escape, all he could do was attempt to come to terms with the situation.

Although he was down, he wasn't out. Lennon was often at his best when exploring the darker side of his psyche. Whether it was the traumatic experience of heroin withdrawal or the after affects of primal therapy, he often shone when all around him seemed gloomy. As raw and honest as anything he'd written, 'Going Down On Love' finds him in a rare moment of contrition, praying for redemption and forgiveness. With Ono no longer there to control him, Lennon must have felt completely lost. Without a guiding hand, he forgoes any attempt to strip away illusions or to analyse the cause of his suffering. Rather there is blind acceptance of the fact that there is no magic cure, no quick fix, but only the fleeting experience of human existence at its darkest.

Having formulated the bare bones of the song, Lennon recorded several demos, developing the lyrics, melody, middle eight, and arrangement as he went. Moving to the piano, he recorded a strident, pounding arrangement that, when he shifted to the studio, would be forsaken in favour of the muted tone of his earlier guitar-based demo recordings. Rehearsing at the Record Plant in early July, Lennon recorded a stripped-down version of the song with just guitarist Jesse Ed Davis, bassist Klaus Voormann, and drummer Jim Keltner in support. Without the gloss of overdubs, the rehearsal take reeks of melancholia and Lennon sounds audibly vulnerable. (Some of these rehearsals were issued later on the *Menlove Ave.* album.)

Between bouts of drinking, drugging, and trouble-making, Lennon and Harry Nilsson managed to stay sober long enough to write 'Old Dirt Road'. Lennon suggested that his collaboration with Nilsson was "just to write a song. You know, 'seein' as we're stuck in this bottle of vodka together, we might as well try and do something'." But he was being disingenuous. Lennon's admiration for the singer's talents was considerable – he wouldn't have offered to produce Nilsson had he not liked him and his work. Although 'Old Dirt Road' is not the best song in his oeuvre, Lennon was too quick to dismiss it. Perhaps he associated the song with a period in his life that he would rather forget and therefore dismissed it as a song written while he was not at his creative best. Although it is not explicitly about the 'lost weekend', it does capture an atmosphere of listless intoxication that must have permeated their days.

Speaking on BBC radio in 1990, Nilsson recalled how he helped Lennon finish the song. Remarkably, it was completed while discussing business with some 'suits'. Nilsson: "When you said something that was either clever or good, [Lennon] would just jump on it. When he was writing 'Old Dirt Road', he'd started the tune, and he was up past the first verse, I guess, and some 'suit people' came in, and he said, 'Harry, what's a good Americanism?' And why this came about [I don't know], it came into my mind, but it was like, 'Trying to shovel smoke with a pitchfork in the wind.' And he said, 'Oh great, great. Fantastic! You're burning man, go for it.' And he talked to the suits over the piano, and wrote another verse, and I'd check in with him every few minutes like a secretary, go back to the piano, and he'd be going, 'Yeah, yeah you're on fire now.'"

The rehearsal take, issued later on *Menlove Ave.*, is the most basic of sketches but allows the listener to eavesdrop on the session as the song takes shape. An outtake issued on the *John Lennon Anthology* is considerably more formed and, with the addition of acoustic guitar, closer to the finished master.

Next up is 'What You Got', a slice of New York funk inspired by The O' Jays' 'Money, Money, Money' and, despite its apparent joie de vivre, a rather sad lament. Lennon restates a lyrical theme beloved of blues singers – "you don't know what you got until you lose it" – and in the process expresses real fears. Acknowledging that his drunken capers with Nilsson were rapidly getting him a reputation as a 'drag', he nevertheless had the sense to recognise the fact and do something about it. Not only were the hangovers becoming too much, but so was his separation from Ono. Delivered with an emotionally charged vocal, 'What You Got' may not have had much new to say lyrically, but it said it musically in the most fashionable way possible.

At the time, Lennon was listening to a lot of dance music and planned to record his next album with Afro-American musicians. Although disco came in for a lot of criticism, dance music was where it was at, and Lennon loved it. Apple executive Tony King remembers stocking Lennon's jukebox with contemporary disco records, and one in particular, 'Shame Shame Shame' by Shirley And Company, influenced his later contribution to David Bowie's *Fame*. Like much dance music, 'What You Got' appears up-beat, but scratch the surface and you'll find a song as honest and self-explanatory as anything Lennon had written.

Paul McCartney didn't have a monopoly on romantic ballads. Lennon was equally capable of writing tender love songs. Like McCartney's 'My Love' from the previous year, 'Bless You' was a heartfelt expression of love and every bit as romantic. But its writing was tempered with the knowledge that both parties had grown apart and could no longer be described as John-and-Yoko. While Lennon was in Los Angeles with May Pang, Ono was in New York City and, Albert Goldman later alleged, was infatuated with guitarist David Spinozza. The Lennons now seemed engaged in a very open relationship, and whereas Lennon would have once been filled with rage and jealousy, he now had the grace to bless his usurper.

Unlike earlier songs dedicated to Ono, which were in effect one-sided expressions of love, 'Bless You' reveals a subtle change in attitude, a recognition that love is not a static emotion but one that is experienced and expressed in many shades and hues. "In a way, it's about Yoko and I," he explained. "And in a way it's about a lot of couples or all of us who go through that (whatever it's called) love experience. You know, the way love changes, which is one of the surprises of life that we all find out: that it doesn't remain exactly the same all the time, although it's still love. It comes in mysterious forms, its wonders to perform. And 'Bless You' expresses one side of it."

As with some of Lennon's best work, 'Bless You' came to him quickly. Speaking just after the release of *Walls And Bridges*, he revealed that he hadn't laboured over it as he had others. "As a song, I think it's the best piece of work on the album, although I worked harder on some of the other tracks. In retrospect, that seems to be the best track, to me."

Lennon took considerable care in shaping it, transforming the song from a rather maudlin ballad to a shimmering statement of regret that bypassed schmaltz for simple honesty. Although he allowed the musicians to develop their own parts, he made himself clear when he heard something he didn't like. While rehearsing 'Bless You', Lennon chastised guitarist Jesse Ed Davis for playing a chord with too many notes in it, even if they were the right ones. After the over-production of *Mind Games* and the Spector 'Back To Mono' sessions, Lennon returned to a simpler recording practice that struck the right balance between artifice and honesty.

As honest and analytical as anything written for *John Lennon/Plastic Ono Band*, 'Scared' was the product of a deepening depression brought on by Lennon's separation from Ono. This wasn't the first time he'd experienced crippling feelings of isolation and alienation brought about by drink, drugs, and fragmenting relationships. He'd expressed similar fears in 'Help!', a literal cry for succour written during a similar bout of personal torment. Like 'Help!', 'Scared' is a distillation of the pain he was experiencing during its writing. "I am scared a lot of the time, I think we all are," he said, "but I'm not always scared. I do have vindictive sides as well."

Adrift from Ono and with little else to do other than hit the bottle, Lennon had plenty of time to contemplate the meaning of life, the universe, and everything. What he found was of little comfort. Had his life's work been in vain? Was he nothing more than an uncommitted phoney, afraid to practice what he preached? Redemption seemed unobtainable, and the questions Lennon asked remained unanswered until he was reunited with Ono.

Musically, Lennon restates what he had originally intended for 'Help!'. Unhappy with The Beatles' up-tempo treatment of 'Help!', he attempted a brooding remake in 1970 when he taped a piano-based home demo at his Tittenhurst home. He also spoke of re-recording the song professionally, but the nearest he got to it was the moody setting he fashioned for 'Scared'. Unadorned by overdubs, the rehearsal take (later issued on *Menlove Ave.*) wouldn't have seemed out of place on *John Lennon/Plastic Ono Band*. It also has slightly different lyrics. Alluding to Dylan's 'Rainy Day Women #12 & 35' and his own recent indulgences, Lennon sings "I'm stoned" in place of "I'm scared".

The ethereal '#9 Dream' began as a string arrangement that Lennon wrote for Harry Nilsson's recording of 'Many Rivers To Cross'. However, this melody was too good to use just once and then discard. Reworking the arrangement, Lennon developed a dreamlike motif that's hangs like a veil between consciousness (reality) and unconsciousness (fantasy). The phantasmagorical atmosphere Lennon created was inspired, in part, by a dream in which he heard the nonsensical phrase "Ah! böwakawa poussé, poussé" and two women (Yoko Ono and May Pang?) calling his name. Combining his skills as a lyricist and melodist, Lennon perfectly captured that moment between sleeping and awakening in which reality and fantasy merge. The lyric was his most poetic for some time, packed with romantic allusions that evoke the dream state that inspired them.

To many listeners, '#9 Dream' has all the hallmarks of a classic. However, when speaking with Andy Peebles in 1980, Lennon was quick to dismiss the song. "That's what I call craftsmanship writing, meaning, you know, I just churned that out," he said. "I'm not putting it down, it's just what it is, but I just sat down and wrote it, you know, with no real inspiration, based on a dream I'd had." If '#9 Dream' was nothing more than "craftsmanship writing", it was a remarkable piece of work.

Lennon began by recording rough work-in-progress demos. But it was only when he took the song into the studio that it really came to life. Once he'd recorded the basic track, to which a lush orchestral arrangement by Ken Ascher and backing vocals were added, he began work on developing the song's dreamy texture, achieved with a great deal of post-production work. Jimmy Iovine recalled that a huge amount of effects were used to create the finished track. "On '#9 Dream', that's an incredible vocal sound. There's a lot of very interesting things done to that vocal sound to make it sound like that. There was so much echo on his voice in the mix, and doubling and tape delay." The results were spectacular. Washes of sound envelop the listener, drawing them into Lennon's narcoleptic dream world.

A song inspired by Lennon's new beau, 'Surprise, Surprise (Sweet Bird Of Paradox)' was written in New York City at the beginning of his relationship with May Pang. Lennon had several affairs, and occasionally wrote about them – 'Norwegian Wood' being an early example – but few were as explicitly revealed as this. Compared with his recent musings on Ono, 'Surprise, Surprise (Sweet Bird Of Paradox)' brims with warmth and emotion. He was clearly besotted with his new sweetheart. Although Pang experienced Lennon at his most depraved, she too was deeply in love with him. However, no sooner had Lennon issued the song than he was back with Ono. What happened to make him abandon Pang so quickly and utterly has never been explained. Whatever it was, Lennon and Ono seemed to pick up their relationship as if nothing had happened. Within months of Lennon moving back to the Dakota, Ono was pregnant and Lennon bound for five years of househusbandry. (The Dakota was the apartment block in New York City to which the pair had moved from their Bank Street apartment in May 1973.)

'Surprise, Surprise' began as little more than an extended exploration of what became the song's middle eight. Accompanying himself on electric guitar, Lennon recorded a demo based on this motif. This early version seemed to question the strength of his relationship with Pang rather than celebrate it. Next he reworked the song to the point where it resembled the finished composition. He made a demo recording of the reworked song, this time accompanying himself with an acoustic guitar. Both demos feature musical elements that were discarded once he moved to the Record Plant. When recording began, the track took on a lighter tone – a version issued later on the *John Lennon Anthology* reveals just how far the song had developed once the band began work on it. With the backing track complete, Lennon began adding overdubs, which included a vocal contribution from Elton John.

'Steel And Glass' was Lennon's attempt to update 'How Do You Sleep?', and many believed that on this occasion his target was his ex-manager, Allen Klein. By the mid 1970s, Lennon's infatuation with Klein had waned considerably, to the extent that neither he nor Harrison nor Starr wanted Klein to manage their affairs any longer. Although Klein had probably made more money for them than Brian Epstein ever did, by 1974 Lennon, Harrison, and Starr were back in the courts attempting to disentangle themselves from his managerial grip. More than anything else, it was this litigation that caused Lennon to attack Klein with such obvious pleasure. Lennon and Klein may have been battling it out in the courts, but that didn't mean that they couldn't still be friends.

Even as Lennon was writing 'Steel And Glass', he was happy to visit and stay with Klein at his Westhampton home. But when asked about the song, Lennon refused to admit that it had anything to do with Klein, only that he may have used him as inspiration to write something nasty. "It actually isn't about one person in particular," he said, "but it has been about a few people and, like a novel writer, if I'm writing about something other than myself, I use other people I know or have known as examples. If I want to write a 'down' song, I would have to remember being down, and when I wrote 'Steel And Glass' I used various people and objects. If I had listed who they were, it would be a few people, and you would be surprised. But it really isn't about anybody. I'm loathe to tell you this, because it spoils the fun. I would sooner everybody think, 'Who's it about?' and try and piece it together. For sure, it isn't about Paul and it isn't about Eartha Kitt."

Before taking it to the studio, Lennon recorded a pounding piano demo with different lyrics to the finished song. He had a habit of rewriting lyrics, often making changes right up to the moment before recording his final vocal. A rehearsal take, recorded at the Record Plant and issued later on *Menlove Ave.*, has Lennon abandoning the piano for an acoustic guitar, slowing the tempo, and leading his small band through a version of the song that still lacked a finished lyric.

If the 'lost weekend' had a signature tune, it was 'Nobody Loves You (When You're Down And Out)'. Written during Lennon's first few weeks in Los Angeles, it is an honest and revealing exploration of his fragile mental state. His feelings of rejection and alienation are etched deep into this song. Battered by critics, abandoned by Ono, cheated by the music industry, and ignored by the public, Lennon had come a long way from being the toppermost of the poppermost, and 'Nobody Loves You (When You're Down And Out)' reveals the effect this had on him.

From where he was standing, it seemed that he'd been abandoned. Derelict and depressed, Lennon muses that he will only be truly valued when he's "six foot in the ground". Exhausted by the demands placed upon him, Lennon found himself staring into a black hole of despair that threatened to swallow him whole. Like his ex-partner Paul McCartney, he'd suffered many dark nights of the soul, but he had survived and was looking for a way out.

Early versions of the song reveal the depth of Lennon's depression. From the earliest of home demos to the group rehearsals held before recording proper, Lennon sounds world-weary and fragile. The rehearsal take issued later on *Menlove Ave.* is dark and melancholic. Lennon's introductory whistling lends the song a sense of lonely isolation, but when guitarist Davis exacts palpable moans and cries of despair from his instrument, the song moves deeper into the shadows. An alternative take issued later on the *John Lennon Anthology* features extra musicians, second guitar, keyboards, and percussion not present on the rehearsal take and runs close to the finished master.

Lennon included a cover of 'Ya Ya' in an attempt to appease music publisher Morris Levy, who was suing over an alleged breech of copyright. It didn't work. Levy wanted something more than an ad-libbed 59-second snippet for him to drop legal proceedings. Lennon's next album, *Rock 'N 'Roll*, would settle the matter once and for all. (See that entry, later, for more details.) Although it was probably tagged on to the album as an afterthought, 'Ya Ya' captures a rare moment of intimacy between Lennon and his first son, Julian (who'd stayed with his mother, Cynthia, when she divorced his father in the late 1960s).

The album sessions produced one outtake. 'Move Over Ms L' was intended to sit between 'Surprise Surprise' and 'What You Got', before Lennon decided to alter the track listing. 'Move Over' was released six months later as the B-side of the single 'Stand By Me'. It was also given to drinking buddy Keith Moon, who recorded a version for his debut and only solo album, *Two Sides Of The Moon*.

Walls And Bridges data

Apple issued *Walls And Bridges* with generic Apple labels and a unique fold-over cover. Lennon had intended to use the paintings he made as a boy for the cover of his 'oldies' album, but as that was postponed he told Roy Kohara to base the design for *Walls And Bridges* on the images already supplied. The package also included a printed inner sleeve and eight-page full colour booklet.

British pressings appear to have been manufactured from lacquer masters supplied by Capitol, as the album's US catalogue number, SW 3416, appears crossed out in the dead wax.

American copies of the LP were produced with three label variations. The first has a medium green Apple label; bold text with the first song title above the spindle hole; B-side label with title at 10 o'clock; artist credit at two o'clock.

The second has a medium green Apple label; plain text with all song titles below the spindle hole; B-side label with title and artist credit on two lines at 10 o'clock.

And the third has a medium green Apple label; bold text with all song titles below the spindle hole; B-side label with title and artist credit on three lines at 10 o'clock.

The album was reissued in America by Capitol in 1978 with purple Capitol labels and again in 1982 with black/colour band Capitol labels. In 1989, Capitol reissued the album with purple Capitol labels with a small Capitol logo. In 1999, EMI released *Walls And Bridges* as a limited-edition 'Millennium' 180 gram audiophile vinyl LP (4994641).

The album was issued in the USA on 8-track cartridge in both stereo (8XW-3416) and quadraphonic (Q8W-3416). In Britain, the 8-track was issued in stereo only (8X-PCTC 253).

Walls And Bridges first appeared on CD in Britain in July 20 1987 (CDP 7 46768 2) with an eight-page booklet. The CD was issued in the USA on April 19 1988. The album was remixed, remastered, and issued by EMI/Capitol with three bonus tracks and revised cover and label artwork on November 22 2005.

The album's respectable chart placing was achieved by Lennon's willingness to engage in promotional duties; he made guest appearances on several American radio stations, and an array of promotional material appeared included badges, stickers, posters, press kits, and photographs, all with the theme 'Listen To This'. Additionally, a 59-second 'Listen To This Radio Spot', featuring both Lennon and Ringo Starr, was distributed to American radio stations. In Britain, EMI issued an interview single (PSR 369), which it gave to its sales reps. The interview with Bob Merger was produced by Lennon and issued as a white-label 7-inch with the EMI logo and the legend 'An Apple record'. The interview was eventually issued as a bonus track on the 2005 remastered CD.

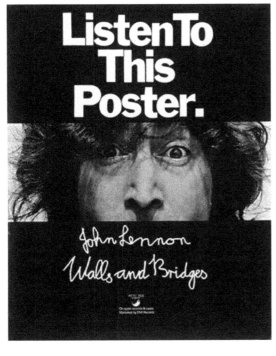
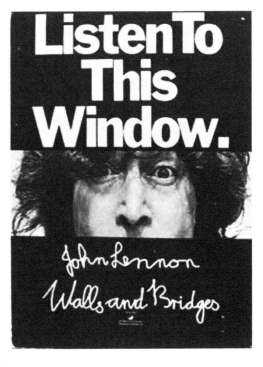

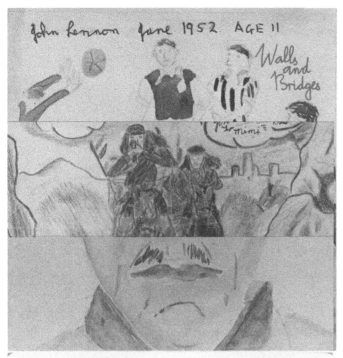

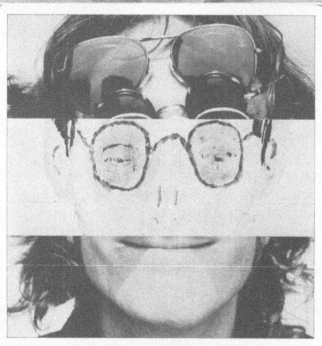

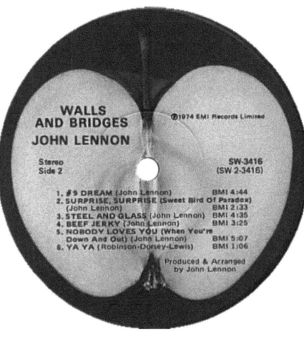

'#9 DREAM' / 'WHAT YOU GOT'
JOHN LENNON

UK release January 24 1975; Apple R 6003; chart high No.23.
US release December 16 1974; Apple APPLE 1878; chart high No.9.

'#9 DREAM'

This was the second and last single issued from *Walls And Bridges*, and like Lennon's previous single it was a bigger hit in the USA than in Britain. Neither American nor British pressings were issued in picture covers.

Promotional copies were issued in both countries. In America, Apple issued mono/stereo promotional singles of '#9 Dream' (P-1878), the stereo mix being a 2:55 edit. They also issued the B-side as a mono/stereo promotional single, 'What You Got' (P-1878) (PRO-8030).

Capitol reissued the single with orange Capitol labels in 1978 and again a few years later with purple Capitol labels.

In Britain, Apple issued two different versions of the promotional single, making '#9 Dream' available in edited and un-edited versions. Commercial copies of the single were also produced with minor label variations; some copies omitted the reference to the song being from the album *Walls And Bridges*.

(from the LP "WALLS AND BRIDGES" SW-3416)

℗ 1974 EMI Records Limited

Lennon Music/ATV Music Corp. BMI

MONO

P-1878
(PRO-8029)

NOT FOR SALE

Intro.–:18
2:58

Produced & Arranged by John Lennon

★ #9 DREAM
(John Lennon)
JOHN LENNON

(from the LP "WALLS AND BRIDGES" SW-3416)

℗ 1974 EMI Records Limited

Lennon Music/ATV Music Corp. BMI

STEREO

P-1878
(SPRO-8035)

NOT FOR SALE

Intro.–:18
2:58

Produced & Arranged by John Lennon

★ #9 DREAM
(John Lennon)

JOHN LENNON

(from the LP "WALLS AND BRIDGES" SW-3416)

℗ 1974 EMI Records Limited

Lennon Music/ATV Music Corp. BMI

MONO

P-1878
(PRO-8030)

NOT FOR SALE

Intro.–:16
3:06

Produced & Arranged by John Lennon

★ WHAT YOU GOT
(John Lennon)
JOHN LENNON

(from the LP "WALLS AND BRIDGES" SW-3416)

℗ 1974 EMI Records Limited

Lennon Music/ATV Music Corp. BMI

STEREO

P-1878
(S45-48821)

NOT FOR SALE

Intro.–:16
3:06

Produced & Arranged by John Lennon

★ WHAT YOU GOT
(John Lennon)
JOHN LENNON

(from the LP "WALLS AND BRIDGES" SW-3416)

℗ 1974 EMI Records Limited

Lennon Music/ATV Music Corp.-BMI

STEREO

1878
(S45-48824)

Intro.–:18
4:44

Produced & Arranged by John Lennon

#9 DREAM
(John Lennon)
JOHN LENNON

(from the LP "WALLS AND BRIDGES" SW-3416)

℗ 1974 EMI Records Limited

Lennon Music/ATV Music Corp.-BMI

STEREO

1878
(S45-48821)

Intro.–:16
3:06

Produced & Arranged by John Lennon

WHAT YOU GOT
(John Lennon)
JOHN LENNON

ROCK'N'ROLL
JOHN LENNON

Side 1 'Be-Bop-A-Lula', 'Stand By Me', 'Rip It Up / Ready Teddy', 'You Can't Catch Me', 'Ain't That A Shame', 'Do You Want To Dance', 'Sweet Little Sixteen'.
Side 2 'Slippin' And Slidin'', 'Peggy Sue', 'Bring It On Home To Me / Send Me Some Lovin'', 'Bony Maronie', 'Ya Ya', 'Just Because'.
UK release February 21 1975; LP Apple PCS 7169; 8-track cartridge Apple 8X-PCS 7169; chart high No.6 (re-enters January 17 1981 chart high No.64).
US release February 17 1975; LP Apple SK 3419; 8-track cartridge Apple 8XK-3419; chart high No.6.

'Be-Bop-A-Lula' (Davis, Vincent)
John Lennon (vocals, guitar), Jesse Ed Davis (guitar), Eddie Mottau (acoustic guitar), Ken Ascher (piano), Klaus Voormann (bass), Arthur Jenkins (percussion), Jim Keltner (drums).
'Stand By Me' (King, Leiber, Stoller)
John Lennon (vocals, guitar), Jesse Ed Davis (guitar), Eddie Mottau (acoustic guitar), Peter Jameson (guitar), Ken Ascher (piano), Klaus Voormann (bass), Arthur Jenkins (percussion), Joseph Temperley (saxophone), Dennis Morouse (tenor saxophone), Frank Vicari (saxophone), Jim Keltner (drums).
'Rip It Up / Ready Teddy' (Blackwell, Marascalco)
John Lennon (vocals, guitar), Jesse Ed Davis (guitar), Eddie Mottau (acoustic guitar), Ken Ascher (piano), Klaus Voormann (bass), Arthur Jenkins (percussion), Joseph Temperley (saxophone), Dennis Morouse (tenor saxophone), Frank Vicari (saxophone), Jim Keltner (drums).
'You Can't Catch Me' (Berry)
John Lennon (guitar, vocals), Art Munson (guitar), Ray Neapolitan (bass), Michael Omartian (keyboards), William Perkins (woodwind), William Perry (guitar), Mac Rebennack (keyboards), Louie Shelton (guitar), Phil Spector (piano, guitar), Nino Tempo (saxophone, keyboards), Anthony Terran (trumpet), Andy Thomas (piano), Michael Wofford (piano), Jim Horn (saxophone), Plas Johnson (saxophone), Joseph Kelson (horn), Jim Keltner (drums), Bobby Keys (saxophone), Ronald Kossajda (instrument unknown), Michael Lang (piano), Ronald Langinger (saxophone), Barry Mann (piano), Julian Matlock (clarinet), Michael Melvoin (piano), Donald Menza (saxophone), Dale Anderson (guitar), Jeff Barry (piano), Hal Baine (drums), Jim Calvert (instrument unknown), Conte Candoli (trumpet), Frank Capp (drums), Larry Carlton (guitar), Gene Cipriano (saxophone), David Cohen (guitar), Gary Coleman (percussion), Steve Cropper (guitar), Jesse Ed Davis (guitar), Alan Estes (percussion), Chuck Findley (trumpet), Steven Forman (percussion), Terry Gibbs (piano or percussion), Bob Glaub (bass), Jim Gordon (drums), Robert Hardaway (woodwind), Leon Russell (keyboards), Jose Feliciano (guitar), Michael Hazelwood (instrument unknown), Thomas Hensley (bass), Dick Hieronymus (instrument unknown).
'Ain't That A Shame' (Domino, Bartholomew)
Personnel as 'Rip It Up / Ready Teddy'.
'Do You Want To Dance' (Freeman)
Personnel as 'Rip It Up / Ready Teddy'.
'Sweet Little Sixteen' (Berry)
Personnel as 'You Can't Catch Me'.
'Slippin' And Slidin'' (Penniman, Bocage, Collins, Smith)
Personnel as 'Rip It Up / Ready Teddy'.
'Peggy Sue' (Holly, Allison, Petty)
John Lennon (vocals, guitar), Jesse Ed Davis (guitar), Eddie Mottau (acoustic guitar), Ken Ascher (piano), Klaus Voormann (bass), Arthur Jenkins (percussion), Jim Keltner (drums).
'Bring It On Home To Me' (Cooke) / 'Send Me Some Lovin'' (Price, Marascalco)
Personnel as 'Rip It Up / Ready Teddy' except Klaus Voormann (bass and backing vocals).
'Bony Moronie' (Williams)
Personnel as 'You Can't Catch Me'.
'Ya Ya' (Robinson, Dorsey, Lewis)
Personnel as 'Bring It On Home To Me / Send Me Some Lovin''.

'Just Because' (Price)
Personnel as 'You Can't Catch Me'.

All recorded at Record Plant East, New York City, NY, USA and produced by John Lennon, except 'You Can't Catch Me', 'Sweet Little Sixteen', 'Bony Moronie', 'Just Because' recorded at A&M Studios or Record Plant West, Los Angeles, CA, USA and produced by Phil Spector, arranged by John Lennon and Phil Spector.

ROCK'N'ROLL

Like The Beatles' ill-fated *Get Back* project, which was recorded before but issued after *Abbey Road*, *Rock 'N 'Roll* spiralled out of control: production moved from one producer to another; an album of entirely new material (*Walls And Bridges*) was recorded and issued before it was completed; and Lennon returned to his roots.

With *Mind Games* yet to be released, Lennon began recording what he thought would be its follow-up. Holed up in Los Angeles, he decided the time was right to record an album of his favourite rock'n'roll oldies. Tired of having to write songs of his own, he wanted simply to be the singer. "I've had enough of this 'be deep and think'," he explained. "Why can't I have some fun?" Having fun was right at the top of Lennon's list or priorities, but he had another more important reason for recording an album of oldies. He was contractually obliged to record three songs published by Big Seven Music.

As writer of 'Come Together', a track from The Beatles' *Abbey Road* album, Lennon was being sued for copyright infringement. Big Seven Music Corp., owned by Morris Levy (the man who had tried, unsuccessfully, to copyright the phrase 'rock'n'roll'), claimed that Lennon had appropriated lyrics from Chuck Berry's 'You Can't Catch Me'. Lennon's habit of borrowing from other songs to kick-start his writing had caught up with him. 'Come Together', originally intended as a campaign song for Timothy Leary, displayed more than a passing resemblance to Berry's primal rocker. Although Lennon's lawyers agreed that both songs shared similar lyrics, they argued that the meaning had been substantially changed and therefore there was no case to answer. The case dragged on for over two years, by which time Lennon was spending almost as much time in the courts as he was in the studio. Growing tired of Levy's litigation, Lennon instructed his lawyers to settle out of court. The agreement with Levy stipulated that "John Lennon agrees to record three songs by Big Seven publishers on his next album. The songs [he] intends to record at this time are 'You Can't Catch Me', 'Angel Baby', and 'Ya Ya', [and he] reserves the right to alter the last two songs to any other songs belonging to Big Seven."

Having reached an agreement with Big Seven and mapped out the record in his head, Lennon needed someone to produce it. Who better than rock's greatest producer, Phil Spector? It wasn't as if Lennon and Spector hadn't worked together before. However, Lennon had always controlled Spector's more eccentric tendencies. But this time, in order to get Spector to produce the album, Lennon gave him total control. Besides selecting some of the songs, Spector booked the studios and chose the musicians to record with. Slipping into megalomaniac mode, Spector called on a small army of top flight players to back Lennon. Spector believed that these sessions were going to be historic; consequently, everything had to be on a grand scale.

Sessions took place at A&M Studios in Los Angeles on the nights of October 17, 18, 20, 22, 24, 26, and 28 and November 28 1973. They quickly descended into chaos. With upwards of 30 musicians at each session, set-up times were tedious affairs. To relieve the boredom of Spector's relentless recording technique, and with Lennon intent on having fun, the sessions took on a party atmosphere. Drummer Jim Keltner recalled that a typical night at the studio would descend into disorder, with Lennon the lead hedonist. "He was drinking too much, and as the evening progressed John would get a little out of control – the whole thing would deteriorate." Spector attempted to maintain control by rehearsing the band for hours on end, but he was fighting a losing battle. For someone who had always insisted on professionalism in the studio, Lennon was now concerned with only thing: having a good time, at the expense of both his reputation and career.

Dr. John, who played on several of the Spector sessions, recalled how everyone was hell-bent on indulging Lennon's excesses. "Instead of sayin', 'Hey man, you're fuckin' up your own date,' they let it happen. It was the first time in my life that I ever felt sorry for the producer. There was nothin' that Spector could do. He would try and dole out the lush to John – and the cat would have it smuggled in. Next night,

Phil would get somebody to make sure that John didn't drink more than a certain amount. The cat wouldn't cut 'til he had his taste. But when he had his taste, he *couldn't* cut!"

Several outtakes from the sessions reveal just how intoxicated Lennon became. Yet, despite this, he attempted to maintain some control over the sessions. During one exchange between singer and producer, Lennon pleaded: "Phil, it's our big chance at A&M, now let's not fuck it." Spector may not have been drinking, but he was no more stable than Lennon. He would arrive each night dressed in a different outfit and often carrying a handgun. One night, a minor incident between Spector and ex-Beatles road manager Mal Evans flew out of control. Spector pulled out his pistol and fired into the ceiling. Everyone, including Spector himself, was shocked into silence. The drunken chaos had been perfectly acceptable, all part of the hedonistic LA scene, but the gun incident was too much. Lennon and Spector had indeed fucked their chances at A&M. After a short break, recording resumed at Record Plant West. After three days (December 3, 11, and 14) everything came to an abrupt end. Spector had disappeared and the tapes with him.

Lennon didn't know it, but Spector had removed the tapes from the studio each night and taken them home with him. He then made a series of bizarre claims. First, he said that the studio had burned down. Next, he said that he had the John Dean Watergate tapes and that his house was surrounded. Finally, that he'd been involved in a serious car accident. The sessions were over and the project on hold until the tapes could be recovered. However, the chaos continued.

Looking for something to do, Lennon offered to produce an album for Harry Nilsson. The sessions for *Pussy Cats* were no less chaotic than they had been for *Rock 'N' Roll*. The only way Lennon could finish his album was to move back to New York City. Convinced that he would never see the Spector tapes again, he began planning his next album, which he started to record in July 1974.

As fate would have it, the Spector tapes arrived out of the blue just days before Lennon entered the studio to begin work on *Walls And Bridges*. Capitol executive Al Coury had secured the tapes by paying Spector $90,000 and guaranteeing a three percent royalty on any of the tracks used. Lennon was hardly in the mood to start wading through hours of tape when he had a brand new album to record. Better to leave the Spector tapes until he'd finished work on his current project. This would have been fine, had he not agreed to include three Big Seven songs on his follow-up to *Mind Games*, which, it now turned out, would be *Walls And Bridges*. Lennon had no intention of including a batch of oldies on his new album; consequently, he was in breech of his agreement with Morris Levy, who expected to see three of his songs on John Lennon's next album.

No sooner had Lennon finished *Walls And Bridges* than he began work on completing his *Rock 'N' Roll* album. His first task was to explain to Levy the reasons behind the delay. A meeting was arranged for October 8, at which Lennon and Levy discussed the project. Lennon recalled: "Harold Seider [Lennon's lawyer] told me that Morris wasn't too happy about the situation, about me not doing the songs or whatever I was supposed to do for that agreement we had made, and he wasn't too happy about 'Ya Ya' on *Walls And Bridges*. And it would be sort of cool if I came along and explained what happened to the Spector tapes … explain what happened to the *Rock 'N' Roll* album."

During the meeting, Levy mentioned that he was developing his empire to include mail-order albums advertised on television. A lucrative business, it removed the need for distributors and retailers. The idea also appealed to Lennon, who made enquiries about selling his album through mail-order. "I was thinking perhaps I could put it straight on TV and avoid the critics and avoid going through the usual channels. And Morris told me that is what he does. … I said that's cool with me as long as it is all right with the record company." However, after he spoke to Capitol CEO Bhaskar Menon, Lennon abandoned the idea.

Lennon decided to finish his rock'n'roll album with the band he'd used for *Walls And Bridges*, some of whom had played on the Spector sessions. To keep Lennon sweet and to ensure that the album didn't drag on any longer, Levy invited him and the band to rehearse at his farm in the Catskills (about 100 miles north of New York City). Ten days after his initial meeting with Levy, Lennon and band were busy rehearsing new material to complete the album. The band set up in a high-ceilinged room in Levy's farmhouse and ran through the songs Lennon intended to record to complete the album. They also rehearsed 'C'Mon Everybody', 'Thirty Days', and 'That'll Be The Day', and played a couple of impromptu jams. The weekend over, Lennon entered the Record Plant on October 21 and in just four days cut enough material to finish the record. The John Lennon of old had returned: the New York *Rock 'N' Roll* sessions were the model of professionalism.

Jim Keltner said: "It was fantastic. … He wasn't drinking – he was very controlled during those sessions and that made a huge difference." With the exception of 'Do You Want To Dance', Lennon insisted that the band stick as close as possible to the original arrangements. Keltner: "He liked that we played the songs as faithfully as we could to the original arrangement." This was fine, providing that the original songs featured similar instrumentation to the band Lennon was recording with. When it came to recording Buddy Holly's 'Peggy Sue', keyboards man Ken Ascher pointed out that the original recording didn't have a piano on it. Lennon was typically pragmatic, as Ascher recalled. "John said never mind, make it simple and play the changes."

With work on the basic tracks finished, Lennon concentrated on editing and mixing the tracks until mid November. On November 14 he had another meeting with Levy, at which he delivered rough mixes of the work-in-progress to the publisher. Levy now had the tapes, and later he would allege that a verbal agreement was made with Lennon to issue them on his Adam VIII mail order record label.

By January 1975, the Apple/Capitol version of *Rock'N'Roll* was nearing completion. The running order had been finalised and the artwork was well on the way to being completed. Lennon had chosen a stunning black-and-white photograph taken of him in Hamburg in 1960 by Jurgen Vollmer. Beside using Vollmer's photograph for the cover, Lennon invited him to design the album package, which was originally intended as an elaborate gatefold. However, Levy's Adam VIII version of the album, titled *John Lennon Sings The Great Rock'n'Roll Hits: Roots*, was issued on February 8, ahead of Apple/Capitol's release date. Consequently, the official version was brought forward and Vollmer's grand design scrapped.

The Adam VIII version was issued in a cheap yellow cover with a poorly cropped image of Lennon on the front and advertisements for another two Adam VIII albums on the rear. It included two tracks, 'Angel Baby' and 'Be My Baby', that were cut from Lennon's version of the album (both would later be issued, on *Menlove Ave.* and the *John Lennon Anthology* respectively).

Lennon immediately issued a cease and desist notice to Adam VIII, but not before the album had been advertised on television and a slow trickle of LPs shipped through the post. Lennon, an avid collector of his own bootlegs, ordered some copies for himself. "I've sent away for the other version of the album, but they haven't arrived yet," he told *Melody Maker*. "It's almost the same, with a couple of slight differences. It'll become a collectors item, I suppose, but it's nowhere near as good." *Roots* did become a collectors' item. Only 1,270 copies of the album and 175 copies of the 8-track were shipped by Adam VIII. Within days of Levy's version being made available, the official Apple/Capitol album had hit the shops, but this didn't sell particularly well either. Capitol's first pressing of *Rock'N'Roll* was of just 2,444 LPs and 500 8-track cartridges. Although *Rock'N'Roll* eventually sold in excess of 340,000 units, it shifted considerably fewer copies than either the previous *Walls And Bridges* or the *Shaved Fish* compilation issued eight months after *Rock'N'Roll*.

With both versions of the album available, each party sued the other. Levy sued Lennon for breach of a verbal agreement, claiming $42 million in damages. Lennon sued for unauthorised use of his recordings and image. He also sued for damages, claiming that his reputation had been marred by Levy's cheap packaging. Levy's case eventually came to court on January 12 1976, but failed as Levy's lawyer caused a mistrial when he began inspecting the cover of Lennon and Ono's *Two Virgins* in front of the jury. Levy vs Lennon round two began the following day, with the same judge who had presided over the original 1973 trial for copyright infringement. This new trial ended on February 5 and Judge Griesa gave his ruling 15 days later, in Lennon's favour. He said: "I conclude on the basis of the evidence about the October 8, 1974 meeting … that no contract was entered into."

A month later, Lennon's counterclaim against Levy went to court. Lennon and his record company sued for lost income and Lennon for punitive damages for the harm that the unofficial *Roots* album had caused his reputation. Again, the case went in Lennon's favour. After Levy appealed, Lennon was eventually awarded $40,259 for lost sales, $14,567 for monies lost due to the reduced price of *Roots*, and $35,000 in punitive damages.

Rock'N'Roll songs

Lennon said: "'Be-Bop-A-Lula' was one of the first songs I ever learned, and I actually remember singing it the day I met Paul McCartney. I was singing at the church [fete] and McCartney was in the audience." Recorded by Gene Vincent in 1956, 'Be-Bop-A-Lula' became Vincent's biggest hit and signature tune. Issued by Capitol (F 3450) with 'Woman Love' in '56, it reached Number 7 in the charts. It was issued by Capitol in Britain, where it went to Number 17. The Beatles eventually met up with Vincent in Hamburg, where they performed the song regularly. A recording of the group performing the song at the Star-Club there, with Fred Fascher on vocals, was issued on *The Beatles Live At The Star-Club In Hamburg, Germany; 1962*.

(Lennon's new version was issued as a single in France, backed with 'Move Over Ms. L'. Sticking closely to Vincent's original arrangement but with additional piano, Lennon romps through this classic rocker with obvious delight. An alternative take was issued on the *John Lennon Anthology*.)

Another favourite, Lennon claimed 'Stand By Me' was "one of my big songs in the dance halls in Liverpool. That was a Ben E. King number. And the same goes for 'Be Bop A-Lula' in that I knew these songs as a child." Lennon would return to 'Stand By Me' again and again. He often jammed on the song, and he recorded an informal version during sessions for Harry Nilsson's *Pussy Cats* album with Paul McCartney, Stevie Wonder, Harry Nilsson, and Jesse Ed Davis, prior to cutting the track for *Rock 'N' Roll*.

Issued as a single, Lennon's 'Stand By Me' was a Top 20 hit in America but fared less well in Britain, where it just managed a Top 30 placing. The song was remixed for the single release, with a string overdub that doubled the organ part. It was reissued by Capitol on its Starline imprint (6244) on April 4 1977, backed with 'Woman Is The Nigger Of The World', while the album version was issued in 1988 as a promotional 12-inch single with purple Capitol labels (SPRO-79453). Touted as the "new single from the album *Imagine: John Lennon*", it was never issued commercially.

Next on *Rock 'N' Roll* comes a medley of two songs originally recorded by Little Richard in 1956, 'Rip It Up / Ready Teddy'. Like Gene Vincent, Little Richard was a huge influence on The Beatles (and again, the band were personally introduced to him in Hamburg). Both songs were originally issued by Richard as a single, which gave him a Top 30 hit and million seller. Lennon recorded the song because "'Ready Teddy' was a sort of guitar-type song written by Little Richard and recorded by him". (An alternative take was issued on the *John Lennon Anthology*.)

Chuck Berry's 'You Can't Catch Me' was issued by Chess (1683) in the USA in 1957 and reached Number 2 in the charts. Issued in Britain by London (HLN 8575), the single failed to chart, and although The Beatles recorded several of Berry's songs for their albums and BBC radio performances, they never got around to tackling this classic rocker. Lennon was a huge fan of Berry and got to perform with him on TV on *The Mike Douglas Show* in 1972. Lennon introduced Berry to middle America with the words: "If you tried to give rock'n'roll another name, you might call it – Chuck Berry!" However, speaking just after the release of *Rock 'N' Roll*, Lennon had little to say about the song that caused him so much trouble. "'You Can't Catch Me' was the Morris Levy song, but it was by Chuck Berry, so that was good enough reason to do it."

Fats Domino's classic 'Ain't That A Shame' was issued by Imperial (5348) in 1955. The song was a massive hit: while Fat's recording reached Number 10, Pat Boone's watered-down version hit the top spot in the USA. The song also did very good business in Britain, where it was issued by London (HLU 8173). It charted four times, once for Fats Domino, twice for Pat Boone, and once for The Four Seasons.

Lennon said: "'Ain't That a Shame' was the first rock'n'roll song I ever learned. My mother taught it to me on the banjo before I learned the guitar. Nobody else knows these reasons except me." Lennon's reading was scheduled to be issued as a single but was withdrawn at the last moment. Promotional copies of the single were issued to radio stations, and Apple issued the single in Mexico.

Originally a Number 5 US hit for Bobby Freeman, 'Do You Want To Dance' was issued on the Josie label in 1957, when Freeman was just 17 years old. It was better known in Britain through Cliff Richard's cover version, which he took to Number 2 in 1962. The song was another that Lennon often tried at jam sessions. "We [did it] at some jam sessions on the west coast," he said, "featuring numerous stars not worth mentioning the names of." He also admitted that he had tried, without much success, to get the *Rock 'N' Roll* band to play a reggae version. "'Do You Want To Dance is the only one that I messed around with a bit more. I tried to make it reggae. … This one makes you feel happy, but I don't know if it makes you want to dance, and that's the problem. It's definitely different from the original."

The second Chuck Berry song that Lennon attempted, 'Sweet Little Sixteen', was issued by Chess Records (1683) in 1957 and gave Berry his fifth million-selling single when it hit Number 2 in the charts. London issued it in Britain (HLM 8575), where it reached Number 11. The Beatles included the song in their stage repertoire, and a live recording by them appeared on *The Beatles Live At The Star-Club In Hamburg, Germany; 1962*. The group also recorded the song on July 10 1963 for the BBC, who broadcast the song on *Pop Goes The Beatles* 13 days later.

Issued in the USA on Specialty 572, Little Richard's second single was arguably his greatest and most successful. A million-seller, 'Long Tall Sally' / 'Slippin' And Slidin'' was a Number 1 single on the R&B charts and a Top 10 hit on the pop charts. 'Long Tall Sally' was equally successful in Britain, where, issued by London (HLO 8366), it reached Number 3. It was also a British hit for Pat Boone, who took it to Number 19 for two weeks, and it was covered by The Beatles and became a live favourite for them.

British pressings of the Little Richard single were backed with 'Tutti Frutti', so Lennon tracked down an import copy of the single. "The first time I heard this Little Richard track, a friend of mine imported it from Holland. It came out in Europe first," he recalled. "'Slippin' And Slidin' was the B-side of 'Long Tall Sally', which is the first Little Richard song I ever heard and was also recorded by Buddy Holly, so that covers a little of both. It was a song I knew. It was easier to do songs that I knew than trying to learn something from scratch, even if I was interested in the songs."

Another million-seller, 'Peggy Sue' was originally recorded by Buddy Holly & The Crickets and issued by Coral (60885) in America, where it went to Number 6. Issued by Coral (72293) in England, it was more successful, heading up to Number 4.

Holly's influence on The Beatles cannot be underestimated. Not only did the young Fabs spend their hard-earned cash recording one of his songs, 'That'll Be The Day' (later issued on The Beatles *Anthology 1*), Holly directly influenced their choice of band-name. Although The Beatles recorded several Holly songs during their career, they never got around to cutting 'Peggy Sue'.

It was another song etched into Lennon's consciousness, and he'd perform it for his own amusement. "I have been doing that since I started," he said. "Buddy Holly did it and, in fact, I used to sing every song that Buddy Holly put out." Paul McCartney was so impressed with Holly's songwriting that when his catalogue came up for sale, he bought it.

Next up on *Rock 'N' Roll* is a medley of songs by Sam Cooke and Little Richard. 'Bring It On Home To Me' was issued by RCA (1296) in the USA in 1962 and peaked at Number 3. 'Send Me Some Lovin'' was issued by Specialty (588) in America in 1957 as a single coupled with 'Lucille', reaching Number 27. In Britain the single was issued by London (HLO 8446), where it went to Number 7 in the charts.

Lennon said: "'Bring It On Home To Me' is one of my all-time favourite songs and, in fact, I have been quoted as saying I wish I had written it. I love it that much, and I was glad to be able to do it. 'Send Me Some Lovin'' is a similar kind of song and it was done originally by Little Richard – again, one of my favourites – and also by Buddy Holly."

Not only did Klaus Voormann play bass on the album but also he got to sing backing vocals on 'Bring It On Home To Me'. Speaking in 2001, he confirmed that Lennon was recording at lightning speed and that he was slightly nonplussed when asked to sing backing vocals on the track. "John surprised me by asking me to sing the harmony on 'Bring It On Home'. One take, and John said, 'Thank you very much' – it was good enough. He was very quick with everything."

Not only did The Beatles cover Larry Williams songs, but both Lennon and McCartney recorded his work for solo albums. 'Bony Maronie' was originally issued by Specialty (605) in the USA in 1957. A million-seller, it reached Number 18 in the charts. Issued by London (HLN 8532) in Britain, it made Number 12. Speaking about his reasons for recording the song, Lennon said: "'Bony Maronie' was one of the very earliest songs [I learned] – along with 'Be-Bop-A-Lula' – and I remember singing it the only time my mother saw me perform before she died. So I was hot on 'Bony Maronie'. That is one of the reasons. Also, I liked Larry Williams, who recorded it."

Lee Dorsey's 'Ya Ya' was a Number 1 hit on the R&B charts when issued by Fury (1053) in America in 1960. A year later, a version by Petula Clark, re-titled 'Ya Ya Twist', made the US Top 10 and went to Number 14 in Britain. The song was also a favourite with German audiences: Tony Sheridan recorded a version of the song, without The Beatles, for an EP (Polydor EPH 21485) and this Lennon reading was issued there as a single (1C 006-05 924) backed with 'Be-Bop-A-Lula'.

John had already recorded a spontaneous version of 'Ya Ya' with his son Julian and issued it on *Walls And Bridges*. As it was published by Big Seven, it was one of the songs he was obliged to record. "'Ya Ya' I did because it was Morris's and it was a good song," he explained.

Written by Lloyd Price, 'Just Because' was a truly independent record. Not only did Price write the song but also he played piano, produced the record, and issued it on his own label, Kent. Issued in early 1957, it was a sizeable regional hit before being picked up for national distribution by ABC-Paramount, who re-released the record, which climbed to Number 27 in the US charts. It was not issued in Britain.

Unlike the rest of the material recorded for *Rock 'N' Roll*, Lennon was not familiar with the song. "'Just Because' I did because Phil Spector talked me into it," he said. The combination of unfamiliarity and alcohol meant that Lennon had to re-record his vocal in New York. Indeed, an outtake from the LA sessions, issued on the remastered *Rock 'N' Roll* CD, reveals just how tired and emotional Lennon was when he recorded his vocal with Spector at the controls.

Towards the end of 'Just Because', Lennon signs off: "And so we say farewell from Record Plant East," a closing remark he later claimed was a conscious farewell to the business. Although he had plans to record a new album, it was scrapped when Ono became pregnant. In its place, Lennon issued a collection of hits and near misses. A summation of his career to that point, it was more of a semicolon than a full stop.

Rock'N'Roll data

The album was promoted with a radio spot issued to American radio stations and with trade advertisements placed in British music weeklies. Lennon also gave several interviews, played DJ at WNEW-FM in New York City, and filmed two promotional videos, of 'Stand By Me' and 'Slippin' And Slidin'', for BBC TV's *Old Grey Whistle Test*.

Apple issued promotional copies of 'Slippin' And Slidin'' (P-1883) to radio stations along with 'Ain't That A Shame' (P-1883). Although the American release of this coupling was cancelled, 'Slippin' And Slidin'' / 'Ain't That A Shame' was released in Mexico (Apple 7755). France issued 'Be-Bop-A-Lula' / 'Move Over Ms. L' (2C 004-05799), while 'Ya Ya' / 'Be-Bop-A-Lula' was issued in Germany (1C 006-05 924) and Japan (EAR-10827).

Apple issued *Rock'N'Roll* in the USA on February 17, although as the album was rush-released a few stores may have received copies earlier (and some sources suggest that the album was available as early as February 5). British pressings matched the American version of the album.

US copies were produced with two label variations. The first has a light green Apple label with a large '1' at 9 o'clock and the two song titles above the spindle hole; the second has a dark green Apple label with 'STEREO' and a small 'Side 1' below at 9 o'clock and three song titles above the spindle hole.

Capitol reissued the album in 1978 with purple Capitol labels and in October 1980 at budget price with green labels (SN-15969). The album was also issued at budget price in Britain by EMI subsidiary Music For Pleasure in November 1981 (MFP 50522). As with *Imagine*, *Rock'N'Roll* was reissued as part of EMI's centenary celebrations. Reissued in early 1997, the LP (LPCENT9) featured original packaging, 180 gram virgin vinyl, heavy quality cover, and analogue cutting from analogue tape. The album was issued on 8-track cartridge in Britain (8X-PCS 7169) and the USA (8XK-3419).

EMI and Capitol both issued *Rock'N'Roll* on CD (CDP 7 46707 2) on May 18 1987. A remixed and remastered edition of the CD (542 4252) with four bonus tracks was issued on September 27 2004 (UK) and 2 November 2004 (USA).

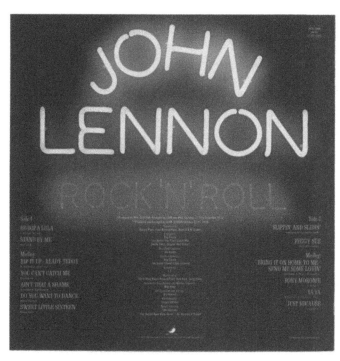

'PHILADELPHIA FREEDOM' / 'I SAW HER STANDING THERE'
THE ELTON JOHN BAND / THE ELTON JOHN BAND FEATURING JOHN LENNON WITH THE MUSCLE SHOALS HORNS

UK release February 28 1975; DJM DJS 354; chart high No.12.
US release February 24 1975; MCA MCA 40364; chart high No.1.

'I Saw Her Standing There' (Lennon, McCartney)
John Lennon (vocals, guitar), Elton John (vocals, piano), Davey Johnstone (guitar), Dee Murray (bass), Nigel Olsson (drums), Ray Cooper (percussion), Muscle Shoals Horns (brass). Live recording at Madison Square Garden, New York City, NY, USA.
Produced by Gus Dudgeon.

'I SAW HER STANDING THERE'

Lennon's first public appearance in a little over three years was as a surprise guest at Elton John's sell-out concert at Madison Square Garden in New York City on November 28 1974. Elton had asked Lennon to appear with him if 'Whatever Gets You Thru The Night' reached Number 1 (Elton had played and sang on it). "I said sure," Lennon recalled, "not thinking in a million years it was gonna get to Number 1."

On November 24 1974, four days before the concert, the two Johns rehearsed with Elton's band at the Record Plant East in New York City. Lennon was to perform three songs, 'Lucy In The Sky With Diamonds', 'Whatever Gets You Thru The Night', and 'I Saw Her Standing There'. Elton originally suggested that Lennon perform 'Imagine', but Lennon rejected the idea, favouring 'I Saw Her Standing There', a song from The Beatles' debut album.

This may have been an attempt by Lennon to publicly re-establish his fractured relationship with Paul McCartney, whose song it was. Lennon intended to visit McCartney in early 1975 while McCartney was recording with Wings in New Orleans. Lennon never made the trip, but this gesture was the next best thing.

Come the day of the concert at Madison Square Garden, Lennon was a nervous wreck. Apple man Tony King recalled that Lennon was constantly running to the toilet because he was so nervous. He hadn't appeared on a concert stage for over two years, and this would be the first time without Ono at his side. Although he was on a roll, with a Number 1 album and single (*Walls And Bridges* and 'Whatever Gets You Thru The Night'), Lennon was unsure how the audience would react when he walked on stage. "I was quite astonished that the crowd was so nice to me," he said, "because I was only judging by what the papers said about me, and I thought I may as well not be around, you know? And the crowd was fantastic." Speaking after the show, Lennon said jokingly: "I had a great time, but I wouldn't want to do it for a living. Actually it was fantastic, so emotional. Everyone was crying and everything."

At the time, Lennon was still separated from Ono. Although he didn't know it, she was in the audience. He said later that if he'd known she was there, he wouldn't have been able to go on. Their meeting after the show was a turning point. Within a few months they were back together as if nothing had happened.

The Beatles originally recorded 'I Saw Her Standing There' at Abbey Road Studios on February 11 1963. Although Lennon later suggested that the song was entirely McCartney's work, it was an early collaboration, written some time in 1962. McCartney supplied the lyrics and initial musical theme; Lennon helped finish the song. Although Lennon said that he had never sung the song, what he meant was that he had not sung the lead vocal. Lennon is vocally present on The Beatles' original recording, providing harmonies to McCartney's lead.

Several live recordings by The Beatles have been issued. *The Beatles Live At the BBC* features a version recorded at the Playhouse Theatre on October 20 1963 and originally broadcast on *Easy Beat. Anthology 1* features a live recording made at Karlaplansstudion, Stockholm, Sweden on October 24 1963, and Paul McCartney included a performance on his 2003 live album *Back In The World*.

'I Saw Her Standing There' data
Lennon's version was first issued as the B-side of this Elton John single, 'Philadelphia Freedom'. All three songs performed by Lennon at Madison Square Garden on November 28 were issued as a 7-inch EP on March 13 1981. They were issued for the first time on CD on the *Lennon* boxed set, in 1990, and in a remixed form on Elton John's *Here And There* live album in 1996.

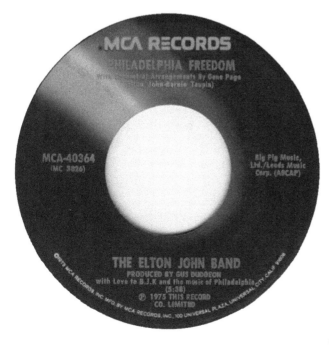

'STAND BY ME' / 'MOVE OVER MS. L'
JOHN LENNON

UK release April 18 1975; Apple R 6005; chart high No. 30.
US release March 10 1975; Apple APPLE 1881; chart high No. 20.

'Move Over Ms. L' (Lennon)

John Lennon (vocals, guitar), Jesse Ed Davis (guitar), Eddie Mottau (acoustic guitar), Ken Ascher (piano), Klaus Voormann (bass), Arthur Jenkins (percussion), Little Big Horns: Bobby Keys, Steve Madaio, Howard Johnson, Ron Aprea, Frank Vicari (horns), Jim Keltner (drums). Recorded at Record Plant East, New York   City, NY, USA. Produced by John Lennon.

'MOVE OVER MS. L'

Originally intended for *Walls And Bridges*, 'Move Over Ms. L' was an up-tempo rocker that saw Lennon poke fun at his estranged wife and several of life's institutions. He wrote the song and recorded home demos some time in 1974. Lennon then gave the song to his erstwhile drinking buddy and drummer with The Who, Keith Moon. He completed his album, *Both Sides Of The Moon*, just after Lennon finished recording *Walls And Bridges*. As Moon's arrangement is close to Lennon's, it's possible that Lennon sent him a rough mix of the track as a reference rather than one of his demos.

Moon's version beat Lennon's to the record stores, but only just. Lennon had planned to include 'Move Over Ms. L' on *Walls And Bridges* but removed it at the last minute. Moon's version hit the shops in April 1975 and was also issued as the B-side of his single 'Solid Gold' (the A-side of which featured another ex-Beatle, Ringo Starr).

An alternative version recorded by Lennon during the *Walls And Bridges* sessions was issued on the *John Lennon Anthology*.

'*Stand By Me*' data

Apple issued 'Stand By Me' with generic Apple labels in the USA and the British single was issued a little over a month later. American pressings were issued with two label variants. The first has a dark green Apple label; song title with composer credit and artist's name centre bottom; 'From the LP "ROCK 'N' ROLL" SK-3914' at 11 o'clock; 'STEREO' at 9 o'clock; catalogue number at eight o'clock; publisher, intro, and total playing time and producer credit on the right side of the label.

The second US label variant has a light green Apple label with the song title and composer credit centre bottom in bold; 'From the LP "ROCK 'N' ROLL" SK-3914' at 11 o'clock; 'STEREO' at 10 o'clock; the catalogue number at 9 o'clock; publisher, intro, and total playing time and producer credit on the right side of the label.

American promotional singles (P-1881) were issued with light green Apple labels with 'from the LP "ROCK 'N' ROLL" SK-3914' at 11 o'clock, 'MONO' at 10 o'clock, catalogue number at 9 o'clock, 'NOT FOR SALE' at 8 o'clock; publisher, introm and total playing time and producer credit on the right side of the label. The song title and composer credit appear centre bottom in bold with a black star placed just above and to the left of the song title.

Capitol reissued 'Stand By Me' (6244) on its Starline label on April 4 1977, backed with 'Woman Is The Nigger Of The World'. Four variations of this single were issued: with tan Starline label, round Capitol 'C' logo, 'All Rights...' in white or black on label perimeter, publishing credit to 'Unichappel Music'; tan Starline label, round Capitol 'C' logo, 'All Rights...' in white or black on label perimeter, publishing credit to 'Belinda Music'; blue Starline label; black/colour band Starline label with perimeter print in colour band.

First pressings of the British single credit the songwriters as King–Glick and the publisher as Trio Music Ltd. Later pressings have a light green label and credit the songwriters as King–Leiber–Stoller and the publisher as Carlin Mus. Corp. British promotional copies of the single replicate the commercial issue with the addition of a large 'A' at 11 o'clock, 'DEMO RECORD NOT FOR SALE' in the centre of the label, and '(18.4.75)' at 5 o'clock.

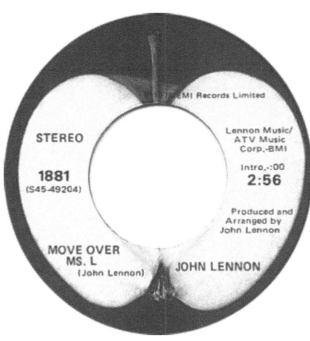

164

'IMAGINE' / 'WORKING CLASS HERO'
JOHN LENNON

UK release October 24 1975; Apple R 6009; chart high No.6 (re-enters December 27 1980 chart high No.1; re-enters December 10 1988 chart high No.45; re-enters December 25 1999 chart high No.3).

'IMAGINE'

'Imagine' was issued as a single in 1971 except in Britain. Bob Mercer, an EMI executive (and later a director), eventually suggested that Lennon issue the song as a single in his home country, primarily to promote his 'best of' album, *Shaved Fish*. A shrewd move, it gave Lennon a much needed hit and the attendant publicity helped push *Shaved Fish* into the Top 10.

The single, Lennon's last for Apple, was issued with generic Apple labels and picture sleeve. Apple issued demonstration copies of the single with 'DEMO RECORD NOT FOR SALE' above the spindle hole and a large 'A' at 2 o'clock, with the date 24.10.75 below.

'Imagine' became Lennon's most successful single ever. In the weeks following his death in 1980, demand for 'Imagine' was such that it reached Number 1. The song was reissued in 1999, when Lennon's lyric was voted Britain's favourite in a BBC poll as part of National Poetry Day.

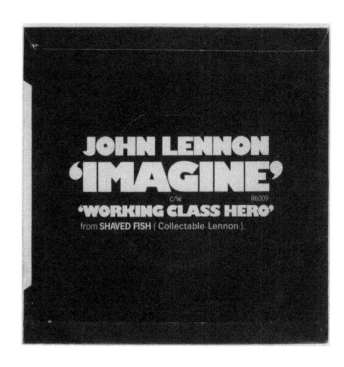

SHAVED FISH
JOHN LENNON/PLASTIC ONO BAND

Side 1 'Give Peace A Chance', 'Cold Turkey', 'Instant Karma!', 'Power To The People', 'Mother', 'Woman Is The Nigger Of The World'.
Side 2 'Imagine', 'Whatever Gets You Thru The Night', 'Mind Games', '#9 Dream', 'Happy Xmas (War Is Over)', 'Give Peace A Chance' (Reprise).

UK release October 24 1975; LP Apple PCS 7173; 8-track cartridge Apple 8X-PCS 7173; chart high No.8 (re-enters January 17 1981 chart high No.11).
US release October 24 1975; LP Apple SW 3421; 8-track cartridge Apple 8XW-3421; chart high No.12.

SHAVED FISH

Shaved Fish was Lennon's last public musical statement for five years. Speaking with Andy Peebles in 1980, he mused on whether or not *Shaved Fish* had been a farewell of sorts. "That was another thing – was it a subconscious move? Did I know I wasn't going to be on Capitol and EMI any more?" With The Beatles' contract with EMI about to expire, Lennon was free to sign with whoever he liked. However, EMI retained the right to issue compilation albums of their own design, which they did with undignified haste. Both group and solo compilations began to leak from EMI like secrets from a government department. Ringo Starr's *Blast From Your Past* followed *Shaved Fish* on December 12 and George Harrison's *The Best Of* was issued a little over a year later. *Wings Greatest* followed in December 1978.

Although Lennon had planned to record an album of new material to follow *Rock 'N' Roll*, when Yoko Ono became pregnant he abandoned the idea and began work on this summation of his solo career. The task should have been easy, but when Lennon began putting the album together he discovered that several of his master tapes were missing. "What I found out was, when I went to look for the 'Cold Turkey' master tapes, nobody knew where they were. I had to use dubs of 'Power To The People' because the tapes were gone. Nobody could give a damn at the record companies because they weren't … you know, that big. Big enough for them to be interested. … I thought if I don't put this package together, some of the work is just going to go … they will be lost forever." That several of the tracks were dubs, presumably from vinyl sources, didn't matter for the vinyl release, but it did when the album was mastered for CD (see below).

Shaved Fish data
Apple issued *Shaved Fish* with generic Apple labels and a cover designed by Roy Kohara with illustrations by Michael Bryan. An inner sleeve with lyrics to Lennon's songs was also included.

US copies of the LP were produced with three label variations. The first has a light green Apple label with 'STEREO' and a small 'Side 1' below at 9 o'clock, and one song title (Medley) above the spindle hole. The second has all song titles below the spindle hole, and the third also has all song titles below the spindle hole and a large '1' at 9 o'clock.

Capitol reissued the album in 1978 with purple Capitol labels in covers with either an Apple or Capitol logo. The album was issued again by Capitol with black/colour band labels, also with covers with either an Apple or Capitol logo. The album was issued once more in 1983 with purple Capitol labels and covers with a Capitol logo. Greek pressings were issued with a gatefold sleeve. In Japan, *Shaved Fish* was reissued by Odeon (EAS-81457) on green vinyl.

The album was issued on 8-track by EMI (8X-PCS 7173) and Capitol (8XW-3421). *Shaved Fish* was the last Lennon album to be issued on 8-track in Britain.

When EMI began to issue The Beatles and related solo albums on CD, the company spent considerable time and effort on mastering The Beatles' CDs, even if it skimped on the packaging, but paid less attention to solo albums. Original copies of *Shaved Fish* were manufactured in Japan, a country known for its high manufacturing standards, and shipped to Britain where they were married up with locally-printed inserts. *Shaved Fish* was issued on CD in Britain on May 25 1987. However, it was found to suffer from poor sound quality. Distribution was halted and the CD remastered. The new 'improved' version was issued in Britain on December 7 1987 and in the USA on May 17 1988.

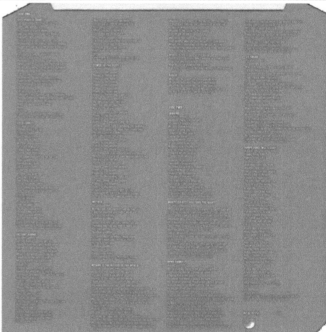

Above: UK 1980s pressing.

1976 to 1980: Cleanup Time

'(JUST LIKE) STARTING OVER' / 'KISS KISS KISS'
JOHN LENNON / YOKO ONO
UK release October 24 1980; Geffen K 79186; chart high No.1.
US release October 20 1980; Geffen GEF 49594; chart high No.1.

'(Just Like) Starting Over' (Lennon)
John Lennon (vocals, guitar), Earl Slick (guitar), Hugh McCracken (guitar), Tony Levin (bass), George Small (keyboards), Arthur Jenkins (percussion), Michelle Simpson, Cassandra Wooten, Cheryl Mason Jacks, Eric Troyer (backing vocals), Andy Newmark (drums).
'Kiss Kiss Kiss' (Ono)
Yoko Ono (vocals), Earl Slick (guitar), Hugh McCracken (guitar), Tony Levin (bass), George Small (keyboards), Arthur Jenkins (percussion), Andy Newmark (drums).

Both recorded at Hit Factory, New York City, NY, USA, and mixed at Record Plant, New York City. Both produced by John Lennon, Yoko Ono, and Jack Douglas.

'(JUST LIKE) STARTING OVER'

Lennon's first single in five years and the first new, original material in almost six was much anticipated. News of Lennon's return to the recording studio made headlines around the world. Music papers were buzzing with speculation. What would he and Yoko Ono have to say? More importantly, how would they say it? The answer came in the form of '(Just Like) Starting Over', a retro-tinged rocker that, after Lennon's five-year silence, was a slight disappointment.

Many expected him to return with an album of blistering rockers. He'd been working with producer Jack Douglas, known for records with Cheap Trick and Aerosmith, but Lennon was playing it safe. This was, after all, his big comeback, and he wasn't going to blow it. Furthermore, Lennon was creeping into middle age and had mellowed considerably. But then so had his fellow ex-Beatles. Compare Lennon's slick craftsmanship with that of McCartney's or Harrison's and one finds Lennon more in step with his ex-bandmates than ever. He may have enjoyed listening to punk rock, but he sure as hell wasn't going to record any.

The Lennons signed with Geffen Records on September 22 1980, and the single was issued a little over four weeks later. There was no promotional video to accompany the release, although John and Yoko were filmed walking through Central Park and pretending to make love. They were also filmed in the studio, but Lennon was apparently unhappy with the footage and it wasn't used. (Footage of Lennon miming guitar to 'I'm Losing You' eventually surfaced in 2016 and was widely circulated.) US record stores received cardboard countertop browser boxes to display the single; British shops were issued with a colourful but plain 21-inch by 8-inch poster.

'(Just Like) Starting Over' was initially more successful in America than in Britain. In the week beginning December 5, the single sat at Number 7 in the US *Cash Box* charts but had started to make its way down the British charts. There it peaked at Number 9, dropping to 11 in the first week of December. However, after Lennon's death on December 8, demand for the single pushed it to the top of the charts on both sides of the Atlantic. By Friday 12, EMI had received orders of 200,000 for both 'Imagine' and 'Happy Xmas (War Is Over)'. Although no figures were given by Warner Bros, they too must have received similar orders for '(Just Like) Starting Over'. The single spent one week at Number 1 on the British charts, being replaced by 'Imagine', and five weeks at the top of the US charts.

Lennon suggested that all the songs on *Double Fantasy* came to him in a rush of inspiration, but the truth was that he'd laboured over '(Just Like) Starting Over' for weeks or maybe months. He developed it from several unfinished fragments that he brought together to form the finished song. This was nothing new, of course: Lennon and McCartney often combined uncompleted bits and pieces to finish a composition. Lennon had reworked several solo songs, but rarely to this extent.

It began as 'My Life', which shared melodic elements with the slow introduction used for the finished item. Over the following weeks, he worked several melodic fragments into new compositions that, when combined, would constitute '(Just Like) Starting Over'. Playing with the melody of Buddy Holly's 'Raining In My Heart', he reworked 'My Life' into another uncompleted song, 'I Watch Your Face'; like 'My Life', this had a melancholic tone.

Lennon then worked on a song called 'Don't Be Crazy', which, with a little revision, would become the verse of '(Just Like) Starting Over'. Finally, he started on 'The Worst Is Over', which would form the chorus. All that remained was for him to combine the various elements into one song, which he did once he'd returned from a holiday in Bermuda. Back home at the Dakota in New York City, he recorded demos of the completed song just days before returning to the studio.

The theme was emotional, spiritual, and creative rebirth. His first solo album had been introduced with the tolling of funeral bells; now, to symbolise this new beginning, he used four rings from a small Japanese wishing bell. However, Lennon's rebirth was firmly rooted in the past. Five years earlier he'd said goodbye with an album of rock'n'roll standards. His return was marked by another dose of rock'n'roll, this time of his own making. Influenced in part by Roy Orbison's 'Only The Lonely', Lennon shaped a comeback single that was as much about his past as it was about the present.

He talked to Andy Peebles about the song's origins. "It was really called 'Starting Over' but, while we're making it, people kept putting things out with the same title. You know, there was a country and western hit called 'Starting Over', so I added 'Just Like' at the last minute. And to me it was like going back to 15 and singing à la Presley. All the time I was referring to John [Smith], the engineer, here in the room I was referring to Elvis Orbison. It's kinda like … 'Only The Lonely', you know … a kind of parody but not really parody."

Not only was this rock'n'roll tempered by parody, but also by age. While there were flashes of the Lennon of old, '(Just Like) Starting Over' revealed that John had developed a little musical middle-age spread.

Ono's 'Kiss Kiss Kiss' is more musically and lyrically adventurous than Lennon's A-side. Although it's more adult-orientated rock than avant-garde, it combined elements from both genres. Ono suggested that the song was about liberation and having the courage to express vulnerability rather than mask it. However, when it came to recording her vocal, she was more than a little embarrassed by her display of openness. The song ends with her double-tracked, recorded at the Hit Factory on September 19, simulating an orgasm, which she found embarrassing to perform in front of a group of men. "I started to do it," she recalled, "and then I suddenly looked and all these engineers were all looking, and I thought, I can't do that, you know? So I said, well, turn off all the lights and put the screen around me, and I did it that way."

'(Just Like) Starting Over' data

The single was issued on both sides of the Atlantic with generic Geffen labels and a black-and-white picture sleeve. Promotional copies featuring mono/stereo mixes of the A-side were issued in America. Canadian promotional copies of the single featured the commercial A and B-sides but had 'PROMOTIONAL COPY' printed on the label at 2 o'clock. The single was also issued as a 12-inch promotional record (PRO-A-919) featuring an extended coda.

'(Just Like) Starting Over' was reissued in the USA on June 5 1981 backed with 'Woman' (GGEF 0408). Warner Bros, distributors of Geffen Records, had a policy of combining hit singles to create double A-side oldies. They issued this pressing with six label variants. Three had a cream label: the first with a thin Geffen Records logo and small perimeter print; the second with bold logo and small print; and the third with bold logo without perimeter print. The others have a black label: the first with silver and white print, issued as part of the Back To Back *Hits* series; the second with the same print but a one-inch by half-inch white box on the label that has no UPC symbol; and the third is the same as this but the box has a UPC symbol.

In 1994, Capitol's Special Markets Division issued '(Just Like) Starting Over' (72438-57894-7) as a jukebox single. Pressed on blue vinyl, it was backed with 'Watching The Wheels'. In 2000, '(Just Like) Starting Over' was issued as part of a CD sampler (DPRO 7087) to promote the remastered versions of *John Lennon/Plastic Ono Band* and *Double Fantasy*.

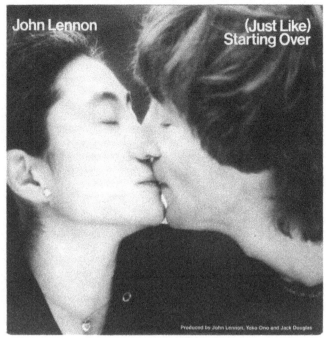

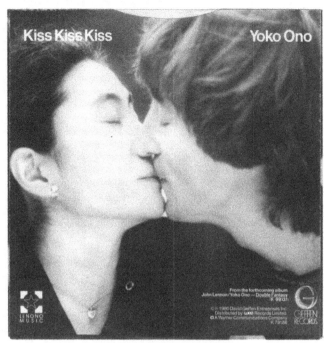

DOUBLE FANTASY
JOHN LENNON AND YOKO ONO

Side 1 '(Just Like) Starting Over', 'Kiss Kiss Kiss', 'Cleanup Time', 'Give Me Something', 'I'm Losing You', 'I'm Moving On', 'Beautiful Boy (Darling Boy)'.
Side 2 'Watching The Wheels', 'Yes, I'm Your Angel', 'Woman', 'Beautiful Boys', 'Dear Yoko', 'Every Man Has A Woman Who Loves Him', 'Hard Times Are Over'.

UK release November 17 1980; Geffen K 99131; chart high No.1.
US release November 17 1980; LP Geffen GHS 2001; 8-track cartridge Geffen GEF-W8-2001; chart high No.1.

'Cleanup Time' (Lennon)
Personnel as 'I'm Losing You' plus Howard Johnson, Grant Hunderford, John Parran, Seldon Powell, George 'Young' Opalisky, Roger Rosenberg, David Tofani, Ronald Tooley (horns).
'Give Me Something' (Ono)
Personnel as 'I'm Moving On' plus Michelle Simpson, Cassandra Wooten, Cheryl Mason Jacks, Eric Troyer (backing vocals).
'I'm Losing You' (Lennon)
John Lennon (vocals, guitar), Earl Slick (guitar), Hugh McCracken (guitar), Tony Levin (bass), George Small (keyboards), Arthur Jenkins (percussion), Andy Newmark (drums).
'I'm Moving On' (Ono)
Yoko Ono (vocals), Earl Slick (guitar), Hugh McCracken (guitar), Tony Levin (bass), George Small (keyboards), Arthur Jenkins (percussion), Andy Newmark (drums).
'Beautiful Boy (Darling Boy)' (Lennon)
Personnel as 'I'm Losing You' plus Robert Greenridge (steel drum).
'Watching The Wheels' (Lennon)
Personnel as 'I'm Losing You' except Lennon (vocals, keyboards) plus Matthew Cunningham (hammer dulcimer), Michelle Simpson, Cassandra Wooten, Cheryl Mason Jacks, Eric Troyer (backing vocals).
'Yes, I'm Your Angel' (Ono)
Personnel as 'I'm Moving On'.
'Woman' (Lennon)
Personnel as 'I'm Losing You' plus Michelle Simpson, Cassandra Wooten, Cheryl Mason Jacks, Eric Troyer (backing vocals).
'Beautiful Boys' (Ono)
Personnel as 'I'm Moving On'.
'Dear Yoko' (Lennon)
Personnel as 'I'm Losing You' plus Michelle Simpson, Cassandra Wooten, Cheryl Mason Jacks, Eric Troyer (backing vocals).
'Every Man Has A Woman Who Loves Him' (Ono)
Personnel as 'I'm Moving On' plus Lennon (vocals).
'Hard Times Are Over' (Ono)
Personnel as 'I'm Moving On' plus Lennon (vocals), Benny Cummings Singer – Kings Temple Choir (choir).

All recorded at Hit Factory, New York City, NY, USA, plus 'Give Me Something' and 'Watching The Wheels' mixed at Record Plant, New York City. All produced by John Lennon, Yoko Ono, and Jack Douglas.

DOUBLE FANTASY

With the birth of Sean Taro Ono Lennon in 1975, John Lennon abandoned record making and released the *Shaved Fish* as a symbolic summation of his career to date. Besides announcing Sean's birth and John's retirement, it drew a line under his career. The dream was well and truly over, but the myth persisted. If anything, Lennon's withdrawal from music making created more column inches than if he'd remained active.

Nevertheless, the birth of his second son gave him the chance to distance himself from the rock'n'roll lifestyle he'd helped define and to consider his future.

Lennon was determined to devote the next five years of his life to bringing up Sean. However, like anyone who finds themselves suddenly removed from the things that give their life meaning, he quickly grew bored. Fatherhood was great for a few months, but the urge to create continued to gnaw away at him and, although he abandoned the recording studio, he continued to write. However, with no specific project in mind, the best he could come up with was a number of half-finished sketches. Far from feeling contented, Lennon sank into a deep depression that manifested itself in his songs as a sense of aimless drifting.

In the summer of 1976, Lennon revived a song he'd started six years earlier. 'Sally And Billy', the story of a couple unable to decide what to do with their lives, mirrored his own sense of purposelessness. Speaking in 1980, he confirmed that he found it hard to cope with his self-imposed silence. "The first half year or year I had this sort of feeling in the back of my mind that I ought to [write] and I'd go through periods of panic … I mean, you know, I just didn't exist any more."

Lennon's early house-husband period saw him returning to the kind of introspective probing that he'd engaged in immediately after The Beatles stopped touring. The only difference was that in 1966 he'd set out on a psychedelic voyage of discovery. What he discovered now was gloomy indeed, and things weren't about to get any better. John and Yoko took an extended holiday to Japan, to meet Yoko's relatives. Feeling increasingly alienated, Lennon allegedly told John Green: "I'm dead. Yoko killed me; this placed killed me." While in Tokyo, he wrote 'Mirror Mirror', a searching piece of self-analysis that alluded to the emptiness he was experiencing. Although he recognised the problem, any solution seemed out of reach. 'Mirror Mirror' offers no hope of redemption, only total abjection.

From the same period came 'I Don't Want To Face It', a song that with a little revision would appear on the posthumous *Milk And Honey*. Like 'Mirror Mirror', it reveals his troubled mind, unable to decide which path to take. Life at the Dakota was proving to be less emotionally and creatively satisfying than Lennon had hoped for. Nevertheless, he continued to amass demos of new songs, many of which formed the basis of *Double Fantasy* and its follow-up, *Milk And Honey*.

In an attempt to ease her husband out of his depression, Ono sent Lennon on a series of holidays. These trips took him on another voyage of self-discovery. For the first time in years, he had to fend for himself. A trip to Hong Kong was a revelation. Lennon found that he was free to walk the streets and enjoyed the experience of being one of the masses. "I wandered around Hong Kong at dawn, alone, and it was a thrill," he said. "It was rediscovering a feeling that I once had as a youngster walking the mountains of Scotland with my auntie. This is the feeling that makes you write or paint."

Further trips followed: South Africa; Egypt. But the turning point came with a holiday to Bermuda. By the time Lennon visited the island in June 1980 his depression had cleared and his thoughts turned to recording again. Further into that summer, Lennon had accumulated a number of incomplete songs, all of which needed a great deal of work before they could be recorded. With his five-year sabbatical drawing to a close, he set about reworking what songs he had, writing new ones, and planning his next album.

A visit to a nightclub, his first in years, exposed Lennon to contemporary pop music. Citing the B-52s' 'Rock Lobster' as a minor epiphany, Lennon convinced himself that the time was right to make his return. "It's time to get out the old axe and wake the wife up!" he told *Rolling Stone*. However, Lennon was keeping his plans close to his chest. When a *New Musical Express* reporter spotted him at Disco 40 and asked if he was planning to make a comeback, Lennon said: "You can't do it if it's not there." In fact it was there, if not in a usable form.

Now that he had an objective in mind, Lennon set about finishing the songs he'd accumulated with an energy he hadn't possessed in years. He cut a number of demos in Bermuda, laying the foundation for *Double Fantasy*, intending them to be a reference source for both the producer and musicians. The producer would be issued with a set prior to entering the studio and Lennon often referred back to them while recording. It was also while he was in Bermuda that Lennon found the title of the new album. While visiting a garden, he came across a variety of freesia. The plant in question was called Double Fantasy, a name that neatly summed up the album's theme of "sexual fantasies between men and women". The fact that the album was almost devoid of songs relating to this theme made no odds. It was a good title and that's what mattered.

While Lennon was putting the finishing touches to his songs, Ono contacted Jack Douglas, who had previously worked for the Lennons as an engineer, to ask if he would like to co-produce the album. Initially, Douglas wanted sole production rights, but consented to a co-production role when Ono agreed to increase his fee. Douglas assembled the band within days of signing with John and Yoko but was sworn to secrecy. The band he assembled was issued with copies of Lennon's demo tape and accompanied Douglas to the

Dakota to rehearse with Lennon before moving to S.I.R. (Studio Instrument Rentals) rehearsal studio in New York to work on the songs without Lennon—Douglas deputising for Lennon. Douglas recorded the band's rehearsals and played them to Lennon who would suggest any changes he wanted made to the arrangements.

While Douglas claims to have selected the band, Lennon maintained that it was he and Ono who picked the musicians, using numerology. What's most likely is that Douglas suggested musicians, which Lennon and Ono then had checked out by their numerologist. Surprisingly, all the names Douglas put forward checked out. The only concession was guitarist Hugh McCracken, whom Lennon insisted on hiring as he wanted to work with at least one musician he had worked with before. Lennon also revealed that he had originally wanted Willie Weeks to play bass, but he was booked for a George Harrison session and unavailable. Nevertheless, Lennon was delighted with Weeks's replacement, Tony Levin, whom he considered the best musician in the group.

Recording proper began three days later on Thursday 7th at New York City's Hit Factory studio. Once Lennon walked into the studio it was business as usual. He quickly established the ground rules: simplicity was the key, there would be no slacking, and there was no room for prima donnas. Just as with *Imagine*, his goal was to record two songs a day, a target they achieved with relative ease. In the first three days, the band cut six songs and completed a total of 22 basic tracks in a little under two weeks. Fourteen songs were selected for *Double Fantasy*; the remainder were earmarked for *Milk And Honey*.

The Lennons' recording sessions were models of efficiency and pragmatism. John and Yoko quickly adopted a routine where Ono worked during the day and Lennon in the late evening. This was not simply an effective use of expensive studio time, but, if Douglas is to be believed, it was the only way Lennon and Ono could work without constantly arguing. Although *Double Fantasy* was a collaborative project, Douglas maintains that the pair did not work well together in the studio. His solution was to think of the record as two solo projects.

"Those two could not work at the same time." he recalled. "If she were there, it would have been impossible. It was just impossible. I had to treat that album as two separate albums. I know that they're both artists on the record, but I had to treat it as a John album and as a Yoko album. My routine was like this. 9:00am, breakfast with John. Yoko from 11:00am, and then John would go home. Yoko from 11 o'clock until about 6:30pm. And then she would go home. John would come in at 7:00pm and would work until about one or two in the morning. I never worked with both of them at the same time. It was impossible. Because she drove John crazy." There are, however, a number of photographs that show the couple working together in the studio, so it couldn't have been all bad. But there is also evidence that Lennon was quick to lose his temper with Ono.

Lennon always recorded quickly, and this time was no exception. He and Ono drove themselves and the band hard, and it's to everyone's credit that they maintained such high standards. However, on this occasion Lennon had an ulterior motive: he was picking up the bill. They had decided to self-finance the album and then offer the finished item to record companies. Lennon didn't want to get himself in the kind of contractual tangle that had beset his earlier career; by financing the project themselves, the Lennons remained in control. Several major labels approached them, but it was the newly formed Geffen Records who won the contract.

David Geffen was making a comeback of his own. Returning to the music business after a cancer scare, he was in the process of setting up his label just as the Lennons were recording their album. He sent them a telegram, with little hope of a response, asking if they would be interested in working with him. Geffen's luck was in, and within weeks of his making contact, he had a contract drawn up and signed by the Lennons. One reason Lennon and Ono signed with Geffen was that, unlike the majors, who were put off by Ono's involvement, Geffen didn't ask to hear the album in advance. Geffen also had the advantage of being an independent, albeit with backing from the massive Warner Bros corporation, who would deal with the Lennons face to face.

The basic tracks were completed by August 19, and by the 25th a provisional track listing had been compiled. Overdub sessions were booked for September, with mixing commencing later in the month at New York's Record Plant. Lennon and Ono then returned to the Hit Factory in October for more mixing, which was completed on the 13th, and the final master was compiled seven days later.

The pair's first album together for eight years marked the end of a self-imposed five-year silence. Their return to public discourse would be made through a series of musical dialogues, of which *Double Fantasy* was the first. Just as their first collaboration, *Two Virgins*, had marked an emblematic beginning, *Double Fantasy* signified rebirth. Lennon was obviously energised by his return and gave several comprehensive interviews to promote the album.

Interviewed by RKO Radio, he said he felt that *Double Fantasy* was "just the start and this was our first album. I know we have worked together before, and we've even made albums before, but we feel like this is the first album". Fuelled by a burst of creative energy, he had high hopes for the album. They both thought the album a Number 1 record – but although it sold well, it looked doubtful that *Double Fantasy* would top the charts. As most of their promotional activities were concentrated on the US market, the album at first performed better there than in Britain.

The record did not go down well with British critics. *Melody Maker* described it as "a god awful yawn! The whole thing positively reeks of an indulgent sterility". *NME* described it thus: '*Double Fantasy* is right: a fantasy made for two... It sounds like a great life. But unfortunately it makes a lousy record." Lennon was particularly keen for the album to succeed in Britain, but within weeks of its release it was slipping down the charts. By the second week of December, *Double Fantasy* had dropped to number 46 in the British charts. Unbelievably, acts like Barry Manilow and Ken Dodd (a Liverpudlian comedian) were outperforming John and Yoko. The success that Lennon hoped for in Britain was only achieved posthumously. The week after his death, *Double Fantasy* climbed to Number 2; the following week it was Number 1.

Double Fantasy songs

As with '(Just Like) Starting Over', 'Cleanup Time' explored the notion of rebirth. This song was inspired by a phone conversation Lennon had with producer Jack Douglas before the two had properly met. "I was in Bermuda," Lennon recalled, "and we were talking about the 1970s and that. We were talking about cleanin' up and gettin' out of drugs and alcohol and those kind of things – not me personally, but people in general. He said, 'Well, it's cleanup time, right?' I said, 'It sure is,' and that was the end of the conversation. I went straight to the piano and started boogieing, and 'Cleanup Time' came out."

Although it took on a universal tone, 'Cleanup Time' reveals how Lennon and Ono set about cleansing themselves of the troubles that beset them. With their trials behind them, all was contentment. They had survived. By following a strict macrobiotic diet and adopting positive thinking, they emerged from the 1970s as well-rounded individuals. At least that's how Lennon chose to present it.

Constructing a picture of comfortable domesticity, as sentimental as any Victorian painting, Lennon's mythologising was, nevertheless, rooted in reality. The pair had cleaned up their act in more ways than one. Thanks to Ono's investment sense and economic acumen, they were financially secure. Lennon had brought up their son and taken on the role of homemaker. Both had kicked debilitating drug habits. They had wiped the slate clean and begun afresh. They were now ready to show the world how it too could clean up, and they offered their relationship as a model of perfect heterosexual harmony. Work to record the basic track began on August 13 at the Hit Factory. The horn section was overdubbed on September 5, and Lennon recorded his vocal on September 17.

Recording for the next track, 'Give Me Something', began on August 18 and was completed on September 23, when Ono cut her vocal. Her blend of hard rock and avant-garde vocalising mirror an equally taught lyric, which with a surgeon's precision cut through Lennon's mawkish efforts. Rather than paint a picture of romantic bliss, Ono alludes to the realities of their relationship.

The two were communication junkies. They loved the telephone and used it incessantly, often preferring to call one another rather than talk face to face. Ono often used the phone to play mind games with Lennon. Her calls were the equivalent of the cryptic messages she sent him when they first met. During his 'lost weekend' – an 18-month alcohol-fuelled Ono-sanctioned separation – she would call him as many as 20 times a day, often with infuriating results.

Lennon, of course, also loved to call Ono, and 'I'm Losing You' stems from his frustration at being unable to contact her while he was on holiday in Bermuda. However, the song had existed in a previous form for some time before he channelled his frustration into finishing it. It was originally titled 'Stranger's Room', which Lennon recorded as a slow, brooding ballad prior to his visit to Bermuda. Speaking later to the BBC, he stressed that he was on the island when inspiration struck. "[I] was actually in Bermuda. I called [Ono] and I couldn't get through. I got really mad, and I wrote this song in the heat of passion, as it were."

In reality, all he did was rework 'Stranger's Room', which already had the verse, chorus, and theme that formed the basis of 'I'm Losing You'. Its lyric even contained a reference to the telephone, although in this instance it was Lennon who wasn't answering. His lyric also included a reference to bleeding, which, in light of the shocking events of December 8, became even more unnerving and seemingly prophetic. But Lennon probably intended it as a metaphor for the emotional pain he was experiencing at being separated from Ono. During this period he may have felt as if his emotional and creative energies were draining from him, as he explained. He said the song "is expressing the losing you, of the 18 months lost … it was everything … losing one's mother, losing one's everything – everything, losing everything you've ever lost is in that song."

'I'm Losing You' was, then, as angst-ridden as anything on *John Lennon/Plastic Ono Band*, and Lennon intended to give it an abrasive reading. To reinforce his sense of loss and perhaps in an attempt to reconnect with the pain he experienced while recording that earlier album, he cites 'Long Lost John', a song he'd improvised with Ringo Starr and Klaus Voormann during those sessions.

Unlike most of what appeared on *Double Fantasy*, 'I'm Losing You' was somewhat difficult to capture successfully. The first attempt at recording the song took place on August 12 1980 at the Hit Factory. Jack Douglas called on the talents of guitarist Rick Nielsen and drummer Bun E. Carlos from Cheap Trick to bring an edge to the proceedings. With Lennon providing second guitar and Tony Levin bass, the quartet recorded two tracks, 'I'm Losing You' and Ono's 'I'm Moving On'. Lennon was unhappy with the results, reasoning that they were too gritty and too close to his early *Plastic Ono Band*/'Cold Turkey' period. He decided to scrap these tracks and start again. (That first version of 'I'm Losing You' would eventually be issued on the *John Lennon Anthology*, albeit in an edited form and without Nielsen's guitar overdub. The edit also appeared on the 1998 collection *Wonsaponatime* and the British two-track promotional CD 'I'm Losing You' / 'Only You' [LENNON 001]. The unedited version appeared on *Howtis* [DPRO-13515], a CD issued to promote the *John Lennon Anthology* boxed set.)

Work on the remake of 'I'm Losing You' began on August 18, with Lennon playing the band his earlier attempt and giving them instructions as to how he wanted it played. However, this session did not go well either, and a third and final attempt at recording the song was booked for August 26. Satisfied that he had at last captured the definitive version, Lennon overdubbed a horn arrangement on September 5 and added his vocal to the track on the 22nd. The horns were then removed at Lennon's insistence because of a large bill he received from the musicians for their services, but artistic reasons must have also played a part when he decided to delete this part of the arrangement.

Ono had rejected the first version of 'I'm Moving On', also recorded with Nielsen and Carlos from Cheap Trick, and re-recorded the song on August 26. She completed it on September 19, adding her vocals to the backing track. It establishes a musical dialogue between husband and wife, and indeed this song and 'I'm Losing You' both speak of loss but from different perspectives. If Lennon felt traumatised at the thought of losing his partner, the same cannot be said for Ono. Her sense of independence is writ large in this song, which she told David Sheff of *Playboy* magazine is about "the sense of 'Well, I've had enough. I'm moving on.' But it's not about any specific incident. It's just the feeling: 'I don't want to play the games. I like everything straight.' That's a feeling I have had. I'm proud of the song."

Next on *Double Fantasy* is 'Beautiful Boy (Darling Boy)', a lullaby for Lennon's son, Sean, that reveals the extent of his feelings for his second-born. To say that he doted on Sean would be an understatement. Sean was the apple of his eye, but to begin with he found it difficult to write a song that described how he felt. It was only when he gave up thinking about the idea that the song took shape. He appears to have finished 'Beautiful Boy (Darling Boy)' in Bermuda, where he recorded several takes of the song with help from his assistant, Fred Seaman. Back in New York City, Lennon recorded the basic track on August 12 and added his vocal on September 17. (An alternative take, without the numerous overdubs that were applied to the master version, was issued on the *John Lennon Anthology*.)

Many found Lennon's five-year silence unfathomable. Why would someone make a conscious decision to squander their talent and distance themselves from friends and the razzmatazz of showbiz? Extended career breaks were almost unheard of in the late 1970s. Artists were expected to remain on the album-tour-album treadmill to satisfy both record company and public. But Lennon had long since stopped playing that game. The Beatles broke with tradition in 1966 by demanding a cessation of their hectic touring schedule, and by his own admission Lennon had grown tired of having to produce an album every year.

'Watching The Wheels' was an attempt to answer his critics while promoting the myth that all was light and happiness during his five-year break. "It's a song version of the love letter from John and Yoko," he told David Sheff. "It's an answer to: 'What have you been doing?' 'Well, I've been doing this – watchin' the wheels.'" But Lennon had been contemplating more than the fast-turning wheels of showbiz. Religion and spirituality had influenced him. Where previously he'd tried to imagine a world without religion, he now found himself drawn to it. The Bahá'í Faith may have affected Lennon: its central belief, that humanity is one single race and that the day has come for its unification in one global society, was condensed into a pithy aphorism, "One World, One People", and inscribed into the dead wax of the '(Just Like) Starting Over' single. The wheels Lennon found himself contemplating were, more often than not, those governing destiny: the karmic wheels that influence the spiritual evolution of humanity as a whole.

Lennon developed 'Watching The Wheels' from a song he'd written in 1975. 'Tennessee', inspired by his fondness for the writer Tennessee Williams, was intended for the follow-up to *Walls And Bridges*. It then formed part of a new song, 'Memories', written some time in 1977 or '78. This developed into 'Watching The Wheels', although it too was reworked and revised on several occasions before Lennon was satisfied. He made several demo recordings of the song but appears to have made the definitive demo while in Bermuda. The song was finally committed to tape at the Hit Factory on August 18: nine takes of the basic track were recorded, number eight being marked best. Lennon added his vocal on September 20 and mixed the track at the Record Plant nine days later.

'Yes, I'm Your Angel' was intended as a joke, a pastiche of the kind of show tunes that populated Hollywood films from the 1930s. In fact, Ono's pastiche was so successful that the publishers of Gus Kahn's 'Makin' Whoopee' sued. While Ono's blend of avant-gardism and hard rock placed her at the centre of New York City's post-punk scene, 'Yes, I'm Your Angel' must have sent all but the most hardened fans reaching for the fast-forward button.

Songs asking for forgiveness are scattered throughout Lennon's oeuvre. Writing in the 1960s, he tended to view women as mere objects of desire. Ono opened his eyes to feminism, and by the early 1970s he'd began a slow transition from chauvinist to pseudo-feminist. Women, or more specifically Ono, were more likely to be referred to as equals and occasionally as enlightened goddesses. He began to express his feelings of regret as apologies, developing the theme with a string of songs that found their way onto his later albums.

Written for Ono, 'Woman' states, very simply and precisely, how Lennon was still struggling to come to terms with his actions. He explained: "['Woman'], that's to Yoko and to all women in a way. My history of relationships with women is very poor – very macho, very stupid, but pretty typical of a certain type of man, which I was, I suppose: a very insecure, sensitive person acting out very aggressive and macho. Trying to cover up the feminine side, which I still have a tendency to do, but I'm learning. I'm learning that it's all right to be soft and allow that side of me out."

A combination of 'Jealous Guy' and 'Aisumassen (I'm Sorry)', 'Woman' extends Lennon's self-criticism and takes the art of apologising to new highs. Exquisitely constructed, if a little sentimental, it has the melodic edge over anything Lennon wrote for this album, reflecting the depth of emotion that he felt for Ono. An extremely personal song, it was given universal appeal by extending the concept to embrace all women.

Lennon knew he'd written something special and constantly referred to the song as the album's Motown/Beatles track. Its melodic simplicity and rich arrangement lent it a sophisticated tone that echoed The Beatles at their best. It is the equivalent of George Harrison's 'Something' or Paul McCartney's 'Here There And Everywhere': a classic love song. It may not be the greatest song John Lennon ever wrote, but it reaffirmed his talent and established a benchmark for others to match.

Before he recorded the song at the Hit Factory, Lennon made several demo recordings, perfecting the melody, lyrics, and phrasing each time. Recording proper began on August 8. With the basic tracks recorded, the process of sweetening began with a number of overdubs. He re-recorded his acoustic guitar part and went to considerable lengths to refine his vocal, double-tracking it and dropping in certain key words to create the perfect take. To complete the track, an overdub session was booked for September 15, during which the backing vocal arrangement was refined to Lennon's satisfaction.

'Beautiful Boys' was Ono's answer to Lennon's 'Beautiful Boy (Darling Boy)', inspired by her husband and their son but also addressing a wider audience. "It's a message to men," she explained. "John and Sean inspired me, but the third verse is about all the beautiful boys of the world. That's sort of like the extension of the idea. I had relationships with men, but it was always: 'You know where the door is.' I didn't really trouble to find out what their needs were, what their pains were. With John, that changed. He found out my pain, and I had to find out his pain." Ono's analysis of her relationship with Lennon was insightful and honest. It flattered and encouraged, expressing everything that a loving wife would wish for her husband. It was also a pretty good description of men in general that neatly companioned Lennon's 'Woman'.

Just as Lennon signed off his *Imagine* album with a song inspired by his wife, he chose to conclude his contribution to *Double Fantasy* in similar style. 'Dear Yoko', referred to by Lennon as 'Oh Yoko!' part two, reaffirms his love for Ono but also reveals that its author craved reassurance at times of self-doubt. Every bit as jubilant and celebratory as 'Oh Yoko!', it lacks the poetic allusions that lifted that song from a work of craft to something approaching art.

He made demo recordings of 'Dear Yoko' at his Cold Spring Harbour home on Long Island in the spring of 1980, unusually performing directly to a video camera, and again while on holiday in Bermuda. The studio recording took place on August 14 and was completed in six takes. One of these, possibly take

1, was issued on the *John Lennon Anthology*. Instrumental overdubs were recorded in late August before John added his vocal on September 22.

Ono's 'Every Man Has A Woman Who Loves Him' restates much of what had already been said with 'Beautiful Boys'. All that she had to say about the song was "it's about love". The track features a harmony vocal by Lennon that was later presented as a bona fide lead vocal, which it is not. (Remixed in 1984, it was issued with Lennon's vocal on the Ono tribute album *Every Man Has A Woman Who Loves Him* [823 490-1 Y-1]. Polydor also issued it as a single [881 378-7 US and POSP 712 UK]. Lennon's version was included on the four-CD boxed set *Lennon* [CDS 79 5220 2], issued by EMI on October 30 1990. Both versions of the song were issued as a promotional single by Capitol [7PRO 6 15898 7] in 2001 to promote the remastered *Double Fantasy* and *Milk And Honey* CDs.)

Just as Lennon revived old songs, so did Ono. 'Hard Times Are Over' was the oldest song on the album. Dating from 1973, it was destined for the follow-up to *Feeling The Space*, *A Story*, which remained unreleased until 1997. It was inspired by a cross-country car journey that the pair took while attempting to kick their drug habit. Speaking with Gillian Gaar in 1997, Ono confirmed that the hard times referred to in the song were the result of drug use. "We were going to withdraw. And we were withdrawing while we were going cross-country. Can you imagine that? It was a station-wagon [that] Peter Bentley, our assistant was driving, and we were trying to get off drugs. And it was really frightening! So we're standing on a corner looking at each other and saying, 'OK, we're going to get off drugs,' it's great." The basic track was recorded on August 19 with overdubs added on September 11 (choir), 19th (Ono's vocals) and 23rd (Lennon's vocals).

In Early 2010, Ono contacted Jack Douglas and commissioned him to remix *Double Fantasy*. Ono's idea was to produce a 'stripped down' version of the album, similar to The Beatles' *Let It Be… Naked* that had been issued in 2003. Douglas returned to his original tapes, originally he'd record onto a 16-track machine synched to a 24-track machine, which he transferred to Pro Tools to remix the album.

By stripping away the layers of overdubs, Douglas' new mix reveals many of Lennon's vocal asides which show just how much fun Lennon was having recording this album. By far the most revealing is the new mix of 'Cleanup Time'. Here numerous Lennon vocals can be heard clearly for the first time. Clearly Lennon never intended these to be heard, otherwise he would have made them more audible when he mixed the album in 1980. However, making them audible has given the album an new intimacy and, at times, vibrancy.

Yoko Ono claimed: "*Double Fantasy Stripped Down* really allows us to focus our attention on John's amazing vocals. Technology has advanced so much that, conversely, I wanted to use new techniques to really frame these amazing songs and John's voice as simply as possible. By stripping down some of the instrumentation the power of the songs shines through with an enhanced clarity. Double Fantasy Stripped Down will be complemented by the original album in the 2CD format. It was whilst working on the new version of this album that I was hit hardest emotionally, as this was the last album John released before his passing."

Essentially what's on offer is the basic tracks, this is how the album sounded before the overdubs were added, and if nothing else it's worth hearing if only to witness Lennon enjoying himself in a recording studio for the first time in five years. The real disappointment is that it would be his last.

Double Fantasy data

Geffen Records issued *Double Fantasy* with generic Geffen labels, inner sleeve with lyrics, and black-and-white cover. Initial copies of the LP were issued with an incorrect track listing on the rear cover, an indication of the speed with which the album was completed.

Double Fantasy was mastered by George Marino at Sterling Sound, New York City, and British pressings were produced from lacquers cut in the USA. Several sets were cut for each country that issued the record. British first pressings were manufactured from UK set 1 (side 2) and UK set 2 (side 1). As demand for the album skyrocketed, the LP was repressed with UK set 3 (side 2) with side 1 being produced from a new lacquer. When the LP was repressed in America, the label had no perimeter text and a slightly larger logo.

Double Fantasy was issued as a Columbia Record Club edition with the track listing corrected on the rear cover. Three editions were manufactured with and without 'CH' on the cover. A black-label edition without 'CH' on the cover was also issued. RCA Music Service also issued the LP (R 104689). In November 1982, the LP was issued by Nautilus Recordings (NR-47) as a half-speed master edition, with a sepia-tone cover, corrected track listing, and a full-colour poster.

The album was reissued in 1989 by Capitol/Columbia House with black/colour band labels (C-1-581425, USA, and EST 2083, UK).

Although by the late 1970s British record companies had dropped the 8-track cartridge format, *Double Fantasy* was issued in the USA in this form. Three variants were issued. The first by Geffen (GEF-W8-2001), the second by Columbia Record Club (W8-2001), and the third by RCA Record Club in 1981 (S-104689).

Double Fantasy was issued on CD in the USA on September 15 1987 and came in three variations. Most of the CDs were manufactured in Germany and have 'Made in West Germany' printed on the disc. A very small number of the first pressing were manufactured in America and have 'Made in USA' printed on the disc. The CD was also issued by Columbia Record Club (M2G-2001). This version has 'Manufactured by Columbia House under license' added to the backing-tray card. *Double Fantasy* was issued on CD (299131-2) in Britain on October 13 1986, with the first pressing manufactured in Britain. In 1989, EMI/Capitol obtained the rights to issue *Double Fantasy* and released the album on LP, cassette, and CD (CDP 7 91425 2). Next to issue the CD were MFSL Original Master Recordings (UDCD-1-590), in 1994. The album was remastered and reissued by EMI/Capitol on October 9 2000 with three bonus tracks ('Help Me To Help Myself', 'Walking On Thin Ice', and 'Central Park Stroll').

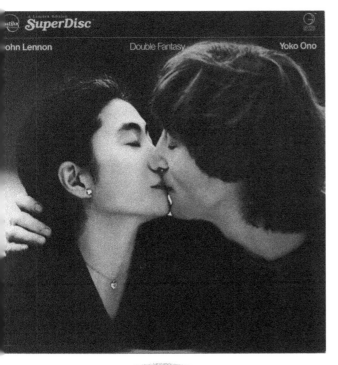

Above: Japan edition
Below: East German edition

188

'WOMAN' / 'BEAUTIFUL BOYS'
JOHN LENNON / YOKO ONO
UK release January 16 1981; LP Geffen K 79195; cassette Geffen K 79195M; chart high No.1.
US release January 12 1981; Geffen GEF 49644; chart high No.2.

'WOMAN'

Selected by Lennon as the follow-up to '(Just Like) Starting Over', 'Woman' was the first posthumous release taken from *Double Fantasy* and a massive hit. Number 1 on both sides of the Atlantic, it spent 11 weeks in the British charts and 17 weeks in the US.

It was issued in the UK and USA with generic Geffen labels and a black-and-white picture sleeve. The single was released in Britain as a cassette single, a format then in its infancy and being heavily promoted as a possible replacement for the vinyl single. 'Woman' was reissued in America on June 5 1981 backed with '(Just Like) Starting Over' (GGEF 0408) as part of Geffen's Back To Back hits series.

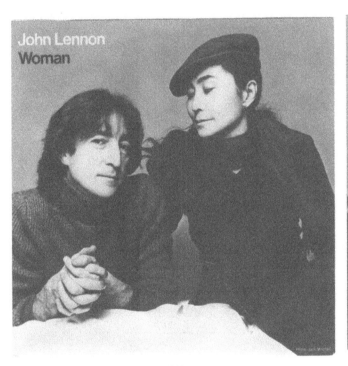

'I SAW HER STANDING THERE' / 'WHATEVER GETS YOU THRU THE NIGHT', 'LUCY IN THE SKY WITH DIAMONDS'
THE ELTON JOHN BAND FEATURING JOHN LENNON WITH THE MUSCLE SHOALS HORNS

UK release March 13 1981; DJM DJS 10965; chart high No.40.

'Lucy In The Sky With Diamonds' (Lennon, McCartney)
John Lennon (vocals, guitar), Elton John (vocals, piano), Davey Johnstone (guitar), Dee Murray (bass), Nigel Olsson (drums), Ray Cooper (percussion), Muscle Shoals Horns (brass). Live recording at Madison Square Garden, New York City, NY, USA. Produced by Gus Dudgeon.

'LUCY IN THE SKY WITH DIAMONDS'

Although EMI suggested that it had no plans to exploit Lennon's back catalogue, the fact that its pressing plant was working overtime to fulfil demand for his records and that a boxed set was planned obviously didn't count as exploitation. Other record companies were quick to issue archive material. DJM Records issued three songs Lennon performed with Elton John on November 28 1974 at Madison Square Garden. This turned out to be his last concert performance (although his last public appearance was on June 13 1975 at a Lew Grade tribute, where he sang a live vocal over pre-recorded backing tracks).

The A-side of this three-track EP had previously been issued as the B-side of Elton John's 'Philadelphia Freedom', but the remaining two live recordings were unreleased. Lennon had of course written 'Lucy In The Sky With Diamonds' in 1967 for The Beatles' groundbreaking *Sgt. Pepper's Lonely Heart's Club Band* album. He was inspired by a painting that his son, Julian, brought home from school. Lennon's dreamy melody and shimmering vocal made it a psychedelic classic, and many assumed that it was influenced by LSD. Its powerful hallucinogenic imagery seemed to confirm as much, but Lennon was adamant that it was not.

Elton John had started performing 'Lucy' in concert in 1974. The song went down remarkably well with British audiences, but John discovered that many Americans were unfamiliar with the song. He decided to record his version while in the USA and asked Lennon to play on it. Gus Dudgeon, who produced the record, recalled that Lennon contributed the reggae middle-eight and played guitar on the track, although Gudgeon was only able to use Lennon's guitar part for the middle-eight because the rest was too ragged. Lennon also contributed backing vocals. Elton's reading was issued as a single in 1974, reaching Number 1 in the US charts. The live recording faithfully reproduces the studio arrangement, with Lennon taking lead vocals during the extended chorus.

'Lucy In The Sky With Diamonds' data
DJM prepared white-label test pressings of this 'Saw Her Standing There' EP with the A-side cut at 45 rpm and the B-side at 33 rpm. Commercial pressings of the EP were issued with both sides of the record cut at 33 rpm. Two label variants were produced, one with black text on a white backdrop and one with red text on a black backdrop. DJM placed full-page advertisements in a number of British music weeklies and issued a poster to shops that ordered 25 or more copies. Twelve-inch pressings of the record were issued in Germany and Mexico, where it was pressed on green vinyl.

45 RPM

A1.
'I Saw Her Standing
There'

33⅓ RPM

A1.   'Whatever Gets
You Through The Night'.
A2.   'Lucy In The Sky
With Diamonds'.

ELTON JOHN BAND featuring
JOHN LENNON and the Muscle Shoals Horns

Produced by
Gus Dudgeon

John Lennon
appears by
arrangement with
EMI Records Ltd

33⅓ RPM
DJS 10965
DJS 10965-A
℗ 1975 This
Record Co Ltd

I SAW HER STANDING THERE
(Lennon/McCartney) (Northern Songs Ltd)

ELTON JOHN BAND featuring
JOHN LENNON and the Muscle Shoals Horns

Produced by
Gus Dudgeon

John Lennon
appears by
arrangement with
EMI Records Ltd

33⅓ RPM
DJS 10965
DJS 10965-B
℗ 1981 This
Record Co Ltd

1. WHATEVER GETS YOU THROUGH THE NIGHT
(John Lennon) (John Lennon/ATV Music Ltd)
2. LUCY IN THE SKY WITH DIAMONDS
(Lennon/McCartney) (Northern Songs Ltd)

ELTON JOHN BAND featuring
JOHN LENNON and the Muscle Shoals Horns

Produced by
Gus Dudgeon

John Lennon
appears by
arrangement with
EMI Records Ltd

33⅓ RPM
DJS 10965
DJS 10965-A
℗ 1975 This
Record Co Ltd

I SAW HER STANDING THERE
(Lennon/McCartney) (Northern Songs Ltd)

ELTON JOHN BAND featuring
JOHN LENNON and the Muscle Shoals Horns

Produced by
Gus Dudgeon

John Lennon
appears by
arrangement with
EMI Records Ltd

33⅓ RPM
DJS 10965
DJS 10965-B
℗ 1981 This
Record Co Ltd

1. WHATEVER GETS YOU THROUGH THE NIGHT
(John Lennon) (John Lennon/ATV Music Ltd)
2. LUCY IN THE SKY WITH DIAMONDS
(Lennon/McCartney) (Northern Songs Ltd)

'WATCHING THE WHEELS' / 'YES, I'M YOUR ANGEL'
JOHN LENNON / YOKO ONO

UK release March 27 1981; LP Geffen K 79207; cassette Geffen K 79207M; chart high No.30.
US release March 13 1981; Geffen GEF 49695; chart high No.10.

'WATCHING THE WHEELS'

The third and final single lifted from *Double Fantasy*, 'Watching The Wheels' was issued on both sides of the Atlantic with generic Geffen labels and a full-colour picture cover. As with the previous Geffen single, it was issued in Britain as a cassette single. It was reissued by Geffen backed with 'Beautiful Boy (Darling Boy)' in 1982 (GGEF 0415) and again in 1986 with black Geffen labels with silver and white print but without the 'Back To Back Hits' logo.

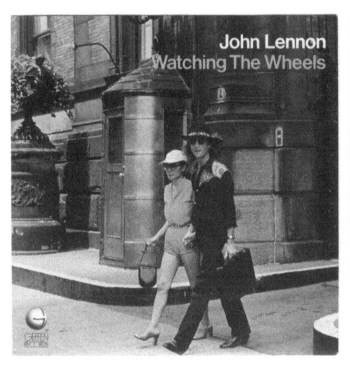

JOHN LENNON
JOHN LENNON

Boxed set, includes seven albums: *Plastic Ono Band – Live Peace In Toronto 1969*; *John Lennon/Plastic Ono Band*; *Imagine*; *Some Time In New York City*; *Mind Games*; *Walls And Bridges*; *Rock'N'Roll*; *Shaved Fish*.
UK release June 15 1981; EMI JLB8; failed to chart.

JOHN LENNON

Despite EMI's statement that it had no plans to issue any posthumous material, temptation was too great and this monumental but disappointing boxed set was issued in the summer of 1981. Impressive as it is, it contains eight of Lennon's solo albums, his avant-garde output is conspicuous by its absence. The set contained no new material with the only incentive being a glossy 20-page magazine produced by *The Liverpool Echo* newspaper. All the albums came with their original covers and inserts, except for *Plastic Ono Band – Live Peace In Toronto 1969*, which did not include the calendar, and *John Lennon/Plastic Ono Band* and *Imagine*, which did not have printed inner sleeves.

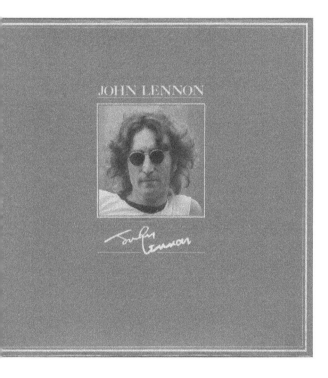

1982 to 2016: Something Precious and Rare

THE JOHN LENNON COLLECTION
JOHN LENNON

Side 1 'Give Peace A Chance', 'Instant Karma!', 'Power To The People', 'Whatever Gets You Thru The Night', '#9 Dream', 'Mind Games', 'Love', 'Happy Xmas (War Is Over)'.
Side 2 'Imagine', 'Jealous Guy', 'Stand By Me', '(Just Like) Starting Over', 'Woman', 'I'm Losing You', 'Beautiful Boy (Darling Boy)', 'Watching The Wheels', 'Dear Yoko'.
The US release does not include 'Happy Xmas' or 'Stand By Me', and 'Dear Yoko' precedes 'Watching The Wheels'.
UK release November 1 1982; LP Parlophone EMTV 37; CD Parlophone CDEMTV 37 released October 23 1989; chart high No.1.
US release November 8 1982; LP Geffen GHSP 2023; 8-track cartridge Geffen GEF-L8-2023; chart high No.33.

THE JOHN LENNON COLLECTION

The second overview of Lennon's career, this album updated the previous compilation, *Shaved Fish*, with the addition of songs from his last album, *Double Fantasy*. Because it included material issued by Geffen Records, the album was delayed by almost a year – it had been planned for late 1981. The problem was solved by EMI/Parlophone issuing the album in Britain and Geffen in the USA. Perhaps because Geffen had fewer tracks to licence, the American release did not include 'Happy Xmas (War Is Over)' or 'Stand By Me'. However, Geffen did issue 'Happy Xmas' as a single (7-29855) to promote the album. In Britain, *The John Lennon Collection* was promoted with the single release of 'Love' (R 5958).

Geffen also issued Quiex II audiophile pressings to promote the album. These promotional records have a Quiex II sticker, track list sticker, and gold embossed text 'Lent For Promotional Use Only' on the front cover.

In Britain, EMI promoted the album with television advertising and in-store displays that featured 12-inch-square cover flats, 20-inch by 30-inch full-colour posters, and life-size cut-outs of Lennon. The campaign was a huge success. *The John Lennon Collection* sold 300,000 copies in its first week and a million by its third.

EMI issued the LP with generic Parlophone labels and full-colour inner sleeve with lyrics. Two label variants exist, one with the boxed Parlophone label, the other without. Geffen issued the LP with generic Geffen labels and cover and inner sleeves identical to the British release. EMI issued the CD (CD EMTV 37) on October 23 1989 with two extra songs, 'Move Over Ms. L' and 'Cold Turkey'. Geffen did not have the rights to issue the album on CD, and instead it was issued by Capitol (CDP 7 91516 2) on January 29 1990.

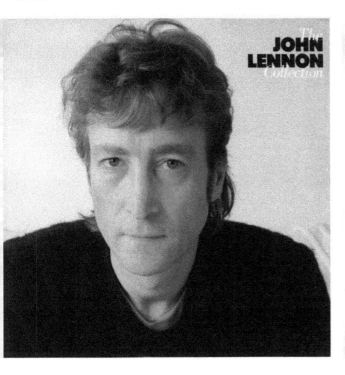

'LOVE' / 'GIVE ME SOME TRUTH'
JOHN LENNON

UK release November 15 1982; Parlophone R 6059; chart high No.41.

'LOVE'

Issued to promote *The John Lennon Collection*, 'Love' was released by Parlophone with generic labels and a full-colour picture cover. It was remixed for single release, with the quiet piano intro and fade-out placed much higher in the mix in an attempt to make it radio-friendly.

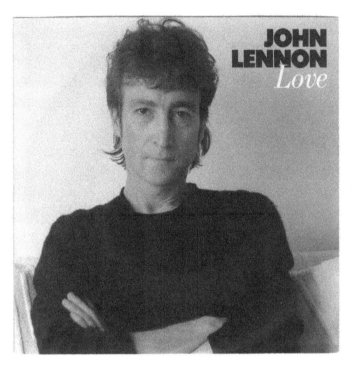
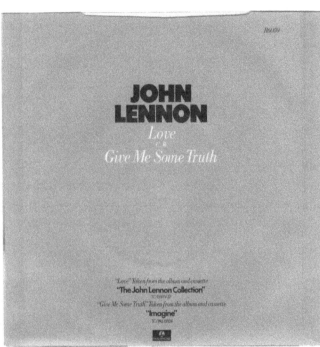

HEART PLAY – UNFINISHED DIALOGUE
JOHN LENNON AND YOKO ONO

Side 1 'Section One', 'Section Two', 'Section Three'.
Side 2 'Section Four', 'Section Five', 'Section Six', 'Section Seven'.
UK release December 16 1983; Parlophone 817 238-1; failed to chart.
US release December 5 1983; Polydor 817 238-1 Y-1; chart high No.95.

HEART PLAY

Yoko Ono's first record for Polydor was a solo album, *It's Alright*. It was followed by a series of archive releases, beginning with this John and Yoko interview recorded with David Sheff for *Playboy* magazine. Sheff's interview with the Lennons took place over several days, and he recorded over 22 hours of conversation during September 1980, 42 minutes of which were selected for the album. Parts of the interview had been published in the January 1981 issue of *Playboy*, and a longer version appeared in the book *The Playboy Interviews With John Lennon And Yoko Ono*. As much of the interview had already been published, there was little of revelation on the album.

Polydor issued *Heart Play – Unfinished Dialogue* in the USA with generic red Polydor labels and a four-inch by two-and-a-quarter-inch rectangular black sticker with white text 'SPECIAL LOW PRICE 1980 Conversations With John Lennon & Yoko Ono' adhered to the front cover. An insert in the form of a letter from Yoko explaining each section was included with the LP.

Polydor issued the album in Britain with labels and sleeve identical to the American release. To promote the album, half-page advertisements appeared in British music weeklies, and although it failed to chart, *Heart Play – Unfinished Dialogue* generated advance publicity for the much anticipated *Milk And Honey*.

'NOBODY TOLD ME' / 'O' SANITY'
JOHN LENNON / YOKO ONO

UK release January 9 1984; Polydor POSP 700; chart high No.6.
US release January 9 1984; Polydor 817 254-7; chart high No.5.

'Nobody Told Me' (Lennon)
John Lennon (vocals, guitar), Earl Slick (guitar), Hugh McCracken (guitar), Tony Levin (bass), George Small   (keyboards), Arthur Jenkins (percussion), Andy Newmark (drums). Recorded at Hit Factory, New York City, NY, USA. Produced by John Lennon and Yoko Ono.
'O' Sanity' (Ono)
Yoko Ono (vocals), John Tropes (guitars), Steve Love (guitars), Elliot Randall (guitars), Paul Griffin (piano), Neil Jason or Wayne Pedziwiatr (bass guitar), Yogi Horton or Allan Schwartzberg (drums). Recorded at A&R Studios or Sterling Sound, New York City, NY, USA, or The Automat, San Francisco, CA. Produced by Yoko Ono.

'NOBODY TOLD ME'

As with '(Just Like) Starting Over', 'Nobody Told Me' was greeted with considerable media and fan anticipation. Everyone knew that there were unreleased songs from the *Double Fantasy* sessions ready to be issued and it was only a matter of time before they would appear. News that Ono was preparing material for record began to appear in the press in mid 1983. By early autumn that year, it had been confirmed that mixing was almost complete and that *Milk And Honey*, the follow-up to *Double Fantasy* that Lennon and Ono had discussed prior to Lennon's death, would be issued early in 1984.

'Nobody Told Me' was another song that Lennon had hanging about and revived for the *Double Fantasy* sessions. He had begun to write it in 1976 and may have intended it for the aborted album he planned to follow *Walls And Bridges*. Originally titled 'Everybody', it underwent considerable revision. The song remained unfinished until 1980, when he began to rework it.

To begin with, Lennon simply overdubbed a new vocal and guitar onto the existing piano demo of 'Everybody' and sang new lyrics over the chorus. Next he reworked the verses and recorded a new demo, this time backing himself on acoustic guitar and rhythm box. The reworked verses offer the listener a number of conflicting images and paradoxes to contemplate. They are a mixture of the banal and the bizarre, evoking a sense of discontinuity that the revised chorus summarised and reinforced. To complete the song, Lennon fashioned a jumpy riff to link the verse and chorus, which provides the song with its melodic hook and matches the sense of suspension established in the verses.

Before deciding to keep 'Nobody Told Me' for himself, Lennon considered offering the song to Ringo Starr, who was in the process of recording his *Stop And Smell The Roses* album. But he kept it – and recorded the song at the Hit Factory on the second day of the *Double Fantasy* sessions. As usual, Lennon recorded a live vocal with every take, and that's what appeared on the record. (An alternative take was issued on the *John Lennon Anthology*.)

Ono's 'O' Sanity' was recorded some time after the *Double Fantasy* sessions, as were all her songs on the *Milk And Honey* album. Lacking a memorable melody or lyric, 'O' Sanity' is little more than an adumbrated sketch. It appears even less finished than many of Lennon's songs on the album.

'Nobody Told Me' data
Polydor issued the single in Britain and America. British pressings were manufactured with blue die-cut Polydor labels and full-colour picture sleeve. The company also issued a one-sided white label 7-inch single to radio stations and the media. In the USA the record came with red Polydor labels and a picture sleeve identical to the British release.

Commercial copies of the US single were manufactured with several label variations. The first label has 'Manufactured by Polydor Incorporated...' perimeter print, and 'stereo' on the label. The second has the same perimeter print, without 'stereo' on the label. The third US label variant has 'Manufactured and Marketed by Polygram...' perimeter print, with 'stereo', '45 RPM', and a small '19' to the left of the Ono Music logo. The other four variants are similar to the third, except that one has 'stereo', '45 RPM', and '26' above the Ono Music logo; the next has 'stereo', '45 RPM', and '49'; another has 'stereo', '45 RPM', and '54' left of the Ono Music logo; and the last has 'stereo', '45 RPM', and '72'.

To promote the single in the USA, Polydor issued a promotional 12-inch (PRO 250-1). The single was also promoted with an extensive poster campaign and a specially commissioned video that consisted of clips from the Lennons' personal archive. 'Nobody Told Me' achieved considerable success on both sides of the Atlantic.

Like Geffen, Polydor coupled hit singles and issued them as double A-sides, on its Timepieces imprint. 'Nobody Told Me', backed with 'I'm Stepping Out', was reissued on this imprint in America on April 30 1990 (883927-7). This coupling was reissued in 1992 on the Collectibles label (COL-4307), the B-side incorrectly listing the song title as 'Steppin' Out'.

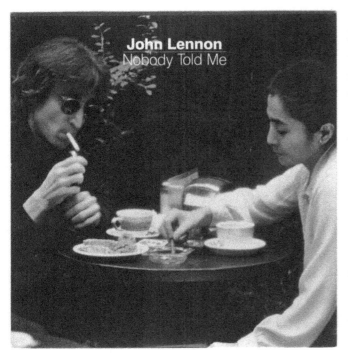

Polydor

Time: 3:34
Ono Music
(BMI)
19

STEREO
45 RPM
817 254-7
83 NP 6541

ONO
MUSIC

NOBODY TOLD ME
(J. Lennon)
From the Polydor album
MILK AND HONEY-A HEART PLAY
422-817 160-1 Y-1
JOHN LENNON
℗ 1983 PolyGram Records, Inc.

MANUFACTURED AND MARKETED BY POLYGRAM RECORDS, INC. • 810 SEVENTH AVENUE, NEW YORK, N.Y. 10019

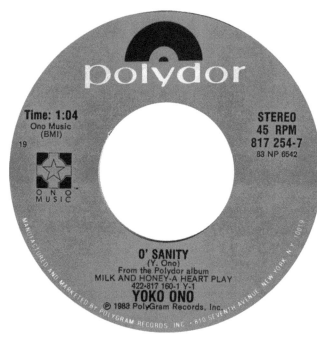

Polydor

Time: 1:04
Ono Music
(BMI)
19

STEREO
45 RPM
817 254-7
83 NP 6542

ONO
MUSIC

O' SANITY
(Y. Ono)
From the Polydor album
MILK AND HONEY-A HEART PLAY
422-817 160-1 Y-1
YOKO ONO
℗ 1983 PolyGram Records, Inc.

MANUFACTURED AND MARKETED BY POLYGRAM RECORDS, INC. • 810 SEVENTH AVENUE, NEW YORK, N.Y. 10019

Polydor

JOHN LENNON

ONO
MUSIC

33 1/3 RPM
STEREO
SIDE 1
26

PRO 250-1
83 NP 6541
PROMOTIONAL COPY
NOT FOR SALE

NOBODY TOLD ME 3:34
(J. Lennon)
Ono Music BMI
From the Polydor album MILK AND HONEY-
A HEART PLAY 422-817 160-1 Y-1
℗ 1983 PolyGram Records, Inc.

JOHN LENNON

"Nobody Told Me"

PROMOTIONAL COPY ONLY

NOT FOR RESALE

ALL RIGHTS OF THE MANUFACTURER AND THE OWNER OF THE RECORDED WORK RESERVED. UNAUTHORISED COPYING, PUBLIC PERFORMANCE AND BROADCASTING OF THIS RECORD PROHIBITED

Collectables

"BACK TO BACK HIT SERIES"

COL 4307

SEND FOR
FREE
CATALOG

Side A

Manufactured by
PolyGram Special
Products, a division of
PolyGram Group
Distribution, Inc.,
825 Eighth Ave.,
New York, N.Y. 10019

NOBODY TOLD ME
JOHN LENNON
This compilation ℗ 1992 PolyGram Records, Inc.
© 1992 COLLECTABLES, INC.

MANUFACTURED BY POLYGRAM SPECIAL PROJECTS

Collectables

"BACK TO BACK HIT SERIES"

COL 4307

SEND FOR
FREE
CATALOG

Side B

Manufactured by
PolyGram Special
Products, a division of
PolyGram Group
Distribution, Inc.,
825 Eighth Ave.,
New York, N.Y. 10019

STEPPIN' OUT
JOHN LENNON
This compilation ℗ 1992 PolyGram Records, Inc.
© 1992 COLLECTABLES, INC.

MANUFACTURED BY POLYGRAM SPECIAL PROJECTS

MILK AND HONEY – A HEART PLAY
JOHN LENNON AND YOKO ONO

Side 1 'I'm Stepping Out', 'Sleepless Night', 'I Don't Wanna Face It', 'Don't Be Scared', 'Nobody Told Me', 'O' Sanity'.
Side 2 'Borrowed Time', 'Your Hands', '(Forgive Me) My Little Flower Princess', 'Let Me Count The Ways', 'Grow Old With Me', 'You're The One'.

UK release January 23 1984; LP Polydor POLH 5; picture disc Polydor POLHP5 released March 26 1984; CD Polydor 817 159-2; chart high No.3.
US release January 23 1984; LP Polydor 817 159-1 Y-1; CD Polydor 817 159-2; chart high No.11.

'I'm Stepping Out' (Lennon)
John Lennon (vocals, guitar), Earl Slick (guitar), Hugh McCracken (guitar), Tony Levin (bass), George Small (keyboards), Arthur Jenkins (percussion), Andy Newmark (drums). Recorded at Hit Factory, New York City, NY, USA. Produced by John Lennon and Yoko Ono.
'Sleepless Night' (Ono)
Yoko Ono (vocals), John Tropes (guitars), Steve Love (guitars), Elliot Randall (guitars), Ed Walsh (synthesisers), Pete Cannarozzi (synthesisers), Paul Griffin (piano), Neil Jason (bass), Wayne Pedziwiatr (bass), Howard Johnson (baritone sax), Billy Alessi, Bob Alessi, Carlos Alomar, Gordon Grody, Kurt Yahijan, Pete Thom (backing vocals), Jimmy Maelen (percussion), Yogi Horton (drums), Allan Schwartzberg (drums). Recorded at A&R Studios or Sterling Sound, New York City, NY, USA or The Automat, San Francisco, CA, USA. Produced by Yoko Ono.
'I Don't Wanna Face It' (Lennon)
Personnel, location, and production as 'I'm Stepping Out'.
'Don't Be Scared' (Ono)
Personnel, location, and production as 'Sleepless Night'.
'Borrowed Time' (Lennon)
Personnel, location, and production as 'I'm Stepping Out'.
'Your Hands' (Ono)
Personnel, location, and production as 'Sleepless Night'.
'(Forgive Me) My Little Flower Princess' (Lennon)
Personnel, location, and production as 'I'm Stepping Out'.
'Let Me Count The Ways' (Ono)
Yoko Ono (vocals, piano). Recorded at The Dakota, New York City, NY, USA. Produced by Yoko Ono.
'Grow Old With Me' (Lennon)
John Lennon (vocals, piano). Recorded at The Dakota. Produced by John Lennon and Yoko Ono.
'You're The One' (Ono)
Personnel, location, and production as 'Sleepless Night'.

MILK AND HONEY – A HEART PLAY

This was the long awaited follow-up to *Double Fantasy*, issued by Polydor in January 1984. Lennon had recorded his songs while making *Double Fantasy* and had planned to return to them early in 1981. He'd spoken about the album in interviews just before his death, and rumours about its imminent release began to circulate as early as 1981. However, Ono found the task of compiling the album too distressing. Instead, she set about recording her solo album, *Season Of Glass*, and put *Milk And Honey* on hold. Had it appeared so soon after Lennon's death it would have smacked of cash-in, and Ono was careful to avoid such allegations.

When the album was issued, Lennon's songs were presented as he had left them, without the layers of sonic dressing he'd applied to *Double Fantasy*. Because his songs are presented 'naked', *Milk And Honey* has a vitality, freshness, and wit that would have been lost had he ever returned to it. Although the songs required a little fixing, they remained as works-in-progress (apart from adding echo to Lennon's vocal to give the impression of double-tracking). Although Jack Douglas was responsible for producing the basic tracks, he was not involved in mixing or sequencing *Milk And Honey*. Nor did he receive a production credit. Having fallen out with Ono over money, he was suing for unpaid royalties. Consequently, production credits went to John Lennon and Yoko Ono.

Milk And Honey songs

While on holiday in Bermuda, Lennon visited a nightclub with his personal assistant, Fred Seaman. He hadn't been to a disco in years but returned from his night out enthused, a little hung over, and inspired. Determined to document his adventures in clubland, he set about writing 'I'm Stepping Out'. The experience obviously had a marked effect on him. It's obvious that he yearned to escape the stultifying self-imposed lifestyle he had grown into.

A good time rock'n'roll song, 'I'm Stepping Out' crackles with pent-up excitement and anticipation. Besides dispelling the myth that Lennon spent all his time as a househusband locked away in the Dakota, it reveals that he'd lost none of his sense of humour, hedonism, or joie de vivre.

He'd made several demo recordings of the song while in Bermuda, one of which was used as a reference source on the first day of recording at the Hit Factory, August 6 1980. 'I'm Stepping Out' was the first song Lennon recorded with his new band. Despite it being the first day, his confidence was high and, leading the musicians through the song, he coaxed a tight performance from them (take 2 was strong enough to be issued later on the *John Lennon Anthology*). The only problem they encountered was a tendency to speed up when coming out of the verses. The original recording featured an additional verse, which was edited from the commercial release. It is unclear if Lennon decided to remove the offending verse at an early stage in the recording or if it was removed when the song was mixed in 1983.

Ono had been honing her skills as a writer of pop songs since the early 1970s. The avant-garde compositions and free-form music that had her labelled as a musical weirdo were replaced by a slick pop voice that was obviously intended to elevate her from experimental ghetto land into the pop mainstream. She embraced pop music, and the technology that drove it, to ever greater heights of sophistication, and her albums had grown increasingly accomplished. Yet despite the sophisticated production of 'Sleepless Night', when one compares it to the two Lennon songs that sit either side of it, it sounds downright amateurish and prosaic.

'I Don't Want To Face It' took Lennon full circle. *John Lennon/Plastic Ono Band* found him exploring a side of his personality that he preferred to hide behind a mask. 'I Don't Want To Face It' explored similar ground and was no less honest or revealing. However, the post-primal angst that informed Lennon's songwriting in 1970 had been replaced by a more relaxed attitude.

The song had its roots in a much earlier composition, 'Mirror Mirror (On The Wall)', written in 1977 after a less than enjoyable holiday in Japan. This study in melancholia remained unfinished, but provided the kernel of an idea that became 'I Don't Want To Face It'. Lennon began work on the song before his visit to Bermuda but continued to tinker with it while there.

As with 'Nobody Told Me', Lennon presents the listener with a series of paradoxes, but here they summarise his butterfly personality. Lampooning his foibles, he seems better to understand the contradictions that fame had brought him. Like George Harrison, he had learnt to deal with life's contradictions, balancing emotional, physical, and mental desires that had previously disturbed him. Yet while Harrison used his knowledge to guide himself spiritually, here Lennon used his to psychologically unburden himself.

Recorded with much exuberance, 'I Don't Want To Face It' developed into a spiky, hard-nosed rocker that rivalled anything in Lennon's oeuvre. He was still fine tuning the song while recording; an alternative version issued on the *John Lennon Anthology* has an extended introduction and coda.

Double Fantasy found the Lennons reassuring themselves and imagining a future together. In the weeks and months after John's death, Ono had to reassure both herself and their son Sean and imagine a future without her husband. Naturally, she wrote a number of songs that expressed her deepest feelings. 'Don't Be Scared' was not only a paean of reassurance, it advocated positive personal projection, a credo that lay at the heart of John and Yoko's philosophy.

Lennon never did get any of New York's session musicians to play reggae convincingly, but that didn't stop him from trying. Jamaican music had a strong influence on Lennon and The Beatles. The middle eight in 'I Call Your Name' was directly influenced by ska, a predecessor of reggae. Lennon experimented with dub when producing Ono's 'Paper Shoes' from her *Yoko Ono/Plastic Ono Band* album, and attempted reggae with another of her songs, 'Sisters, O Sisters'. He tried to assimilate the style into several of his own songs, but no matter how hard he tried he couldn't get NYC's white rockers to understand the genre. His attempts at recording reggae were always hampered by the musicians he worked with, and 'Borrowed Time' suffered a similar fate.

He wrote the song while in Bermuda and had been influenced by Bob Marley. Inspired by a line from Marley's 'Hallelujah Time', which contained the phrase "We got to keep on living / Living on borrowed time", Lennon began work on his own song. Recording at the Hit Factory, he guided the musicians through the arrangement by referring them to The Isley Brothers' 'Twist And Shout' and 'Spanish Twist'. Those two songs were also his reference points for a horn arrangement he planned to add to the song. Several takes were recorded, with take 3 being marked best and given a guitar overdub by Lennon.

'Borrowed Time' was a song that celebrated life; the fact that Lennon's would be taken from him so senselessly only added poignancy to the song. He depicts himself as contented, more relaxed, and accepting of his past. Where previously he may have turned to outsiders for help, here he looks inwards. Reflecting on his life, he concludes that it's good to be older. The future looked bright, everything was clear, and now was the time to act. He was not yet 40 when he wrote the song, but he was obviously thinking of the future and growing older. In the interviews he gave in the weeks before he died, Lennon spoke longingly of growing old with Yoko and living out the rest of his days in peace. Sadly, this wasn't to be.

Ono sings 'Your Hands' in Japanese and English, mourning her late husband. Focusing on parts of his body – hands, skin, mouth, arms, and eyes – to represent the whole, she reflects that losing him was not made any easier by the time they spent together. At least, that's how one reads it in this context. As *Milk And Honey* was intended to develop the theme of "sexual fantasies between men and women" begun with *Double Fantasy*, it could be read entirely differently.

Lennon's oeuvre is scattered with songs asking Ono for forgiveness. It's a theme that appears to have haunted him, as he returned to it again and again. '(Forgive Me) My Little Flower Princess' revisits this theme but adds little. The song was never completed satisfactorily. Lennon made demo recordings while in Bermuda but had still to finalise the lyrics by the time he entered the Hit Factory to record the song. Although he was only interested in recording the backing track, he seemed indifferent to the task and allowed the band to wander through the song without any real enthusiasm. The least distinguished recording to emerge from the *Double Fantasy*/*Milk And Honey* sessions, it would have been better left in the archives.

The album ends with a pair of demo recordings made by Lennon and Ono that are central to the record's theme. The couple liked to imagine themselves as reincarnations of Robert and Elizabeth Barrett Browning. The Brownings expressed their love for one another as publicly as the Lennons. Each published volumes of poetry that expressed how they had been affected by the other's love. Inspired by the Brownings' romantic relationship and poetry, the Lennons wrote a song each based on poems by the Brownings. Ono's borrowed from Elizabeth Barrett Browning's Sonnet 43 *How Do I Love Thee? Let Me Count The Ways* from *Sonnets From The Portuguese* (1850). As with Lennon's *Grow Old With Me*, Ono here evokes a number of adolescent metaphors to describe how she feels about her husband. Perhaps both of them would have been better advised to set the Brownings' poems to music rather than attempt their own.

Lennon based 'Grow Old With Me' on a line from Robert Browning's poem *Rabbi Ben Ezra*. Like Ono's Browning-influenced song, it's romantic and personal; it also restates much of what he'd said previously. Ono suggested that Lennon continued to work on the song while recording *Double Fantasy* but that he never completed a satisfactory arrangement. She alleged that he had planned a rich orchestral arrangement for the song, which it eventually received when she asked George Martin to write an orchestral setting for it. 'Grow Old With Me' would duly appear with Martin's orchestral backing on 1998's *John Lennon Anthology*. However, it is Lennon's original piano demo that has the charm and pathos. Martin's orchestral counterpart fails to improve the song and one suspects that, had he survived, Lennon would have rejected Martin's somewhat overblown arrangement.

Ono's 'You're The One', a love song with a contemporary pop feel, brought *Milk And Honey* to a close. Like the songs Lennon wrote for her, it reinforces the myth that they were just like everyone else, a boy and girl in love. By her own admission, Ono knew this to be a fiction. As if to reinforce the strength and pre-eminence of their relationship, she juxtaposes the media perspective of John and Yoko with how they saw themselves, as romantic, magical, and quixotic. The fight to prove that their love was true had been long and hard, but for Ono they had prevailed. The world may have lost a Beatle, but Ono had lost the one person who gave her life meaning.

Milk And Honey data

Polydor issued the album with generic red Polydor labels, an inner sleeve with lyrics, a poster, and a gatefold cover. The original concept for the cover was to have 200 heart-shaped photographs of Lennon and Ono. This idea was dropped and an outtake from the *Double Fantasy* photo session used instead.

The album was issued in Britain as a picture disc (POLHP 5) in an edition of 2,000, and a second pressing of 1,000 was produced as demand quickly outstripped supply. Coloured vinyl pressings of the album also appeared, although these were unauthorised editions probably made by an employee at Polydor's pressing plant during downtime. The record was pressed on yellow, green and gold vinyl.

Milk And Honey was the first album by any of The Beatles to be issued on CD. First pressings of the CD (817 159-2) were manufactured in Germany and came with a full-colour four-page booklet. EMI issued a remastered version of the CD (535 9582) with four bonus tracks on September 27 2001.

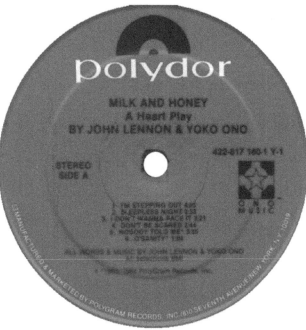

BORROWED TIME' / 'YOUR HANDS'
JOHN LENNON / YOKO ONO

UK release March 9 1984; Polydor POSP 701; 12-inch Polydor POSPX 701; 7-inch with poster Polydor POSPG 701 released March 16; chart high No.32.
US release May 14 1984; Polydor 821-204-7; chart high No.108.

'BORROWED TIME'

Polydor issued this single in Britain as the follow-up to 'Nobody Told Me' in several variants. The 7-inch single was issued with silver die-cut labels and a picture sleeve. An edition of 10,000 came with a poster sleeve (POSPG 701). Promotional copies (PODJ 701) were issued with an edit of the A-side in stock copies of the picture sleeve. 'Borrowed Time' was also issued as a 12-inch (POSPX 701) with a 15-inch by 11-inch full-colour poster and Ono's 'Never Say Goodbye' (not on *Milk And Honey*) included as a bonus track on the B-side.

In the USA, Polydor issued 'Borrowed Time' with generic red Polydor labels and a picture sleeve that was later used for the British release of 'I'm Stepping Out'. There were three variants, the first with a small number '19' printed above the Ono Music logo and '45 RPM' printed on the label, the second with a small number '26' printed on the label, without '45 RPM' and the third with a small '72' printed on the label below the album credits at 9 o'clock. Promotional copies (821-204-7 DJ) were issued with an edit of the A-side and the full album version on the other.

A promotional video was made for this and the two other singles taken from *Milk And Honey* consisting of footage from the Lennons' archives, and it received considerable television exposure. This did little to help the single on its chart journey.

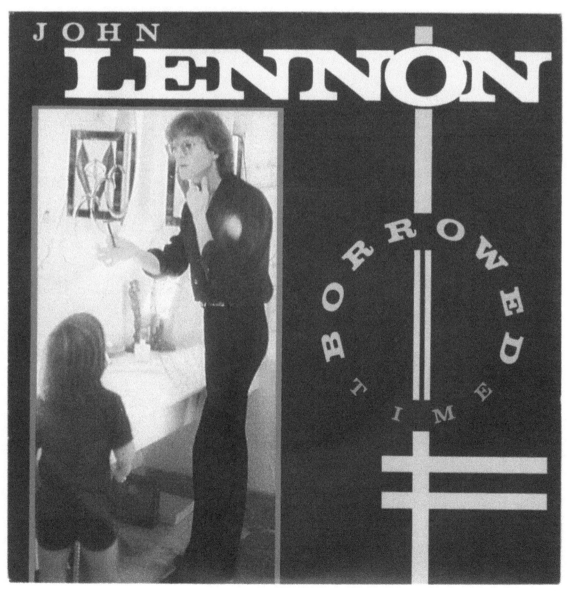

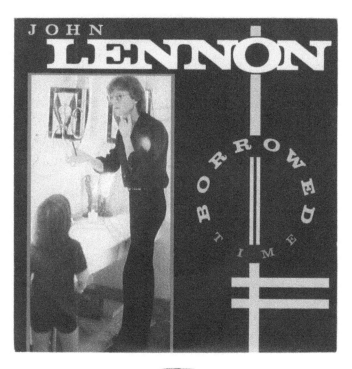

214

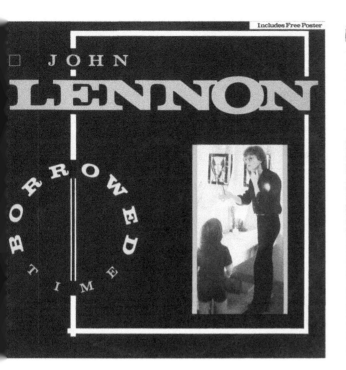

POSPX 701

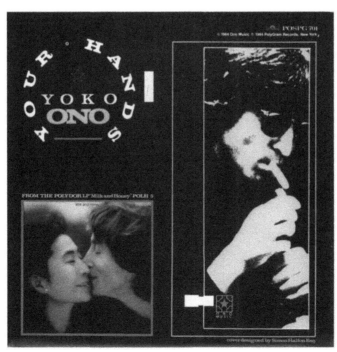

215

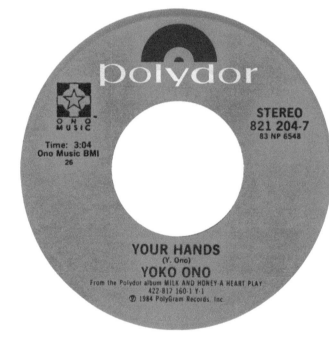

'GIVE PEACE A CHANCE' / 'COLD TURKEY'
PLASTIC ONO BAND

UK release March 12 1984; Apple G45 2; failed to chart.

'GIVE PEACE A CHANCE'

As part of a short-lived golden-oldies reissue campaign, EMI released two early Lennon solo A-sides as a double A-side 7-inch single. Although put out by EMI, the picture-sleeved single was manufactured with Apple labels.

'I'M STEPPING OUT' / 'SLEEPLESS NIGHT'
JOHN LENNON / YOKO ONO

UK release July 15 1984; Polydor POSP 702; 12-inch Polydor POSPX 702; failed to chart.
US release March 19 1984; Polydor 821-107-7; chart high No.55.

'I'M STEPPING OUT'

Polydor issued this single in Britain as the third and final one from *Milk And Honey*. British 7-inch pressings were issued with silver die-cut labels and a picture sleeve based on the American sleeve for 'Borrowed Time'. As with the previous single, it was issued as a 12-inch with the added 'bonus' of Yoko's 'Loneliness', taken from her *It's Alright* album.

Polydor issued the single in the USA with a picture sleeve and generic red Polydor labels, with or without '45 RPM' and with the numbers '19', '26' or '54' printed on the label. Polydor also issued a demonstration 7-inch single (821 107-7-DJ) with album and edited versions of the song. Issued with the commercial picture sleeve, the demonstration record was manufactured with a small number '26' on the label.

JOHN LENNON

I'M
STEPPING
OUT

POSP 702
©1983 Ono Music ℗1984 PolyGram Inc

ONO
MUSIC

taken from the polydor LP 'milk and honey'
POLH5

YOKO ONO

SLEEPLESS NIGHT

sleeve design-simon halfon

219

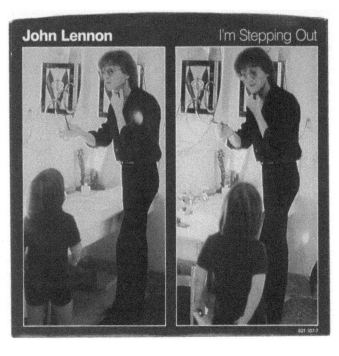

EVERY MAN HAS A WOMAN
VARIOUS ARTISTS

John Lennon 'Every Man Has A Woman Who Loves Him'; **Spirit Choir** 'Now Or Never'.

UK release September 21 1984; LP Polydor POLH 13; CD Polydor 823 490-2 released November 16; failed to chart.
US release September 17 1984; LP Polydor 422-823 490-1 Y-1; CD Polydor 823 490-2 released November   19; failed to chart.

'Every Man Has A Woman Who Loves Him' (Ono)
John Lennon (vocals, guitar), Earl Slick (guitar), Hugh McCracken (guitar), Tony Levin (bass), George Small   (keyboards), Arthur Jenkins (percussion), Andy Newmark (drums). Recorded at Hit Factory, New York City, NY, USA. Produced by John Lennon.
'Now Or Never' (Ono)
John Lennon (guitar), Stan Bronstein (saxophone), George Young (saxophone), Gary Van Scyoc (bass), Adam Ippolito (piano, organ), Wayne 'Tex' Gabriel (guitar), Richard Frank Jr. (drums, percussion). Recorded at The Record Plant East, New York City. Produced by John & Yoko Plastic Ono Band with Elephant's Memory.

EVERY MAN HAS A WOMAN

Issued to mark Yoko Ono's 50th birthday (actually it was a little late), *Every Man Has A Woman* was conceived as a tribute album featuring both new and archive recordings from an eclectic group of musicians.

Despite record company hype, Lennon's reading of his 'Every Man Has A Woman Who Loves Him', did not feature a lead vocal. Rather, his harmony to Ono's lead vocal was remixed at Sigma Sound in July 1984 with the intention of presenting it as a genuine lead vocal. At around the same time, Ono revealed that there was a version of 'Hard Times Are Over' with Lennon taking the lead vocal; this remains unreleased. Whether or not it is a genuine lead vocal or another harmony vocal remixed and presented as the real thing is not clear.

Lennon's other contribution to the album was his guitar-playing on a middle-of-the-road version of Ono's 'Now Or Never'. Recorded in February and March 1972 while the Lennons were in full-on political mode, it was, perhaps, an attempt to engage with middle America. The pair had already appeared on *The Mike Douglas Show* in an effort to reach the masses, so this may have been intended to spread the message beyond the small circle of Lennon fans and counterculture rebels who were their main audience in 1972.

The album was issued with generic red Polydor labels and lyric sheet, as well as on CD.

'EVERY MAN HAS A WOMAN WHO LOVES HIM' / 'IT'S ALRIGHT'
JOHN LENNON / SEAN ONO LENNON

UK release November 16 1984; Polydor POSP 712; failed to chart.
US release October 8 1984; Polydor 881 387-7; failed to chart.

'EVERY MAN HAS A WOMAN WHO LOVES HIM'

Polydor issued this as a single in Britain with silver die-cut labels and picture sleeve. Some copies were also put out with a poster similar to that issued with the 12-inch pressing of 'Borrowed Time'.

The single was issued by Polydor in the USA with red Polydor labels and picture sleeve identical to the British release. Commercial pressings were manufactured with minor typographical differences: stock copies can be found with the numbers '19', '22', or '172' printed on the label. Polydor also issued a demonstration 7-inch single (881 378-7-DJ) with the stereo version on both sides of the disc. A small number '22' was printed on the label.

EVERY MAN HAS A WOMAN WHO LOVES HIM
John Lennon
JOHN LENNON

881 378-7

881 378-7

b/w IT'S ALRIGHT
Sean Ono Lennon
SEAN ONO LENNON

From The Polydor Album "EVERY MAN HAS A WOMAN" 823 490-1 Y-1

℗ 1984 PolyGram Records, Inc.
© 1984 PolyGram Records, Inc.
Manufactured and Marketed by PolyGram Records, Inc.
810 Seventh Avenue, New York, New York 10019. Printed in
U.S.A. All Rights Reserved. Unauthorized Duplication Is
A Violation Of Applicable Laws.

Manufactured and Marketed by
PolyGram Records

Polydor

PROMOTIONAL
COPY
NOT FOR SALE
Time: 3:32
Lenono Music
(BMI)

22

STEREO
45 RPM
881 378-7 DJ
84 NP 6747
Produced by
John Lennon

EVERY MAN HAS A WOMAN WHO LOVES HIM
(Yoko Ono)
JOHN LENNON
From the Polydor album 422-823 490-1 Y-1
"EVERY MAN HAS A WOMAN"
℗ 1984 PolyGram Records, Inc.

PROMOTIONAL
COPY
NOT FOR SALE
Time: 3:32
Lenono Music
(BMI)

22

STEREO
45 RPM
881 378-7 DJ
84 NP 6747
Produced by
John Lennon

EVERY MAN HAS A WOMAN WHO LOVES HIM
(Yoko Ono)
JOHN LENNON
From the Polydor album 422-823 490-1 Y-1
"EVERY MAN HAS A WOMAN"
℗ 1984 PolyGram Records, Inc.

Time: 3:32
Lenono Music
(BMI)

19

ONO
MUSIC

STEREO
45 RPM
881 378-7
84 NP 6747
Produced by
John Lennon

EVERY MAN HAS A WOMAN WHO LOVES HIM
(Yoko Ono)
From the Polydor album 422-823 490-1 Y-1
"EVERY MAN HAS A WOMAN"
JOHN LENNON
℗ 1984 PolyGram Records, Inc.

MANUFACTURED AND MARKETED BY POLYGRAM RECORDS, INC. • 810 SEVENTH AVENUE, NEW YORK, N.Y. 10019

Time: 2:26
Ono Music
(BMI)

19

ONO
MUSIC

STEREO
45 RPM
881 378-7
84 NP 6755
Produced by
Yoko Ono and
Sean Ono Lennon

IT'S ALRIGHT
(Yoko Ono)
From the Polydor album 422-823 490-1 Y-1
"EVERY MAN HAS A WOMAN"
SEAN ONO LENNON
℗ 1984 PolyGram Records, Inc.

MANUFACTURED AND MARKETED BY POLYGRAM RECORDS, INC. • 810 SEVENTH AVENUE, NEW YORK, N.Y. 10019

'JEALOUS GUY' / 'GOING DOWN ON LOVE'
JOHN LENNON

UK release November 18 1985; Parlophone R 6117; 12-inch Parlophone 12 R 6117 'Jealous Guy' / 'Going Down', 'Oh Yoko!'; chart high No.65.

'JEALOUS GUY'

Issued in the UK to promote the release on home video of *Imagine – The Film*, 'Jealous Guy' had already hit the Number 1 spot in Britain when covered by Roxy Music. This time, however, the song barely scraped into the lower end of the charts. Issued by Parlophone with generic labels as 7 and 12-inch singles, it was released in a picture sleeve designed by Shoot That Tiger!. A video compiled from footage from the *Imagine* film was used to promote the single. EMI provided stores with a 20-inch by 30-inch full-colour poster that advertised the *Imagine* video, the 'Jealous Guy' single, the *John Lennon Collection*, and the *Imagine* album.

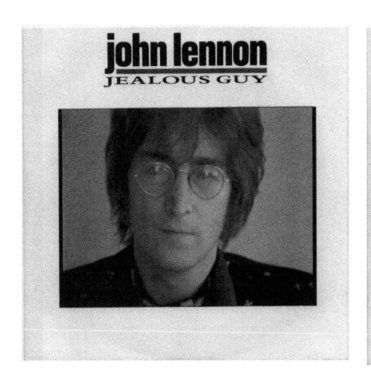
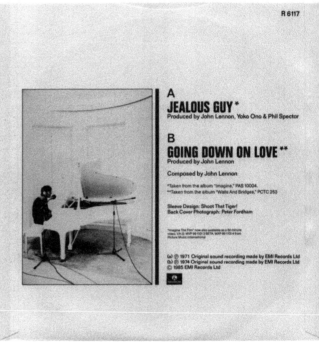

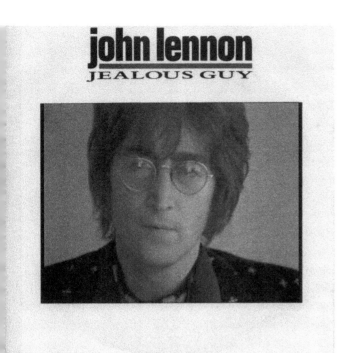

LIVE IN NEW YORK CITY
JOHN LENNON

Side 1 'New York City', 'It's So Hard', 'Woman Is The Nigger Of The World', 'Well Well Well', 'Instant Karma! (We All Shine On)'.
Side 2 'Mother', 'Come Together', 'Imagine', 'Cold Turkey', 'Hound Dog', 'Give Peace A Chance'.
UK release February 24 1986; LP Parlophone PCS 7301; CD Parlophone CDP 7 46096 2 released April 28 1986; chart high No.55.
US release January 24 1986; LP Capitol SV-12451; CD Capitol CDP 7 46096 2 released May 26 1986; chart high No.41.

'Come Together' (Lennon, McCartney)
'Hound Dog' (Leiber, Stoller)

Both with John Lennon (vocal, guitar), Yoko Ono (piano), Stan Bronstein (saxophone), Gary Van Scyoc (bass), John Ward (bass), Adam Ippolito (piano), Richard Frank Jr. (drums and percussion), Jim Keltner (drums). Both recorded live at Madison Square Garden, New York City, NY, USA. Both produced by Yoko Ono; original recordings supervised by Phil Spector.

LIVE IN NEW YORK CITY

Her contract with Polydor having expired, Ono re-signed with EMI and began work on releasing more Lennon material from the archives. *Live In New York City* was the first of two albums consisting of archive material that she issued in 1986. The recording here was taken from the Lennons' One To One concert, which took place at Madison Square Garden on August 30 1972. It was now made available on LP and CD, and the concert was also issued on video with extra material, including Ono's 'Sisters, O Sisters' and 'Born In A Prison'.

The One To One concert took place on the cusp of the Lennons' retreat from radical left-wing politics. Lennon was under FBI surveillance and was being threatened with deportation. Although they had plans to tour and continue with their political activities, John and Yoko were desperate to remain in America, and the only way they could achieve this was to appear less threatening and more like caring members of society. By the time President Nixon was re-elected, Lennon's commitment to the radical left was all but extinguished. However, before Nixon made it into the White House for a second term, the Lennons gave their final full-length concert together.

Lennon and Ono were approached by Geraldo Rivera, who invited them to participate in a charity event he was organising to benefit the Willowbrook Hospital. Rivera had discovered the terrible conditions in which mentally handicapped children were living and wanted to do something about it. As the Lennons had already appeared at several charity concerts, and were desperate to do whatever it took to stay in the USA, Rivera had few problems in securing their services for the event.

The concert was arranged at short notice. Rivera made contact with the pair in late July, which left less than four weeks to arrange everything. Rehearsals with Elephant's Memory were held at Butterfly Studios and the Fillmore East concert hall in New York City. As usual, Lennon taped everything. The rehearsals at Butterfly Studios were recorded and those at the Fillmore East filmed. During the rehearsal period, Lennon, Ono, Elephant's Memory, and Rivera recorded radio spots for broadcast, informing the public that a second matinee performance had been added due to the huge demand for tickets.

On the afternoon of August 30, hundreds of mentally handicapped children enjoyed the One To One festival in Central Park. At 2 o'clock, the matinee performance at Madison Square Garden kicked off with Sha Na Na, Roberta Flack, and Stevie Wonder; John and Yoko topped the bill. That evening, the entire concert was repeated. The Lennons also donated $59,000 to the charity because Rivera felt that not enough money was being raised by the event. He really needn't have worried: Lennon and Ono's generosity helped raise over $1,500,000. Besides giving their time and the money from ticket sales, the Lennons arranged for both matinee and evening shows to be filmed and recorded. The rights to broadcast the concert film were sold to ABC Television for $350,000, which also went to the charity.

Compared with his previous appearances, Lennon's performance at the One To One concert was stunning. He was in fine voice and was particularly animated. Dressed in army fatigues, he looked every bit the king of the counterculture. The rehearsals had paid off. Nothing had been left to chance. The stage set was minimal but beautifully lit, and the sound in the concert hall was spectacular. Although it is generally accepted that the evening performance was the superior of the two, with Lennon referring to the matinee performance as "the rehearsal", it was that matinee show that was used for this album. Tapes of the evening concert proved to have unacceptable levels of tape hiss, which is why they were not used. Later, with the advance of digital technology, the tapes were digitally enhanced, and three songs from the evening concert were included on 1998's *John Lennon Anthology*.

Prior to the release of *Live In New York City*, only a brief extract of 'Give Peace A Chance', performed at the evening concert only, had been made commercially available, cross-faded with 'Happy Xmas (War Is Over)' on the *Shaved Fish* compilation. Part of the Lennons' performance was broadcast by the ABC network as one of their *In Concert* series on December 14 1972. The show was also broadcast by the *King Biscuit Flower Hour*, which provided bootleggers with a good audio source. An edited version of the original ABC Television broadcast, which drew on the evening rather than the matinee concert, was issued by BMG on laserdisc in 1992.

Live In New York City songs

Issued in 1969 by Apple as the B-side to 'Something', 'Come Together' was a swampy, blues-based rocker recorded as The Beatles spiralled out of control. Lennon had been inspired by Dr. Timothy Leary's political campaign slogan, fashioning a potent brew of sexual innuendo and political rhetoric. The lyric echoed Lennon's previous psychedelic utterances, which no doubt delighted Leary, for whom the song was originally intended. There was, however, a more symbolic meaning to Lennon's nonsense verse. The coming together he envisioned was, perhaps, the coming together of the counterculture tribes. Woodstock was just around the corner and the Establishment was looking unstable. In light of the Lennons' peace campaign, it may also have been a plea for global harmony.

That it was the only song from The Beatles' repertoire that Lennon chose to perform during the One To One concert suggests that he intended it as a rallying call of some kind. Performed while he was still committed to radical change, it retained its political impact. But within the context of the concert, it could have also been an appeal for a socially equal society, where those with handicaps are no different from those without them.

Musically, Lennon borrowed from Chuck Berry's 'You Can't Catch Me' as a way into his song. He did this all the time and wasn't alone in doing so. George Harrison borrowed from The Edwin Hawkins Singers' 'Oh Happy Day' when writing 'My Sweet Lord', for which he was sued; not because it resembled 'Oh Happy Day' but because, it was claimed, of similarities with The Chiffons' 'He's So Fine'. Usually, Lennon had the sense to disguise his borrowings. This time, however, he retained a line from Berry's original and was sued for breach of copyright. The case dragged on for years and Lennon ended up in court – although he eventually came out the winner.

A massive hit for Elvis Presley, 'Hound Dog' was originally recorded by Big Mama Thornton in 1953. Elvis heard a reworked version by Freddie Bell & The Bellboys and decided to have a go at recording the song himself. The result was a defining moment in rock'n'roll history. Like Presley, Lennon loved the song, which is why he decided to perform it at the One To One concert. If not the best version ever captured on tape, it is one of the most committed and spirited. Lennon was having fun, and that's what comes across.

The other songs Lennon performed at the One To One concerts don't improve on the original studio versions, but they are among the best live recordings he made. Performing material from his *Plastic Ono Band*, *Imagine*, and *Some Time In New York City* albums, Lennon, backed by Elephant's Memory, was on top form. Previous live shows had been ragged affairs, but the One To One concerts were models of professionalism. He delivered a virtuoso performance that matched the equally stunning performance that George Harrison gave at the Concert For Bangla Desh at the same venue the previous year.

Live In New York City data

Parlophone issued the album in the UK with generic labels and full-colour inner sleeve. The CD, issued two months after the vinyl, was manufactured by Nimbus and issued with a four-page booklet.

In the USA, Capitol issued the LP with black/colour band labels and full-colour inner sleeve. The LP was also issued as a Columbia House edition (SV-512451) and as a RCA Music Service edition (R-144497). RCA Music Service also issued a white-shell 8-track cartridge (S-144497).

Although no singles were pulled from the album for commercial release, Capitol issued a 12-inch promotional single to radio stations. 'Imagine', backed with 'Come Together', was issued in a plain white card sleeve with a three-and-a-quarter-inch by seven-inch sticker attached to the top left corner. The 33 rpm record (SPRO-9585 / 9586) was issued with black/colour band labels. 'Imagine' / 'Come Together' was also issued as a promotional 7-inch single (PRP-1163) in Japan. In-store displays and promotional posters advertising both the record and video were issued to record stores.

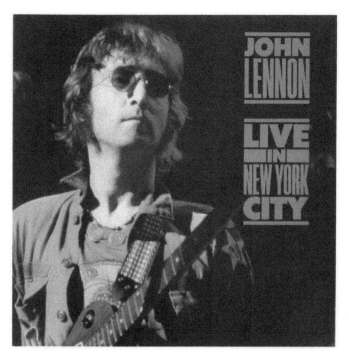

Columbia House edition has SV-512451 on front, spine, back and inner sleeve. SV-512451 on labels. Cover & spine read: Live In New York City. Labels read: John Lennon Live In New York City.

RCA Music Club edition has R144497 as the catalogue number on the front and back cover as well as the spine and labels. SV-12451 is also listed as a catalogue number on the labels. The back cover has a blank white rectangle where the barcode would be.

MENLOVE AVE.
JOHN LENNON

Side 1 'Here We Go Again', 'Rock And Roll People', 'Angel Baby', 'Since My Baby Left Me', 'To Know Her Is To Love Her'.

Side 2 'Steel And Glass', 'Scared', 'Old Dirt Road', 'Nobody Loves You (When You're Down And Out)', 'Bless You'.

UK release November 3 1986; LP Parlophone PCS 7308; CD Parlophone CDP 7 46576 2 released April 13 1987; chart high No.119.

US release October 27 1986; LP Capitol SJ-12533; CD Capitol CDP 7 46576 2 released April 7 1987; chart high No.127.

'Here We Go Again' (Lennon, Spector)

John Lennon (vocals), Art Munson (guitar), Ray Neapolitan (bass), Michael Omartian (keyboards), William Perkins (woodwind), William Perry (guitar), Mac Rebennack (keyboards), Louie Shelton (guitar), Phil Spector (piano, guitar), Nino Tempo (saxophone, keyboards), Anthony Terran (trumpet), Andy Thomas (piano), Michael Wofford (piano), Jim Horn (saxophone), Plas Johnson (saxophone), Joseph Kelson (horn), Jim Keltner (drums), Bobby Keys (saxophone), Ronald Kossajda (instrument unknown), Michael Lang (piano), Ronald Langinger (saxophone), Barry Mann (piano), Julian Matlock (clarinet), Michael Melvoin (piano), Donald Menza (saxophone), Dale Anderson (guitar), Jeff Barry (piano), Hal Baine (drums), Jim Calvert (instrument unknown), Conte Candoli (trumpet), Frank Capp (drums), Larry Carlton (guitar), Gene Cipriano (saxophone), David Cohen (guitar), Gary Coleman (percussion), Steve Cropper (guitar), Jesse Ed Davis (guitar), Alan Estes (percussion), Chuck Findley (trumpet), Steven Forman (percussion), Terry Gibbs (piano or percussion), Bob Glaub (bass), Jim Gordon (drums), Robert Hardaway (woodwind), Leon Russell (keyboards), Jose Feliciano (guitar), Michael Hazelwood (instrument unknown), Thomas Hensley (bass), Dick Hieronymus (instrument unknown).

'Rock And Roll People' (Lennon)

John Lennon (vocals and guitar), Ken Ascher (keyboards), David Spinozza (guitar), Gordon Edwards (bass), Jim Keltner (drums).

'Angel Baby' (Hamlin)

Personnel as 'Here We Go Again'.

'Since My Baby Left Me' (Crudup)

Personnel as 'Here We Go Again'.

'To Know Her Is To Love Her' (Spector)

Personnel as 'Here We Go Again'.

All recorded at A&M Studios or Record Plant West, Los Angeles, CA, USA and produced by Phil Spector/arranged by John Lennon and Phil Spector, except 'Rock And Roll People' recorded at Record Plant East, New York City, NY, USA and produced by John Lennon.

MENLOVE AVE.

This album drew on outtakes from two albums that bookend a turbulent period in Lennon's solo career. *Rock 'N' Roll* and *Walls And Bridges* each had their own unique atmosphere influenced by events in Lennon's life. He rode an emotional roller-coaster during the nine months in which these recordings were made, and the emotions he experienced and expressed then appear all the more concentrated here.

The *Rock 'N' Roll* outtakes reveal Phil Spector's chaos-and-control production technique and dispel Lennon's assertions that they were unusable. Lennon may have described these outtakes as unworkable, but the sense of relief and joy he found while recording a soundtrack to his youth leaps from the speakers. They may not be the greatest songs either Lennon or Spector made, but they reveal that not all was doom and gloom during Lennon's LA sojourn.

The recordings that followed his return to New York City reveal just how down Lennon was in the wake of his 'lost weekend'. Recorded during rehearsals for *Walls And Bridges*, they are suffused with a depth of loneliness and pain that is almost palpable. Lacking the sophisticated production of the finished masters, these rehearsal takes are stripped-to-the-bone renditions that expose Lennon's inner darkness. When issued on *Walls And Bridges* they lost some of the psychological gloom audible on these early cuts, but still revealed a troubled mind. That doesn't mean that there is no light to illuminate the proceedings here: Lennon improvised several lyrics, often with hilarious results.

Unlike *Live In New York City*, the *Menlove Ave.* album was a relative flop. It failed to enter the top 100 in either Britain or America and received minimal to no publicity.

Menlove Ave. songs

'Here We Go Again' is the only Lennon–Spector song to emerge from their four-year partnership. What or how much Spector contributed to the song is difficult to confirm. A solo Lennon demo, recorded before he entered the studio with Spector, reveals little of the producer's influence. Recorded during the infamous *Rock 'N' Roll* sessions, 'Here We Go Again' bears no resemblance to anything else recorded at these sessions. Obviously, it was not intended for Lennon's proposed album of rock'n'roll standards, and its monumental wall-of-sound production excluded it from *Walls And Bridges*. The reason for its recording, like Spector's co-author credit, remains a mystery.

From its serpentine introductory notes that seem to spiral into eternity, to its swirling brass arrangement, 'Here We Go Again' finds Lennon contemplating the meaning of life. It is both a personal and philosophical examination of the eternal question, and it also echoes George Harrison's meditations on the theme of eternal return. However, unlike Harrison, Lennon sounds resigned to the fact that we are bound by karmic laws and unable to transcend them. The song seems to undermine what he'd proposed only three years earlier with 'Instant Karma!'. The egalitarianism of that song is replaced by a vision of disparate also-rans. Lennon's dream of global harmony through positive projection appears tarnished by a realisation, perhaps brought about by the efforts of the American authorities to deport him, that far from reaching a state of enlightenment, mankind is doomed to repeat its mistakes, forever.

Lennon had been attempting to perfect his 'Rock And Roll People', an outtake from the *Mind Games* album, for some time. He began work on the song in late 1970, when he made a demo recording at his Tittenhurst home. It remained dormant for almost three years before he attempted another demo recording.

With the song foremost in this mind, Lennon tried to record it with the band of session players he was using to record *Mind Games*. It both celebrates and belittles rock musicians, and it never really caught fire. As with McCartney's account of life in a rock'n'roll band, 'Famous Groupies', Lennon's attempts at humour and wordplay for once eluded him. Several takes were attempted, but even Lennon grew tired of the band's inability to *rock* and gave up on the track. Obviously, the band were having an off day. The predictable arrangement verges on third-rate pub-rock, and Jim Keltner's drum fills verge on the amateur.

For some reason, 'Rock And Roll People' was issued as a promotional single for the *Menlove Ave.* album and must have done more harm than good. Almost any other track from side one would have made a better advertisement than this. ('Rock And Roll People' had first appeared commercially on Johnny Winter's 1974 album *John Dawson Winter*. Shelly Yakus, who engineered several of Lennon's albums including *Mind Games*, produced Winter's album and suggested that he might record the song. Lennon agreed, but did not contribute to Winter's recording.)

'Angel Baby' had been intended for *Rock 'N' Roll* and was issued on the *Roots* version but pulled from the official release at the last moment. Originally recorded by Rosie & The Originals in 1959, it was written by Rosie Hamlin at the age of 14. The song started life as a poem about a boyfriend before she added the melody. The original was recorded on a 2-track tape machine in an aircraft hangar and by necessity was a model of simplicity. Issued by the independent Highland Records (H-5001), 'Angel Baby' became a huge hit, reaching Number 5 on the *Billboard* charts. Issued in Britain by London Records (HL-U 9266) it did not make an impact on the British charts but become a classic must-have among rock'n'roll aficionados.

Although Lennon decided against including 'Angel Baby' on his *Rock 'N' Roll* album, it would not have sounded out of place. A typical Phil Spector production transforms the original teen ballad into a monolithic slab of rock'n'roll.

Elvis Presley recorded 'Since My Baby Left Me' in 1956 as an act of recognition and rebellion. Already tiring of the Tin Pan Alley material his record company were suggesting he record, Presley turned to Arthur Crudup's rustic blues in an attempt to distance himself from the mainstream he was slowly drifting toward. It was also an act of solidarity with the blues singer. Presley had already cut Crudup's 'That's Alright Mama', and by recording 'Since My Baby Left Me' he consolidated his allegiance with Crudup and pushed up a notch his claim for authenticity. The song was issued in Britain by HMV as the B-side of Presley's 'I Want You, I Need You, I Love You' (POP 235), which reached Number 9 in the UK charts. Issued in America by RCA, it was a Number 1. Spector transformed Presley's slice of rockabilly for Lennon: slashing the tempo, he created a call-and-response party record that might have been difficult to dance to but which sounded monumental.

'To Know Him Is To Love Him' was a 1957 hit for Phil Spector's first group, The Teddy Bears, for whom he played guitar and wrote their sole hit in tribute to his late father. It was issued by Dore Records (45-503) and became Spector's first American Number 1. Issued in Britain by London Records (HL 8733), the song reached Number 2.

It was another long-standing favourite of Lennon's, and featured in The Beatles' pre-fame repertoire. When the group auditioned for Decca at the company's London studio it was a nervous John Lennon who sang lead on this Spector ballad. The Beatles' recording, with Pete Best on drums, was briefly issued by AFE Records (AFELP 1047) in 1982. A few years earlier, a live recording, this time with Ringo Starr on drums, was issued by Lingasong Records on the two-LP set *Live! At The Star-Club In Hamburg, Germany: 1962* (LNL1). The Beatles also taped the song for the BBC, recording a version at the Corporation's Paris Theatre (in London) on July 16 1963. This recording was issued by Apple on *Live At The BBC* (PCSP 726) in 1994.

As with 'Since My Baby Left Me', Spector slowed the tempo, turning 'To Know Him Is To Love Him' into a pop requiem for his father. Lennon adds to the sense of loss with a vocal loaded with vulnerability. Set against Spector's echoing volley of drums and trademark wall-of-sound, he presents a masterclass in how to deliver a song and manipulate the listener's emotions.

Menlove Ave. data

Capitol issued a promotional 12-inch single of 'Rock And Roll People' (SPRO-9917) to American radio stations, but no commercial singles were pulled from the album. *Menlove Ave.* seems to have been assembled in something of a hurry. Ono's sleevenotes are minimal, and the American LP cover credits the author of 'Since My Baby Left Me' as "unknown". It was of course written by Arthur Crudup. This error appeared on cover proofs printed in Britain but was corrected for commercial copies of the LP (and these early proofs also have the EMI box logo in the bottom right corner of the rear cover, rather than the Parlophone logo that appeared on finished copies). British pressings of the LP were issued with generic black labels; American pressings with Capitol's black/colour band labels. The album was issued on CD in Britain on April 13 1987 and in America on April 7 1987.

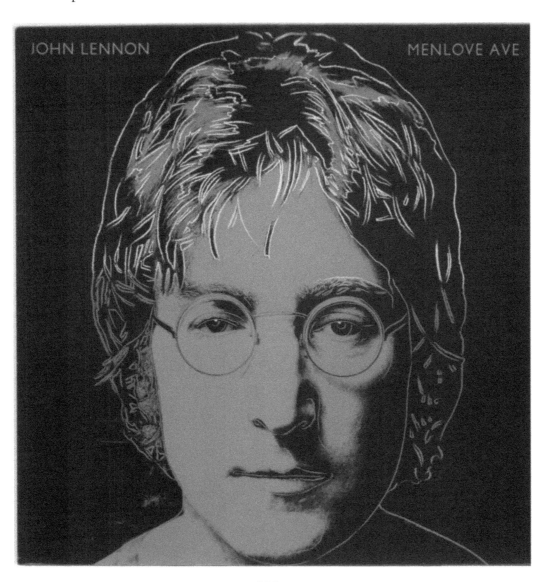

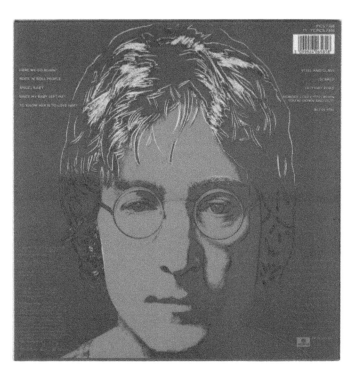

IMAGINE: JOHN LENNON, MUSIC FROM THE MOTION PICTURE
JOHN LENNON

Side 1 'Real Love', 'Twist And Shout', 'Help!', 'In My Life', 'Strawberry Fields Forever', 'A Day In The Life'.
Side 2 'Revolution', 'The Ballad Of John And Yoko', 'Julia', 'Don't Let Me Down', 'Give Peace A Chance'.
Side 3 'How?', 'Imagine' (Rehearsal) / 'God', 'Mother', 'Stand By Me'.
Side 4 'Jealous Guy', 'Woman', 'Beautiful Boy (Darling Boy)', '(Just Like) Starting Over', 'Imagine'.

UK release October 10 1988; LP Parlophone PCSP 722; CD Parlophone CD PCSP 722; chart high No.64.
US release October 4 1988; LP Capitol C1-90803; CD Capitol CDP 7 9080302; chart high No.31.

'Real Love' (Lennon)
Personnel: John Lennon (vocals and guitar). Recorded at The Dakota, New York. Produced by John Lennon.

IMAGINE: JOHN LENNON

This was a career overview that doubled as the soundtrack to the Lennon biopic, *Imagine: John Lennon*. Work on the Ono-sanctioned documentary began in 1988 when David Wolper and Andrew Solt were given unrestricted access to the Lennons' extensive film archive. A forerunner to The Beatles' *Anthology* project, the film featured much rare footage, and old interviews with Lennon were used to provide a narrative. As with The Beatles' *Anthology*, the film was marketed with a home video release, a soundtrack album, and a large, glossy book. Although intended as such, the album did not qualify as a soundtrack, because the musical performances in the film differed from those issued on the record. Furthermore, the album presented the songs in a different sequence to the film. EMI insisted on this to make the listening experience as enjoyable as possible.

For the first time, songs from The Beatles' catalogue appeared on a John Lennon album, but it was not the first time that group and solo material had been mixed on an album. *The Best Of George Harrison* (PAS 10011), issued by Parlophone in 1976, featured one side of songs performed by The Beatles and another of solo compositions.

Even before it was transformed into a new Beatles single, 'Real Love' had a remarkable history. The song was, in fact, a composite of two pieces that eventually metamorphosed into a charming Lennon ballad. Lennon began by combining elements of ' The Way The World Is' and 'Baby Make Love To You'. Once he had glued the various melodic fragments together, he wrote a lyric that recounted his day-to-day routine.

Lennon's early attempts at the lyric reflected his desire to chronicle his activities with a chorus of "it's real life", which he later changed to "it's real love". He made more changes to the lyrics as work on the song progressed. Once he'd rewritten the verses and changed the chorus, Lennon began to make more demo recordings. The version used for the later Beatles recording was piano-based, but the version presented here was performed on guitar. Despite some interesting chord changes and an intimate atmosphere, 'Real Love' has nothing new or significant to say. Having run out of things to say about himself, Lennon seemed to have had little to say on other matters either. As compelling as it is, 'Real Love' is craftsman-like but uninspired.

Imagine: John Lennon data

Parlophone issued the album as a two-record set with generic black labels, printed inner sleeves, and gatefold cover. The Capitol issue featured purple Capitol labels. Capitol issued 'Stand By Me' as a promotional 12-inch single (SPRO-79453) with a rectangular white sticker that proclaimed "'Stand By Me' The new single from the album Imagine John Lennon Music From The Original Motion Picture". The single was not issued commercially.

REAL LOVE
TWIST AND SHOUT*
HELP!*
IN MY LIFE*
STRAWBERRY FIELDS FOREVER*
A DAY IN THE LIFE*

REVOLUTION*
THE BALLAD OF JOHN AND YOKO*
JULIA*
DON'T LET ME DOWN*
GIVE PEACE A CHANCE

*PERFORMED BY THE BEATLES

HOW?
IMAGINE (Rehearsal)
GOD
MOTHER
STAND BY ME

JEALOUS GUY
WOMAN
BEAUTIFUL BOY
(JUST LIKE) STARTING OVER
IMAGINE

I M A G I N E
John Lennon

MUSIC FROM THE MOTION PICTURE

PARLOPHONE

IMAGINE—JOHN LENNON

Music from the motion picture

Original sound recordings
made by EMI Records
Ltd except *Original
sound recordings made
by Yoko Ono under
exclusive licence to
Capitol Records Inc.
This compilation ℗ 1988
EMI Records Ltd

RECORD 2
SIDE 1
33⅓ r.p.m.
STEREO
PCSP 722
PCSP 722C

1. HOW? ℗ 1971   2. IMAGINE (Short Rehearsal)* ℗ 1988
3. GOD ℗ 1970   4. MOTHER* ℗ 1986
5. STAND BY ME ℗ 1975

Composed by: 1-4. John Lennon, 5. King/Leiber/Stoller

Produced by: 1, 3. John & Yoko and Phil Spector,
4. Yoko Ono, 5. John Lennon

1, 3, 4. Northern Songs Ltd, 2. Chappell Music Ltd,
5. Trio Music Ltd

PARLOPHONE

IMAGINE—JOHN LENNON

Music from the motion picture

Original sound recordings
made by EMI Records
Ltd except *Original
sound recordings made
by Yoko Ono under
exclusive licence to
Capitol Records Inc.
This compilation ℗ 1988
EMI Records Ltd

RECORD 2
SIDE 2
33⅓ r.p.m.
STEREO
PCSP 722
PCSP 722D

1. JEALOUS GUY ℗ 1971   2. WOMAN* ℗ 1980
3. BEAUTIFUL BOY* ℗ 1980   4. STARTING OVER* ℗ 1980
5. IMAGINE ℗ 1971

Composed by John Lennon

Produced by: 1, 5. John & Yoko and Phil Spector,
2-4. John Lennon, Yoko Ono and Jack Douglas

Chappell Music Ltd

'JEALOUS GUY' / 'GIVE PEACE A CHANCE'
JOHN LENNON

US release September 19 1988; Capitol B-44230; chart high No.91.

'JEALOUS GUY'

Capitol released 'Jealous Guy' / 'Give Peace A Chance' to promote the *Imagine: John Lennon* album, issued as a 7-inch single with generic purple labels and a picture sleeve. Demonstration copies of the A-side were issued as a one-track CD single (DPRO-79417).

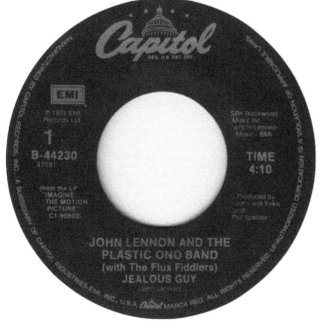

'IMAGINE' / 'JEALOUS GUY', 'HAPPY XMAS (WAR IS OVER)'
JOHN LENNON

UK release November 28 1988; Parlophone R 6199; picture disc Parlophone RP 6199 released December 5; 12-inch Parlophone 12 R 6199; CD single CDR 6199; chart high No.45.

'IMAGINE'

Parlophone issued a three-track 7-inch single, 'Imagine' / 'Jealous Guy', 'Happy Xmas (War Is Over)' with generic black labels and a picture sleeve. They also issued it as a 7-inch picture disc, 12-inch, and a CD single. The CD featured a bonus track, 'Give Peace A Chance'. However, this was merely the live version from the One To One concert cross-faded with 'Happy Xmas (War Is Over)', as on the *Shaved Fish* album. Parlophone had planned to issue a 12-inch picture disc but did not. Due to consumer demand for Lennon product on the tenth anniversary of his death, EMI reissued the CD single in Europe on November 19 1990. Although identical to the original issue, it was given a new catalogue number, 20415242.

LENNON
JOHN LENNON

Disc 1 'Give Peace A Chance', 'Blue Suede Shoes', 'Money (That's What I Want)', 'Dizzy Miss Lizzy', 'Yer Blues', 'Cold Turkey', 'Instant Karma! (We All Shine On)', 'Mother', 'Hold On', 'I Found Out', 'Working Class Hero', 'Isolation', 'Remember', 'Love', 'Well, Well, Well', 'Look At Me', 'God', 'My Mummy's Dead', 'Power To The People', 'Well (Baby Please Don't Go)'.
Disc 2 'Imagine', 'Crippled Inside', 'Jealous Guy', 'It's So Hard', 'Give Me Some Truth', 'Oh My Love', 'How Do You Sleep?', 'How?', 'Oh Yoko!', 'Happy Xmas (War Is Over)', 'Woman Is The Nigger Of The World', 'New York City', 'John Sinclair', 'Come Together', 'Hound Dog', 'Mind Games', 'Aisumasen (I'm Sorry)', 'One Day (At A Time)', 'Intuition', 'Out The Blue'.
Disc 3 'Whatever Gets You Thru The Night', 'Going Down On Love', 'Old Dirt Road', 'Bless You', 'Scared', '#9 Dream', 'Surprise, Surprise (Sweet Bird Of Paradox)', 'Steel And Glass', 'Nobody Loves You (When You're Down And Out)', 'Stand By Me', 'Ain't That A Shame', 'Do You Want To Dance', 'Sweet Little Sixteen', 'Slippin' And Slidin'', 'Angel Baby', 'Just Because', 'Whatever Gets You Thru The Night' (Live Version), 'Lucy In The Sky With Diamonds' (Live Version), 'I Saw Her Standing There' (Live Version).
Disc 4 '(Just Like) Starting Over', 'Cleanup Time', 'I'm Losing You', 'Beautiful Boy (Darling Boy)', 'Watching The Wheels', 'Woman', 'Dear Yoko', 'I'm Stepping Out', 'I Don't Wanna Face It', 'Nobody Told Me', 'Borrowed Time', '(Forgive Me) My Little Flower Princess', 'Every Man Has A Woman Who Loves Him', 'Grow Old With Me'.

UK release October 1 1990; Parlophone CDS 7 95220 2; failed to chart.
US release July 1991; Capitol CDS 7 95220 2; failed to chart.

LENNON

Issued to celebrate what would have been Lennon's 50th birthday, this was a 73-track, four-CD set that covered his solo career from 1969 to 1980. The compilation, which takes tracks from every Lennon album from *Live Peace In Toronto – 1969* to *Menlove Ave.*, was compiled by Beatles expert Mark Lewisohn and approved by Yoko Ono.

It contained seven tracks issued on CD for the first time, four from *Live Peace In Toronto – 1969* and three from Lennon's performance with Elton John at Madison Square Garden in 1974. All of the tracks were digitally remastered, with several treated with a 'No Noise' system to eliminate tape hiss.

The four CDs were issued in a substantial card case with a booklet featuring lyrics and photographs. Although the set was issued worldwide on October 1 1990, large numbers manufactured by EMI in Britain were exported. Capitol, for example, imported the set from Britain and didn't get around to officially issuing it until July 1991.

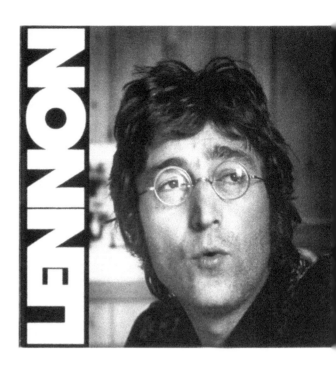

242

ROCK AND ROLL CIRCUS
VARIOUS ARTISTS

The Dirty Mac 'Yer Blues'; **Yoko Ono, Ivy Gitlis & The Dirty Mac** 'Whole Lotta Yoko'.
UK release October 14 1996; CD Mercury 526 771-2; failed to chart.
US release October 15 1996; CD Mercury 8 21954 2; chart high No.92.

'Yer Blues' (Lennon, McCartney)
John Lennon (vocals, guitar), Eric Clapton (guitar), Keith Richards (bass), Mitch Mitchell (drums). Recorded on Olympic Mobile Recording Truck at InterTel Television, London, England. Produced by Jimmy Miller, Jody Klein, and Lenne Alink.

'Whole Lotta Yoko' (Ono)
John Lennon (vocals, guitar), Yoko Ono (vocals), Ivy Gitlis (violin), Eric Clapton (guitar), Keith Richards (bass), Mitch Mitchell (drums). Recorded on Olympic Mobile Recording Truck at InterTel Television, London, England. Produced by Jimmy Miller, Jody Klein, and Lenne Alink.

ROCK AND ROLL CIRCUS

Back in 1968, The Rolling Stones were looking for a way to promote their soon-to-be-released album *Beggar's Banquet*, and they hired Michael Lindsey-Hogg to make a one-hour television special to feature them and their friends. Lindsey-Hogg suggested that the film take the form of a travelling circus, but with pop stars in place of lion-tamers. Established acts and newcomers mixed with circus performers and a one-off supergroup fronted by John Lennon.

Rehearsals began on Tuesday December 10 at Stonebridge House, Wembley, north-west London before filming began the next day. The audience was admitted to the studio from the early afternoon, but Lennon didn't take to the stage until late in the evening. Speaking to John Peel on the night of December 11, Lennon suggested that he'd agreed to appear at the last moment. Stevie Winwood had cancelled abruptly and Jagger asked Lennon if he could fill the gap.

Forming The Dirty Mac, Lennon was backed by Eric Clapton on guitar, Keith Richards on bass, and Mitch Mitchell on drums, and they took to the stage at around 10:00pm, performing a blistering version of 'Yer Blues', not dissimilar to Lennon's version on Live Peace In Toronto, except it is a little tighter. Several takes later, it was Yoko Ono's turn. Backed by The Dirty Mac, she was joined by Ivry Gitlis on violin, and they jammed on a simple blues riff for 'Whole Lotta Yoko'. Ono gives her usual vocalisations and Gitlis scrapes away in the vain hope of keeping up with the band. While this kind of jamming could occasionally produce spectacular results, as on *Yoko Ono/Plastic Ono Band*, here it fails to impress.

The Stones eventually performed in the early hours of the morning of December 12, and although their performance was said to be one of their best, the film was scrapped. It's been suggested that they were unhappy with their performance and felt up-staged by The Who, who delivered a powerful reading of 'A Quick One (While He's Away)'.

Rock And Roll Circus data
Scheduled for release in 1995, the CD and video of the performances were put on hold until 1996. Issued by Mercury Records, the CDs were manufactured in America and imported into Britain. The album was not issued on vinyl. A DVD of the film was issued on October 12 2004 and featured bonus previously-unseen footage of the backstage meeting between Jagger and Lennon plus an alternative take of Lennon performing 'Yer Blues'.

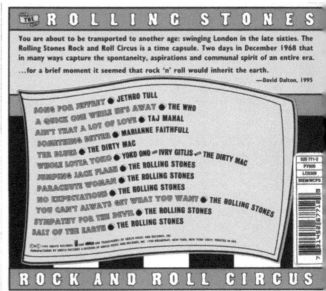

LENNON LEGEND – THE VERY BEST OF JOHN LENNON
JOHN LENNON

Side 1 'Imagine', 'Instant Karma!', 'Mother', 'Jealous Guy', 'Power To The People'.
Side 2 'Cold Turkey', 'Love', 'Mind Games', 'Whatever Gets You Through The Night', '#9 Dream'.
Side 3 'Stand By Me', '(Just Like) Starting Over', 'Woman', 'Beautiful Boy (Darling Boy)', 'Watching The Wheels'.
Side 4 'Nobody Told Me', 'Borrowed Time', 'Working Class Hero', 'Happy Xmas (War Is Over)', 'Give Peace A Chance'.

UK release October 27 1997; LP Parlophone 8 21954 1; CD Parlophone 8 21954 2; chart high No.4.
US release February 24 1998; CD Capitol 8 21954 2; LP Capitol 8 21954 1 released March 10 1988; chart high No.65.

LENNON LEGEND

This was a remastered and revamped version of 1982's *The John Lennon Collection*. As with that previous best-of, this overview of his solo career sold extremely well, due in part to a massive advertising campaign and careful remastering, which made this the best-sounding Lennon album issued so far.

Parlophone issued it as a two-record set in a gatefold cover with printed inner sleeves and black labels. The LP set was also issued in America by Parlophone with 'Made in U.S.A.' printed on the back cover.

The CD, manufactured by EMI, was issued with a ten-page booklet that included rare photographs taken during the recording of *Imagine*. 'Advance Listening' copies of the CD (CDPP 037) were issued prior to the official release date. The CD was re-promoted in 2003 with a new colourised outer sleeve and catalogue number (595 0672).

In Britain, the album was promoted with TV advertising, in-store displays, and billboard-size posters in major British cities and on the London Underground. Parlophone issued two one-track promotional CD singles; 'Imagine' (IMAGINE 001), limited to 2,000 copies, and 'Happy Xmas (War Is Over)' (IMAGINE 002), issued in the run-up to Christmas. In Spain, the album was promoted with a one-track promo CD single of *God* (PE 98030).

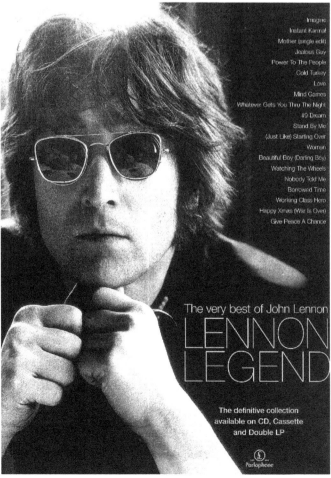

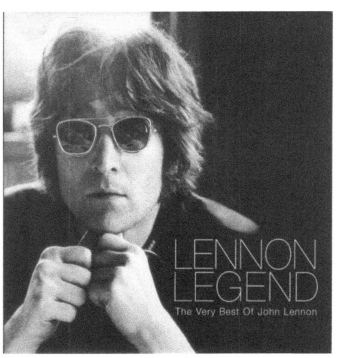

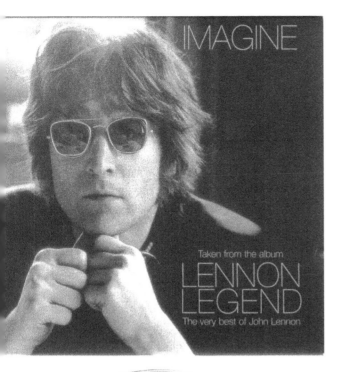

IMAGINE

Taken from the album
LENNON
LEGEND
The very best of John Lennon

IMAGINE
John Lennon and The Plastic Ono Band (with the Flux Fiddlers)
Written by John Lennon

Taken from the album

LENNON
LEGEND
The very best of John Lennon

Imagine
Instant Karma!
Mother (single edit)
Jealous Guy
Power To The People
Cold Turkey
Love
Mind Games
Whatever Gets You Thru The Night
#9 Dream

Stand By Me
(Just Like) Starting Over
Woman
Beautiful Boy (Darling Boy)
Watching The Wheels
Nobody Told Me
Borrowed Time
Working Class Hero
Happy Xmas (War Is Over)
Give Peace A Chance

For Promotion Only
Not For Sale

Lenono Music administered by BMG Music Publishing · Produced by John & Yoko and Phil Spector
℗ 1971 the copyright in this sound recording is owned by EMI Records Ltd.
Photography: Spud Murphy
Design & Artwork: PLinard Marketing and Advertising Ltd.

Parlophone

ALL RIGHTS OF THE PRODUCER AND OF THE OWNER OF THE RECORDED WORK RESERVED. UNAUTHORISED COPYING, HIRING, RENTING, PUBLIC PERFORMANCE AND BROADCASTING OF THIS RECORD PROHIBITED. © 1997 THE COPYRIGHT IN THIS COMPILATION IS OWNED BY EMI RECORDS LTD. ©1997 EMI RECORDS LTD. MADE IN UK. STEREO.

IMAGINE

For Promotion Only
Not For Sale

IMAGINE 001

Parlophone

Taken from the album
LENNON
LEGEND
The very best of John Lennon

ALL RIGHTS OF THE PRODUCER AND OF THE OWNER OF THE RECORDED WORK RESERVED. UNAUTHORISED COPYING, HIRING, RENTING, PUBLIC PERFORMANCE AND BROADCASTING OF THIS RECORD PROHIBITED. © 1997 THE COPYRIGHT IN THIS SOUND RECORDING IS OWNED BY EMI RECORDS LTD. ℗ 1971 THE COPYRIGHT IN THIS SOUND RECORDING STEREO. MADE IN UK.

HAPPY XMAS
(WAR IS OVER)

For Promotion Only
Not For Sale

IMAGINE 002

Parlophone

Taken from the album
LENNON
LEGEND
The very best of John Lennon

HAPPY XMAS
(WAR IS OVER)

Taken from the album
LENNON
LEGEND
The very best of John Lennon

HAPPY XMAS
(WAR IS OVER)
John & Yoko and The Plastic Ono Band
with The Harlem Community Choir
Written by John Lennon & Yoko Ono

Taken from the album
LENNON
LEGEND
The very best of John Lennon

For Promotion Only
Not For Sale

Lenono Music/Ono Music administered by
BMG Music Publishing
Produced by John & Yoko and Phil Spector
℗ 1971 the copyright in this sound recording is owned by
EMI Records Ltd.

Photography: Spud Murphy
Design & Artwork: PLinard Marketing and Advertising Ltd.

Parlophone

247

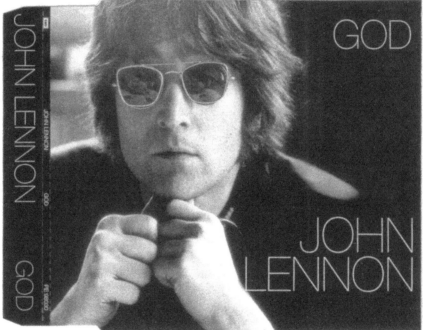

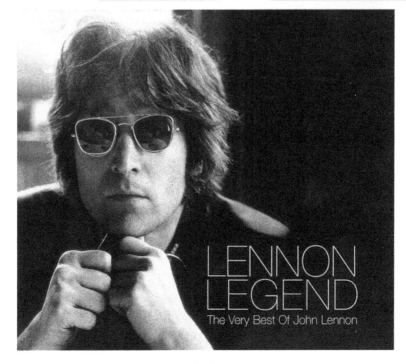

2003 colourised outer sleeve.

248

JOHN LENNON ANTHOLOGY
JOHN LENNON

Disc 1 (Ascot) 'Working Class Hero', 'God', 'I Found Out', 'Hold On', 'Isolation', 'Love', 'Mother', 'Remember', 'Imagine' (Take 1), 'Fortunately', 'Well (Baby Please Don't Go)', 'Oh My Love', 'Jealous Guy', 'Maggie Mae', 'How Do You Sleep?', 'God Save Oz', 'Do The Oz', 'I Don't Want To Be A Soldier', 'Give Peace A Chance', 'Look At Me', 'Long Lost John'.
Disc 2 (New York City) 'New York City', 'Attica State' (Live), 'Imagine' (Live), 'Bring On The Lucie (Freda Peeple)', 'Woman Is The Nigger Of The World', 'Geraldo Rivera – One to One Concert', 'Woman Is The Nigger of The World' (Live), 'It's So Hard' (Live), 'Come Together' (Live), 'Happy Xmas (War Is Over)', 'Luck of the Irish' (Live), 'John Sinclair' (Live), 'The David Frost Show', 'Mind Games (I Promise)', 'Mind Games (Make Love, Not War)', 'One Day At A Time', 'I Know', 'I'm The Greatest', 'Goodnight Vienna', 'Jerry Lewis Telethon', 'A Kiss Is Just A Kiss', 'Real Love', 'You Are Here'.
Disc 3 (The Lost Weekend) 'What You Got', 'Nobody Loves You When You're Down And Out', 'Whatever Gets You Thru the Night' (Home), 'Whatever Gets You Thru the Night' (Studio), 'Yesterday (Parody)', 'Be-Bop-A-Lula', 'Rip It Up', 'Ready Teddy', 'Scared', 'Steel And Glass', 'Surprise, Surprise (Sweet Bird of Paradox)', 'Bless You', 'Going Down On Love', 'Move Over Ms. L', 'Ain't She Sweet', 'Slippin' And Slidin'', 'Peggy Sue', 'Bring It On Home To Me', 'Send Me Some Lovin'', 'Phil And John 1', 'Phil And John 2', 'Phil And John 3', 'When In Doubt, Fuck It', 'Be My Baby', 'Stranger's Room', 'Old Dirt Road'.
Disc 4 (Dakota) 'I'm Losing You', 'Sean's Little Help', 'Serve Yourself', 'My Life', 'Nobody Told Me', 'Life Begins At 40', 'I Don't Wanna Face It', 'Woman', 'Dear Yoko', 'Watching The Wheels', 'I'm Stepping Out', 'Borrowed Time', 'The Rishi Kesh Song', 'Sean's Loud', 'Beautiful Boy', 'Mr. Hyde's Gone (Don't Be Afraid)', 'Only You', 'Grow Old With Me', 'Dear John', 'The Great Wok', 'Mucho Mungo', 'Satire 1', 'Satire 2', 'Satire 3', 'Sean's In The Sky', 'It's Real'.

UK release November 2 1998; CD Capitol 830 6042; chart high No.62.
US release November 3 1998; CD Capitol C2 830 6042; chart high No.99.

'Maggie Mae' (trad arr Lennon)
John Lennon (vocals, guitar). Recorded at The Dakota, New York City, NY, USA.
'Long Lost John' (trad arr Lennon)
John Lennon (vocals, guitar), Klaus Voormann (bass), Ringo Starr (drums). Recorded at Abbey Road Studios, London, England.
'I'm The Greatest' (Lennon)
John Lennon (vocals, piano), George Harrison (guitar), Klaus Voormann (bass), Ringo Starr (drums). Recorded at Sunset Sound, Los Angeles, CA, USA
'Goodnight Vienna' (Lennon)
John Lennon (vocals, piano), Lon Van Eton (guitar), Jesse Ed Davis (guitar), Ringo Starr (drums). Recorded at Record Plant West, Los Angeles, CA, USA.
'Yesterday' (Lennon, McCartney)
John Lennon (vocals, guitar). Recorded at Record Plant East, New York City, NY, USA.
'Ain't She Sweet' (Yellen, Ager)
John Lennon (vocals, guitar), Nicky Hopkins (piano). Recorded at Record Plant East, New York City.
'Be My Baby' (Spector, Greenwich, Barry)
John Lennon (vocals), Art Munson (guitar), Ray Neapolitan (bass), Michael Omartian (keyboards), William Perkins (woodwind), William Perry (guitar), Mac Rebennack (keyboards), Louie Shelton (guitar), Phil Spector (piano, guitar), Nino Tempo (saxophone, keyboards), Anthony Terran (trumpet), Andy Thomas (piano), Michael Wofford (piano), Jim Horn (saxophone), Plas Johnson (saxophone), Joseph Kelson (horn), Jim Keltner (drums), Bobby Keys (saxophone), Ronald Kossajda (instrument unknown), Michael Lang (piano), Ronald Langinger (saxophone), Barry Mann (piano), Julian Matlock (clarinet), Michael Melvoin (piano), Donald Menza (saxophone), Dale Anderson (guitar), Jeff Barry (piano), Hal Baine (drums), Jim Calvert (instrument unknown), Conte Candoli (trumpet), Frank Capp (drums), Larry Carlton (guitar), Gene Cipriano (saxophone), David Cohen (guitar), Gary Coleman (percussion), Steve Cropper (guitar), Jesse Ed Davis (guitar), Alan Estes

(percussion), Chuck Findley (trumpet), Steven Forman (percussion), Terry Gibbs (piano or percussion), Bob Glaub (bass), Jim Gordon (drums), Robert Hardaway (woodwind), Leon Russell (keyboards), Jose Feliciano (guitar), Michael Hazelwood (instrument unknown), Thomas Hensley (bass), Dick Hieronymus (instrument unknown). Recorded at A&M Studios or Record Plant West, Los Angeles, CA, USA.

'Serve Yourself' (Lennon)

John Lennon (vocals, guitar). Recorded at The Dakota.

'Life Begins At 40' (Lennon)

John Lennon (vocals, guitar). Recorded at The Dakota.

'The Rishi Kesh Song' (Lennon)

John Lennon (vocals, guitar). Recorded at The Dakota.

'Sean's Loud'

John Lennon (spoken word), Sean Lennon (guitar). Recorded at The Dakota.

'Mr. Hyde's Gone (Don't Be Afraid)' (Lennon)

Personnel: John Lennon (vocals, piano). Recorded at The Dakota.

'Only You' (Ram, Rand)

John Lennon (vocals, guitar), Steve Cropper (guitar), Jesse Ed Davis (guitar), Billy Preston (electric piano), Harry Nilsson (backing vocals), Ringo Starr (drums). Recorded at Sunset Sound, Los Angeles, CA, USA.

'Dear John' (Lennon)

John Lennon (vocals, guitar). Recorded at The Dakota.

'Mucho Mungo' (Lennon)

John Lennon (vocals, guitar). Recorded at The Dakota.

'Satire 1/2/3' (Lennon)

John Lennon (vocals, guitar). Recorded at The Dakota.

'Sean's In The Sky'

John Lennon, Yoko Ono, Sean Lennon (spoken word). Recorded at The Dakota.

'It's Real' (Lennon)

John Lennon (vocals, guitar). Recorded at The Dakota.

All produced by John Lennon, except: 'Long Lost John' produced by John & Yoko and Phil Spector; 'I'm The Greatest', 'Only You' produced by Richard Perry; 'Be My Baby' produced by Phil Spector/arranged by John Lennon and Phil Spector.

JOHN LENNON ANTHOLOGY

The vogue for retrospective multi-disc boxed sets, often with unreleased material, hit its peak in the late 1990s. Some of the world's greatest musicians, as well as many minor players, had their careers reviewed and neatly packaged in well designed boxes, often with generous booklets stuffed with scholarly essays about the artist. John Lennon was the first ex-Beatle to have his entire solo career condensed and issued in a boxed set. (George Harrison's solo work would be reissued as a boxed set after his death, but, unlike the *Lennon Anthology*, *George Harrison: The Dark Horse Years* and the later *George Harrison: Apple Years* consisted of remastered solo albums with little in the way of unreleased material. The only real bonus was the inclusion of a DVD featuring rare footage.)

The *John Lennon Anthology* was issued in November 1998, but the idea had been around for almost a decade. The project began to take form when EMI acquired the master tapes that Lennon recorded in America while contracted to them. Although EMI had paid for Lennon's sessions, their London archives only held the stereo masters, not the multi-track tapes. However, in the late 1980s, EMI had 477 reels of Lennon studio outtakes shipped to Abbey Road for safekeeping.

At around the same time, Yoko Ono sanctioned what would become a long-running weekly radio programme, *The Lost Lennon Tapes*, syndicated by Westwood One, which featured unheard material from the Lennon archives. Perhaps aware that the programmes would be bootlegged, EMI and Ono agreed to produce a Lennon boxed set that would draw on the best material from *The Lost Lennon Tapes* and the recently acquired studio outtakes.

EMI's next move was to employ Beatles expert Mark Lewisohn to listen to everything that had been shipped from the USA and compile a proposed track listing for a CD boxed set. Between 1991 and 1993, Lewisohn set about compiling what he considered to be the best of the studio outtakes and demo recordings from Lennon's personal tape archive. Lewisohn completed his task in 1994, and then, for some unknown reason, the project ground to a halt.

Enter Rob Stevens, a New Yorker, who had worked on several projects with Ono. It was now Stevens' turn to trawl through the Lennon archive and compile his version of the boxed set. Having listened to everything, he selected about 50 hours of recordings, which he then began to present to Ono so that she could make the final selection. Stevens had one advantage over Lewisohn; he was a studio engineer. Unlike Lewisohn, whose job it was to compile the set, Stevens was also charged with restoring and mixing the tapes. Some of the recordings were cleaned using the Cedar system to remove tape hiss, while the multi-track tapes were mixed at Quad Recording Studios using a variety of vintage consoles.

Besides selecting which songs and takes to include in the boxed set, Ono sequenced the CDs. Stevens maintains that she put a lot of work into this part of the project, sequencing the discs many times until she was completely happy with them. Yet despite her hard work, several discs have anomalies. Disc 2, for example, which focuses on the 1971–73 period, features 'Real Love', recorded around 1979/'80, spoiling the continuity and narrative of the set.

The Stevens/Ono set differed from that complied by Lewisohn. Several songs, including outtakes of 'Cold Turkey', the home demo of 'Give Me Some Truth', 'Just Because' with Lennon greeting his old friends, Paul, George, and Ringo, and an early version of 'The Luck Of The Irish', all failed to make the set. Despite this, the *John Lennon Anthology* was packed with great performances and oodles of unreleased material. Ono noted that there was a lot of good material left off the set that may be issued in the future. "I found that there were many more takes and stuff that really were very presentable," she told *Beatles Monthly*. "In the beginning, I was thinking that this was going to be the ultimate John Lennon box. And I thought, no, we shouldn't call it the ultimate, because there's so much more there. There are still more beautiful songs, but I couldn't fit them all in there. It's possible that this is not the last presentation of John's work."

John Lennon Anthology songs

Much of the best-of material on this set has been dealt with elsewhere in this book, of course, and here we concentrate on the unreleased material it collected. First of these is 'Maggie Mae', famously ad-libbed during The Beatles' *Get Back* sessions. But it was a warm-up favourite that Lennon returned to while taping a batch of home demos for what would become *Double Fantasy*, and the song was obviously haunting him as he attempted this further casual reading.

While Lennon often found it difficult to remember his own lyrics, he had no trouble recalling those of other artists that he'd performed as a youth in Liverpool. 'Long Lost John', a traditional folk song given an up-tempo treatment by Lonnie Donegan, was probably based on the story of Long John Green, a convict with an amazing ability to outrun his pursuers. The version here was recorded during the *Plastic Ono Band* sessions, with Lennon, Starr, and Voormann giving a convincing, spontaneous performance that suggests they were all well acquainted with it. Lennon returned to the song while recording his vocal for 'I'm Losing You', ad-libbing it as the song fades.

Before he donated 'I'm The Greatest' to Ringo Starr, Lennon may have considered recording it himself. He began the song in late 1970. Having just finished his *Plastic Ono Band* album, Lennon recorded a brace of piano demos at his Tittenhurst home along with several new compositions destined for what would become his *Imagine* album. During sessions for that record, he attempted a studio demo of 'I'm The Greatest', the lyrics to which he either hadn't finished or couldn't remember. Once completed, 'I'm The Greatest' was both autobiographical and a statement of self-assurance. Knowing that if he issued the song himself it might be read as merely arrogant, Lennon offered it to Starr.

Starr was in Los Angeles working on his third and arguably best album, *Ringo*. It featured contributions from a raft of great musicians, including Lennon, McCartney, and George Harrison. By the time John and Yoko arrived to record 'I'm The Greatest', Harrison had already contributed to the *Ringo* sessions. Harrison happened to call the studio, to see how things were going, on the evening that Lennon and Starr were scheduled to record 'I'm The Greatest'. Lennon seized the opportunity to involve Harrison and told him to hightail it down to the studio to help finish the song. For the first time in three years, three of The Beatles found themselves in the same studio and recording together. Starr's reading of 'I'm The Greatest' was a tour de force and set the trend for future collaborations. Lennon's guide vocal was never intended to be released, but issued on this *Anthology* it reveals that he never gave less than 100 percent – even when he knew that his vocal would not be used.

The follow-up to Starr's *Ringo* album took its title from another Lennon composition written especially for the drummer. Lennon wrote 'Goodnight Vienna' (a Liverpudlian expression meaning "let's get out of here") and recorded this studio demo while producing Harry Nilsson's *Pussy Cats* album. Starr took the song away with him and recorded his version at Sunset Sound on August 6 1974, with Lennon adding piano. Issued as a single (Apple 1882) in the USA only it reached Number 29, becoming Starr's penultimate Top 30 *Billboard* hit.

'Yesterday' offers a brief parody of Paul McCartney's most successful song. Although it was of course written by and will forever be associated with McCartney, Lennon grew to accept the fact that, despite having nothing to do with its creation, he would also be associated with it. He often quipped that he'd be serenaded with 'Yesterday' when he entered restaurants or bars. Here it's performed just for laughs.

A favourite of Lennon's, 'Ain't She Sweet' was his first professionally recorded lead vocal. The Beatles' version was recorded in Hamburg, Germany, in June 1962. Issued at the height of Beatlemania, it made Number 29 in Britain and 19 on the US charts. At the time, The Beatles were none to happy at having something as old as 'Ain't She Sweet' issued as a single. But that's not to say that it didn't remain a favourite. While recording *Abbey Road*, The Beatles returned to the song, performing a ragged but authentic reading that paid homage to Gene Vincent's 1956 version, which had inspired them in the first place. Fast-forward five years, and Lennon returned to the song once again, this time with Nicky Hopkins on piano. Rough, ready, and played for laughs, the song sees Lennon hamming it up for the guys in the studio.

'Be My Baby' was written by Phil Spector with Jeff Barry and Ellie Greenwich as a showcase for Ronnie Bennett. Recorded by The Ronettes for Spector's Philles label, the majestic song screamed pop classic. From the moment the needle hit the vinyl, the much imitated drum intro and rich, echo-laden production ensured its greatness. A Top 5 hit in America and Britain, it marked the high point in The Ronettes' career. Although they would have several other hit singles, they would never again equal the success of 'Be My Baby'.

Spector's reworking of The Ronettes' greatest moment for Lennon's *Rock 'N' Roll* sessions was every bit as grandiose as the original. Outtakes from the sessions reveal just how unfocused Lennon could be at that time. That Spector managed to coax acceptable vocals from him is a testament to his skill as a producer and of Lennon's ability to perform even when severely relaxed. The scale of wantonness during those sessions did little to ground Lennon and in all probability pushed him close to the edge.

His reading of 'Be My Baby' reveals just how alienated he'd become. Unlike the original, Lennon's version is a primal plea for forgiveness and redemption. It should come as no surprise that he decided to leave this track out from his *Rock 'N' Roll* album – not because of any musical deficiencies, but because it exposes a fragile and fracturing psyche that he would rather forget. Lennon, however, had the strength of will to overcome his demons and Spector's eccentricities to emerge from the sessions a wiser and more sober person.

Inspired by Bob Dylan's conversion to Christianity, Lennon composed 'Serve Yourself'. It's a stinging parody that set out to answer Dylan's 'Gotta Serve Somebody', the sharpest and funniest song Lennon had written for years. He obviously enjoyed the song, as can be heard by the giggles from him and Ono at the end of the recording. Indeed, he had so much fun that he made several more demo recordings, but none caught the spirit and vitriol of this spontaneous take.

Lennon wrote 'Life Begins At 40' speculatively for Ringo Starr, who like Lennon was facing 40, but he never got further than the simple sketch presented here. It's little more than a throwaway, and even Starr would have been hard pushed to make it sound convincing.

Although Lennon spent a good deal of his househusband period travelling, very few of the places he visited seem to have impressed him enough to write about them. Instead, he decided to compose a song inspired by a visit he made to India 12 years previously. The Beatles' visit to India, to study with the Maharishi, inspired many of the songs they recorded for the *White Album*. In fact, Lennon, McCartney, and Harrison wrote so many songs while in India that they were unable to include them all on that mammoth double album.

After the group split up, songs from that trip continued to turn up on solo albums by McCartney and Harrison, but Lennon appeared content to keep them private. What he intended to do with 'The Rishi Kesh Song' is unclear. There was no obvious place for it on *Double Fantasy* or *Milk and Honey*. However, he certainly seemed preoccupied with India. Besides writing the still unreleased 'India', a song that fused the melodies of 'Memories' and 'Serve Yourself' with a new set of lyrics, he also wrote 'The Maharishi Song' and made passing references to the country in 'The Great Wok', also included on this *Anthology*.

On 'Sean's Loud', Sean Lennon plays guitar, very badly and loudly. An intimate moment between father and son, it's charming but far from essential. 'Mr. Hyde's Gone (Don't Be Afraid)' is a home demo from 1980 that finds Lennon once again contemplating his self-image and relationship with Ono. However, this tired pastiche suggests that his talent for probing self-analysis had temporarily deserted him. Perhaps it was intended to answer Ono's equally tired 'Yes, I'm Your Angel'. Both songs share a similar musical style – and

Mr. Hyde was a fitting metaphor for Lennon's own split personality. Certainly, Lennon's self view could be read as opposing Ono's vision of herself as an angel. If Lennon did intend this as a companion to her song, even he had to laugh at his hackneyed, improvised clichés, which suggests that he was being less than serious when he committed this rough draft to tape. If it was intended to answer Ono, the picture it paints is too simplistic. Thankfully, Lennon had the good sense to drop the idea and leave the song in his personal tape archive.

Having written the title song for Starr's *Goodnight Vienna* album, Lennon suggested he record The Platters' 'Only You', and to help, he recorded a guide vocal. However, 'Only You', with Lennon's vocal in place of Starr's, almost didn't make it onto the *John Lennon Anthology*. The multi-track tape only came to light two days before the album was due to be mastered, which accounts, perhaps, for it being placed out of sequence on disc 4. The track was mixed, authorised by Ono, and minor adjustments made just hours before the mastering deadline.

Starr's version was issued by Apple as a single in 1974. A hit on both sides of the Atlantic, it reached Number 6 in the US charts but only 28 in his home country.

'Dear John' is an unfinished song that Lennon recorded at home some time in 1980, in effect a lazy rewrite of 'Hold On', which he'd written some ten years earlier. Like its predecessor, it finds Lennon reassuring himself. However, here he sounds tired and world-weary. Lacking either a chorus or middle eight, this is the most synoptic of sketches, and Lennon never returned to it.

Lennon wrote 'Mucho Mungo' with guitarist Jesse Ed Davis in mind but eventually gave it to Harry Nilsson, who, with the help of both Davis and Lennon, recorded it for his *Pussy Cats* album. A pleasant song, typical of the kind Lennon donated to his friends, it formed the first half of a medley with 'Mt. Elga', a Nilsson composition. Lennon had already made demo recordings of the song in 1973, so why he decided to make further home recordings three years after the event is unclear. Perhaps, like the 'satires' that follow, it was just for fun.

On the three 'Satire' pieces, Lennon pokes fun at his old pal, Bob Dylan. They're hardly essential listening and not even very funny, and so it's hard to imagine why these recordings were issued, or, indeed, what Dylan thought of them. On 'Sean's In The Sky' Lennon and Ono share the facts of life with an inquisitive Sean, while 'It's Real' has Lennon playing the guitar and whistling. That's all.

John Lennon Anthology data

The boxed set was promoted with a media blitz that included specially prepared videos, electronic press kits (EPKs), and a dedicated *Anthology* website. Launched on what would have been Lennon's 50th birthday, the site featured press releases, excerpts from Anthony DeCurtis's liner notes, audio and video clips, and photographs. A lavish *Lennon Anthology* press pack was issued to the media. It consisted of a gatefold A4 presenter, two-track promo CD of 'I'm Losing You' / 'Only You' (LENNON 001) in a slim-line jewel case, seven assorted colour and black-and-white 5-inch by 7-inch lustre-finish photographs (all printed on Kodak paper), two A4 pages of immediate release information (dated September 11 1998), one A4 page of immediate release information with more details on the boxed set (dated September 3 1998), ten A4 pages of introduction to the *Lennon Anthology* by Yoko Ono, seven A4 pages of a John Lennon mini biography by DeCurtis, and two A4 pages of immediate release information on the *Wonsaponatime* album (dated October 13 1998).

Ono recorded an interview that was issued as *Howtis* (DPRO-13515), a promotional CD that included an unedited version of 'I'm Losing You'. The interview was also filmed for use as an EPK. A second promotional CD, *Excerpts From John Lennon Anthology* (DPRO-13507), issued in early October 1998, featured 'I'm Losing You', 'Working Class Hero', 'God', 'How Do You Sleep', 'Imagine', 'Only You', and 'Sean's In The Sky'. Finally, 'Happy Xmas (War Is Over)' and 'Be-Bop-A-Lula' were issued as a promotional CD single (LENNON 002) to promote both the *John Lennon Anthology* and the *Wonsaponatime* album.

To promote the boxed set on television, Capitol produced a video of 'I'm Losing You' that featured Rick Nielsen, Bun E. Carlos, and Tony Levin. Lennon was represented by his animated drawings that float through the video and interact with the musicians.

This onslaught of promotional activity had the desired effect. The *John Lennon Anthology* was certified gold in December 1998, having sold 125,000 copies in the USA (each set counted as four CDs making a total of 500,000 units). It also received critical acclaim: *Rolling Stone* voted it Boxed Set Of The Year. In Britain, sales were also strong, with the boxed set climbing to Number 62 in the charts, a remarkable feat for an expensive four-CD set. Originally issued in a 'cube' with the four CDs and booklet in digi-pack sleeves, the boxed set was repackaged in October 2004 in the more conventional 'long box' format.

255

WONSAPONATIME
JOHN LENNON

Side 1 'I'm Losing You', 'Working Class Hero', 'God', 'How Do You Sleep?'.
Side 2 'Imagine' (Take 1), 'Baby Please Don't Go', 'Oh My Love', 'God Save Oz', 'I Found Out'.
Side 3 'Woman Is The Nigger Of The World' (Live), 'A Kiss Is Just A Kiss (As Time Goes By)', 'Be-Bop-A-Lula', 'Rip It Up', 'Ready Teddy', 'What You Got', 'Nobody Loves You When You're Down And Out'.
Side 4 'I Don't Wanna Face It', 'Real Love', 'Only You', 'Grow Old With Me', 'Sean's In The Sky', 'Serve Yourself'.

UK release November 2 1998; CD Capitol CDP 4 97639 2; LP Capitol 497 6391 released January 18 1999; chart high No.76.
US release November 3 1998; CD Capitol CDP 4 97639 2; failed to chart.

WONSAPONATIME

A best-of of the *John Lennon Anthology*, this was issued for the casual listener rather than the committed fan. It was released as a two-record set and a single CD. The LP was issued with customised labels, printed inner sleeves, and gatefold cover. The CD came in a card digi-pack.

WONSAPONATIME
JOHNLENNON
selections from Lennon Anthology

SIDE ONE
1 I'M LOSING YOU 3:56
2 WORKING CLASS HERO 3:58
3 GOD 3:15
4 HOW DO YOU SLEEP? 5:00

WONSAPONATIME
JOHNLENNON
selections from Lennon Anthology

SIDE TWO
1 BEAUTIFUL BOY 3:04
2 CLEANUP TIME/MIND GAMES 4:03
3 OH MY LOVE 1:39
4 GOODNIGHT VIENNA 2:58
5 I FOUND OUT 3:43

WONSAPONATIME
JOHNLENNON
selections from Lennon Anthology

SIDE THREE
1 WOMAN IS THE NIGGER OF
   THE WORLD (live) 5:16
2 "A KISS IS JUST A KISS" 0:12
3 BE BOP A LULA 2:40
4 RIP IT UP/READY TEDDY 2:26
5 WHAT YOU GOT 1:15
6 NOBODY LOVES YOU WHEN
   YOU'RE DOWN AND OUT 5:02

WONSAPONATIME
JOHNLENNON
selections from Lennon Anthology

SIDE FOUR
1 I DON'T WANNA FACE IT 3:31
2 REAL LOVE 4:09
3 ONLY YOU 3:25
4 GROW OLD WITH ME 3:19
5 SEAN'S "IN THE SKY" 1:25
6 SERVE YOURSELF 3:49

'IMAGINE', 'HAPPY XMAS (WAR IS OVER)', 'GIVE PEACE A CHANCE', 'IMAGINE' (VIDEO)
JOHN LENNON

UK release December 13 1999; CD single Parlophone CDR 6534; chart high No.3.

'IMAGINE'

Reissued in the UK "due to massive public demand", 'Imagine' once again found its way into the higher reaches of the British charts. It was issued as an enhanced CD single, including the original video for 'Imagine'. A promotional CD single (CDRDJ 6534) was issued in a card sleeve with the classic photograph of Lennon at his white baby-grand piano.

IMAGINE
JOHN LENNON AND THE PLASTIC ONO BAND (WITH THE FLUX FIDDLERS)

'Imagine', 'Crippled Inside', 'Jealous Guy', 'It's So Hard', 'I' Don't Want To Be A Soldier', 'Give Me Some Truth', 'Oh My Love', 'How Do You Sleep?', 'How?', 'Oh Yoko!'

UK release: 17 February 2000. Parlophone Records (UK): (CD) 5 24857 2, (LP [27 March 2000]) 5 248571. Highest UK chart position: Failed to chart.
US release: 11 April 2000. Capitol Records (US): (CD) COP 5 25757 2. Highest US chart position: Failed to chart.

In 2000, Yoko Ono began the task of remixing and remastering John's albums for release on CD. When Lennon's back catalogue was first issued on CD, there were problems with poor sound, due to the inferior quality of the original master tapes. *Shaved Fish* had to be withdrawn because it suffered from tape hiss and other audio defects; several other albums also suffered from poor sound quality. Lennon could never have foreseen the advances in technology that took place during the 1980s. Consequently, he mastered his albums, including his last, *Double Fantasy*, for vinyl. When issued on CD, the minor defects in Lennon's analogue masters were clearly audible. Ironically, the same technological advances that exposed the weakness in analogue masters could also be used to repair them. In late 1999, Yoko returned to Abbey Road to oversee the remixing of *Imagine*. Returning to the original master tapes, re-mix engineer Peter Cotton produced new mixes that replicated the originals, but with improved stereo separation, richer bass response and crisper high tones. "*Imagine* is such an incredibly important album, and I wanted to keep it as close to the original as possible. We can do so much more than in 1985 when *Imagine* was first issued on CD. I thought it would be much better to use the newest mechanical power (sic) to make sure the sound is clean and in maximum good condition," Yoko explained.

The CD was issued with a fourteen-page booklet and newly designed custom label. The remixed version of Imagine was issued by MFSL Original Master Recordings as an Ultradisc II 24 kt. gold CD on 22 August 2003. EMI also issued a vinyl pressing of the album with generic Apple labels, although the album was actually issued by Parlophone, a printed inner sleeve, almost identical to the original, and gatefold cover. MFSL Original Master Recordings also issued a 180 gram GAIN 2 Ultra Analog, half speed master vinyl pressing of the remixed album in February 2004 (LMF277).

JOHN LENNON/PLASTIC ONO BAND
JOHN LENNON

'Mother', 'Hold On', 'I Found Out', 'Working Class Hero', 'Isolation', 'Remember', 'Love', 'Well Well Well', 'Look At Me', 'God', 'My Mummy's Dead', 'Power To The People', 'Do The Oz'

UK release: 9 October 2000. Parlophone Records (UK): (CD) 528 7402. Highest UK chart position: Failed to chart.
US release: 9 October 2000. Capitol Records (US): (CD) 7243 5 28740 2. Highest US chart position: Failed to chart.

John Lennon/Plastic Ono Band and *Double Fantasy* were both given the remix treatment and issued on what would have been Lennon's sixtieth birthday. As with *Imagine*, the idea was to present superior sounding albums. Several songs on the original *John Lennon/Plastic Ono Band* album were in mono and these were mixed to stereo for the CD. However, in at least one case, 'Well Well Well', the new stereo mix failed to improve on the original. What it reveals is an appalling Lennon guitar overdub that wasn't used for the original mix. A minor irritation but somewhat startling when encountered for the first time. In addition, some of the songs run a little longer than on the original album, again revealing elements not heard on the 1970 release.

The CD was issued with a new booklet that featured many rare photographs and Lennon's hand-written lyrics. 'Power To The People' and 'Do The Oz' were added as 'bonus' tracks. MFSL Original Master Recordings issued *John Lennon/Plastic Ono Band* as an Ultradisc II 24 kt. gold CD in January 2004 (UDCD-759). They also issued a vinyl edition (MFSL 1-280) in November 2004. The reissues of *John Lennon/Plastic Ono Band* and *Double Fantasy* were promoted with a CD *John Lennon Starting Over* (DPRO 7087 6 156702 1).

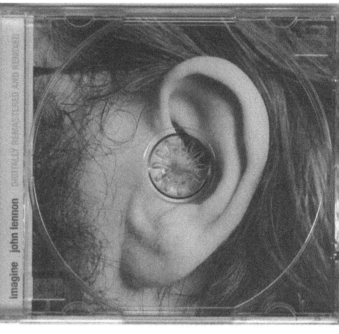

Above: MFSL 1-153 and MFSL 1-277

1. MOTHER
2. HOLD ON
3. I FOUND OUT
4. WORKING CLASS HERO
5. ISOLATION
6. REMEMBER
7. LOVE
8. WELL WELL WELL
9. LOOK AT ME
10. GOD
11. MY MUMMY'S DEAD
12. POWER TO THE PEOPLE
13. DO THE OZ

Above: MFSL 1-280

Above: 2010 re-issue

DOUBLE FANTASY
JOHN LENNON AND YOKO ONO

'(Just Like) Starting Over', 'Kiss Kiss Kiss', 'Cleanup Time', 'Give Me Something', 'I'm Losing You', 'I'm Moving On', 'Beautiful Boy (Darling Boy)', 'Watching The Wheels', 'Yes, I'm Your Angel', 'Woman', 'Beautiful Boys', 'Dear Yoko', 'Every Man Has A Woman Who Loves Him', 'Hard Times Are Over', 'Help Me To Help Myself', 'Walking On Thin Ice', 'Central Park Stroll'

UK release: 9 October 2000. Capitol Records (UK): (CD) 528 7392. Highest UK chart position: Failed to chart.
US release: 9 October 2000. Capitol Records (US): (CD) 7243 5 28739 2. Highest US chart position: Failed to chart.

What was perhaps Lennon's best sounding album, *Double Fantasy*, was overhauled, extended with 'bonus' tracks and reissued on CD. In truth, only the unreleased 'Help Me To Help Myself' was of any real interest. 'Walking On Thin Ice' was already available on CD, and 'Central Park Stroll', although not available on CD, had been issued as the preamble to 'It Happened' on the b-side of 'Walking On Thin Ice'. The CD was issued with an improved eighteen-page booklet that included photographs of John and Yoko from the summer/autumn of 1980. *Double Fantasy* and *Milk and Honey* were issued as a double CD (EBX23) with a card slip sleeve on 13 September 2004 (UK).

'Help Me To Help Myself' (Lennon)
John Lennon (vocals, piano). Recorded at The Dakota, New York City, NY, USA. Producer: John Lennon

'HELP ME TO HELP MYSELF'

Issued as a bonus track on the remastered *Double Fantasy*, 'Help Me To Help Myself' had previously been broadcast on the Lost Lennon Tapes and issued on bootlegs. One of the better unissued songs Lennon wrote and recorded while preparing the album, this is a gospel-style ballad that finds him contemplating his acquisitiveness and self-destructive nature.

Reviewing his life, Lennon avows that now is the time to accept some divine intervention. While his relationship with God and organised religion was ambivalent at best, this was no radical U-turn. 'Help Me To Help Myself' was more than a plea for redemption, it was a pragmatic statement of protestant self-help that restates the maxim "heaven helps those who help themselves".

Seen in this light, the song extends the theme of personal projection and individual development that had occupied Lennon from the outset. Stripping away the lyrical ambivalence that made 'Imagine' so appealing, he offers his own experiences as a paradigm for others to employ as they journey through life.

'HAPPY XMAS (WAR IS OVER)'
JOHN LENNON & YOKO ONO/PLASTIC ONO BAND WITH THE HARLEM COMMUNITY CHOIR

'Happy Xmas (War Is Over)', 'Imagine', 'Instant Karma!'*, 'Imagine'* (instrumental + photo gallery)
John Lennon & Yoko Ono / Plastic Ono Band with The Harlem Community Choir
CD only *

UK release 12 December 2003; Parlophone Records (UK): R 6627, (CD) CDR 6627; chart high No. 33.

Christmas comes but once a year and when it does there's usually some Beatles related product ready for release. In 2003, there was no Lennon reissue to tempt fans from their hard-earned cash. Rather there was a new DVD, *Lennon Legend*, that up-dated the previous *John Lennon Collection*. Naturally, the CD of the same name was re-promoted and the Lennon evergreen, 'Happy Xmas (War Is Over)', re-promoted for the umpteenth time to give both DVD and CD a little boost.

The single was issued as an enhanced CD and 7-inch single. As with the original single, EMI pressed the record on green vinyl. However, this time the record was manufactured with black Parlophone labels with white print and backed with 'Imagine'. The original picture sleeve was also employed but with minor differences. The rear cover now sported a bar code and a reference to the Lennon Legend DVD and CD.

The single was mastered using new masters and included an alternative version of 'Instant Karma!'. The 2003 master features Lennon's live vocal from Top of the Pops, the knitting version (actually, to be pedantic, Yoko is crocheting). It was also marginally longer as it did not fadeout. The enhanced CD single also featured an instrumental version of 'Imagine' – basically the finished master sans Lennon's vocal – that accompanied a photo gallery.

MILK AND HONEY
JOHN LENNON AND YOKO ONO

'I'm Stepping Out', 'Sleepless Night', 'I Don't Wanna Face It', 'Don't Be Scared', 'Nobody Told Me', 'O' Sanity', 'Borrowed Time', 'Your Hands', '(Forgive Me) My Little Flower Princess', 'Let Me Count The Ways', 'Grow Old With Me', 'You're The One', 'Every Man Has A Woman Who Loves Him', 'Stepping Out' (Home Version), 'I'm Moving On', 'Interview with J & Y December 8th 1980'

UK release: 8 October 2001. Parlophone Records (UK): (CD) 535 9582. Highest UK chart position: Failed to chart.
US release: 23 October 2001. Capitol Records (US): (CD) 7243 535858 2. Highest US chart position: Failed to chart.

Remastered and extended, *Milk and Honey* now included John's vocal of 'Every Man Has A Woman Who Loves Him', a home demo of 'Stepping Out' and 'I'm Moving On', plus an extract from John and Yoko's 8 December 1980 interview with RKO. As with the previous reissue CDs, it also benefited from a twenty-four page booklet.

MIND GAMES
JOHN LENNON (WITH THE PLASTIC U.F.ONO BAND)

'Mind Games', 'Tight As', 'Aisumasen (I'm Sorry)', 'One Day (At A Time)', 'Bring On The Lucie (Freda Peeple)', 'Nutopian International Anthem', 'Intuition', 'Out The Blue', 'Only People', 'I Know (I Know) You Are Here', 'Meat City', 'Aisumasen (I'm Sorry)' (Home version), 'Bring On The Lucie (Freda Peeple)' (Home version), 'Meat City' (Home Version)

UK release: 7 October 2002. Parlophone Records (UK): (CD) 542 4252. Highest UK chart position: Failed to chart.
US release: 5 November 2002. Apple Records (US): (CD) 7243 542425 2. Highest US chart position: Failed to chart.

The John Lennon reissue campaign rolls on with the release of his 1973 album, *Mind Games*. As with previous CD reissues, *Mind Games* was upgraded and expanded. The album was remixed from the original multi-track tapes at Abbey Road, overseen by Yoko Ono. Three previously un-issued home recordings were also included, along with a thirty-two-page booklet, which included lyrics, photographs, drawings and trade advertisements.

The original album included Lennon's tongue-in-cheek 'Nutopian International Anthem', which consisted of 5 seconds of silence. For this CD release, the silence was replaced with 5 seconds of tape hiss, to replicate the experience of listening to the original vinyl edition. As with the previous reissued CDs, *Mind Games* sounded fantastic, and the remixing brought out subtle nuances in the arrangements that had been lost to Lennon's original dense production The reissue was given little in the way of promotion and failed to make any impact on the charts. The remixed version of *Mind Games* was issued by MFSL Original Master Recordings as an Ultradisc 11 24 kt. gold CD on 23 November 2004 (UDCD 761).

MILK AND HONEY

Yoko Ono

1 I'm Stepping Out 2 Sleepless Night 3 I Don't Wanna Face It 4 Don't Be Scared
5 Nobody Told Me 6 O' Sanity 7 Borrowed Time 8 Your Hands
9 (Forgive Me) My Little Flower Princess 10 Let Me Count The Ways
11 Grow Old With Me 12 You're The One
13 Every Man Has A Woman Who Loves Him
14 Stepping Out (Home Version) 15 I'm Moving On
16 Interview with J & Y December 1980

7243 5 35959 2 0

7 24353 59592 9

7243 5 35959 2 0

℗ 2001 The copyright in this sound recording is owned by Yoko Ono Lennon under exclusive licence to EMI Records Ltd.
© 2001 Yoko Ono Lennon under exclusive licence to EMI Records Ltd.

© 2001 EMI Records Ltd. This label copy information is the subject of copyright protection.
All rights reserved.

Artwork and Design: P. Linard Marketing and Advertising Ltd

On behalf of John and myself, I'd like to thank the following people for their efforts in re-introducing this album to the world.
Rupert Perry, Tony Wadsworth, Mike Heatley, Andy Slater, Dave Ayers, Allan Rouse, Peter Mew, Murray Chalmers,
George Marino, Shun Mori, and Michiko Fujimura.

MIND GAMES
JOHN LENNON

JOHN LENNON
MIND GAMES
NOW INCLUDES 3 EXTRA TRACKS,
RARE JOHN LENNON DRAWINGS,
PHOTOGRAPHS
AND MEMORABILIA
7243 5 42425 2 5

MIND GAMES 4:13
TIGHT A$ 3:37
AISUMASEN (I'm Sorry) 4:43
ONE DAY (At A Time) 3:08
BRING ON THE LUCIE (Freda People) 4:11
NUTOPIAN INTERNATIONAL ANTHEM 0:03
INTUITION 3:07
OUT THE BLUE 3:22
ONLY PEOPLE 3:23
I KNOW (I Know) 3:48
YOU ARE HERE 4:06
MEAT CITY 2:45

Bonus Tracks:
AISUMASEN (I'm Sorry) home version 3:35
BRING ON THE LUCIE (Freda People) home version 1:02
MEAT CITY home version 2:36

Total Time 47:58

7 24354 24252 6

267

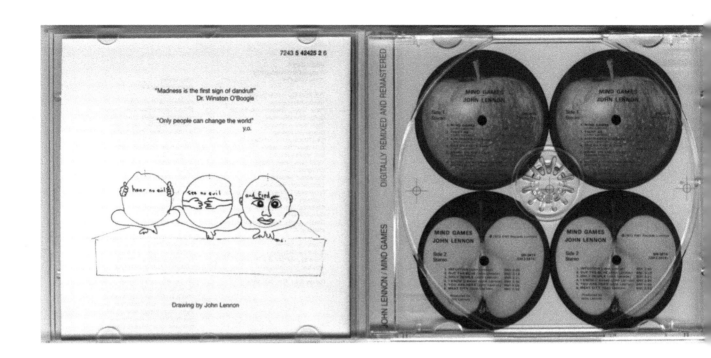

ROCK'N'ROLL
JOHN LENNON

'Be-Bop-A-Lula', 'Stand By Me', 'Rip It Up', 'Ready Teddy', 'You Can't Catch Me', 'Ain't That A Shame', 'Do You Want To Dance', 'Sweet Little Sixteen', 'Slippin' And Slidin'', 'Peggy Sue', 'Bring It On Home To Me', 'Send Me Some Lovin'', 'Bony Maronie', 'Ya Ya', 'Just Because', 'Angel Baby', 'To Know Her Is To Love Her', 'Since My Baby Left Me', 'Just Because' (Reprise)

UK release: 27 September 2004. Parlophone Records (UK): (CD) 874 3292. Highest UK chart position: Failed to chart.
US release: 2 November 2004. Capitol Records (US): (CD). Highest US chart position: No. 17 (The Billboard Pop Catalogue Chart).

Remixed and remastered, *Rock'N'Roll* was reissued in Britain on 27 September 2004. The American release took place on 2 November to coincide with the release of a 'new' Lennon album, *Acoustic*.

As with the previous reissue CDs, *Rock'N'Roll* was remixed from the original masters. Consequently, there are several differences between this version and the original Lennon produced mix. 'Be-Bop-A-Lula', for example, now has a count in, while 'You Can't Catch Me' appears to feature a lead guitar part that was either not used or buried in the original mix. Lennon's vocals are placed much higher in this mix and the brass section, now given greater stereo separation, sounds crisp, bright and clear.

The CD has four bonus songs, two of which, 'Angel Baby' and 'To Know Her Is To Love Her', were previously issued on *Menlove Avenue* and the *John Lennon Anthology*. 'Since My Baby Left Me' is a previously unreleased alternative take with a loose live feel, which leads one to speculate that it is an early take, although no documentation concerning the songs appears in the sleeve notes. Speaking of which, this reissue has just a four-page booklet. Lennon's plans for the original album had been to include copious sleeve notes. But because the LP was rush released in 1975 he didn't get the opportunity to write them. However, he gave enough interviews at the time which could have been used to complete his original vision. The booklet features some early photographs of John taken in Hamburg, but none from the original sessions.

Also included is a reprise of 'Just Because', which features an alternative salutation to the original *Rock'N'Roll* version. Lennon proffers greetings to his former band mates Ringo Starr, Paul McCartney and George Harrison and the people of Great Britain. While Lennon sounds fine for the first 44 seconds, he sounds more than a little inebriated from then on. As Lennon replaced his original vocal when he resumed the project in New York, it's probable that the version issued here consists of an overdub (0'00 - 0'43) and the original vocal (0'44 - 1'22). This reprise had been programmed for the *John Lennon Anthology*, but was dropped when the boxed set was reprogrammed.

The CD was issued with a custom label based on the neon lettering that appears on the front cover. The CD booklet has both Parlophone and Apple logos. A line drawing by Lennon of a two headed rocker was used for the inner CD tray.

ACOUSTIC
JOHN LENNON

'Working Class Hero', 'Love', 'Well Well Well', 'Look At Me', 'God', 'My Mummy's Dead', 'Cold Turkey', 'The Luck Of The Irish', 'John Sinclair' (live), 'Woman Is The Nigger Of The World', 'What You Got', 'Watching The Wheels', 'Dear Yoko', 'Real Love', 'Imagine' (live), 'It's Real'

UK release 1 November 2004; Parlophone Records (CD) 874 4282; failed to chart.
US release 2 November 2004; Capitol Records (CD) 874 4282; chart high No. 28 (No. 6 on the Billboard Internet Album Chart).

'Well Well Well', 'God' and 'My Mummy's Dead'
Personnel: John Lennon (vocals and acoustic guitar).
Recording Studio: Bel Air, California.
Recording data: home recording.
Producer: Yoko Ono.

'Cold Turkey'
Personnel: John Lennon (vocals and acoustic guitar).
Recording Studio: Tittenhurst Park, Ascot.
Recording data: home recording.
Producer: Yoko Ono.

'What You Got'
Personnel: John Lennon (vocals and electric guitar).
Recording Studio: home studio.
Recording data: home recording.
Producer: John Lennon.

'Dear Yoko'
Personnel: John Lennon (vocals and acoustic guitar).
Recording Studio: home studio, Bermuda.
Recording data: home recording.
Producer: Yoko Ono.

'Real Love'
Personnel: John Lennon (vocals and acoustic guitar).
Recording Studio: The Dakota, New York.
Recording data: home demo.
Producer: John Lennon.

ACOUSTIC

A new compilation of John Lennon demos and live recordings. Issued in Britain and America on 2 November, the CD was issued in Japan (TOPC-67483) on 29 September to coincide with a tribute concert that took place there, and was originally planned for Japanese consumption only. 'I was just going to release *Acoustic* in Japan to coincide with a John Lennon tribute concert that was a week or two ago, and I was there for that tribute,' explained Yoko. 'But then Capitol heard it and said, 'Can we release it here, too?' A Japanese only release was never a feasible option, which Capitol, if not Yoko, knew too well. Sales would have been lost to CDs imported from Japan or illegal downloads. With the music industry already suffering from a slump in sales, even an album with limited sales potential was worth issuing.

Of the sixteen songs on the album, nine had been previously issued on the *John Lennon Anthology*. The remaining seven songs had been available on bootlegs, but were presented in superior sound quality. Although some of the songs were treated with noise reduction and reverb, as most were recorded on mono tape recorders, most of the recordings could not be remixed.

The majority of the songs on *Acoustic* were recorded as home demos and never intended for public consumption. Unable to write music, Lennon's home demos were the foundations upon which the finished recordings would be based. 'With the acoustic songs, first he would play them to me, then he would say, 'Yoko, let's record this,'' Ono recalled. 'And he would set up the microphone in such a way that his voice and his guitar sound was very balanced. At first I wanted to collect some acoustic stuff on guitar and piano, but the piano tracks were not in good enough condition to put out. When he was banging the piano, he would put the microphone on top of the piano, so that you'd hear the piano much more than his voice. The balance was not good at all, so I could not rescue those songs. But with the guitar, he did a beautiful job of balancing the sound. Considering that most of Lennon's demo recordings were made on domestic cassette recorders, they sound remarkable.

Acoustic songs

This demo recording of 'Well Well Well' was made on 28 July 1970 while Lennon was undergoing Primal Therapy in California. The recording was first aired on *The Lost Lennon Tapes* programme broadcast on 14 August 1989, it later appeared on the bootleg *The Dream Is Over* (Pegboy 1006).

Also originating from the cassette of demo recordings John made on 28 July 1970, this demo of 'God' reveals it to be a work-in-progress. After a light-hearted introduction, that recalls the rock'n'roll records of his youth, Lennon performs a version of the song lacking the closing 'dream is over' verse. As with 'Well Well Well', this demo, along with three further takes, appeared on the bootleg *The Dream Is Over* (Pegboy 1006).

An alternative take of Lennon's haunting lament for his dead mother, 'My Mummy's Dead', issued commercially for the first time. Like the previous two songs, 'My Mummy's Dead' first appeared on the bootleg *The Dream Is Over* (Pegboy 1006).

Lennon's acoustic home demo of 'Cold Turkey' sounds not unlike the kind of music being made by then up-and-coming hippie duo Tyrannosaurus Rex. Lennon's vocalisations sound remarkably similar to those of the group's lead singer and future super star, Marc Bolan. While obviously influenced by Yoko, John would surely have been aware of Tyrannosaurus Rex, the duo were championed by British DJ John Peel on his Perfumed Garden show, and he may have decided to adapt Bolan's vibrato for his demo recording. This version of the song has double tracked guitars, John having added a second guitar part to his original recording. The track was first aired on *The Lost Lennon Tapes* broadcast on 5 June 1989 and appeared on the bootleg *Gone From This Place* (Vigotone VT-CD 01).

Performed using an unamplified electric guitar, rather than an acoustic model, this demo recording of 'What You Got' was first broadcast on the 5 June 1989 edition of *The Lost Lennon Tapes*. A longer, unedited version appeared on the Vigotone bootleg *Listen To This...* (VT-175-7). However, the version presented on *Acoustic* has been edited and treated with noise reduction.

Recorded while Lennon was on holiday in Bermuda, this demo recording of 'Dear Yoko' features an alternative introduction based on the song's chord structure. It also suffers from slight distortion, John having set the input level too high while recording. This was Lennon's second attempt at recording the song. Two months earlier he'd taped several takes in front of a home video camera. Attempting the song again, he recorded three takes, the first two breaking down and therefore incomplete. This version of 'Dear Yoko' was first aired on *The Lost Lennon Tapes* on 12 August 1991.

Another acoustic guitar version of 'Real Love', the first having been issued on *Imagine: John Lennon, Music From The Motion Picture*. This take, take 4 dating from June 1980, does not improve on the previously issued versions. This recording was first broadcast on *The Lost Lennon Tapes* on 12 June 1989, and was issued on the bootleg *Free As A Bird: The Dakota Beatles Demos* (Pegboy 1001).

Acoustic data

Acoustic was issued by Capitol on CD with an eight-page booklet and customised label that featured one of Lennon's drawings. To promote both *Acoustic* and the reissued *Rock 'N' Roll*, Capitol issued a promotional CD, John Lennon: *Two Sides Of Lennon* (DPRO-70876). The CD featured a one-hour radio show based on a conversation between Yoko and Jody Denberg. Both albums are discussed with three songs from each release used to highlight the unique nature of each CD.

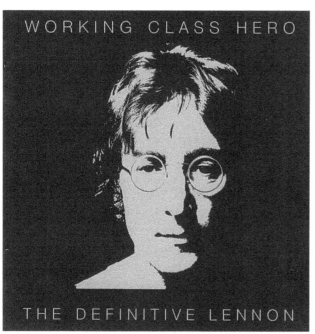

WORKING CLASS HERO – THE DEFINITIVE LENNON
JOHN LENNON

Disc 1: '(Just Like) Starting Over', 'Imagine', 'Watching The Wheels', 'Jealous Guy', 'Instant Karma! (We All Shine On)', 'Stand By Me', 'Working Class Hero', 'Power To The People', 'Oh My Love', 'Oh Yoko!', 'Nobody Loves You (When You're Down And Out)', 'Nobody Told Me', 'Bless You', Come Together', 'New York City', 'I'm Stepping Out', 'You Are Here', 'Borrowed Time', 'Happy Xmas (War Is Over)'
Disc 2: 'Woman', 'Mind Games', 'Out The Blue', 'Whatever Gets You Thru The Night', 'Love', 'Mother', 'Beautiful Boy', 'Woman Is The Nigger Of The World', 'God', 'Scared', '#9 Dream', 'I'm Losing You', 'Isolation', 'Cold Turkey', 'Intuition', 'Gimme Some Truth', 'Give Peace A Chance', 'Real Love', 'Grow Old With Me'

UK release 3 October 2005. Parlophone Records (UK): 340 0802; chart high number 11.
US release 4 October 2005. Capitol Records (US): 094634039123; chart high number 135.

Issued a few days before what would have been Lennon's 65th birthday, *Working Class Hero – The Definitive Lennon* reworked earlier 'best of' compilations into the most comprehensive collection of Lennon's hit singles and key album tracks so far. A top twenty album in Britain, it faired less well in America where it reached 135 on the charts. The release of this compilation also saw the entire Lennon solo catalogue issued via legitimate digital music sites for the first time.

THE U.S. VS JOHN LENNON
JOHN LENNON

'Power To The People', 'Nobody Told Me', 'Working Class Hero', 'I Found Out', 'Bed Peace', 'The Ballad Of John & Yoko' - The Beatles, 'Give Peace A Chance', 'Love', 'Attica State' (live previously unreleased), 'Happy Xmas (War Is Over)', 'I Don't Want To Be A Soldier', 'Imagine', 'How Do You Sleep?' (instrumental previously unreleased), 'New York City', 'John Sinclair' (live), 'Scared', 'God', 'Here We Go Again', 'Gimme Some Truth', 'Oh My Love', 'Instant Karma!'

UK release 26 September 2006. Parlophone Records (UK): 3749122; chart high failed to chart.
US release 26 September 2006. Capitol Records (US): chart high failed to chart.

Lennon's back catalogue raided once more, this time for the soundtrack to the feature-length documentary film, *The U.S. vs John Lennon*. Co-written, directed and produced by David Leaf and John Scheinfeld, the documentary sets out to explore the American government's attempts at silencing Lennon during the early 1970s. It also attempted to draw parallels between the early '70s and the Bush administration management of the Iraq war. It does so through archival film clips, new interviews and Lennon's music. Some of Lennon's songs were remixed to provide the film with its score. "We were allowed to 'strip' lead vocals from Lennon's original recordings, so that we could use his own instrumental work as the score for the movie," explained David Leaf. "I think it's the first time that John's solo catalogue can be heard in this way." However, only the instrumental version of 'How Do You Sleep?' was issued on the album. Also included was the previously unreleased live recording of 'Attica State' from the John Sinclair Freedom Rally in Ann Arbor, Michigan.
Parlophone and Capitol issued *The U.S. vs John Lennon* as a standard CD with liner notes by Yoko Ono.

REMEMBER
JOHN LENNON

'#9 Dream', 'Instant Karma! (We All Shine On)', 'Working Class Hero', 'Hold On' (Anthology version), 'Watching the Wheels', 'Remember', 'God', 'Mother', 'Sean's Little Help' (from John Lennon Anthology), 'Imagine', 'Steel and Glass', 'I'm Losing You' (Anthology version), 'Going Down On Love' (Instructions only from John Lennon Anthology), 'Nobody Told Me', 'Isolation' (Anthology version), 'Nobody Loves You (When You're Down and Out)' (Anthology version), 'Jealous Guy', '(Just Like) Starting Over'

US release 3 January 2007. Capitol Records/Hear Music (US): 71108-2-9; chart high failed to chart.

And would you like a John Lennon CD with your coffee, sir? Lennon's solo back catalogue revisited and newly compiled for global coffee purveyors, Starbucks. Compiled by EMI-Capitol Special Markets division, *Remember* comprises eighteen tracks that span his solo career and was available exclusively from Starbucks coffee shops.

This isn't as odd as it may at first appear. Starbucks has become more than just about selling coffee. In 1999 the company bought Hear Music, an independent record retailer, and invested in new retail outlets that are music stores first and coffee-houses second. And they seem to have done OK.

When Ray Charles' *Genius Loves Company* CD went platinum in America, Starbucks was responsible for one-third of its sales. Having cracked the adult music market, which many record companies ignored, it made perfect sense for Capitol's Special Markets division to compile a Lennon CD for sale exclusively through America's largest chain of coffee shops.

Drawing heavily on Lennon first solo album proper, *Remember* mixes familiar versions of Lennon's music with alternative takes from the *Lennon Anthology*. The inclusion of two spoken word extracts is superfluous and does little to enhance the listening pleasure of what is otherwise a solid compilation.

EMI Music Special Markets/Hear Music issued Remember with a tri-fold digi-pack cover, 12-page booklet, and screen-printed CD.

JOHN LENNON
JOHN LENNON

'Power To The People', 'Jealous Guy', 'New York City', 'Mind Games', 'Bless You', 'Slippin' and Slidin'', 'Here We Go Again', 'Beautiful Boy', 'Nobody Told Me', 'Imagine' (Take 1), 'Give Peace A Chance', 'Grow Old With Me'
UK release 18 January 2009. The Mail On Sunday/EMI: UPJLEN001; chart high failed to chart.

Another in a long line of Lennon compilations, this time a freebie given away with *The Mail On Sunday*. The music business was changing and artists, or in this case the keepers of their estate, had to think of new ways of marketing their work. As it has becoming increasingly difficult to make money from recorded music, why buy music when it's available to download for nothing? The only way to make money was to perform. That was impossible, even for the god-like Lennon. The other option was to get somebody else to pay to give the music away for free.

SINGLES BAG
JOHN LENNON

Single 1: 'Mother' / 'Why'
Single 2: 'Imagine' / 'It's So Hard'
Single 3: 'Watching the Wheels' / 'Yes, I'm Your Angel'

UK release 17 April 2010. Capitol Records 29697 72; chart high failed to chart.
US release 17 April 2010. Capitol Records 29697 72; chart high failed to chart.

On Record Store Day (17 April), EMI Music released a limited edition John Lennon vinyl package that was sold 'exclusively' by participating independent music retailers. The *John Lennon Singles Bag* comprised three 45 rpm singles in picture sleeves housed in an individually numbered Kraftpak envelope with a string and button closure. The package also contained a 24 x 36 inch poster, three postcards and a custom plastic adaptor hub.

Despite its supposed 'exclusively' to Record Store Day, the *John Lennon Singles Bag* was available through a well know online auction site well in advance of it hitting the shops, which somewhat undermined the idea behind the release. Also some copies came with a standard plastic adaptor hub, rather than the 'custom' hub that had been promised.

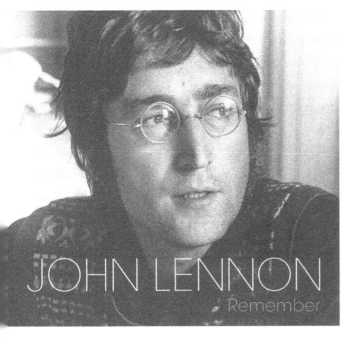

JOHN LENNON
Remember

JOHN LENNON

JOHN LENNON SINGLES BAG

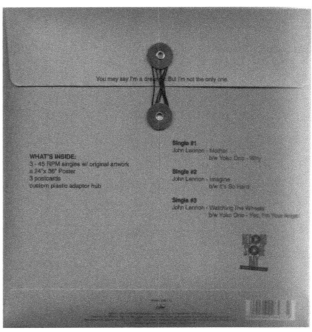

SIGNATURE BOX
JOHN LENNON

IMAGINE
SOME TIME IN NEW YORK CITY
MIND GAMES
WALLS AND BRIDGES
ROCK'N'ROLL
DOUBLE FANTASY
MILK AND HONEY

Bonus Disc 1: 'Power To The People', 'Happy Xmas (War Is Over)', 'Instant Karma! (We All Shine On)', 'Cold Turkey' (Single Version), 'Move Over Ms L', 'Give Peace A Chance'
Bonus Disc 2: 'Mother'*, 'Love',* 'God',* 'I Found Out',* 'Nobody Told Me',# 'Honey Don't',*
'One Of The Boys',# India, India',# 'Serve Yourself',# 'Isolation',* 'Remember',* 'Beautiful Boy',#
'I Don't Wanna Be A Soldier Mama I Don't Wanna Die'*
* (STUDIO OUTTAKE) # (HOME RECORDING)

UK release 4 October 2010. EMI: 5099990650925; chart high failed to chart.
US release 5 October 2010. EMI: 5099990650925; chart high failed to chart.

GIMME SOME TRUTH (4 CD COMPILATION)
Disc: 1: 'Working Class Hero', 'Instant Karma (We All Shine On)', 'Power To The People', 'God', 'I Don't Wanna Be A Soldier Mama I Don't Wanna Die', 'Gimme Some Truth', 'Sunday Bloody Sunday', 'Steel And Glass', 'Meat City', 'I Don't Wanna Face It', 'Remember', 'Woman Is The Nigger Of The World', 'I Found Out', 'Isolation', 'Imagine', 'Happy Xmas (War Is Over)', 'Give Peace A Chance', 'Only People'
Disc: 2: 'Mother', 'Hold On', 'You Are Here', 'Well Well Well', 'Oh My Love', 'Oh Yoko', 'Grow Old With Me', 'Love', 'Jealous Guy', 'Woman', 'Out The Blue', 'Bless You', 'Nobody Loves You (When You're Down And Out)', 'My Mummy's Dead', 'I'm Losing You', 'Just Like Starting Over', '#9 Dream', 'Beautiful Boy (Darling Boy)'
Disc: 3: 'Mind Games', 'Nobody Told Me', 'Cleanup Time', 'Crippled Inside', 'How Do You Sleep', 'How', 'Intuition', 'I'm Stepping Out', 'Whatever Gets You Thru The Night', 'Old Dirt Road', 'Scared', 'What You Got', 'Cold Turkey', 'New York City', 'Surprise Surprise (Sweet Bird Of Paradox)', 'Borrowed Time', 'Look At Me', 'Watching The Wheels'
Disc: 4: 'Be Bop A Lula', 'You Can't Catch Me', 'Rip It Up/Ready Teddy', 'Tight A$', 'Ain't That A Shame', 'Sweet Little Sixteen', 'Do You Wanna Dance', 'Slippin' And Slidin', 'Peggy Sue', 'Bring It On Home/Send Me Some Lovin'', 'Yer Blues', 'Just Because', 'Boney Moronie', 'Beef Jerky', 'Ya Ya', 'Hound Dog', 'Stand By Me', 'Here We Go Again'

UK release 4 October 2010. EMI: 5099990664229; chart high failed to chart.
UK release 5 October 2010. EMI: 5099990664229; chart high failed to chart.

POWER TO THE PEOPLE - THE HITS (REMASTERED) (CD+DVD)
Disc: 1: 'Power To The People', 'Gimme Some Truth', 'Woman', 'Instant Karma (We All Shine On)', 'Whatever Gets You Thru The Night', 'Cold Turkey', 'Jealous Guy', '#9 Dream', 'Just Like Starting Over', 'Mind Games', 'Watching The Wheels', 'Stand By Me', 'Imagine', 'Happy Xmas (War Is Over)', 'Give Peace A Chance'
Disc: 2: 'Power To The People', 'Gimme Some Truth', 'Woman', 'Instant Karma (We All Shine On)', 'Whatever Gets You Thru The Night', 'Cold Turkey', 'Jealous Guy', '#9 Dream', 'Just Like Starting Over', 'Mind Games', 'Watching The Wheels', 'Stand By Me', 'Imagine', 'Happy Xmas (War Is Over)', 'Give Peace A Chance'

UK release 4 October 2010. EMI: 5099990664021; chart high failed to chart.
UK release 5 October 2010. EMI: 5099990664021; chart high failed to chart.

DOUBLE FANTASY STRIPPED DOWN/DOUBLE FANTASY
JOHN LENNON & YOKO ONO

'(Just Like) Starting Over' 'Kiss Kiss Kiss', 'Cleanup Time', 'Give Me Something', 'I'm Losing You', 'I'm Moving On', 'Beautiful Boy (Darling Boy)', 'Watching The Wheels', 'Yes, I'm Your Angel', 'Woman', 'Beautiful Boys', 'Dear Yoko', 'Every Man Has A Woman Who Loves Him', 'Hard Times Are Over'

UK release 4 October 2010; EMI: 5099990937224; chart high failed to chart.
US release 5 October 2010; EMI: 5099990937224; chart high failed to chart.

'India, India' and 'One Of The Boys' (Lennon)
Personnel: John Lennon (vocals and acoustic guitar).
Recording Studio: Dakota apartments, New York City.
Recording data: home recording.
Producer: Yoko Ono.

Issued to celebrate what would have been Lennon's 70th birthday, the *Lennon Signature Box* featured eight of his solo albums in digi-sleeves that mirror the original packaging, plus an EP of non-album singles and a 'bonus disc' of rare and previously unreleased recordings. The set also featured a collectible limited edition art print and a hardbound book with rare photos, poetry, artwork and new liner notes by Anthony DeCurtis. However, the *Lennon Signature Box* was far from comprehensive, preferring to focus on his 'pop' recordings rather than his more challenging 'avant-garde' releases. Lennon's early albums with Ono are, once again, conspicuous by their absence. For this set of re-issues, Lennon's original mixes rather than the Ono sanctioned remixes were used.

In case packaging alone wasn't enough to get Lennon fans rushing for their credit cards, a CD of unreleased Lennon outtakes and demos was included with the boxed set. This disc comprised outtakes from *Plastic Ono Band, Imagine,* and home demos. Of the 'new songs' presented on this disc, only 'One Of The Boys' and 'India, India' had not been issued commercially, although both recordings had been available on bootlegs for years. 'Serve Yourself' had previously been issued on the *Lennon Anthology*, but here features Lennon on piano. 'Nobody Told Me' is an acoustic guitar/drum box version which had also been previously bootlegged.

'India, India' had featured in the troubled 2005 Lennon musical and was originally intended for a musical the Lennons had planned called *The Ballad of John and Yoko*. Written in the late '70s, it features Lennon on acoustic guitar and vocals. It's a pleasant enough song that combines melodies from 'Memories' and 'Serve Yourself', but as pleasing as it is, 'India, India' remains an incomplete sketch.

'One Of The Boys' dates from late 1977 or early '78 and is little more than another rough sketch, Lennon fumbles part of the song but keeps going rather than starting anew. Clearly he never finished the song as it's comprised of no more than a brief verse, chorus and lots of adlibbing. Nor did he show much interest in it because he only record two takes before abandoning it.

The 11 disc set was accompanied by a less expensive 4 disc set, *Gimme Some Truth*, that presented Lennon's work on four themed discs.

'Roots' – John's rock 'n' roll roots and influences
'Working Class Hero' – John's socio-political songs
'Woman' – John's love songs
'Borrowed Time' – John's songs about life

A new 'best of' *Power to the People - the Hits* presented 15 of Lennon's most popular songs as either a 15-track single-disc or as an 'Experience Edition' with what was essentially a DVD of the 2003 'Best Of John Lennon' disc and access to a web-site.

To round things off, *Double Fantasy* was issued as a two-disc set in its original mix and a new 'Stripped Down' version remixed by Jack Douglas.

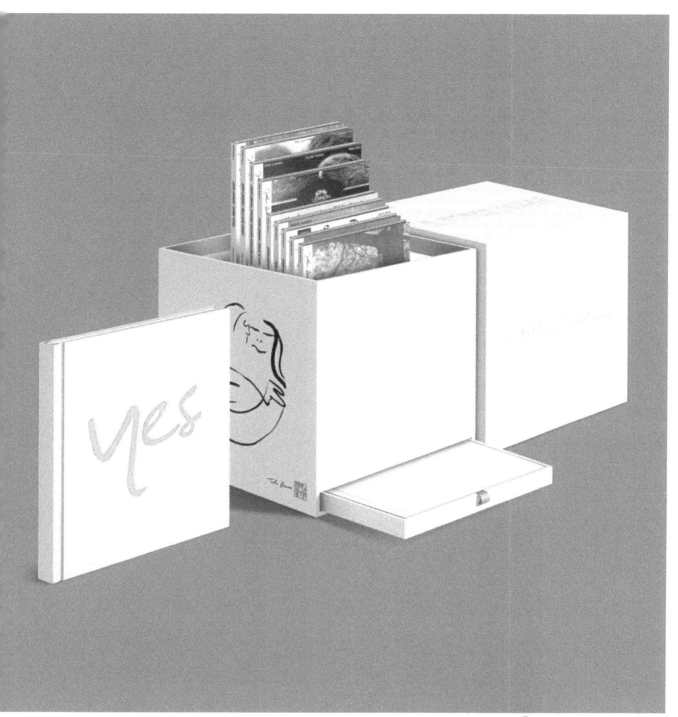

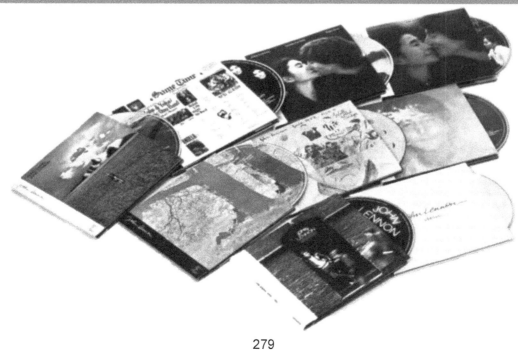

John Lennon
Gimme Some Truth

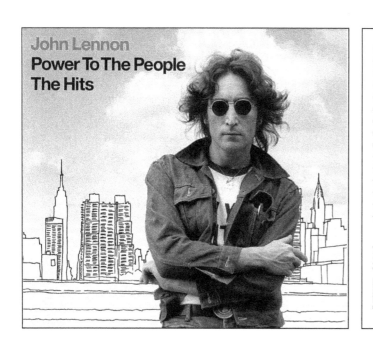

John Lennon
**Power To The People
The Hits**

01. Power To The People
02. Gimme Some Truth
03. Woman
04. Instant Karma! (We All Shine On)
05. Whatever Gets You Thru The Night
06. Cold Turkey (Live)
07. Jealous Guy
08. #9 Dream
09. (Just Like) Starting Over
10. Mind Games
11. Watching The Wheels
12. Stand By Me
13. Imagine
14. Happy Xmas (War Is Over)
15. Give Peace A Chance

John Lennon
**Power To The People
The Hits**

CD: The Music

Ⓟ 2010 The copyright in this audio compilation is owned by EMI Records Ltd and Yoko Ono Lennon. © 2010 EMI Records Ltd. This label copy information is the subject of copyright protection. All rights reserved. © 2010 EMI Records Ltd. 5099990955020. 5099990955129.

John Lennon
**Power To The People
The Hits**

DVD: The Videos

Ⓟ 2010 The copyright in this audio-visual compilation is owned by EMI Records Ltd and Yoko Ono Lennon. © 2010 EMI Records Ltd. This label copy information is the subject of copyright protection. All rights reserved. © 2010 EMI Records Ltd. 5099990864120. 5099990955099.

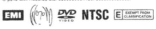

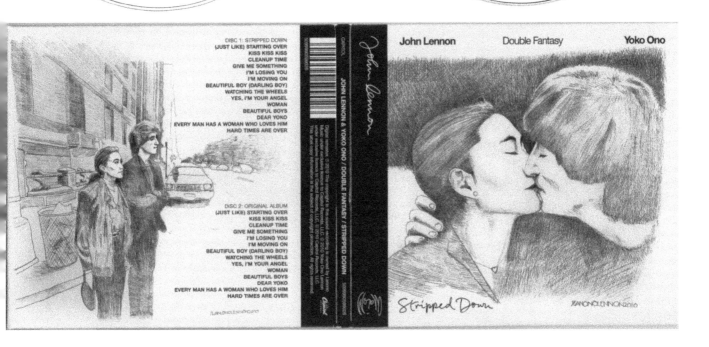

281

IMAGINE
JOHN LENNON AND PLASTIC ONO BAND (WITH THE FLUX FIDDLERS)

Side 1 'Imagine', 'Crippled Inside', 'Jealous Guy', 'It's So Hard', 'I Don't Want To Be A Soldier'.
Side 2 'Give Me Some Truth', 'Oh My Love', 'How Do You Sleep?', 'How?', 'Oh Yoko!'.

IMAGINE SESSIONS
Side 1 'Baby Please Don't Go', 'Imagine', 'How Do You Sleep?'
Side 2 'Jealous Guy', 'Oh My Love', 'I Don't Want To Be A Soldier'

US release 25 November 2011; LP Capitol 5099967887316; chart high failed to chart.

Released for Record Store Day 2011, also the 40th anniversary of the *Imagine* album, this two record boxed set contains a reproduction of the original album, complete with poster, and postcard and a 6 track white vinyl 12-inch 'Imagine Sessions'. Although manufactured in the U.S.A., this album was available worldwide.

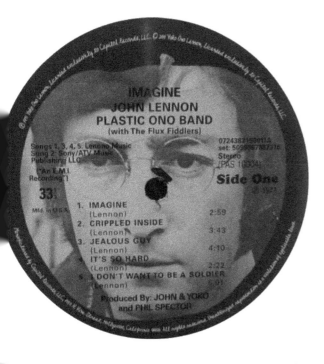

LENNON
JOHN LENNON

UK release 8 June 2015; LP Universal 00600753570937; chart high failed to chart.

Remastered editions of eight of John Lennon's albums pressed on heavyweight, 180-gram vinyl with authentically replicated original artwork. The eight LPs were issued individually on 21 August 2015. Despite going to considerable lengths to ensure that each LP was an authentic reproduction of its original UK pressing, faithfully replicated to the smallest detail, copies of *Rock 'N 'Roll* were mastered with 'Sweet Little Sixteen' repeated, where 'You Can't Catch Me' should have been. Universal Music issued a form so customers with proof of purchase could get a corrected pressing.

The set contains:

John Lennon / Plastic Ono Band
Imagine
Some Time In New York City
Mind Games
Walls And Bridges
Rock 'N 'Roll
Double Fantasy
Milk And Honey

'IMAGINE'
JOHN LENNON AND PLASTIC ONO BAND (WITH THE FLUX FIDDLERS)

UK release May 10 2016; Secret 7" S733; chart high failed to chart.

'IMAGINE'

Secret 7" takes 7 tracks from 7 of the world's best-known musicians and presses each one 100 times to 7" vinyl. It then invites artists from around the world to interpret the tracks in their own style for every 7". 700 sleeves are exhibited and then sold for £50 each. You don't know who created the sleeve, or even which song it's for, until you have parted with your cash - the secret lies within.

In 2016, Secret 7" chose 'Imagine' and 100 one-sided 7-inch singles were pressed, each with a unique sleeve designed by 100 different artists. Secret 7" also auctioned a test pressing signed by Yoko Ono.

LENNON DISCOGRAPHY

Over these pages we list John Lennon's album, CD, and single releases and promos issued in the UK, the USA, and Japan. Please note that release dates are shown in UK format: day, month, year.

UK LPs

29.11.68 *Unfinished Music No. 1: Two Virgins* Apple APCOR 2
29.11.68 *Unfinished Music No. 1: Two Virgins* Apple SAPCOR 2
02.05.69 *Unfinished Music No. 2: Life With The Lions* Zapple ZAPPLE 01
14.11.69 *The Wedding Album* Apple SAPCOR 11
12.12.69 *Plastic Ono Band – Live Peace In Toronto 1969* Apple CORE 2001
11.12.70 *John Lennon/Plastic Ono Band* Apple PCS 7124
07.10.71 *Imagine* Apple PAS 10004
00.06.72 *Imagine* Apple Q4PAS 10004
15.09.72 *Some Time In New York City* Apple PCSP 716
16.11.73 *Mind Games* Apple PCS 7165
04.10.74 *Walls And Bridges* Apple PCTC 253
21.02.75 *Rock'N'Roll* Apple PCS 7169
24.10.75 *Shaved Fish* Apple PCS 7173
17.11.80 *Double Fantasy* Geffen K 99131
28.11.80 *Mind Games* MFP MFP 50509
15.06.81 *John Lennon* EMI/Apple JLB8
25.11.81 *Rock'N'Roll* MFP MFP 50522
01.11.82 *The John Lennon Collection* Parlophone EMTV 37
16.12.83 *Heart Play* – Unfinished Dialogue Polydor 817 238-1
23.01.84 *Milk And Honey* Polydor POLH 5
26.03.84 *Milk And Honey* Polydor POLHP 5
02.07.84 *John Lennon/Plastic Ono Band* EMI/FAME FA 41 3102 1
21.09.84 *Every Man Has A Woman* Polydor POLH 13
24.02.86 *Live In New York City* Parlophone PCS 7301
03.11.86 *Menlove Ave.* Parlophone PCS 7308
10.10.88 *Imagine: John Lennon, Music From The Motion Picture* Parlophone PCSP 722
00.00.89 *Double Fantasy* Capitol EST 2083
17.02.96 *Rock'N'Roll* EMI/Apple LPCENT 9
27.10.97 *Lennon Legend – The Very Best Of John Lennon* Parlophone 8 21954 1
17.11.97 *Imagine* EMI/Apple LPCENT 27
18.01.99 *Wonsaponatime* Capitol 497 6391
22.03.99 *Walls And Bridges* millennium edition EMI/Apple 4994641
14.02.00 *Imagine* Apple 5 24858 1
08.06.2015 *Lennon* 8 LP boxed set Universal 00600753570937

UK 8-TRACK CARTRIDGES

11.12.70 *John Lennon/Plastic Ono Band* Apple 8X-PCS 7124
00.11.71 *Imagine* Apple 8X-PAS 10004
00.03.72 *Imagine* Apple Q8-PAS 10004
15.09.72 *Some Time In New York City* Apple 8X-PCSP 716
00.01.74 *Mind Games* Apple 8X-PCS 7165
04.10.74 *Walls And Bridges* Apple 8X-PCTC 253
21.02.75 *Rock'N'Roll* Apple 8X-PCS 7169
24.10.75 *Shaved Fish* Apple 8X-PCS 7173

UK CDs

03.06.97 *Unfinished Music No. 1: Two Virgins* Rykodisc RCD10411

03.06.97 *Unfinished Music No. 2: Life With The Lions* Rykodisc CD10412
03.06.97 *The Wedding Album* Rykodisc RCD10413
01.05.95 *Plastic Ono Band – Live Peace In Toronto 1969* Apple CDP 7 90428 2
04.04.88 *John Lennon/Plastic Ono Band* Apple CDP 7 46770 2
18.05.87 *Imagine* Apple CDP 7 46641 2
10.08.87 *Some Time In New York City* Apple CDS 7 46782 8
03.08.87 *Mind Games* Apple CDP 7 46769 2
20.07.87 *Walls And Bridges* Apple CDP 7 46768 2
18.05.87 *Rock 'N' Roll* Apple CDP 7 46707 2
25.05.87 *Shaved Fish* Apple CDP 7 46642 2
13.10.86 *Double Fantasy* Geffen 299 131
23.10.89 *The John Lennon Collection* Parlophone CD EMTV 37
23.01.84 *Milk And Honey* Polydor 817 160-2
19.11.84 *Every Man Has A Woman* Polydor 823 490-2
28.04.86 *Live In New York City* Parlophone CDP 7 46196 2
13.04.87 *Menlove Ave.* Parlophone CDP 7 46576 2
10.10.88 *Imagine: John Lennon, Music From The Motion Picture* Parlophone CD PCSP 722
01.10.90 *Lennon* Parlophone CDS 7 95220 2
14.10.96 *Rock And Roll Circus* Mercury 526 771-2
27.10.97 *Lennon Legend – The Very Best Of John Lennon* Parlophone 8 21954 2
02.11.98 *Anthology* Capitol 830 6142
03.11.98 *Wonsaponatime* Capitol CDP 4 97639 2
14.02.00 *Imagine* remastered Parlophone 524 8582
09.10.00 *John Lennon/Plastic Ono Band* remastered Parlophone 528 7402
09.10.00 *Double Fantasy* remastered Capitol 528 7392
08.10.01 *Milk And Honey* remastered Parlophone 535 9592
07.10.02 *Mind Games* remastered Parlophone 542 4252
27.10.03 *Lennon Legend – The Very Best Of John Lennon* Parlophone 595 0672
13.09.04 *Milk And Honey / Double Fantasy* Parlophone EBX23
27.09.04 *Rock 'N' Roll* remastered Parlophone 8743292
01.11.04 *Acoustic* Parlophone 8744282
03.10.05 *Working Class Hero (The Definitive Lennon)* Parlophone 340 0802
26.09.06 *The U.S. vs John Lennon* Parlophone 3749122
18.01.09 *John Lennon* The Mail On Sunday/EMI: UPJLEN001
04.10.10. *Signature Box* EMI: 5099990650925
04.10.10 *Gimmie Some Truth* EMI: 5099990664229
04.10.10 *Power To The People - The Hits Remastered* EMI: 5099990664021
04.10.10 *Double Fantasy Stripped Down* EMI: 5099990937224

UK 7-INCH SINGLES

04.07.69 'Give Peace A Chance' / 'Remember Love' Apple APPLE 13
24.10.69 'Cold Turkey' / 'Don't Worry Kyoko (Mummy's Only Looking For A Hand In The Snow)' Apple APPLES 1001
05.12.69 'You Know My Name (Look Up The Number)' / 'What's The New Mary Jane' withdrawn Apple APPLES 1002
06.02.70 'Instant Karma!' / 'Who Has Seen The Wind?' Apple APPLES 1003
12.03.71 'Power To The People' / 'Open Your Box' Apple R 5892
16.07.71 'God Save Us' / 'Do The Oz' Apple APPLE 36
24.11.72 'Happy Xmas (War Is Over)' / 'Listen The Snow Is Falling' Apple R 5970
05.12.72 'Woman Is The Nigger Of The World' / 'Sisters, O Sisters' Apple R 5953*
16.11.73 'Mind Games' / 'Meat City' Apple R 5994
04.10.74 'Whatever Gets You Thru The Night' / 'Beef Jerky' Apple R 5998
24.01.75 '#9 Dream' / 'What You Got' Apple R 6003
28.02.75 'Philadelphia Freedom' (Elton John Band) / 'I Saw Her Standing There' (Elton John Band featuring Lennon with Muscle Shoals Horns) DJM DJS 354

18.04.75 'Stand By Me' / 'Move Over Ms. L' Apple R 6005
24.10.75 'Imagine' / 'Working Class Hero' Apple R 6009
24.10.80 '(Just Like) Starting Over' / 'Kiss Kiss Kiss' Geffen K 79186
16.01.81 'Woman' / 'Beautiful Boys' Geffen K 79195
13.03.81 'I Saw Her Standing There' / 'Whatever Gets You Thru The Night', 'Lucy In The Sky With Diamonds' (Elton John Band featuring Lennon with Muscle Shoals Horns) DJM DJS 10965
27.03.81 'Watching The Wheels' / 'Yes, I'm Your Angel' Geffen K79207
15.11.82 'Love' / 'Give Me Some Truth' Parlophone R 6059
09.01.84 'Nobody Told Me' / 'O' Sanity' Polydor POSP 700
16.03.84 'Borrowed Time' / 'Your Hands' Polydor POSP 701
12.03.84 'Give Peace A Chance' / 'Cold Turkey' Apple G45 2
15.07.84 'I'm Stepping Out' / 'Sleepless Night' Polydor POSP 702
16.11.84 'Every Man Has A Woman Who Loves Him' / 'It's Alright' Polydor POSP 712
18.11.85 'Jealous Guy' / 'Going Down On Love' Parlophone R 6117
28.11.88 'Imagine' / 'Jealous Guy' / 'Happy Xmas (War Is Over)' Parlophone R 6199
05.12.88 'Imagine' / 'Jealous Guy', 'Happy Xmas (War Is Over)' Parlophone RP 6199
14.02.00 'Imagine' / 'Working Class Hero' Parlophone R 6009
12.12.03 'Happy Xmas (War Is Over)' / 'Imagine' Parlophone R 6627
17.04.10 *Singles Bag* Capitol Records 29697 72
10.05.16 'Imagine' Secret 7 S733

UK 12-INCH SINGLES

09.03.84 'Borrowed Time' / 'Your Hands', 'Never Say Goodbye' Polydor POSPX 701
15.07.84 'I'm Stepping Out' / 'Sleepless Night', 'Loneliness' Polydor POSPX 702
18.11.85 'Jealous Guy' / 'Going Down On Love', 'Oh Yoko!' Parlophone 12 R 6117
28.11.88 'Imagine' / 'Jealous Guy', 'Happy Xmas (War Is Over)' Parlophone 12 R 6199

UK CASSETTE SINGLES

16.01.81 'Woman' / 'Beautiful Boys' Geffen K 79195M
27.03.81 'Watching The Wheels' / 'Yes, I'm Your Angel' Geffen K79207M

UK CD SINGLES

28.11.88 'Imagine', 'Jealous Guy', 'Happy Xmas (War Is Over)', 'Give Peace A Chance' Parlophone CDR 6199
23.12.99 'Imagine', 'Happy Xmas (War Is Over)', 'Give Peace A Chance', 'Imagine' (Video) Parlophone CDR 6534
12.12.03 'Happy Xmas (War Is Over)', 'Imagine', 'Instant Karma!', 'Imagine' (Instrumental/Photo Gallery) Parlophone CDR 6627

UK 7-INCH SINGLE PROMOS

05.12.69 'You Know My Name (Look Up The Number)' / 'What's The New Mary Jane' custom Apple labels Apple APPLES 1002
05.12.72 'Woman Is The Nigger Of The World' / 'Sisters, O Sisters' white label test pressing Apple R 5953
00.11.74 'Interview with Lennon by Bob Merger and Message to Salesmen 'EMI/Apple PSR 369
24.01.75 '#9 Dream' (Edit) / 'What You Got' Apple R 6003
13.03.81 'I Saw Her Standing There' / 'Whatever Gets You Thru The Night', 'Lucy In The Sky With Diamonds' white label A-side 45 rpm, B-side 33-1/3 rpm DJM DJS 10965
13.03.81 'I Saw Her Standing There' / 'Whatever Gets You Thru The Night', 'Lucy In The Sky With Diamonds' promo label both sides play at 33-1/3 rpm DJM DJS 10965
09.01.84 'Nobody Told Me' one-sided white label Polydor POSP 70
09.03.84 'Borrowed Time' (Edit) / 'Your Hands' Polydor PODJ 701

UK CD SINGLE PROMOS

00.10.97 'Imagine' Parlophone IMAGINE 001
00.12.97 'Happy Xmas (War Is Over)' Parlophone IMAGINE 002
00.10.98 'I'm Losing You', 'Only You' Capitol LENNON 001
00.12.97 'Happy Xmas (War Is Over)', 'Be-Bop-A-Lula' Capitol LENNON 002
00.00.00 'Imagine', 'Happy Xmas (War Is Over)', 'Give Peace A Chance' Parlophone CDRDJ6534

US LPs

06.01.69 *Unfinished Music No. 1: Two Virgins* Apple T 5001
26.05.69 *Unfinished Music No. 2: Life With The Lions* Zapple ST 3357
20.10.69 *The Wedding Album* Apple SMAX 3361
12.12.69 *Plastic Ono Band – Live Peace In Toronto 1969* Apple SW 3362
11.12.70 *John Lennon/Plastic Ono Band* Apple SW 3372
09.09.71 *Imagine* Apple SW 3379
12.06.72 *Some Time In New York City* Apple SVBB 3392
02.11.73 *Mind Games* Apple SW 3414
26.09.74 *Walls And Bridges* Apple SW 3416
17.02.75 *John Lennon Sings The Rock & Roll Hits: Roots* Adam VIII A8018
17.02.75 *Rock 'N' Roll* Apple SK 3419
24.10.75 *Shaved Fish* Apple SW 3421
17.11.80 *Double Fantasy* Geffen GHS 2001
00.10.80 *Mind Games* Capitol SN-16068
00.10.80 *Rock 'N' Roll* Capitol SN-16069
17.11.81 *Double Fantasy* corrected back cover, no 'CH' on label Columbia House GHS 2001
00.00.81 *Double Fantasy* RCA Music Service R 104689
00.00.82 *Double Fantasy* Nautilus NR-47
00.00.82 *Double Fantasy* experimental sepia cover Nautilus NR-47
08.11.82 *The John Lennon Collection* Geffen GHSP 2023
08.11.82 *The John Lennon Collection* promo, Quiex II audiophile vinyl Geffen GHSP 2023
05.12 .83 *Heart Play – Unfinished Dialogue* Polydor 817 238-1 Y-1
23.01.84 *Milk And Honey* Polydor 817 160-1 Y-1
17.09 .84 *Every Man Has A Woman* Polydor 422-823 490-1 Y-1
00.00.84 *Reflections And Poetry* Silhouette SM-10012
00.00.84 *Imagine* MFSL 1-153
00.00.86 *Double Fantasy* corrected back cover, no 'CH' on black Geffen label Columbia House GHS 2001
24.01.86 *Live In New York City* Capitol SV-12451
24.01.86 *Live In New York City* Columbia House SV-512451
24.01.86 *Live In New York City* RCA Music Service R-144497
27.10.86 *Menlove Ave.* Capitol SJ-12533
27.10.86 *Menlove Ave.* BMG Direct Marketing R-144136
04.10.88 *Imagine: John Lennon, Music From The Motion Picture* Capitol C1-90803
00.00.89 *Double Fantasy* Columbia House/Capitol C-1-591425
10.03.98 *Lennon Legend – The Very Best Of John Lennon* Parlophone 8 21954 1
00.00.04 *Imagine* MFSL 1-277
15.11.04 *John Lennon/Plastic Ono Band* MFSL 1-280
00.00.05 *Mind Games* MFSL 1-293
00.00.06 *Plastic Ono Band – Live Peace In Toronto 1969* MFSL 1-283
25.11.11 *Imagine* RSD boxed set Capitol 5099967887316
11.11.16 *Unfinished Music No. 1: Two Virgins* Secretly Canadian SC289
11.11.16 *Unfinished Music No. 2: Life With The Lions* Secretly Canadian SC290

US 8-TRACK CARTRIDGES

06.01.69 *Unfinished Music No. 1: Two Virgins* Apple TNM-85001
26.05.69 *Unfinished Music No. 2: Life With The Lions* Zapple 8XT-3357
20.10.69 *The Wedding Album* Apple 8AX-3361
12.12.69 *Plastic Ono Band – Live Peace In Toronto 1969* Apple 8XT-3362
11.12.70 *John Lennon/Plastic Ono Band* Apple 8XW-3372
09.09.71 *Imagine* Apple 8XW-3379
09.09.71 *Imagine* Apple Q8W-3379
12.06.72 *Some Time In New York City* Apple 8XW-3393 and 8XW-3394
02.11.73 *Mind Games* Apple 8XW-3414
26.09.74 *Walls And Bridges* Apple 8XW-3416
26.09.74 *Walls And Bridges* Apple Q8W-3416
17.02.75 *Rock'N'Roll* Apple 8XK-3419
24.10.75 *Shaved Fish* Apple 8XW-3421
17.11.80 *Double Fantasy* Geffen GEF-W8-2001
17.11.80 *Double Fantasy* Columbia Record Club W8-2001
17.11.80 *Double Fantasy* RCA Record Club S-104689
08.11.82 *The John Lennon Collection* Geffen GEF-L8-2023
24.01.86 *Live In New York City* Capitol 8XV 512451

US REEL-TO-REEL TAPES

12.12.69 *Plastic Ono Band – Live Peace In Toronto 1969* Apple L-3362
11.12.70 *John Lennon/Plastic Ono Band* Apple M-3372
09.09.71 *Imagine* Apple L-3379

US CDs

23.01.84 *Milk And Honey* Polydor 817 160-2
19.11.84 *Every Man Has A Woman* Polydor 823 490-2
18.05.87 *Imagine* Apple CDP 7 46641 2
10.08.87 *Some Time In New York City* Apple CDP 7 46782 / 3 8
03.08.87 *Mind Games* Apple CDP 7 46769 2
20.07.87 *Walls And Bridges* Apple CDP 7 46768 2
18.05.87 *Rock'N'Roll* Apple CDP 7 46707 2
25.05.87 *Shaved Fish* Apple CDP 7 466422
13.10.86 *Double Fantasy* Geffen 2001-2
28.04.86 *Live In New York City* Parlophone CDP 7 46196 2
13.04.87 *Menlove Ave.* Parlophone CDP 7 46576 2
04.04.88 *John Lennon/Plastic Ono Band* Apple CDP 7 46770 2
10.10.88 *Imagine: John Lennon, Music From The Motion Picture* Parlophone CDP 7 90803 2
23.10.89 *The John Lennon Collection* Parlophone CDP 7 91516 2
01.10.90 *Lennon* Parlophone CDS 7 95220 2
00.00.91 *Unfinished Music No. 1: Two Virgins* Rock Classics SSI 9999
00.00.94 *Double Fantasy* MFSL UDCD-1-590
01.05.95 *Plastic Ono Band – Live Peace In Toronto 1969* Apple CDP 7 90428 2
14.10.96 *Rock And Roll Circus* Mercury 526 771-2
03.06.97 *Unfinished Music No. 1: Two Virgins* Rykodisc RCD10411
03.06 97 *Unfinished Music No. 2: Life With The Lions* Rykodisc CD10412
03.06.97 *The Wedding Album* Rykodisc RCD10413
27.10.97 *Lennon Legend – The Very Best Of John Lennon* Parlophone 8 21954 2
03.11.98 *Anthology* Capitol C2 8 30614 2
03.11.98 *Wonsaponatime* Capitol CDP 4 97639 2
11.04.00 *Imagine* remastered Capitol CDP 5 24858 2
09.10.00 *John Lennon/Plastic Ono Band* remastered Capitol 528 7402

09.10.00 *Double Fantasy* remastered Capitol 528 7392
08.10.01 *Milk And Honey* remastered Capitol 535 9592
07.10.02 *Mind Games* remastered Capitol 542 4252
22.08.03 *Imagine* remastered Ultradisc II 24 kt. Gold MFSL CMF759
20.01.04 *John Lennon/Plastic Ono Band* remastered Ultradisc II 24 kt. GoldMFSL CMF760
02.11.04 *Rock 'N'Roll* remastered Capitol 542 4252
02.11.04 *Acoustic* Capitol 744292
23.11.04 *Mind Games* remastered Ultradisc II 24 kt. Gold MFSL UDCD 761
04.10.05 *Working Class Hero (The Definitive Lennon)* Capitol 094634039123
08.11.05 *Plastic Ono Band – Live Peace In Toronto 1969* MFSL UDCD 763
26.09.06 *The U.S. vs John Lennon* Capitol 74912-2
03.01.07 *Remember* Capitol/Hear Music 71108-2-9
05.10.10 *Signature Box* EMI: 5099990650925
05.10.10 *Gimmie Some Truth* EMI: 5099990664229
05.10.10 *Power To The People - The Hits Remastered* EMI: 5099990664021
05.10.10 *Double Fantasy Stripped Down* EMI: 5099990937224
11.1116 *Unfinished Music No. 1: Two Virgins* Secretly Canadian SC289,
11.11.16 *Unfinished Music No. 2: Life With The Lions* Secretly Canadian SC290,

US 7-INCH SINGLES

21.07.69 'Give Peace A Chance' / 'Remember Love' Apple 1809
21.07.69 'Give Peace A Chance' / 'Remember Love' Apple/Americom 809P/M-435
20.10.69 'Cold Turkey' / 'Don't Worry Kyoko (Mummy's Only Looking For A Hand In The Snow)' Apple 1813
20.02.70 'Instant Karma!' / 'Who Has Seen The Wind?' Apple 1818
00.00.70 'Song For John', 'Let's Go On Flying', 'Snow is Falling All The Time', 'Mum's Only Looking For Her Hand In The Snow', 'No Bed For Beatle John', 'Radio Play' Aspen Magazine
28.12.70 'Mother' / 'Why' Apple 1827
22.03.71 'Power To The People' / 'Touch Me'Apple 1830
07.07.71 'God Save Us' / 'Do The Oz' Apple 1835
10.10.71 'Imagine' / 'It's So Hard' Apple 1840
01.12.71 'Happy Xmas (War Is Over)' / 'Listen The Snow Is Falling' Apple 1842
24.04.72 'Woman Is The Nigger Of The World' / 'Sisters, O Sisters' Apple 1848
29.10.73 'Mind Games' / 'Meat City' Apple 1868
23.09.74 'Whatever Gets You Thru The Night' / 'Beef Jerky' Apple 1874
16.12.74 '#9 Dream' / 'What You Got' Apple 1878
24.02.75 'Philadelphia Freedom' (Elton John Band) / 'I Saw Her Standing There' (Elton John Band featuring Lennon The Muscle Shoals Horns)MCA MCA 40364
10.03.75 'Stand By Me' / 'Move Over Ms. L' Apple 1881
04.04.77 'Stand By Me' / 'Woman Is The Nigger Of The World' Capitol6244
20.10.80 '(Just Like) Starting Over' / 'Kiss Kiss Kiss' Geffen GEF 49604
12.01.81 'Woman' / 'Beautiful Boys' Geffen GEF 49644
13.03.81 'Watching The Wheels' / 'Yes, I'm Your Angel' Geffen GEF 49695
06.07.81 '(Just Like) Starting Over' / 'Woman' Geffen GGEF 0408
09.11.81 'Watching The Wheels' / 'Beautiful Boy (Darling Boy)' Geffen GGEF 0415
29.11.82 'Happy Xmas (War Is Over)' / 'Beautiful Boy (Darling Boy)' Geffen GEF-7-29855
09.01.84 'Nobody Told Me' / 'O' Sanity' Polydor 817 254-7
19.03.84 'I'm Stepping Out' / 'Sleepless Night' Polydor 821-107-7
14.05.84 'Borrowed Time' / 'Your Hands' Polydor 821-204-7
08.10.84 'Every Man Has A Woman Who Loves Him' / 'It's Alright' Polydor 881 387-7
19.09.88 'Jealous Guy' / 'Give Peace A Chance' Capitol B-44230
30.04.90 'Nobody Told Me' / 'I'm Stepping Out' Polydor 883927-7
00.10.92 'Imagine' / 'It's So Hard' CEMA S7-57849
00.00.92 'Nobody Told Me' / 'I'm Steppin' Out' Collectibles COL-4307
00.00.94 'Give Peace A Chance' / 'Remember Love' CEMA S7-17783

00.00.94 '(Just Like) Starting Over' / 'Watching The Wheels' blue vinyl CEMA 72438-58894-7
00.00.94 'Happy Xmas (War Is Over)' / 'Listen, The Snow Is Falling' green vinyl CEMA S7-17644
00.00.94 'Woman' / 'Walking On Thin Ice' clear vinyl CEMA 72438-58895-7
17.04.10 *Singles Bag* Capitol Records 29697 72

US 7-INCH SINGLE PROMOS

'The KYA Peace Talk' KYA 1260
'Instant Karma'! one-sided Apple 1818
'John Lennon on Ronnie Hawkins – The Short Rap / The Long Rap' Cotillion PR-105
'Mother' / 'Why'Apple P-1827
'Power To The People' / 'Touch Me' Apple P-1830
'God Save Us' / 'Do The Oz' Apple P-1835
'Imagine' / 'It's So Hard' Apple P-1840
'Happy Xmas (War Is Over)' / 'Listen, The Snow Is Falling' white label, black text 'NOT FOR SALE FOR RADIO STATION PLAY ONLY" Apple S-45X-47663
'Woman Is The Nigger Of The World' / 'Sisters, O Sisters' Apple P-1848
'Mind Games' mono/stereo Apple P-1868
'Whatever Gets You Thru The Night' mono/stereo Apple P-1874
'#9 Dream 'mono/stereo Apple P-1878
'What You Got' mono/stereo)Apple P-1878
'Stand By Me' mono/stereo Apple P-1881
'Ain't That A Shame' mono/stereo Apple P-1883
'Slippin' And Slidin' mono/stereo Apple P-1883
'(Just Like) Starting Over' mono/stereo Geffen GEF 49604
'Watching The Wheels' mono/stereo Geffen GEF 49695
'Happy Xmas (War Is Over)' mono/stereoGeffen GEF-7-29855
'Nobody Told Me' / 'O' Sanity' Polydor 817 254-7 DJ
'I'm Stepping Out' 3:33/4:06 Polydor 821-107-7 DJ
'Borrowed Time' / 'Borrowed Time'Polydor 821-204-7 DJ
'Every Man Has A Woman Who Loves Him' / 'Every Man Has A Woman Who Loves Him'Polydor 881 387-7 DJ
'Jealous Guy' / 'Jealous Guy'Capitol P-B-44230
'Every Man Has A Woman Who Loves Him' Lennon/Ono Capitol 7PRO 6 15998 7

US 12-INCH SINGLE PROMOS

'(Just Like) Starting Over' / 'Kiss Kiss Kiss' Geffen PRO-A-919
'Happy Xmas (War Is Over)' / 'Beautiful Boy (Darling Boy)' Geffen PRO-A-1079
'Nobody Told Me' / 'O' Sanity' Polydor PRO 250-1
'Imagine' / 'Come Together' Capitol SPRO-9585 / 6
'Happy Xmas (War Is Over)' / 'Happy Xmas (War Is Over)' 2,000 hand-numbered for Central Virginia Foodbank Capitol SPRO-9894
'Rock And Roll People' / 'Rock And Roll People' Capitol SPRO-9917
'Happy Xmas (War Is Over)' / 'Listen, The Snow Is Falling' silver label, plastic sleeve, limited 1,500 Capitol SPRO-9929
'Stand By Me' / 'Stand By Me'Capitol SPRO-79453

US CD PROMOS

'Jealous Guy' Capitol DPRO-79417
Excerpts From John Lennon Anthology Capitol DPRO-13507
Starting Over conversation with Ono Capitol DPRO-15670
The Lennon/Ono Publishing Catalogue Sampler EMI Music Publishing IFPIL433
John Lennon: Two Sides Of Lennon Capitol DPRO-70876

JAPANESE LPs

Life With The Lions Zapple logo Zapple AP-8782
Life With The Lions no Zapple logoZapple AP-8782
Life With The Lions reissue Zapple EAS-80701
Wedding Album Apple AP-9010
Wedding Album Odeon EAS-80702
Live Peace In Toronto – 1969 Apple AP-8867
Live Peace In Toronto – 1969 Odeon EAS-80703
John Lennon/Plastic Ono Band Apple AP-80174
John Lennon/Plastic Ono Band Odeon EAS-80704
Imagine Apple AP-80370
Imagine quadraphonic Apple EAZ-80006
Imagine Odeon EAS-80705
Some Time In New York City Apple EAP-93049
Some Time In New York City Odeon EAS-67110-11
Mind Games Apple EAP-80950
Mind Games Odeon EAS-80706
Walls And Bridges Apple EAS-80065
Rock 'N 'Roll Apple EAS-80175
Shaved Fish Apple EAS-80380
Shaved Fish green vinyl Odeon EAS-81457
Double Fantasy with/without memorial OBI Geffen P-10948J
Double Fantasy Geffen P-5909
John Lennon 8-LP boxed set Odeon EAS-67161-69
Elton John & John Lennon Live! with poster/insert King K28P-200
The John Lennon Collection Odeon EAS-91055
Heart Play – Unfinished Dialogue Polydor 20MM-9250
Milk And Honey Polydor 25MM-0260
Milk And Honey Nice Price Polydor 18MM 0609
Every Man Has A Woman Polydor P33P-26223
Imagine O.S.T. Odeon R P15-5690-91
Live In New York City Odeon ECS-9116
Menlove Ave. Odeon ECS-91197

JAPANESE CDs

Two Virgins Rykodisc VACK 1125
Life With The Lions Rykodisc VACK 1126
Wedding Album Rykodisc VACK 1127
Live Peace In Toronto – 1969 with '95 calendar Odeon TOCP-8560
Live Peace In Toronto – 1969 Odeon TOCP-65533
John Lennon/Plastic Ono Band Odeon CP32-5463
John Lennon/Plastic Ono Band Odeon TOCP-3122
John Lennon/Plastic Ono Band Odeon Super Master Odeon TOCP-6857
Imagine Odeon CP32-5451
Imagine limited 24kt. Gold Odeon CP43-5773
Imagine Odeon TOCP-67483
Sometime In New York City Odeon CP25-5466-67
Some Time In New York City Odeon TOCP-65523/24
Mind Games Odeon CP32-5464
Mind Games Odeon TOCP-3123
Walls And Bridges Odeon CP32-5465
Walls And Bridges Odeon TOCP-65526
Rock 'N 'Roll Odeon CP32-5452
Rock 'N 'Roll Odeon TOCP-65527

Shaved Fish Odeon CP32-5453
Shaved Fish Odeon TOCP-65525
Double Fantasy Geffen 32XD-447
Double Fantasy Geffen CP32-5750
Milk And Honey Polydor POCP-1884
Milk And Honey Odeon TOCP-65535
John Lennon Collection Odeon TOCP-53220
John Lennon Collection promo Odeon SPCD-1615
Lennon 4-CD boxed set Odeon TOCP-6281/84
Imagine – O.S.T. Odeon CP36-5690
Imagine – O.S.T. Odeon TOCP-65532
Live In New York City Odeon CP32-5126
Live In New York City Odeon TOCP-65530
Menlove Ave. Odeon TOCP-7615
Menlove Ave. Odeon TOCP-65531
The Greatest 19-track compilation, embossed jewel case Odeon TOCP-51056
Imagine millennium edition Odeon TOCP-65522
John Lennon/Plastic Ono Band millennium edition Odeon TOCP-65520
Double Fantasy millennium editionOdeon TOCP-65528
Milk And Honey new century edition Odeon TOCP-65535
Milk And Honey promo sampler Odeon PCD-2509
Anthology Odeon TOCP-65002-5
Wonsaponatime Odeon TOCP-65001
Legend Odeon TOCP-51110
Mind Games remastered Odeon TOCP-67075
Rock 'N 'Roll millennium edition OdeonTOCP-67500
Acoustic with white guitar pick Odeon TOCP-67483
John Lennon/Plastic Ono Band remastered Odeon TOCP-65520

JAPANESE 7-INCH SINGLES

Key GS = gatefold sleeve; SS = single-sheet sleeve; TS = trifold sleeve; LSI = lyric sheet insert; PS = pocket sleeve; 4 = ¥400 on sleeve; 5 = ¥500 on sleeve; 6 = ¥600 on sleeve; 7 = ¥700 on sleeve.

'Give Peace A Chance' / 'Remember Love' GS, 4 or 5, red or black vinylApple AR-2324
'Give Peace A Chance' / 'Remember Love' GS, 7Odeon EAS-17120
'Cold Turkey' / 'Don't Worry Kyoko (Mummy's Only Looking For A Hand In The Snow)' GS, 4 or 5, red or black vinylApple AR-2399
'Cold Turkey' / 'Don't Worry Kyoko (Mummy's Only Looking For A Hand In The Snow)' SS, 7Odeon EAS-17121
'Instant Karma!' / 'Who Has Seen The Wind?' GS, 4 or 5, red or black vinyl Apple AR-2462
'Instant Karma!' / 'Who Has Seen The Wind?' Odeon SS, 7 Odeon EAS-17122
'Mother' / 'Why' SS, 4 or 5, red or black vinyl Apple AR-2734
'Mother' / 'Why' SS, 7 Odeon EAS-17123
'Power To The People' / 'Open Your Box' GS, 4 or 5 Apple AR-2773
'Power To The People' / 'Open Your Box' SS, 7 Odeon EAS-17124
'Imagine' / 'It's So Hard' GS, 4 and 5, red or black vinyl Apple AR-2929
'Happy Xmas (War Is Over)' / 'Listen, The Snow Is Falling' SS, 4 or 5, red or black vinyl Apple AR-2943
'Happy Xmas (War Is Over)' / 'Listen, The Snow Is Falling' 7 Odeon EAS-17126
'Woman Is The Nigger Of The World' / 'Sisters, O Sisters' TS, 1st issue, '1972 Apple Records Inc.' Apple EAR-10082
'Woman Is The Nigger Of The World' / 'Sisters, O Sisters' 2nd issue '1972 Gramophone Company Limited', 5 Apple EAR-10082
'Woman Is The Nigger Of The World' / 'Sisters, O Sisters' SS, 7 Odeon EAS-17127
'Mind Games' / 'Meat City' PS, LSI, 5, red or black vinyl Apple EAR-10474
'Mind Games' / 'Meat City' SS, 7 Odeon EAS-17128

'Whatever Gets You Thru The Night' / 'Beef Jerky' SS, 5, red or black vinylApple EAR-10650
'Whatever Gets You Thru The Night' / 'Beef Jerky' SS, 7 Odeon EAS-17129
'#9 Dream' / 'What You Got' SS, 5 Apple EAR-10700
'#9 Dream' / 'What You Got' SS, 7 Odeon EAS-17130
'Stand By Me' / 'Move Over Ms. L' SS, 5Apple EAR-10750
'Stand By Me' / 'Move Over Ms. L' SS, 7 Odeon EAS-17131
'Be-Bop-A-Lula' / 'Ya Ya' SS, 5 Apple EAR-10827
'Be-Bop-A-Lula' / 'Ya Ya' SS, 7 Odeon EAS-17132
'Imagine' / 'Working Class Hero' PS, LSI, 5 Apple EAR-10880
'Imagine' / 'Working Class Hero' PS, LSI, 7 or ¥659 Odeon EAS-17125
'(Just Like) Starting Over' / 'Kiss Kiss Kiss' SS, 6 Geffen P-645W
'Woman' / 'Beautiful Boys' SS, 7 Geffen P1502J
'Watching The Wheels' / 'Yes, I'm Your Angel' SS, 7 Geffen P-1527J
'Jealous Guy' / 'Going Down On Love' SS, 7 Odeon EAS-17133
'Love' / 'Give Me Some Truth' PS, LSI, 7 Odeon EAS-17295
'Nobody Told Me' / 'Your Hands' GS, 7 Polydor 7DM0100
'I'm Stepping Out' / 'Sleepless Night' SS, 7 Polydor 7DM0107
'Every Man Has A Woman Who Loves Him' / 'It's Alright' SS, 7 Polydor 7DM0128

JAPANESE CD SINGLES

'Beautiful Boy (Darling Boy)', 'Beautiful Boys' 3-inch Capitol TODP-2360
'(Just Like) Starting Over', 'Beautiful Boy (Darling Boy)' 3-inch Capitol TODP-2544
'Love', 'Stand By Me' 3-inch Parlophone TOCP-51110
'Love' 3-inch EMI TODP-2555
'Love' 5-inch EMI PCD-2014

JAPANESE SINGLE PROMOS

John Lennon And Yoko Ono Interview 7-inch 33-1/3rpm, limited 1,000Toshiba/Apple 3ER-282
John Lennon And Yoko Ono Interview same as above, reissued 1998 3-inch CD BCDS-1046
'I Saw Her Standing There', 'Lucy In The Sky With Diamonds' 7-inch live with Elton John King 17DY-5611-1
'Imagine', 'Come Together' 7-inch from Live In New York CityToshiba/Capitol PRP-1163
'Beautiful Boy (Darling Boy)' 3-inch CD plus cover by Japanese band Dreams Come True Capitol PCD-0942
'Love', 'Stand By Me' 5-inch CD from Acoustic EMI PCD-3014

UK SINGLES CHARTS

	Music Week	NME
'Give Peace A Chance'	2	2
'Cold Turkey'	14	13
'Instant Karma (We All Shine On)'	5	5
'Power To the People'	7	6
'Happy Xmas (War Is Over)'	4	2
'Mind Games'	26	19
'Whatever Gets You Thru the Night'	36	24
'#9 Dream'	23	23
'Stand By Me'	30	30
'Imagine'	6	5
'(Just Like) Starting Over'	1	1
'Woman'	1	2
'I Saw Her Standing There'	40	24
'Watching The Wheels'	30	7
'Love'	41	FTC
'Nobody Told Me'	6	2
'Borrowed Time'	32	30
'I'm Stepping Out'	FTC	49
'Every Man Has A Woman'	FTC	49
'Jealous Guy'	62	36

US SINGLES CHARTS

	Billboard	Cashbox
'Give Peace A Chance'	14	11
'Cold Turkey'	30	32
'Instant Karma (We All Shine On)'	3	3
'Mother'	43	19
'Power To the People'	11	10
'Imagine'	3	2
'Happy Xmas (War Is Over)'	FTC	36
'Woman Is The Nigger Of The World'	57	93
'Mind Games'	18	10
'Whatever Gets You Thru the Night'	1	1
'#9 Dream'	9	10
'Stand By Me'	20	20
'(Just Like) Starting Over'	1	1
'Woman'	2	1
'Watching The Wheels'	10	7
'Nobody Told Me'	5	6
'I'm Stepping Out'	55	57
'Borrowed Time'	108	FTC
'Jealous Guy'	91	FTC

JAPANESE CHARTS*
Albums

Date	Album title	Highest chart position	Weeks on the chart
23.02.70	*Plastic Ono Band - Live Peace In Toronto 1969*	29	12
15.03.71	*John Lennon/Plastic Ono Band*	05	25
08.11.71	*Imagine*	01	34
04.12.72	*Sometime In New York City*	15	13
28.01.74	*Mind Games*	06	18
02.12.74	*Walls And Bridges*	14	18
14.04.75	*Rock 'N' Roll*	15	20
08.12.75	*Shaved Fish*	22	10
15.12.80	*Double Fantasy*	02	25
20.12.82	*The John Lennon Collection*	08	12
06.02.84	*Heart Play - Unfinished dialogue*	50	02
06.02.84	*Milk and Honey*	03	10
10.03.86	*Live In New York City*	13	08
08.12.86	*Menlove Avenue*	32	06
02.05.88	*John Lennon/Plastic Ono Band* (reissue)	83	03
17.10.88	*Imagine* (soundtrack)	10	33
01.12.89	*The John Lennon Collection* (reissue)	38	19
08.10.90	*John Lennon* 4 CD Set	53	12
05.06.95	*Plastic Ono Band - Live Peace In Toronto 1969* (reissue)	78	01
24.11.97	*Lennon Legend*	94	03
18.10.98	*Lennon Legend - The Very Best Of*	46	35
16.11.98	*Anthology*	30	03
23.11.98	*Wonsaponatime*	57	02
28.02.00	*Imagine* (millennium edition)	11	05
16.10.00	*John Lennon/Plastic Ono Band* (millennium edition)	17	04
16.10.00	*Double Fantasy* (millennium edition)	15	04
08.10.01	*Milk and Honey* (new century edition)	70	02
23.10.02	*Mind Games* (remixed edition)	60	01

Singles

Date		Highest chart position	Weeks on the chart
18.08.69	'Give Peace A Chance'	81	02
02.02.70	'Cold Turkey'	91	03
13.04.70	'Instant Karma!'	58	10
08.03.71	'Mother'	30	15
19.04.71	'Power To The People'	66	09
22.11.71	'Imagine'	14	19
27.12.71	'Happy Christmas'	30	04
25.09.72	'Woman Is The Nigger Of The World'	38	11
21.01.74	'Mind Games'	46	17
02.12.74	'Whatever Gets You Thru The Night'	72	09
24.02.75	'#9 Dream'	97	01
19.05.75	'Stand By Me'	74	09
24.11.80	'Starting Over'	37	14
19.05.97	'Starting Over' (reissue)	40	08
19.10.98	'Love'	58	07

* Japanese chart positions taken from from 'Oricon'.

LENNON COLLABORATIONS

Here we list John Lennon's contributions to the recorded work of other artists, as a producer and/or a musician.

YOKO ONO
Yoko Ono/Plastic Ono Band
Lennon co-produces with Ono, performs on all tracks except 'AOS'
Released December 17 1970
UK Apple SAPCOR17
US Apple SW3391

YOKO ONO
Fly
Lennon co-produces with Ono, performs on most tracks
Released December 3 1971
UK Apple SAPTU 101/2
US Apple SVBB-3380

DAVID PEEL & THE LOWER EAST SIDE
The Pope Smokes Dope
Lennon produces
Released April 1972
US Apple SW3391

DAVID PEEL & THE LOWER EAST SIDE
'F Is Not A Dirty Word' / 'The Ballad Of New York City' / 'John Lennon-Yoko Ono'
Lennon produces
Released April 1972
US Apple PRO-6498 / SPRO-6499

DAVID PEEL & THE LOWER EAST SIDE
'Hippy From New York City' / 'The Ballad Of New York City' / 'John Lennon-Yoko Ono'
Lennon produces
Released April 1972
US Apple SPRO-6545 / SPRO-6546

ELEPHANT'S MEMORY
Elephant's Memory
Lennon co-produces with Yoko Ono, performs on several tracks (with Ono)
Released September 1972
UK Apple SAPCOR22
US Apple SMAS 3389

ELEPHANT'S MEMORY
'Liberation Special' / 'Madness'
Lennon produces, performs
Released November 1972
US Apple 1854

ELEPHANT'S MEMORY
'Power Boogie' / 'Liberation Special'
Lennon produces, performs
Released December 1 1972
UK Apple APPLE45

MICK JAGGER
'Too Many Cooks'
The Very Best Of Mick Jagger
Lennon produces
Released October 1 2007
UK Rhino 8122-79961-0
US Rhino R2 74640

YOKO ONO
Approximately Infinite Universe
Lennon co-produces with Ono, plays guitar on 'Move On Fast', 'Is Winter Here To Stay'
Released February 16 1973
UK Apple SAPDO1001
US Apple SVBB-3399

YOKO ONO
Feeling The Space
Lennon performs on 'She Hits Back', 'Woman Power'
Released November 23 1973
UK Apple SAPCOR 26
US Apple SW-3412

RINGO STARR
Ringo
Lennon performs on 'I'm The Greatest'
Released November 23 1973
UK Apple PCTC 252
US Apple SWAL-3413

HARRY NILSSON
Pussy Cats
Lennon produces and arranges, performs on a few tracks
Released August 19 1974
UK RCA APL1-0570
US RCA CPL1-0570

RINGO STARR
Goodnight Vienna
Lennon performs on 'Goodnight Vienna', 'All By Myself', 'Only You (And You Alone)'
Released November 15 1974
UK Apple PCS 7168
US Apple SW-3417

ELTON JOHN
'Lucy In The Sky With Diamonds' / 'One Day At A Time'
Lennon performs on A-side
Released November 12 1974
UK DJM DJS340
Released November 18 1974
US MCA MCA 40344

DAVID BOWIE
Fame
Lennon performs on 'Across The Universe', 'Fame'
Released March 1975
UK RCA APL1 1006
US RCA 0998

DAVID BOWIE
'Fame' / 'Right'
Lennon performs on A-side
Released August 1975
UK RCA 2579
US RCA PB-10320

LORI BURTON
'Answer Me, My Love'
Lennon co-produces with Roy Cicala, performs
Released with Engelhardt *Beatles Undercover* book September 1998
CAN CGPINT8008

LORI BURTON AND PATRICK JUDE
'Let's Spend The Night Together'
Lennon co-produces with Roy Cicala, performs
Released with Engelhardt *Beatles Undercover* book September 1998
CAN CGPINT8008

DOG SOLDIER AND PATRICK JUDE
'Incantation'
Lennon co-produces with Roy Cicala
Released with Engelhardt *Beatles Undercover* book September 1998
CAN CGPINT8008

RINGO STARR
Ringo's Rotogravure
Lennon plays piano on 'A Dose Of Rock'n'Roll', performs on 'Cookin' (In The Kitchen Of Love)'
Released September 17 1976
UK Polydor 2302 040
US Atlantic 82417-2

YOKO ONO
'Walking On Thin Ice' / 'It Happened'
Lennon co-produces with Ono and Jack Douglas
Released February 20 1981
UK Geffen K 79202
US Geffen 49683

SONG INDEX

Lightning Source UK Ltd.
Milton Keynes UK
UKHW020323260819
348473UK00012B/46/P

9 780995 515437